THE LORD OF THE ENTIRE WORLD

New Testament Monographs, 31

Series Editor
Stanley E. Porter

THE LORD OF THE ENTIRE WORLD

LORD JESUS, A CHALLENGE TO LORD CAESAR?

Joseph D. Fantin

SHEFFIELD PHOENIX PRESS

2011

Copyright © 2011 Sheffield Phoenix Press

Published by Sheffield Phoenix Press
Department of Biblical Studies, University of Sheffield
45 Victoria Street, Sheffield S3 7QB

www.sheffieldphoenix.com

A CIP catalogue record for this book
is available from the British Library

Typeset by the HK Scriptorium
Printed by Lightning Source

Hardback 978-1-907534-12-6

ISSN 1747-9606

To Robin, Jillian and David

You are greatly cherished

CONTENTS

PREFACE

The majority of this work was completed as a PhD thesis for the University of Sheffield (2007). Therefore, those who have contributed to the original also deserve the most significant recognition here. My supervisor, Professor Loveday Alexander at the University of Sheffield, was a constant source of encouragement and support. Her direction and patience were essential during this process and I am not sure whether I would have been able to complete it under another advisor. Her example as a teacher, scholar and writer have impacted me in more ways than can be expressed. Throughout my Sheffield experience in various contexts, when it was revealed that Professor Alexander was my supervisor, responses of envy were often expressed. This was well founded. In addition to scholarly competence, I feel what makes an excellent supervisor is the ability to encourage and motivate students. To her I express my gratitude.

My examiners, Jorunn Økland (Sheffield) and Peter Oakes (Manchester), helped me clarify my thoughts and challenged me in many positive ways. Peter Oakes also deserves thanks for help and direction early in the project, which included providing me with an important chapter of his monograph on Philippians prior to its publication.

In addition, many others deserve thanks. The entire Department of Biblical Studies at the University of Sheffield has contributed to both the content and the method of this work. The New Testament faculty of Dallas Theological Seminary, of which I am proud to be a part, has been a source of encouragement and stimulation. David Horrell chaired the Social World Seminar at the British New Testament Society meeting in September 2001, which was devoted to the topic of the imperial cult. I gained a great deal from the other participants' contributions and their feedback on my work. Involvement in the Relevance Theory and Biblical Interpretation group at the International Society of Biblical Literature meetings over the years has provided me with an opportunity to present my use of relevance theory to scholars with much more experience in the theory than myself. This has provided support for part of the linguistic aspect of this book. Various exchanges over scholarly Internet lists such as B-Greek, the relevance theory list, and a directed seminar hosted by the Corpus Paulinum group with Richard Horsley in April–May 2002 have been helpful as well. I am thankful for all who have taken an interest in my work and have contributed to its final form through these means.

Regarding the revision for publication, I express my thanks to Stanley Porter, the editor of the New Testament Monographs series, for his encouraging comments, helpful suggestions to improve the work, and for choosing to include this book in the series. All those I had contact with at Sheffield Phoenix Press were very helpful, especially David Clines and Ailsa Parkin. I have not changed any conclusions from the original. However, the revision process has given me the opportunity to clarify and further support the conclusions in this work.

Concerning imperial cults, I am of course indebted to the ground-breaking work of Simon Price (*Rituals and Power*, 1984). The two authors I have found most helpful are Steven Friesen (*Twice Neokoros*, 1993, and *Imperial Cults and the Apocalypse of John*, 2001) and Ittai Gradel (*Emperor Worship and Roman Religion*, 2002). Dr Gradel was kind enough to send me the final proofs of his book while this thesis was in its formative stage. The influence of these authors on this work cannot be exaggerated. Late in the final revision stage for publication, I discovered the work of Fernando Lozano Gómez of the University of Seville. He kindly provided me with a number of his articles on imperial cults including one in press but not published at the time of this book's completion. He also contributed helpful insights through e-mail. I am thankful for his input into my research.

Many others have contributed to aspects of this thesis as well. At the risk of missing many, I wish to thank Dorian Coover Cox, Buist Fanning, Malcolm Gill, John Hilber, John Pulliam, Robert Rezetko, Jay Smith, Rick Taylor, Dan Wallace, Bruce Winter and N.T. Wright for various contributions. I also would like to thank Jim Harrison, whose friendship and insights through our discussions have been a constant source of encouragement. I also thank him for making available the proofs of his book, *Paul and the Imperial Authorities,* so it could be included in this work. My intern during the 2004–2005 school year, Matt Jones, as well as April Stier (now Frazier) helped in proofreading the original thesis. I am also thankful to Jonathan Murphy who read the entire thesis and also provided important proofreading assistance. David Houser and my intern during the Fall 2010 semester, Stephen Tiu, read through the proofs of this book and provided helpful feedback. Two PhD students, Steven Sanders and Luke Tsai, proofread the book and created the indexes. I am confident that I will see these two names in print again very soon. I wish to thank my children, Jillian and David, who helped by proofreading the prologue and epilogue and providing helpful comments. Additionally, my parents, David and Jane Fantin, were always supportive as well as helped in practical ways at various stages while we were resident in Sheffield. I would also like to mention my brothers Greg Fantin and Mark Fantin. Greg knows why.

Access to resources is essential for any research project. I am thankful for the University of Sheffield's library and especially for the Turpin Library at Dallas Theological Seminary, which had most of what I needed. Debbie Hunn was able to get everything else through interlibrary loan. Thank you.

As I reflect on the PhD process, I am convinced that success in a PhD programme is highly dependent on a supportive spouse. I uprooted my family with our one-year-old daughter to come to Sheffield. Our son was born there as well. My wife's sacrifices at a time of uncertainty were great and I can only begin to understand them. It takes a special woman to participate in this process. It takes an unimaginably special woman to go through the PhD process twice! Perhaps, the dedication of this work can serve as a small token of my gratitude. Many spouses have a PhD thesis dedicated to them. This is an acknowledgment for their support, a small compensation for an enormous sacrifice. No spouse should have a second! But with sincere gratitude I dedicate this book, as I did the original PhD thesis, to Robin; and this time it is also dedicated to my children, Jillian and David, who have been passengers on this journey. This was a family project.

Finally and most importantly, the grace of our Lord Jesus has sustained me in unimaginable ways. I am glad that this seems to be part of his plan.

Soli Deo gloria
Joe Fantin

ἵνα ἐν τῷ ὀνόματι Ἰησοῦ
πᾶν γόνυ κάμψῃ . . .
καὶ πᾶσα γλῶσσα ἐξομολογήσηται
ὅτι κύριος Ἰησοῦς Χριστὸς
εἰς δόξαν θεοῦ πατρός (Phil. 2.10-11).

ABBREVIATIONS

Bible verses, Apocrypha, and Dead Sea Scrolls texts follow standard SBL abbreviations. Titles of works of ancient literature are not abbreviated. Ancient non-literary sources are abbreviated. For some papyri and ostraca, texts were viewed using PHI CD 7. In these cases and on the rare occasion in which a non-literary source is cited through a secondary source (such instances are noted in the text), the bibliographic data in this list are taken from Paul Bureth, *Les titulatures impériales dans les papyrus, les ostraca et les inscriptions d'Egypte (30 a.C.–284 p.C.)* (Brussels: Fondation Egyptologique Reine Elisabeth, 1964), pp. 11-17, and/or John F. Oates, *et al.* 'Checklist of Editions of Greek, Latin, Demotic and Coptic Papyri, Ostraca and Tablets' (web edition: http://scriptorium.lib.duke.edu/papyrus/texts/clist.html [updated: 11 September 2008]). In one case (PNovio), bibliographic data were not available. The abbreviation title is in full form here.

AB	Anchor Bible
AHB	*Ancient History Bulletin*
AJA	*American Journal of Archaeology*
AJAH	*American Journal of Ancient History*
AJP	*American Journal of Philology*
ANRW	Temporini, H., and W Haawe (eds.), *Aufstieg und Niedergang der römischen Welt: Geschichte und Kultur Roms im Spiegel der neueren Forschung* (Berlin: W. de Gruyter. 1972–).
ANTC	Abingdon New Testament Commentaries
Arch. f. Pap.	*Archiv für Papyrusforschung und verwandte Gebiete* (Leipzig/Berlin: Teubner).
AYB	Anchor Yale Bible
BBR	*Bulletin for Biblical Research*
BCE	Before the Common Era (BC)
BCH	*Bulletin de correspondance hellénique*
BDAG	Bauer, W., F.W. Danker, W.F. Arndt, and F.W. Gingrich, *A Greek–English Lexicon of the New Testament and Other*

	Early Christian Literature (Chicago: University of Chicago Press, 3rd edn, 2000).
BECNT	Baker Exegetical Commentary on the New Testament
BEFAR	Bibliothèque des écoles françaises d'Athènes et de Rome
BGU	*Aegyptische Urkunden aus den Staatlichen Museen zu Berlin* (Berlin: Weidmann, 1895-1937).
Bib	*Biblica*
BibInt	*Biblical Interpretation*
BibNotiz	*Biblische Notizen*
BibOr	Biblica et orientalia
BMCR	*Bryn Mawr Classical Review* [http://bmcr.brynmawr.edu]
BMCRE	Mattingly, H., *et al.* (eds.), *Coins of the Roman Empire in the British Museum* (London: Trustees of the British Museum, 1923-62).
BNTC	Black's New Testament Commentaries
BSac	*Bibliotheca Sacra*
BT	*The Bible Translator*
BTB	*Biblical Theology Bulletin*
BZNW	Beihefte zur *Zeitschrift für die neutestamentliche Wissenschaft*
CAH	Cook, S.A., *et al.* (eds.), *Cambridge Ancient History* (Cambridge: Cambridge University Press, 1st edn, 1923–39; 2nd edn, 1961–).
CBQMS	*Catholic Biblical Quarterly* Monograph Series
CBR	*Currents in Biblical Research*
CCS	Cincinnati Classical Studies
CE	Common Era (AD)
CFA	John Scheid, *Commentarii Fratrum Arvalium qui supersunt: Les copies épigraphiques des protocoles annuels de la Confrérie Arvale (21 AV.–31 AP. J.-C.)* (Roma Antica, 4; Rome: École Française de Rome, Soprintendenza Archeologica di Roma, 1998).
CIL	Mommsen, Th., *et al.* (eds.), *Corpus inscriptionum latinarum* (Berlin: G. Reimer, 1863–).
CILT	Current Issues in Linguistic Theory
ConBNT	Coniectanea neotestamentica/Coniectanea biblica: New Testament Series
CP	*Classical Philology*
CPR	*Corpus papyrorum Raineri* (Vienna, 1895)
CQ	*Classical Quarterly*
CSL	Cambridge Studies in Linguistics
CTL	Cambridge Textbooks in Linguistics
CTR	*Criswell Theological Review*

DJD	Discoveries in the Judaean Desert (Oxford: Clarendon Press, 1955–).
DPL	Hawthorne, G.F., R.P. Martin, and D.G. Reid (eds.), *Dictionary of Paul and his Letters* (Downers Grove, IL: InterVarsity Press, 1993).
DSD	*Dead Sea Discoveries*
EPRO	Etudes préliminaires aux religions orientales dans l'empire romain
Exp	*The Expositor*
FilolNT	*Filología neotestamentaria*
GNS	Good News Studies
HDR	Harvard Dissertations in Religion
Hellenica	*Hellenica: Recueil d'épigraphie, de numismatique, et d'antiquités grecques*
HNTC	Harper's New Testament Commentaries
HTR	*Harvard Theological Review*
HTS	Harvard Theological Studies
IBC	Interpretation: A Bible Commentary for Teaching and Preaching
IBS	*Irish Biblical Studies*
ICC	International Critical Commentary
ICLW	Fishwick, Duncan, *The Imperial Cult in the Latin West: Studies in the Ruler Cult of the Western Provinces of the Roman Empire* (3 vols. [vols. 1–2: EPRO; vol. 3: RGRW]; Leiden: E.J. Brill, 1987–2005).
IG	*Inscriptiones graecae* (Berlin: G. Reimer, 1903–).
IGRR	Cagnat, R., *et al.* (eds.), *Inscriptiones graecae ad res romanas pertinentes* (Paris: E. Leroux, 1906–27; repr., Chicago: Ares, 1975).
ILS	Dessau, H. (ed.), *Inscriptiones latinae selectae* (3 vols.; Berlin: Weidmann, 1892–1916; repr., Chicago, 1979).
IPriene	*Inschriften von Priene* (Berlin: G. Reimer, 1906).
Jastrow	Jastrow, M., *A Dictionary of the Targumim, the Talmud Babli and Yerushalmi, and the Midrashic Literature* (New York: Pardes, 2nd edn, 1903).
JBL	*Journal of Biblical Literature*
JETS	*Journal of the Evangelical Theological Society*
JHS	*Journal of Hellenic Studies*
JLin	*Journal of Linguistics*
JRS	*Journal of Roman Studies*
JSNT	*Journal for the Study of the New Testament*
JSNTSup	*Journal for the Study of the New Testament*, Supplement Series

JSOTSup	*Journal for the Study of the Old Testament,* Supplement Series
JTS	*Journal of Theological Studies*
KEK	Kritisch-exegetischer Kommentar über das Neue Testament
Klio	*Klio: Beiträge zur alten Geschichte*
LCL	Loeb Classical Library
LinPhil	*Linguistics and Philosophy*
LN	Louw, J.P., and E.A. Nida (eds.), *Greek–English Lexicon of the New Testament: Based on Semantic Domains* (New York: United Bible Societies, 2nd edn, 1989).
LNTS	Library of New Testament Studies
LXX	Septuagint (Greek Old Testament)
LSJ	Liddell, H.G., R. Scott, H.S. Jones and R. McKenzie, *A Greek–English Lexicon* (Oxford: Clarendon Press, 9th edn, 1940).
MM	Moulton, J.H., and G. Milligan, *The Vocabulary of the Greek Testament: Illustrated from the Papyri and Other Non-Literary Sources* (London: Hodder & Stoughton, 1930; repr., Peabody, MA: Hendrickson, 1997).
MNTC	Moffatt New Testament Commentary
MT	Masoretic Text (Hebrew Old Testament)
NA[27]	*Novum Testamentum graece,* 27th rev. edn
NCB	New Century Bible
NCBC	New Cambridge Bible Commentary
NIB	*The New Interpreter's Bible* (Nashville: Abingdon Press, 1994–2004).
NICNT	The New International Commentary on the New Testament
NIDNTT	Brown, C. (ed.), *The New International Dictionary of New Testament Theology* (4 vols.; Grand Rapids: Regency Reference Library, 1975–85).
NIGTC	The New International Greek Testament Commentary
NotesLin	*Notes on Linguistics*
NotesTrans	*Notes on Translation*
NovT	*Novum Testamentum*
NovTSup	Supplements to *Novum Testamentum*/*Novum Testamentum* Supplements
NTM	New Testament Monographs
NTOA	Novum Testamentum et orbis antiquus
NTOA/ StUNT	Novum Testamentum et orbis antiquus/Studien zur Umwelt des Neuen Testaments
NTS	*New Testament Studies*

OBerl   *Ostraka aus Brüssel und Berlin* (Berlin: W. de Gruyter, 1922).

OBodl   *Greek Ostraca in the Bodleian Library at Oxford* (ed. J.G. Tait, *et al.*; London, 1930-1964)

OBrux   *Ostraka aud Brüssel und Berlin* (Berlin, 1922)

OCamb   Tait, J.G., *et al.* (eds.), *Greek Ostraca in the Bodleian Library at Oxford* (3 vols.; London: Egypt Exploration Society, 1930–64), I, pp. 153-73.

ODeiss   Meyer, P. (ed.), *Griechische Texte aus Ägypten. I. Papyri des neutestamentlichen Seminars der Universität Berlin. II. Ostraka der Sammlung Deissmann* (Berlin: Weidmann, 1916; repr., Milan, 1973).

OECT   Oxford Early Christian Texts

OGIS   Dittenberger, W. (ed.), *Orientis graeci inscriptiones selectae* (2 vols.; Leipzig: S. Hirzel, 1903, 1905; repr., Chicago: Ares, 2001).

OPetr   Tait, J.G., *et al.* (eds.), *Greek Ostraca in the Bodleian Library at Oxford* (3 vols.; London: Egypt Exploration Society, 1930–64), I, pp. 82-152.

OStras   *Griechische und griechisch-demotische Ostraka der Univer-sitäts- und Landesbibliothek zu Strassburg im Elsass* (Berlin: Weidmann, 1923–).

OTheb   Milne, J.G. (ed.), *Theban Ostraca. III. Greek Texts* (Toronto: University of Toronto Library, 1913).

OTS   Old Testament Studies

OWilck   Wilcken, U. (ed.), *Griechische Ostraka aus Aegypten und Nubien: Ein Beitrag zur antiken Wirtschaftsgeschichte* (2 vols.; Leipzig: Gieseke & Debrient, 1899; repr., New York: Arno Press, 1979).

P&Bns   Pragmatics & Beyond, New Series

PBSR   *Papers of the British School at Rome*

PColl.Youtie   *Collectanea papyrologica. Texts Published in Honor of H.C. Youtie* (Papyrologische Texte und Abhandlungen, 19, 20; 2 vols.; Bonn: Habelt, 1976).

PFlor   Vitelli, G. (ed.), *Papiri greco-egizii. I. Papiri Fiorentini* (Milan: U. Hoepli, 1905).

PFouad   *Les papyrus Fouad* (Cairo: Institut français d'archéologie orientale, 1939).

PHeid   *Griechische Papyrusurkunden und Ostraka der Heidelberger Papyrus-Sammlung* (Heidelberg: C. Winter, 1963).

PHI   *PHI Greek Documentary Texts*

PhilRev   *Philosophical Review*

PLond	*Greek Papyri in the British Museum* (London: Trustees of the British Museum, 1893–)
PMAAR	Papers and Monographs of the American Academy in Rome
PMert	Bell, H. Idris, and C.H. Roberts (eds.), *A Descriptive Catalogue of the Greek Papyri in the Collection of Wilfred Merton* (3 vols.; London: E. Walker, 1948-67).
PMich	*Michigan Papyri* (Ann Arbor: University of Michigan Press, 1933–).
PMil.Vogl	*Papiri della Università degli Studi di Milano* (Milan: Cisalpino, 1937–).
PNovio	*The Noviomagensis Papyri*
PNTC	Pillar New Testament Commentary
POslo	*Papyri osloënses* (ed. S. Eitrem [and Leiv Amundsen]; Oslo: Dybwad, 1925–).
POxy	Grenfell, B.P., A.S. Hunt *et al.* (eds.), *The Oxyrhynchus Papyri* (London: Egypt Exploration Society, 1898–).
PPrinc	*Papyri in the Princeton University Collection* (Baltimore: Johns Hopkins University Press, 1931; Princeton, NJ: Princeton University Press, 1936, 1942).
PRyl	*Catalogue of the Greek and Latin Papyri in the John Rylands Library Manchester* (Manchester: Manchester University Press, 1915–).
PStras	*Griechische Papyrus der Kaiserlichen Universitäts- und Landesbibliothek zu Strassburg* (Leipzig: Hinrichs, 1912–20).
PTebt	Grenfell, B.P., A.S. Hunt *et al.* (eds.), *The Tebtunis Papyri* (London: Egypt Exploration Society, 1902–76).
RB	*Revue biblique*
RBL	*Review of Biblical Literature* [http://www.bookreviews.org]
RelSRev	*Religious Studies Review*
ResQ	*Restoration Quarterly*
RevExp	*Review and Expositor*
RGRW	Religions in the Graeco-Roman World
RIC	Mattingly, H., *et al.* (eds.), *The Roman Imperial Coinage* (London: Spink, 1923–94).
RT	Relevance theory
RTR	*Reformed Theological Review*
SB	*Sammelbuch griechischer Urkunden aus Aegypten* (Strassburg: Trübner, 1915–).
SBAlt	Schweizerische Beiträge zur Altertumswissenschaft
SBG	Studies in Biblical Greek
SBL	Society of Biblical Literature
SBLSP	Society of Biblical Literature Seminar Papers

SBT	Studies in Biblical Theology
SEG	*Supplementum epigraphicum graecum* (Leiden/Amsterdam: Giessen, 1923–).
SemeiaSt	Semeia Studies
SIG³	Dittenberger, W. (ed.), *Sylloge inscriptionum graecarum* (Leipzig: Hirzel, 3rd edn, 1915–24).
SIL	Summer Institute of Linguistics
SJLA	Studies in Judaism in Late Antiquity
SMSR	*Studi e materiali di storia delle religioni*
SNTSMS	Society for New Testament Studies Monograph Series
SP	Sacra pagina
SR	*Studies in Religion/Sciences religieuses*
TANZ	Texte und Arbeiten zum neutestamentlichen Zeitalter
TAPA	*Transactions and Proceedings of the American Philological Association*
TDNT	Kittel, G., and G. Friedrich (eds.), *Theological Dictionary of the New Testament* (trans. G.W. Bromiley; 10 vols.; Grand Rapids: Eerdmans, 1964–76).
TLG	*Thesaurus linguae graecae*
TNTC	Tyndale New Testament Commentaries
trans.	translated by
TS	*Theological Studies*
TynBul	*Tyndale Bulletin*
UBS⁴	*The Greek New Testament* (United Bible Societies, 4th rev. edn).
VC	*Vigiliae christianae*
VCSup	Supplements to *Vigiliae christianae*
VerbEccl	*Verbum et ecclesia*
VT	*Vetus Testamentum*
WBC	Word Biblical Commentary
WUNT	Wissenschaftliche Untersuchungen zum Neuen Testament
ZPE	*Zeitschrift für Papyrologie und Epigraphik*

Prologue

PLACE: CORINTH. DATE: MID 50s CE

Demetrios was in a hurry. He had been attending a gathering of a relatively new religious sect for over three months. He had come to believe that a Jewish man named Jesus who had been crucified two decades earlier had been raised to life again by God. Demetrios had not seen this Jesus, but some people he had met at the gathering knew people who had seen him. Stranger things have happened. He was drawn to the group by their communal spirit and enjoyed the food and conversation at the gatherings. Although he did not understand all the teaching (actually he did not understand much at all) he was drawn to the meetings, and what he did understand was very satisfying. He could not explain it, but he knew that Jesus was alive and somehow was at these meetings.

Demetrios was in a hurry because a day earlier a letter had arrived from the founder of the community. This Paul was a bit controversial. Some liked him, but others felt that he overstepped his authority. The letter was supposed to answer some long-standing questions the group had on many practical matters. Demetrios had not yet formulated an opinion about Paul. He was not concerned with some of the disputes among the members, but he did respect Paul as the founder of the community. This had to grant him a measure of authority.

Now at the east end of the Agora, despite his haste, Demetrios stopped briefly at the Julian Basilica with its statue of the late emperor Augustus in which the emperor was involved in a sacrifice. He enjoyed looking at this statue. Its artistic beauty was captivating, and its message clear—Augustus interceded for his people. This statue stood between statues of Augustus's grandchildren Gaius and Lucius Caesar. These statues reminded Demetrios of the Dioscuroi, which was probably intended. Demetrios admired Augustus and had often wished that one of his grandchildren had been able to succeed him as emperor. Tiberius had been acceptable, but Caligula was an embarrassment to the imperial family. Claudius had also been fairly good, but Demetrios still could not help but wonder how things could have been different if Gaius and/or Lucius had followed Augustus.

All in all the relationship between Corinth and Rome was really very good. And things were looking even better. Recently young Nero had just become emperor and, by every measure thus far, he showed promise. He appeared to be following in Augustus's footsteps. In fact, Demetrios had heard that the young emperor loved Greece and hoped to visit Corinth. Excitement filled the air.

Demetrios had to move on west through the Agora, but in front of the small temples of Apollo and Venus he saw some children eating figs and he remembered that he wanted to bring some grapes home that night for tomorrow morning's breakfast. The market selling the fruit that he most enjoyed was not far, but he would have to backtrack a little. It would be closed when the meeting was concluded. Thus, despite his hurry, he made a right turn, passed an old temple and saw the fruit stand on his right. The fruit looked especially good today; maybe he would get a little extra to have a small taste before the meeting. This would be a treat. Demetrios reached into his moneybag and pulled out the only coin in the bag. He stopped and looked at the coin. It was the old coin that his father had given him. The coin had been in the family since his grandfather's grandfather fought for Augustus at Actium. Augustus rewarded his soldiers in part with this coin. It remained in the family and was passed on to the firstborn son. The coin offered an opportunity for Demetrios to talk to others about his connection to that great victory over Antony and Cleopatra. Demetrios was proud of the coin and what it represented. He was proud to have a relative who had fought for Augustus. In long conversations, he might even mention that the father of this soldier (also named Demetrios) was one of the original Greek settlers who had come to the city when it was refounded by Julius Caesar as a Roman colony. Augustus was important to Demetrios. He was like a great benefactor to his family and his city. He had brought peace to the region that had lasted now for over 80 years. The title *saviour* was certainly applicable. If anyone deserved to be a god, it was Augustus.

Forgetting to bring spending money was a disappointment; he would have to forgo grapes and probably breakfast. The coin was too important. Maybe he could bring some bread back from the meeting he was attending. He returned to the Agora and passed between the fountain of Poseidon and the little temple of Apollo. He turned left but not before gazing at the new temple dedicated to the imperial family. This temple had really excited him while it was being built and even more so when it was first opened. However, during the past few months he had not felt quite as enthusiastic about it. Maybe it was because of the new community he was involved in. They rarely spoke of traditional or imperial gods and never in a manner of worship. To be honest, Demetrios was beginning to feel uncomfortable in both settings. The imperial family was so important to him and his family; however, what he was learning about Jesus was also very important to him.

Jesus was also a *saviour*, and if it was true that he died to satisfy the wrath of God on his behalf, such a gift could not go without some type of reciprocity.

Generally speaking, Demetrios felt that the two types of worship were compatible. He really had not thought much about it. Was it not just like his short commitment to Isis five years ago? He had happily honoured both the Caesars and Isis (and the traditional gods of course). However, this did not last. In fact, just after the cute Spartan girl stopped coming to the Isis temple, his interest waned. Nevertheless, his attraction to Jesus seemed different in some way. This seemed very real. Although it was not intentional, he sometimes wondered what roles the Roman gods had in the life of his new friends. He thought at times he heard these gods called 'idols' among them. This certainly seemed like a negative attitude. He figured that he must have been mistaken. People did not discuss the Roman gods in this manner.

Now Demetrios was really late. His host would certainly have begun the meal by now so he hurried to the meeting. To his surprise he had not even missed the prayer of thanks. After reclining at the table and finishing his meal, he awaited the reading of the letter.

One of the servants brought the letter to the host and after a slight pause, the letter began,

Παῦλος κλητὸς ἀπόστολος Χριστοῦ Ἰησοῦ διὰ θελήματος θεοῦ . . .

Paul, called an apostle of Christ Jesus through the will of God . . .

This Paul did not hold anything back. He clearly believed in his role as a special messenger of God. Demetrios was listening with interest for a while. However, when the discussion turned to court cases, his interest was diminishing. Even the discussion of marriage was not that important. He was happy at present and expected to be married in a year or two. He was in no rush. However, just as he began to get restless, the reader of the letter stated, Περὶ δὲ τῶν εἰδωλοθύτων, ('now concerning things sacrificed to idols'). This seemed to remotely touch on some of what he had been thinking about. He listened closely. Then the reader stated,

καὶ γὰρ εἴπερ εἰσὶν λεγόμενοι θεοὶ εἴτε ἐν οὐρανῷ εἴτε ἐπὶ γῆς, ὥσπερ εἰσὶν θεοὶ πολλοὶ καὶ κύριοι πολλοί, ἀλλ᾽ ἡμῖν εἷς θεὸς ὁ πατὴρ ἐξ οὗ τὰ πάντα καὶ ἡμεῖς εἰς αὐτόν, καὶ εἷς κύριος Ἰησοῦς Χριστὸς δι᾽ οὗ τὰ πάντα καὶ ἡμεῖς δι᾽ αὐτοῦ.

for even if [it is true] there are those called gods whether in heaven or on earth, just as there are many gods and many lords, but to us there is one God, the Father, from whom all things are and we exist in him, and there is one Lord, Jesus Christ, through whom all things are and we exist through him.

Demetrios focused on these words to the point that he failed to follow the message of the letter after the passage. The words echoed in his mind:

'there are many gods and many lords, but to us there is one God, the Father, ... and there is one Lord, Jesus Christ'. 'There is one Lord Jesus Christ.' 'There is one Lord Jesus Christ.' ...

***

This study is intended to attempt to understand what response Demetrios (and others) would have had to statements such as this one in 1 Corinthians. It will attempt to reconstruct the first-century context of certain recipients of Paul's letters through ancient sources and modern theory. The sources will be used to help (re-)create a thought world into which we can enter by exposure to some of the same history, ideas, physical remains and so on that Demetrios would have experienced. Modern theory will be used to understand and utilize these data in a responsible manner. Our task is to construct a picture of relevant aspects of the ancient world that can provide us with a grid or foundation through which we can respond to passages like 1 Cor. 8.5-6 in the way that Demetrios himself would respond.

I recognize that such an idealized goal is impossible. We cannot presume to enter in any objective way into the mind of those with whom we communicate on a daily basis, let alone the mind of the ancient individual. This exercise to some extent is an attempt to become aware of and to set aside our own worldview as much as possible when approaching the text. Although this can be only marginally achieved, the attempt nevertheless provides a better and more accurate view of the first century than we can achieve without this process.

***

The first part of the title of this work, 'lord of the entire world,' is a quotation from an inscription written approximately ten years after 1 Corinthians (SIG³ 814; 67 CE). It was found not far from Corinth. The referent of the phrase from this inscription is the ruling emperor Nero. Lordship terminology is complex and can be used for many different people in a society without confusion. The question I am attempting to answer is whether passages like 1 Cor. 8.5-6, referring to Jesus, and SIG³ 814, referring to Caesar, can exist without conflict or whether the concept in one is a direct challenge to the concept in the other.

Chapter 1

Introduction

In the second century of the Common Era, a battle clearly raged for the allegiance of the individual hearts, minds and souls of the Roman empire. Conflicting claims of lordship demanded a choice to be made between the claim of Christ and the claim of Caesar. This decision was most acute for the young Christian communities spread throughout the empire. The (apparently) safe decision would be to confess allegiance to Caesar. However, this position was unacceptable to those who believed that Christ was the true saviour and lord despite the present political situation in which the propaganda and ideology claimed these roles for the emperor. This claim was supported by the might of imperial Rome, which placed in the emperor's hands the power over physical life and death. Christians believed that there was a role for the emperor, but it was not one that usurped the roles exclusive to God and Christ. Thus, choice for Christ was a rejection of the emperor and the young church's Lord demanded nothing less. Given the political realities, the Christians' choice was offensive to the emperor and to those whose allegiance was committed to him. Therefore, the position of the Christian was dangerous and could result in dire consequences. The *Martyrdom of Polycarp* describes the events preceding the death of Polycarp. The aged protagonist is presented with the following question:

Τί γὰρ κακόν ἐστιν εἰπεῖν, Κύριος Καῖσαρ, καὶ ἐπιθῦσαι (καὶ τὰ τούτοις ἀκόλουθα) καὶ διασώζεσθαι; (8.2; see also 9.2–10.1).[1]

For what harm is there to say 'Caesar is Lord' and to offer incense (and so forth) and [thus] escape death[2]?

---

1. Unless otherwise noted, all non-biblical ancient Greek and Latin texts are from the Loeb Classical Library, and all translations are my own.

2. The voice of the present infinitive διασώζεσθαι is middle/passive. It seems common to translate this verb as a direct middle (so Ehrman [LCL], 'to save yourself'; and Michael Holmes, 'saving yourself' [Michael W. Holmes [ed. and trans.], *The Apostolic Fathers: Greek Texts and English Translation* [after the earlier work of J.B. Lightfoot and J.R. Harmer; Grand Rapids: Baker Book House, 3rd edn, 2007]). This is how I originally translated it. However, Stanley Porter suggested to me the passive 'be saved'. After considering this option for a while, I concluded that in light of the rare

Polycarp of course rejects the offer and thus is put to death for his devotion to his Lord, Jesus. From this example, two points can be drawn. First, approximately one hundred years after Paul wrote his letters, at least some Christians' commitment to the lordship of Jesus brought them into direct conflict with the imperial system. Specifically, the Christians' submission to Jesus prohibited them from acknowledging Caesar as lord. This was offensive to the ruling power and resulted in persecution. For some, this conflict was fatal. Second, the recording and circulating of this detailed account suggest that, around this same time,[3] Christianity rejected a syncretistic (and even pluralistic) relationship with the imperial cult(s) and was explicitly attempting to counter it. The account in the *Martyrdom of Polycarp* probably served as an example to be followed.

Although this recorded conflict took place almost one hundred years after Paul, it is unlikely that this friction was new. It probably had been growing for some time. The more visible the church had become and the more distinct its identity from Judaism (which, although not immune from difficulties, was somewhat exempt from imperial religion), the more likely for conflict to occur. The problem is primarily one with the Christians. Imperial religion was polytheistic, syncretistic and pluralistic. It probably would have tolerated Christianity as long as the followers of Christ also honoured the Roman gods (including the emperor). Where do the roots of this conflict begin? Could the conviction of later martyrs such as Polycarp have come from the New Testament itself?

Although imperial ideology was already in place when Paul wrote his letters nearly one hundred years earlier, no explicit or direct statement of conflict between Caesar and Christ appears to exist in the Pauline literature. Does this mean that there was no tension for the followers of Christ in light of imperial ideology? Or, was there conflict that has gone unnoticed owing to our distance from the original events?

The purpose of this project is to determine if, in some cases, Paul's use of the term κύριος involves a polemic against the living Roman emperor and, by implication, his (and the Roman state's) claim of sovereignty over every aspect of the lives of those under his authority. The world of Paul was dominated by the ideology of the imperial regime. In addition to other purposes, Paul's message challenged this ideology and its leader. The role of the emperor himself was an essential aspect of this ideology. Whether explicitly acknowledged or not, the emperor was the *lord* of the empire. I

'direct' usage of the middle and the acceptability of the passive, this was preferable. The translation 'escape death' is the passive gloss in BDAG for this verb.

3. The death of Polycarp can be roughly dated to the middle of the second century. See Holmes, *Apostolic Fathers*, pp. 301-302. The *Martyrdom of Polycarp* was probably written shortly after the recorded events (Holmes, *Apostolic Fathers*, p. 298).

intend to explore whether or not Paul's message challenged imperial ideology, the state, and the emperor himself. And, if it did, in what ways was this challenge articulated? Did Paul challenge the emperor's authority and role when it conflicted with the role of God and Christ in the lives of the Christian?

Before proceeding, it is necessary to make a brief statement about terminology. The nature and practice of the worship of the emperor and his family (and occasionally others associated with these) are complex. Unless a specific localized expression of this phenomenon is under consideration, the plural label *imperial cults* (or in some cases the more general *emperor worship*) will be used in this work to avoid misrepresenting these empire-wide phenomena. The singular implies a unified system of belief and practice that did not exist in the first-century Roman empire. Rather, there were many different expressions of emperor (and the imperial family) worship incorporated and practised at various levels of society. Therefore, unless I am speaking of a specific localized practice of imperial worship, I will avoid the singular use of the label. This will be further developed in Chapter 3.

Finally, it is important to make explicit exactly what this study is and is not intending to do. The goal of this study is to determine whether or not it is probable that Paul intended a polemic against the living Caesar in some of his uses of κύριος for Jesus. If a polemic exists, it does not demand that it be the most important aspect of the usage in any context. It would merely demonstrate that the polemic is part of the message. The arguments being suggested seem to be sufficient to persuade some scholars of the existence of a *polemic*. However, others dismiss it entirely. Therefore, I will proceed inductively. First, I will discuss the evidence with the methodology usually used. Although this should provide additional evidence for a polemic, it will not really advance the argument. Those who already maintain the existence of a polemic will be strengthened in their conviction; however, it is questionable whether it will persuade anyone not previously convinced. I will turn to an alternative method that will build on the more traditional approach. To pursue this end, in certain places I will focus my discussion towards critics who have dismissed the possibility of a *polemic*. In particular, I ask whether James D.G. Dunn would be persuaded. Dunn is chosen because his writings demonstrate sensitivity to both the text and the context of a passage and he does not see a polemic in the Pauline text. I can of course in no way know whether Dunn would truly be persuaded by new arguments or approaches. Nevertheless, he serves as a conversation partner. To dialogue with a critic is the best way to assure that the soundest arguments are made. The use of this inductive approach does not suggest that the extant approach is insufficient. The polemical position has many proponents. However, the existence of many doubters suggests that the issue can be pursued with benefit.

Thus, the goal of this study is to determine whether or not a *polemic* exists. This will have a significant impact on exegesis. However, space does not provide that exegetical implications be pursued in any depth. Only minimal exegetical work will be done here. This must be reserved for further development at a later date.

The structure of this book is shaped to reach this goal. Much is devoted to providing background material to help the reader understand the historical, linguistic, religious, and social context of Paul and his churches. Chapters 1 and 2 are introductory but include important preliminary information. Chapter 3 describes imperial cults and the emperor. A significant amount of space is devoted to imperial cults. There are two reasons for this. First, although this topic is only a part of the context, it is an important part. Second, there is much discussion of imperial cults in contemporary New Testament work; however, this often lacks the preciseness necessary for our task. Chapter 4 provides linguistic data on κύριος. Although much traditional word study material and linguistic analysis are included, Chapter 4 is focused on aspects that contribute specifically to our task. The first half of Chapter 5 contributes to the context by looking at κύριος as a title for the emperor. The second half of Chapter 5 begins by providing insights from a communication theory. The contextual material and communication theory are intended to give the reader the necessary background to help determine whether a challenge to the emperor is present in Paul's use of κύριος for Jesus and under what circumstances such a challenge may be present. In other words, I am attempting to re-create as much of the relevant context as possible to help the reader hear the text as the original readers would have heard it. The remainder of Chapter 5 is a discussion of texts. I will attempt to determine with the contextual information whether these texts include a polemic.

1. *Towards Defining 'Polemic'*

There is one further terminological clarification needed before proceeding. What is meant here by 'polemic'? The *Oxford English Dictionary* defines the non-personal substantive 'polemic' as 'A controversial argument or discussion; argumentation against some opinion, doctrine, etc.; aggressive controversy; in *pl.* the practice of this, esp. as a method of conducting theological controversy: opposed to *irenics*'.[4] Perhaps the first noun definition of the *New Oxford American Dictionary* is more precise for our purposes: 'a strong verbal or written attack on someone or something.'[5]

---

4. J.A. Simpson and E.S.C. Weiner (preparers), *The Oxford English Dictionary* (Oxford: Clarendon Press, 2nd edn, 1989), XII, p. 21.

5. E.J. Jewell and F. Abate (eds.), *New Oxford American Dictionary* (Oxford: Oxford University Press, 2nd edn, 2005), p. 1313.

Among other things, these definitions emphasize the controversial nature of the content labelled *polemic* with a view towards a response from an opposing party. The content (i.e. argument, etc.) is what is labelled *polemic*. This content is itself the controversial element. Additionally, any response may or may not be explicit (i.e. it may be only internal or may involve a reaction against the party responsible for the offence). The intended response of the polemic-directed party is out of the control of the communicator. It only predicts that some party may be offended. Nevertheless, the communication offering is intended to produce a response. To some extent, these definitions are helpful for the present purpose. However, they focus on the controversial argument itself. I am not attempting to determine whether the word κύριος, or Jesus himself, is polemical. Of course, Jesus is controversial in many ways; however, the question here is whether or not Paul's use of the title κύριος for Jesus (in some contexts) is a challenge to Caesar (or his position/role in the lives of the addressees[6]). The use of the term suggests that a challenge is being set forth. In this case, the challenge is against a specific person for a specific position or role held within society. The person and/or position (lord) in itself is not what is considered controversial[7] (although, based on the quoted definitions, this would seem to be the case). Rather, I am attempting to determine whether, by the use of a certain term representing a specific position or role, one would be seen as a challenge to another who also has some claim to the same position. Therefore, my definition of 'polemic' can be summed up simply as *a communicative act that challenges and/or gives offence in the form of a challenge to another*. Or slightly more specifically for this work, it may be defined as *a challenge of one party to another through a claim to a role held by the other*. This can vary in directness and strength. It often is a challenge against a specific role or position held by another. In this study I am attempting to determine whether or not Paul's use of κύριος for Jesus in some way challenges the position of the living Caesar. This challenge may be made through a third party on behalf of the challenger. Although this definition (and some of the other terminology here) is general, it will serve until it can be refined in Chapter 5.

2. *The Need for and Value of the Study*

There are at least seven reasons why this study is worth pursuing at this time. First, there is a renewed interest in the Graeco-Roman context of the

---

6. This is why the definition from the *Oxford English Dictionary* was for non-personal usages.

7. Of course, the person of Jesus was and is highly controversial on other grounds. Our task here is focused on a specific type of challenge.

New Testament. This renewed interest is not simply a return to the history-of-religions approach of decades past but rather a more balanced and nuanced approach to the contexts in which the biblical authors and their readers lived. The Graeco-Roman context seems especially important to the Pauline corpus because the churches and individuals to whom Paul wrote were all in Graeco-Roman cities.[8]

Second, since Simon Price's highly influential book *Rituals and Power*,[9] the scholarly community has a better and more informed understanding of imperial cults and the role of the Roman emperor in the daily lives of the people under Roman authority. Price's volume focuses on Asia Minor, which is valuable for the Pauline scholar since many of Paul's letters were written to this area. Nevertheless, it is applicable also to other parts of the Roman empire (especially in the other parts of the eastern empire; e.g. Greece). Price's insights have also been utilized by others who have contributed important works that help us understand imperial cults in other areas of the empire.[10]

Third, advances in technology make studies like this much more manageable. Biblical search engines such as GRAMCORD[11] (and other Bible software) and classical resources such as the TLG and PHI CD-ROMs[12]

---

8. See, e.g., the articles in Troels Engberg-Pedersen (ed.), *Paul beyond the Judaism/ Hellenism Divide* (Louisville: Westminster/John Knox Press, 2001). The renewed interest in Graeco-Roman contexts will be discussed further below and in Chapter 2. Additionally, the renewed interest in Paul and his Graeco-Roman context is evident by the recent reference-like volume edited by J. Paul Sampley, *Paul in the Greco-Roman World: A Handbook* (Harrisburg, PA: Trinity Press International, 2003).

9. Simon R.F. Price, *Rituals and Power: The Roman Imperial Cult in Asia Minor* (Cambridge: Cambridge University Press, 1984). This book and its contribution will be discussed in detail in Chapter 3.

10. See, e.g., Ittai Gradel, *Emperor Worship and Roman Religion* (Oxford Classical Monographs; Oxford: Oxford University Press, 2002). Although not in full agreement with Price, see also Duncan Fishwick, *The Imperial Cult in the Latin West: Studies in the Ruler Cult of the Western Provinces of the Roman Empire* (3 vols. [vols. 1-2: EPRO]; [vol. 3: RGRW]; Leiden: E.J. Brill, 1987–2005) (abbreviated ICLW). Further volumes are planned but their completion is uncertain.

11. GRAMCORD (*GRAMCORD Greek New Testament for Windows 2.4cx with Database 5.3* [Vancouver, WA: Gramcord Institute, 1999]) is a software programme that searches a morphologically tagged Greek New Testament (UBS[4]) yielding results based on selected morphological characteristics. Searches can be simple, comprised of only one word, or complex, including complicated strings of grammatical and lexical detail. GRAMCORD was programmed by Paul Miller and initially tagged by James Boyer.

12. *Thesaurus linguae graecae* E CD-ROM (*Thesaurus Lingua Graecae* [CD ROM E. Software database] [Los Altos, CA: Packard Humanities Institute, 1999]) is a CD-ROM containing Greek texts from Homer to 1453 CE. This CD may be searched for various words and phrases. *PHI Greek Documentary Texts* CD-ROM #7 and CD-ROM

provide the scholar with the ability to search massive amounts of literature in minimal time. What would have taken hundreds of hours just a few years ago can now be accomplished in seconds. This provides accuracy and data to make a project such as this manageable.

Fourth, advances in linguistic and communication theories provide a means of analysing texts that can result in more convincing conclusions. These theories are based on observations of language usage and can supplement more traditional philological approaches to analysis. This added level of analysis provides a framework based not exclusively on Greek but on the act of communication. Thus, conclusions can be tested for validity beyond the traditional understanding of the Graeco-Roman world.

Fifth, we place a high value on the text of the New Testament for Christian life and practice. It is important to understand the original context of Paul and the churches to which he wrote in order to maximize our understanding of the text. If (based on our understanding of the context) Paul's use of κύριος may be a polemic against Caesar, it is worth examining either to verify or to reject this thesis. Additionally, if a polemic can be demonstrated, it will be important to see just how this understanding impacts exegesis. Finally, this study may affect twenty-first-century Christians' ethics. The insights explored here should challenge Christians to examine their own governments and governmental policies and, by careful application of principles drawn from this study, to respond appropriately.

Sixth, unlike terms such as σωτήρ, where the imperial usage is clear, κύριος was not common for emperors until the middle of Nero's reign. There is evidence that all of the emperors before Nero were addressed with this title at some time, but most Julio-Claudians seemed to have rejected it (whether out of actual conviction or pragmatism—this will be discussed in Chapter 5). In addition, the title was common for God in the Septuagint,[13] which undeniably influenced Paul. Therefore, this study will need to push beyond simple word parallels. I acknowledge at the onset that the burden of proof is on those attempting to prove a polemic. However, I hope to gain a clearer picture of the possibility of a polemic through the reconstruction of the context.[14]

#5.3 are searchable CD-ROMs from the Packard Humanities Institute. The first CD contains inscriptions and papyri. The second includes Latin texts and Bible versions (*PHI Greek Documentary Texts* [CD ROM #7 software database] [Los Altos, CA: Packard Humanities Institute, 1991–96]).

13. I am not unaware of the problems with the label 'Septuagint' for the Greek translation of the Old Testament. This will be briefly addressed in Chapter 4.

14. Our understanding of *context* will be defined below. The label *cognitive environment* will be introduced and developed for this purpose.

Finally, as I will highlight in the next section, no extensive research projects have been published on this topic to date. Claims are often made in support of or against a polemical usage of the title in the New Testament, but the basis of these claims is dubious. They seem to be founded on other factors. For example, one who already assumes a Graeco-Roman context to Paul's work may see the polemic as natural. However, if one has rejected the Graeco-Roman context as significant, a polemical option may be dismissed. In many cases, even contextually sensitive works may not consider a potential polemic. For example, while discussing the use of κύριος in his massive Pauline theology, James D.G. Dunn dismisses emperor worship as irrelevant.[15] The present state of the debate is such that those who maintain a polemic must defend it. Those who do not see a polemic need not address the issue at all. Jean Héring goes further than many by acknowledging the view before dismissing it: 'We can rule that the Apostles might have used the term *"kurios"*, even hypothetically, for the Emperor.'[16] The burden of proof rests with those who maintain a polemic. Additionally, the inconclusive nature of the use of the term for the Julio-Claudian emperors contributes to the burden of proof resting upon the pro-polemic proponents. I hope that this work, by considering not only the term but also the wider conceptual and (social) contextual issues, will provide evidence to either maintain the status quo or to balance or even shift the burden of proof with more certainty than we presently maintain.

Further, as we will see below, some scholars use the argument of an anti-imperial polemic with the term as a single point among many to argue other interests. Our research is partially intended to provide solid information to determine if such claims are justified. Finally, there seems to be a naïve understanding of the use of κύριος for the emperors during Paul's ministry. One otherwise careful commentator suggests that the primary titles for the emperor at the time Paul wrote to the Philippians were κύριος and σωτήρ.[17] This apparently incorrect statement (at least as far as κύριος is concerned) is not supported but certainly has implications for the Christology of the book. It is our purpose not only to attempt to reconstruct as much of the context as possible, but also to focus on κύριος itself and determine the potential for a polemic on its own merits.

15. James D.G. Dunn, *The Theology of Paul the Apostle* (Grand Rapids: Eerdmans, 1998), p. 247.

16. Jean Héring, *The First Epistle of Saint Paul to the Corinthians* (trans. A.W. Heathcote and P.J. Allcock; London: Epworth Press, 1962), pp. 69.

17. Gordon D. Fee, *Paul's Letter to the Philippians* (NICNT; Grand Rapids: Eerdmans, 1995), p. 31.

3. *Previous Studies of Importance*

As already stated, no extended discussions exist regarding an anti-imperial polemical use of κύριος in Pauline literature. Additionally, there is little argument against the presence of a polemic. Essentially, the burden of proof is with those who desire to demonstrate the existence of a polemic. Therefore, our discussion here will be both brief and selective.

A number of sources make an imperial connection without significant support. This is often due to the nature of the work.[18] These studies use the argument to support other claims. Marie Keller's work on Philippians is representative; she briefly discusses the use of κύριος and concludes, 'There is evidence that "Caesar is lord" is an imperial proclamation.'[19] She then cites *Martyrdom of Polycarp* 8.2 in support,[20] but this text is too late to lend much support for any usage in Philippians. I suspect it is intended to be illustrative.

One might expect Wilhelm Bousset's famous work *Kyrios Christos* to deal with this issue in some depth.[21] However, his interest is primarily one of derivation. He desires to demonstrate that New Testament usage is derived from Hellenistic concepts (as opposed to Jewish/Palestinian concepts).[22] With this purpose and concluding that the worship of the emperor as κύριος would not have been developed enough at the time of and in the areas where worship of Jesus as κύριος developed, Bousset concludes that it would be wrong to assume that worship of Jesus as the Lord was developed in 'conscious opposition' to emperor worship.[23] Nevertheless, his is an excellent resource for understanding the term in its non-Jewish context.

---

18. See, e.g., N.T. Wright, *What Saint Paul Really Said: Was Paul of Tarsus the Real Founder of Christianity?* (Grand Rapids: Eerdmans, 1997), pp. 56-57, 88. It is of interest to note that Steve Walton makes a claim similar to ours for Luke's literature, 'Luke never mentions Caesar's claim to be lord, but to use κύριος so prominently for Jesus could not but remind readers living in the empire of this claim and would suggest that Luke was making a counter-claim for Jesus over against Caesar (as indeed he was)' ('The State They Were in: Luke's View of the Roman Empire', in Peter Oakes [ed.], *Rome in the Bible and the Early Church* [Carlisle: Paternoster Press, 2002], pp. 1-41 [26]). Again, the purpose of Walton's work does not provide for a significant defence of this claim.

19. Marie Noël Keller, *Choosing What Is Best: Paul, Roman Society and Philippians* (Unpublished ThD diss., Lutheran School of Theology at Chicago, 1995), pp. 139-41.

20. Keller, *Choosing What Is Best*, pp. 141 n. 154.

21. Wilhelm Bousset, *Kyrios Christos* (trans. John E. Steely; Nashville: Abingdon Press, 5th edn, 1970). The first German edition of this work was published in 1913.

22. Bousset, *Kyrios Christos*, pp. 138-47.

23. Bousset, *Kyrios Christos*, p. 141.

Probably the most significant and cited source on this issue remains Adolf Deissmann.[24] He brings together a wealth of primary sources to demonstrate that although the use of words for *lord* was not common throughout the empire until Domitian, as early as Nero it was a common title in the East, and it was not lacking for Augustus, Tiberius, and Claudius. Deissmann concludes,

> It is sufficient for our purpose to have realised the state of affairs in the time of Nero and St. Paul. And then we cannot escape the conjecture that the Christians of the East who heard St. Paul preach in the style of Phil. ii. 9, 11 and I Cor. viii. 5, 6 must have found in the solemn confession that Jesus is 'the Lord' a silent protest against other 'lords,' and against 'the lord,' as people were beginning to call the Roman Caesar. And St. Paul himself must have felt and intended this silent protest. . . .[25]

Deissmann's discussion is too brief to do justice to this conclusion. His discussion of primary sources has demonstrated that by around 60 CE κύριος was a common title for Nero. Depending on the dating of Philippians, his conclusions may apply to Philippians 2 as noted. However, his scant evidence of the title applied to Augustus, Tiberius, and Claudius,[26] the lack of evidence for its use for Gaius,[27] and his own acknowledgment that Augustus and Tiberius 'scorned' the title,[28] demand that his claimed connection for 1 Corinthians be defended more vigorously. Essentially, our study among other purposes is meant to provide further research to examine such claims.

Generally, the field of New Testament studies has not advanced much beyond Deissmann on this issue. Dominique Cuss devotes more than ten pages to the title and produced a helpful and concise summary of the use of κύριος for the emperor and for Christ but does not really advance Deissmann's work.[29] Although I could list others (some will be cited in this work), four works will be noted here as example of studies that discuss κύριος as having a possible polemical nuance. What distinguishes these types of works from those that Keller (above) represents is that the authors interact on a more substantial level with the issue of whether the appearance of κύριος in some contexts has polemical intention or effect.

---

24. Adolf Deissmann, *Light from the Ancient East: The New Testament Illustrated by Recently Discovered Texts of the Graeco-Roman World* (trans. Lionel R. Strachan; New York: George H. Doran, 1927; repr. Peabody, MA: Hendrickson, 1995), pp. 348-63.

25. Deissmann, *Light*, p. 355.

26. Deissmann, *Light*, p. 353.

27. Deissmann, *Light*, p. 353.

28. Deissmann, *Light*, p. 350.

29. Dominique Cuss, *Imperial Cult and Honorary Terms in the New Testament* (Fribourg, Switzerland: University Press, 1974), pp. 53-63.

First is Peter Oakes's important study on Philippians.[30] This work includes a significant chapter entitled 'Christ and the Emperor.'[31] His discussion of κύριος is brief,[32] included in a discussion of Phil 2.9-11.[33] Nevertheless, it is worth noting briefly here (the entire chapter will be used more thoroughly in later portions of our work). Oakes acknowledges that the context of Phil 2.11 (where our term occurs) is both Septuagintal and imperial. Oakes rejects later examples of *dominus* as support for this being an example of an imperial acclamation but nevertheless concludes that the term was 'a common term connected with the Emperor.' The term was probably familiar to the readers as being applied to both Christ and the emperor. However, given the nature of the church at Philippi, the Septuagintal connotations would be more likely to go unnoticed than the imperial.[34]

Second, Mikael Tellbe has produced a very detailed study of Paul's relationship to the Roman state.[35] Tellbe discusses κύριος in the context of 1 Thessalonians, Romans, and Philippians. In 1 Thessalonians (e.g. 5.2), Paul's eschatology is used to counter imperial ideology. Hope is to be placed in the day of the *parousia*, not in imperial propaganda.[36] In Romans, Tellbe discusses κύριος in the context of other terms and concludes that, taken together, Paul's theology is anti-imperial.[37] Like Oakes, Tellbe treats our term in Philippians in the context of a discussion of ch. 2. Tellbe discusses κύριος with σωτήρ and concludes that both terms have 'a political background' and 'connotations'.[38]

Third, it is worth noting Ian Rock's PhD thesis from the University of Wales.[39] This work considers the implications of imperial ideology on the interpretation of Rom. 1.1-17. In the midst of his task, Rock considers Paul's

---

30. Peter Oakes, *Philippians: From People to Letter* (SNTSMS, 110; Cambridge: Cambridge University Press, 2001).

31. Oakes, *Philippians*, pp. 129-74.

32. Oakes, *Philippians*, pp. 171-72.

33. Oakes, *Philippians*, pp. 147-74.

34. Oakes, *Philippians*, pp. 172

35. Mikael Tellbe, *Paul between Synagogue and State: Christians, Jews, and Civic Authorities in 1 Thessalonians, Romans, and Philippians* (ConBNT, 34; Stockholm: Almqvist & Wiksell International, 2001).

36. Tellbe, *Paul between Synagogue and State*, pp. 126-27.

37. Tellbe, *Paul between Synagogue and State*, pp. 200-206 (p. 200 for κύριος specifically).

38. Tellbe, *Paul between Synagogue and State*, pp. 251-53.

39. Ian E. Rock, *The Implications of Roman Imperial Ideology for an Exegesis of Paul's Letter to the Romans: An Ideological Literary Analysis of Exordium, Romans 1:1-17* (Unpublished PhD thesis, University of Wales, 2007). I am in debt to Jim Harrison from the Wesley Institute (Drummoyne, Australia) for providing me with this source.

use of κύριος and concludes that, given the imperial usage of this term, the nature of Jesus' lordship and Paul's propositions about Jesus, his usage of the title was a challenge to Caesar.[40] Rock's treatment is sensitive to κύριος language in the Greek Old Testament as well as the Roman context.

Oakes, Tellbe, and Rock essentially arrive at their conclusions in the same way that Deissmann had before them. They conclude that there is enough evidence in extant Graeco-Roman sources to suggest a (polemical) association of the term's use for Christ and Caesar. They all draw upon apparent (anti-)imperial features in the context. Thus, given the likelihood of an imperial context, κύριος should also have anti-imperial implications. In such a context, some support in the primary sources, and no explicit argument to demand that we reject an imperial understanding of the term κύριος, an imperial understanding can be assumed. This is a valid way to argue the position and works most strongly for Philippians if one dates the letter in the early sixties. However, for Pauline letters such as Romans, 1 Thessalonians, and 1 Corinthians, the isolated association of an anti-emperor polemical use of κύριος is much more strained. Additionally, even if the context can be seen as (anti-)imperial, it does not necessarily follow that the term must have imperial associations or anti-imperial intentions. I will attempt to determine whether the minimal primary source evidence is sufficient to view κύριος as polemical even before 60 CE when the contextual (textual, historical, cultural, etc.) and lexical evidence are considered with proven communicative principles.

Finally, John L. White's Pauline theology defends a significant Graeco-Roman (especially Augustan) influence on Paul.[41] He therefore acknowledges a connection between Christ and Caesar as lord.[42] White's discussion is unique in that the issue of lordship is discussed among many similar concepts and roles mentioned in the literature for the emperor and Christ. These are lord-like roles and may be included under the title lord. These include political lord, head of household, and priestly lord.[43] Additionally, White discusses the role of adoption by divine fathers and its implications for lordship.[44] White's work is helpful because it pushes the argument beyond merely discussing the usage of the term κύριος and widens the debate into related conceptual areas including the concept of *authority*. However, White seems to follow Bousset in his purpose. He is more interested in demonstrating derivation than polemic. This is not a criticism; rather it merely

40. Rock, *Implications of Roman Imperial Ideology*, pp. 178-91.

41. John L. White, *The Apostle of God: Paul and the Promise of Abraham* (Peabody, MA: Hendrickson, 1999).

42. White, *Apostle of God*, pp. 173-206.

43. White, *Apostle of God*, pp. 185-204.

44. White, *Apostle of God*, pp. 179-84.

distinguishes his purpose from ours. Although I feel he may overemphasize the imperial influence on Paul (see Chapter 2), our studies may be seen as complementary in many respects and his work will be helpful in this study.

4. *Method*

In order to pursue our goal successfully, we must reconstruct as much as possible the relevant aspects of the *context* of the first century in which the Pauline documents were produced and read. However, the term 'context' is used for many things. It is too broad and difficult to define beyond a general description. Rather, I will attempt to reconstruct the *cognitive environment* of the participants in Paul's writing ministry. The label 'cognitive environment' is from a communication theory that I will introduce below. A cognitive environment is usually discussed in the context of individuals. In contrast to vague notions of *mutual knowledge* or *shared information*, a cognitive environment is 'the set of assumptions which [a person] is capable of constructing and as accepting as true.'[45] The use of the word 'true' here does not mean *true* in an ontological sense. It refers to a way of perceiving and accepting reality. Different individuals will have different cognitive environments. Where cognitive environments of two or more individuals overlap, there is a *mutual cognitive environment*.[46] Since we are primarily concerned with a group, the more cumbersome label will not be used.[47]

For this work I will slightly modify the concept with a shift in emphasis. A cognitive environment is the conceptual world in which a community lives. It includes features such as historical events, values, opinions, convictions about the way the world is and how it works, and so on. Essentially, it is the manner in which the world and life are perceived and accepted. It includes empirically determined facts but should not be confused with an ideological notion of historical reality (i.e. historical fact). It may include convictions about truth that are not true (e.g. the belief that the world was flat in some communities). Essentially, a cognitive environment is *perceived reality*. It is the cognitive environment that provides the basis for respond-

45. Diane Blakemore, *Relevance and Linguistic Meaning: The Semantics and Pragmatics of Discourse Markers* (CSL, 99; Cambridge: Cambridge University Press, 2002), p. 69. For a comprehensive discussion, see Dan Sperber and Deirdre Wilson, *Relevance: Communication and Cognition* (Oxford: Basil Blackwell, 2nd edn, 1995), pp. 38-46.

46. Sperber and Wilson, *Relevance*, pp. 41-42.

47. The label *mutual cognitive environment* does not seem to be used often outside the Sperber and Wilson introduction noted above.

ing to the world. Thus, it is slightly stronger than more conventional uses of the term 'context'.[48]

It is my contention that a reconstruction of the cognitive environment will provide the opportunity to determine whether a polemical interpretation will naturally arise. Of course, we cannot fully place ourselves in the shoes (or sandals) of these people. Nevertheless, we must do whatever possible to attempt to gain a glimpse (albeit a somewhat blurred glimpse) of the world of the first-century Christian in the Pauline churches. The task of reconstructing a cognitive environment is very similar to that of the historian, but there is one significant difference. Although determining what *actually happened* is important, it is not always essential. How events are perceived by those experiencing them is most important. Thus, a lack of certainty over precisely *what happened* is not necessarily problematic. I will proceed in two ways: historical critical and linguistic.[49]

a. *Method: Historical Critical*
From a historical perspective, the following areas will be explored to recreate relevant aspects of the first-century cognitive environment. First, I will consider Paul, his probable influences, and his role as a Roman Jew during the middle of the first century (Chapter 2). Second, I will consider relevant events and literature of the period (Chapters 2 and 3). This discussion will focus generally on the role of the emperor and imperial cults in Roman society and specifically in areas relevant for our study. We will attempt to understand the place of the emperor in the day-to-day lives and thoughts of the first-century recipients of select letters of Paul. By focusing on formal cults, historical events involving the office of the principate (and its pred-

48. Our description of a cognitive environment is slightly less precise than that presented by Sperber and Wilson. This is intentional. The original term is primarily used for individuals whose limitations are more easily recognized. Additionally, I am not confident that it can be as clearly defined as they suggest. Nevertheless, as refined here, it is a helpful concept for use in this work.

49. Other methodologies may also have contributed to this type of study and yielded fruitful results. These have some influence here. For example, postcolonial theory as described by Edward Said (e.g. Edward W. Said, *Culture and Imperialism* [New York: Vintage Books, 1993]) was used successfully by Steven Friesen as part of his method to understand the book of Revelation (Steven J. Friesen, *Imperial Cults and the Apocalypse of John: Reading Revelation in the Ruins* [Oxford: Oxford University Press, 2001]). Although indirect influence on this project may exist, our needs are focused on a specific word and concept. Thus, the historical-critical and linguistic methods seem most appropriate. Additionally, James C. Scott's *Hidden Transcripts* also may be helpful (James C. Scott, *Domination and the Arts of Resistance: Hidden Transcripts* [New Haven: Yale University Press, 1990]). However, my task is to determine if a polemic existed in Paul's letters; I do not suggest that this polemic was 'hidden'.

ecessor Julius Caesar), recent actions of the emperor, and contemporary literature and other texts revealing first-century ideology, I hope to reconstruct a cognitive environment that will help us more accurately understand the meaning and implication(s) of a term such as κύριος when used by Paul in certain contexts.

My historical approach will be primarily a modified historical-critical method.[50] I will not attempt to describe fully my historical-critical method in this section. Rather, I will mention foundational elements. Specific application in many cases will be discussed while using the historical data themselves. One reason for the limited discussion here is that most New Testament scholars are familiar with the method in some form and excessive discussion here would not be helpful.

Historical criticism is a product of the Enlightenment. Ernst Troeltsch, himself a product of the Enlightenment, developed three principles that are basic to the original (early) approach of historical criticism. (1) The principle of *criticism* acknowledges our limitations when approaching history and suggests that criticism and revision must always be applied to historical interpretation. (2) The principle of *analogy* assumes that only experiences that can be experienced today can be valid history (analogous experiences). (3) A principle of *correlation* views all events as being interconnected (cause–effect).[51] It is acknowledged that these three principles generally describe the way histories are produced and are helpful. Nevertheless, they are not sufficient for our task. The first principle is important. Although it is rather sceptical, it is essential to assure that the pursuit of history does not cease and that refinements are always welcomed and encouraged. The second and third principles however are beneficial as general norms but cannot be adhered to with any conviction. They assume too much knowledge on our part (an Enlightenment weakness). We simply do not have enough experience in the world to limit history by these principles. In addition, they limit any unexplainable phenomena from consideration (including

---

50. I am not unique in using a modified historical-critical approach. For more detail on the historical-critical method and modifications made by some (especially as applied by biblical scholars), see Donald A. Hagner, 'The New Testament, History, and the Historical-Critical Method,' in David Alan Black and David S. Dockery (eds.), *New Testament Criticism and Interpretation* (Grand Rapids: Zondervan, 1991), pp. 73-96; Gerhard Hasel, *New Testament Theology: Basic Issues in the Current Debate* (Grand Rapids: Eerdmans, 1978), pp. 13-57; Edgar Krentz, *The Historical-Critical Method* (Philadelphia: Fortress Press, 1975); and Stephen Neill and N.T. Wright, *The Interpretation of the New Testament 1961–1986* (Oxford: Oxford University Press, new edn, 1988), pp. 13-64, 439-49.

51. Ernst Troeltsch, 'Historical and Dogmatic Method in Theology,' in Ephraim Fischoff and Walter Bense (eds.), *Religion in History* (Minneapolis: Fortress Press, 1991), pp. 11-32 (13-15). The German original of this article was published in 1898.

the possibility of divine intervention). For some this may be an acceptable approach, but for others it is not. This is an issue of presupposition and pre-understanding (of which no one is free) about what *could* happen and not really a matter for historical research. It seems safest to not limit possibility. Finally, Troeltsch's second and third principles make uniqueness and new-ness suspect. As mentioned above, these principles are helpful for general research and in most cases should serve to make the historian cautious of claims that violate them. Nevertheless, with good reason, these principles can be violated. Therefore, my modified historical-critical method may be stated as an attempt to evaluate history by gathering and evaluating all possible relevant data from an event and/or era and presenting them in a coherent manner.

At this stage, it would be helpful to inject a measure of caution into our discussion. Simon Price develops a number of warnings for the study of emperor worship that apply to our project.[52] He points out that literary sources do not explain emperor worship and that non-literary sources such as inscriptions and archaeological materials must play an important role in our understanding.[53] Another warning relates to how the ancients interpreted ritual. Price suggests (building on the work of anthropologists) that ritual was a means of viewing the world.[54] We need to recognize that we may not view ritual matters in the same way as the ancients. Price also includes warnings against viewing emperor worship through Christian lenses,[55] making an anachronistic distinction between religion and politics[56] and maintaining a preference for Roman over Greek.[57] The latter warning seems most relevant to some classical scholarship that seems to have maintained that Romans were somehow more enlightened (like modern scholars) than Greeks in the first century and could not have taken emperor worship very seriously. However, the warning against viewing emperor worship through Christian lenses is very important for the New Testament scholar. Price's warning is not necessarily against more conservative expressions of Christianity that have explicitly interpreted the Christian model as superior to other religions and thus viewed emperor worship against the *high point* in the history or religion (i.e. Christianity). Most New Testament scholars also find fault with this approach. Price's critique is more subtle. Among other things, he demonstrates that many scholars maintain that emperor worship was part of a degradation of religion in the ancient world. This view is based

---

52. Price, *Rituals and Power*, pp. 1-22.
53. Price, *Rituals and Power*, pp. 2-7.
54. Price, *Rituals and Power*, pp. 7-11.
55. Price, *Rituals and Power*, pp. 11-15.
56. Price, *Rituals and Power*, pp. 5-16.
57. Price, *Rituals and Power*, pp. 17-22.

on an underlying Christian assumption about religion. These scholars were not explicitly Christian; rather, their view of religion was shaped by Christianity.[58] As a result, modern Western perspectives on religion often assume that the worship of a human leader is somehow a lower form of religion than the worship of a transcendent being. In the case of Rome, this perspective assumes that the more valid expressions of Roman religious experience occurred early in its history and were corrupted over time. This corruption reached its climax with the worship of the emperors. In this depraved state, the empire was ripe for a religious revolution which ultimately took the form of Christianity.

Price's warnings are important and should not merely be passed over by New Testament scholars as *assumed,* since it is our practice 'to study a text in its own context'. Price's words were intended primarily for classicists, some of whom have made the study of Roman religion a life's pursuit. If such a danger exists for the classicist, those of us devoted to the study of the New Testament should take this warning seriously. Indeed, as we will see in Chapter 3, our entire Western view of 'religion' has a distinctly Protestant Christian flavour. This conditioning is not always easy to recognize, let alone shed. Without passing judgment on any religious worldview, given the sources and methods available, I will consciously attempt to understand emperor worship within a context of first-century Roman religion. I cannot claim to be objective. Rather, I am acknowledging my subjectivity and will attempt to restrain it and, if possible, to compensate for it. As will be developed in later chapters, this approach will yield helpful insights for understanding the context in which Paul wrote his letters.[59]

Historical analysis based on a historical-critical method can provide an important structure with which we can begin to understand the context of the first-century Pauline churches. It will describe important events, people and so on that were present in the cognitive environment of the day. In addition, some measure of critical evaluation can be accomplished to help determine what is historically most plausible, given our sources. Sources can be critiqued for reliability, bias and the like, using common techniques of historical-critical analysis, and in most cases a relatively certain conclusion can be reconstructed from the evidence.

---

58. For example, although attributing great worth to the work of A.D. Nock, Price states, 'but the difficulty with Nock's detailed studies is that the evidence is interpreted largely (as is usual) within a Christianizing framework' (Price, *Rituals and Power*, p. 18).

59. I am not suggesting that a Christian view of the world or of religion is wrong (I am not interested in endorsing modern political notions of correctness). My position is not one of moral judgment. I am merely stating that such conditioning is not helpful for understanding Roman religion generally and the imperial cults specifically.

Any project of this nature is to some extent a writing of history. However, I will avoid debates over whether history *is* the basic facts of the recorded past or whether these facts are history only *when* a historian uses them for such a purpose (positivism versus relativism[60]). For my purposes the raw facts (inscriptions, papyri, contemporary literature, etc.) as well as the ancient historian's use of those raw facts are important. In the case of the ancient historian, most of his raw data are not available to the modern scholar. Nevertheless, his produced work is valuable raw material for our purposes. The types and use of sources will be discussed in more detail in Chapter 2. At this stage, I only wish to make explicit a few general points of method that will be followed. These are general because my purpose does not demand that we reconstruct a precisely accurate picture of the first-century Roman world (which is impossible). I am interested in perception. I will examine sources to help us understand what people would have understood. Although not unimportant, whether or not events actually happened a certain way is less important to this study. Nevertheless, we must strive for continual refining of our understanding of the past. This includes both an understanding of the event and (as emphasized here) an understanding of the perception of the event.

Basically, the application of the historical-critical method here will be to ask what happened and why, to answer these questions by coming to some type of understanding of the historical data through interpretation, and to do this without judgment.[61] I suggest that by attempting to do this, we will recover enough of the 'history' to reconstruct the target worldview sufficiently for our purposes. I acknowledge that not all will agree with the specific modifications of the historical-critical method made here. I also acknowledge that not all will agree with the value placed on the method itself nor the relative confidence that the method can provide usable results.

The modern historian with any hope of getting an accurate picture of the past must recognize that different sources have different strengths and weaknesses for the task (this will be discussed in a general matter in Chapter 2). Also, one must acknowledge differences in worldview between ourselves and the authors and other producers of ancient sources. No writer is without bias, and every piece of writing and other produced remains (e.g. buildings, etc.) were made for a purpose. We must consider each author's biases and

---

60. This is a simplification of these positions; nevertheless, seen as general statements of the approaches, they are helpful. We need not pursue the matter in depth for our purposes. For contrasting approaches see G.R. Elton, *The Practice of History* (Glasgow: Fontana, 1984) (positivism), and E.H. Carr, *What Is History? The George Macaulay Trevelyan Lectures Delivered in the University of Cambridge, January–March 1961* (London: Penguin Books, 2nd edn, 1987) (relativism).

61. Krentz, *Historical-Critical Method*, pp. 35-36.

purposes as much as possible. We must also acknowledge our own biases and purposes. The various ancient sources available for this project will be introduced and briefly discussed for value and usage in Chapter 2.

I am not suggesting that a historical-critical method is without problems, nor that there is a universal recognition of its value. Postmodernism has rightly challenged the emphases on objectivity, certainty, and rationalism in the so-called modern movement.[62] The result is that (pure) modernism is no longer sustainable. However, assertions that minimize a historical-critical method in favour of (or reducing it to be equal with) other types of analysis must be rejected for historical reconstruction. Other types of analysis are not without value. They serve many important purposes; however, a historical-critical method remains of critical importance for historical and historically related work.

b. *Method: Linguistic*

Acknowledging the value of a historical-critical method, especially for reconstructing the broad historical picture, we must concede that as an analytical tool it is somewhat limited for our purposes. Our task demands a more powerful means of understanding language (in this case a specific term) and its implications. Therefore, although our task will be historical it will also be linguistic. I will utilize linguistic analysis in the historical reconstruction as well as in the important task of using our historical reconstruction to demonstrate whether or not the word κύριος is a polemic against the living Roman emperor in some contexts. The linguistic analysis can be described in two related but distinct phases. These phases will use different theoretical frameworks demanded by the tasks for which they are used.

(1) *Linguistics and Biblical Studies.* Before proceeding we must acknowledge that the use of linguistics in biblical studies is a rather new practice and its value is not unquestioned. This is partially due to the state of linguistics itself. Modern linguistics is not a uniform field of study. Many diverse and in some cases contradictory theories are practised. In some cases, these different theories are used among faculty members at the same university. Not much less complicated is the use of linguistics in New Testament studies. Some works seem to utilize linguistics with positive results,[63] and it is

---

62. For a brief description of postmodernism, see the entry in Simon Blackburn, *The Oxford Dictionary of Philosophy* (Oxford: Oxford University Press, 1994), pp. 294-95.

63. See, e.g., Paul L. Danove, *Linguistics and Exegesis in the Gospel of Mark: Applications of a Case Frame Analysis and Lexicon* (JSNTSup, 218; Studies in New Testament Greek, 10; London: T. & T. Clark, 2001); Ivan Shing Chung Kwong, *The Word Order of the Gospel of Luke: Its Foregrounded Messages* (LNTS, 298; Studies in New Testament Greek, 12; London: T. & T. Clark, 2005); Gustavo Martin-Asensio,

generally agreed that linguistics is a permanent member of the New Testament scholar's exegetical toolbox. However, there is little agreement on its use and value. I am not unaware of problems associated with linguistics and its use in New Testament studies.[64] Nor am I willing to dispose of traditional methods of grammatical and lexical analysis (the first phase described below will include some rather traditional analysis). Additionally, my use of linguistics will primarily be the use of specific principles that seem to reflect an accurate view of language. Although these principles are the results of linguistic analysis and theory, they can maintain validity even if the theory from which they are derived is modified and/or ultimately found to be unsatisfactory to explain language. Therefore, it is maintained

Transitivity-Based Foregrounding in the Acts of the Apostles: A Functional-Grammatical Approach to the Lukan Perspective (JSNTSup, 202; Studies in New Testament Greek, 8; Sheffield: Sheffield Academic Press, 2000); Matthew Brook O'Donnell, *Corpus Linguistics and the Greek of the New Testament* (NTM, 6; Sheffield: Sheffield Phoenix Press, 2005); Mari Broman Olsen, *A Semantic and Pragmatic Model of Lexical and Grammatical Aspect* (Outstanding Dissertations in Linguistics; New York: Garland, 1997); Stanley E. Porter, *Verbal Aspect in the Greek of the New Testament with Reference to Tense and Mood* [SBG, 1; New York: Peter Lang, 2nd edn, 1993]); and various articles in Stanley E. Porter and D.A. Carson (eds.), *Biblical Greek Language and Linguistics: Open Questions in Current Research* (JSNTSup, 80; Sheffield: JSOT Press, 1993). Discourse analysis, an application of modern linguistics, has also been applied with success to the New Testament. See, e.g., O'Donnell, *Corpus Linguistics*, pp. 444-85 (on Philemon); Jeffrey T. Reed, *A Discourse Analysis of Philippians: Method and Rhetoric in the Debate over Literary Integrity* (JSNTSup, 136; Sheffield: Sheffield Academic Press, 1997); Ralph Bruce Terry, *A Discourse Analysis of First Corinthians* (Dallas: Summer Institute of Linguistics, 1995); Cynthia Long Westfall, *A Discourse Analysis of the Letter to the Hebrews: The Relationship between Form and Meaning* (LNTS, 297; London: T. & T. Clark, 2005); and various articles in David Alan Black, Katherine Barnwell and Stephen H. Levinsohn (eds.), *Linguistics and New Testament Interpretation: Essays on Discourse Analysis* (Nashville: Broadman, 1992); Stanley E. Porter and D.A. Carson, (eds.), *Discourse Analysis and Other Topics in Biblical Greek* (JSNTSup, 113; Sheffield: Sheffield Academic Press, 1995); Stanley E. Porter and Jeffrey T. Reed (eds.), *Discourse Analysis and the New Testament: Approaches and Results* (JSNTSup, 170; Studies in New Testament Greek, 4; Sheffield: Sheffield Academic Press, 1999).

64. For a more detailed discussion of this and other related issues, see Appendix 1 in Joseph D. Fantin, *The Greek Imperative Mood in the New Testament: A Cognitive and Communicative Approach* (SBG, 12; New York: Peter Lang, 2010), pp. 315-39. This appendix includes a brief history of modern linguistics, its use in New Testament studies, problems with linguistics in general, problems with its use in New Testament studies, suggestions for future use, and a helpful bibliography. For a survey of the use of linguistics in New Testament studies since 1961, see Stanley E. Porter and Andrew W. Pitts, 'New Testament Greek Language and Linguistics in Recent Research', *CBR* 6 (2008), pp. 214-55.

here that the judicious use of modern linguistics can be extremely helpful for certain tasks in New Testament studies.

(2) *Terminology.* Unfortunately for the biblical scholar, a stroll through the linguistic forest is not a simple walk in the park. Rather, it is an adventure through often unfamiliar and sometimes dangerous terrain. Among the problems of applying linguistic method to biblical studies is a lack of uniform terminology. This work is not an exercise in linguistic analysis. Nevertheless, as a study of the use of a word in the Greek New Testament, it must incorporate some linguistic methodology. Therefore, it is helpful to define a few essential terms at this stage of the work.

Our project is partially an exercise in determining meaning. However, even the meaning of 'meaning' is not without problems. The philosopher H. Paul Grice explores the different ways this term is used in his 1957 article entitled simply 'Meaning'.[65] Essentially for the purposes here, the general meaning of the term is its *semantic* meaning. The context-dependent usages of the term is in the domain of *pragmatics*.

For the purposes of this work, 'semantic meaning' can be defined as the inherent linguistic meaning encoded and expressed by the use of language[66] in an utterance without reference to non-linguistic factors such as beliefs, social considerations and so on, or other contextual linguistic elements. It is the linguistic meaning directly involved in the linguistic element under discussion.[67] The use of the phrase 'inherent meaning' here needs clarification. This does not mean that the symbol (i.e. the combination of letters

---

65. H. Paul Grice, 'Meaning', *PhilRev* 66 (1957), pp. 377-88.

66. The term 'language' is also laden with difficulties and can be used in many ways to refer to many different linguistic phenomena. Here the term refers to the linguistic processes such as phonology, grammar (morphology and syntax) and semantics and the interaction of these processes, which are used by a communicator to produce an utterance. This may be termed the *linguistic system* by some. For a discussion of these issues, see Fantin (*Greek Imperative Mood*, p. 18, and the literature cited there).

67. This definition is my own but is based on the work of many others: Diane Blakemore, *Understanding Utterances* (Oxford: Basil Blackwell, 1992), p. 40; Julia S. Falk, 'Semantics', in Virginia P. Clark, Paul A. Escholz, and Alfred F. Rosa (eds.), *Language: Introductory Readings* (New York: St Martins Press, 1981), pp. 319-417 (399); Sperber and Wilson, *Relevance*, pp. 9-10; Adrian Akmajian, Richard Demers and Robert M. Harnish, *Linguistics: An Introduction to Language and Communication* (Cambridge, MA: MIT Press, 2nd edn, 1984), p. 529; John G. Cook, *The Structure and Persuasive Power of Mark: A Linguistic Approach* (SemeiaSt; Atlanta: Scholars Press, 1995), p. 4. Additionally, my understanding of semantic meaning is similar to (but not identical with) and here influenced by Daniel B. Wallace's *unaffected* or *ontological meaning* (Wallace, *Greek Grammar beyond the Basics: An Exegetical Syntax of the New Testament* [Grand Rapids: Zondervan, 1996], pp. 2-3). However, despite the influence of others, any deficiency in the proposed definition is my own.

representing a concept) has some innate meaning. Rather, such meaning is forged in usage. Although possibly too simplistic, John Lyons's words are helpful, 'inherent meaning is determined by its characteristic use'.[68] Nevertheless, in a specific time/place context, terms have an inherent meaning. In the case of a term like κύριος, this is the (aspect of) meaning not affected by the context in which the term appears.[69] Additionally, in light of this discussion on inherent meaning, I can clarify the latter part of the definition to state that *semantic meaning* is the meaning 'without reference to non-linguistic factors such as beliefs, social considerations and so on, or other contextual linguistic elements'.[70] These sociological factors may contribute to the development of an inherent meaning. However, their presence in a context in which the term appears does not affect the semantic meaning. The sociological factors in a context may or may not be the same as those that contributed to the development of the inherent meaning of a given term in a specific time and place.

The aspect of meaning in which sociological and other factors contribute is pragmatics. It is helpful to distinguish between the general study of pragmatics and the resultant meaning of pragmatic factors with the semantic meaning. The former is simply labelled *pragmatics;* the latter, *pragmatic implicatures.* Meaning relating to pragmatics is indirect linguistic (contextual) meaning and non-linguistic meaning including factors such as beliefs, social considerations and so on, and its relationship to the communicators. Pragmatic implicatures are the resultant meaning of any non-linguistic factors such as beliefs, social considerations and so on, and indirect contextual linguistic meaning interacting with the semantic meaning.[71]

---

68. John Lyons, *Language and Linguistics* (London: Cambridge University Press, 1981), pp. 167-68.

69. See also Stephen H. Levinsohn, *Discourse Features of New Testament Greek: A Coursebook on the Information Structure of New Testament Greek* (Dallas: Summer Institute of Linguistics, 2nd edn, 2000), p. ix; and Wallace's clarification of the term 'ontological', which is applicable here (*Exegetical Syntax*, p. 2 n. 8).

70. Fantin, *Greek Imperative Mood*, p. 62.

71. As with the definition of 'semantics', the definitions of 'pragmatics' and 'pragmatic implicature' are my own but are based on the work of many others: Diane Blakemore, *Semantic Constraints on Relevance* (Oxford: Basil Blackwell, 1987), p. 1; Blakemore, *Utterances*, p. 40; Sperber and Wilson, *Relevance*, p. 10; Akmajian, Demers, and Harnish, *Linguistics*, p. 527; Andrew Radford, *Transformational Syntax* (CTL; Cambridge: Cambridge University Press, 1981), p. 3; Cook, *Structure and Persuasive Power*, p. 4. Pragmatic implicature is similar to (but not identical with) and here influenced by Wallace's *affected* or *phenomenological* meaning. However, within *relevance theory* (including some influences listed here), development of this concept goes beyond the definition used here. *Relevance theory* will be described below. Despite the influence of others, any deficiency in the proposed definition is my own.

As noted above, within linguistics terminology varies. In fact, one won-ders whether certain definitions of some terms are compatible. Compare for example the definitions of 'pragmatics' by Wilhelm Egger,[72] Mari Olsen,[73] and John Cook.[74] Each of these authors utilizes linguistics to illuminate bib-lical studies, but it is difficult to understand how all these definitions are explaining the same linguistic term, 'pragmatics'.[75] For this reason I am using my own definition and clearly defining its meaning.

There are a number of reasons for problems with definition. First, an emphasis on semantics and pragmatics is relatively recent in modern lin-guistics (itself a rather new discipline). In 1968 John Lyons stated, 'Many of the more influential books on linguistics that have appeared in the last thirty years devote little or no attention to semantics.'[76] This has changed, and many are now discussing these aspects of linguistics.[77] The influence of Paul Grice and new theories such as *relevance theory* used in this work (see below) are evidence of this increase in interest. However, new areas of inquiry often need time to solidify terminology. This is complicated, because very diverse fields of linguistics and philosophy are all pursuing these areas.

Second, disagreements over the meaning of semantics and pragmatics may result from differing views of where semantics end and pragmatics begin.[78] The line is not clear. Thus, some may take issue with the exclusion here of contextual features from semantics. This may be due to a view that places more emphasis on semantics.[79]

---

72. Wilhelm Egger, *How to Read the New Testament: An Introduction to Linguistic and Historical-Critical Methodology* (ed. Hendrikus Boers; trans. Peter Heinegg; Peabody, MA: Hendrickson, 1996), p. 125.

73. Olsen, *Aspect*, p. 17.

74. Cook, *Structure and Persuasive Power*, p. 4.

75. For a detailed discussion of definition, see Stephen C. Levinson, *Pragmatics* (CTL; Cambridge: Cambridge University Press, 1983), pp. 5-35.

76. John Lyons, *Introduction to Theoretical Linguistics* (London: Cambridge University Press, 1968), p. 400.

77. Important treatments include John Lyons, *Semantics* (2 vols.; Cambridge: Cambridge University Press, 1977); Lyons, *Linguistic Semantics: An Introduction* (Cambridge: Cambridge University Press, 1995); Levinson, *Pragmatics*; and Jacob L. Mey, *Pragmatics: An Introduction* (Oxford: Basil Blackwell, 1993).

78. For a discussion of the distinction between semantics and pragmatics and various views on where the line between them should be drawn, see Geoffrey N. Leech, *Principles of Pragmatics* (London: Longmans, 1983), pp. 5-7.

79. For example, Lyons defines semantics in a much broader way than many linguists (*Linguistic Semantics*, pp. xii-xiii, 1-45). For Lyons, 'semantics' is simply the 'study of meaning' (*Linguistic Semantics*, p. xii). Thus, semantics includes much of what others (including this work) consider the domain of pragmatics.

Within a discussion of semantics of lexical items, some distinguish three types of meaning: symbol, sense, and referent.[80] This view has been followed by New Testament scholars[81] and may be termed *lexical semantics*. In a discussion of semantics and pragmatics proper, these categories are limiting (or possibly misleading) because they are not necessarily all considered in what is labelled *semantics*. Some linguists develop more sophisticated systems. For example, John Lyons discusses *denotation, reference,* and *sense*.[82] For Lyons, what is considered *reference* by others is further distinguished by *denotation* and *reference*.[83] In his discussion, the notion of *symbol* is not directly included.[84] Even Lyons's view is rather simplistic, especially when taken out of his overall discussion of semantics. Our main focus in this book is on the meaning and use of a single term. Thus, for our purposes, it is only necessary to make the distinction between *symbol, sense,* and *reference*. In fact, for our approach as developed here, the notion of *symbol* will be an important element and thus I do not desire to minimize it.[85]

The actual letters and the word formed is a symbol. For example, the letters or sounds: *d-o-g* make up the symbol *dog*. With the exception of onomatopoeic words, symbols are entirely random. A symbol stands for

80. The source of this distinction is C.K. Ogden and I.A. Richards, who use the label *thought or reference* for what is termed *sense* here (*The Meaning of Meaning: A Study of the Influence of Language upon Thought and of the Science of Symbolism* [New York: Harcourt, Brace & World, 8th edn, n.d. (preface dated 1946, 1st edn, 1923)], pp. 8-13). Ogden and Richard's presentation is more detailed and more interested in *symbol* than those who follow them who are cited below.

81. See, e.g., Grant R. Osborne, *The Hermeneutical Spiral: A Comprehensive Introduction to Biblical Interpretation* (Downers Grove, IL: InterVarsity Press, rev. and exp. edn, 2006), pp. 95-96; Moisés Silva, *Biblical Words and their Meanings* (Grand Rapids: Zondervan, 1983), esp. pp. 101-14. Also helpful is James Barr, *The Semantics of Biblical Language* (Oxford: Oxford University Press, 1961; repr. London: Xpress Reprints [SCM Press], 1996), pp. 217-18. For a more popular description, see Darrell L. Bock, 'New Testament Word Analysis', in Scot McKnight (ed.), *Introducing New Testament Interpretation* (Grand Rapids: Baker Book House, 1989), pp. 97-113 (100-101).

82. Lyons, *Semantics,* I, pp. 174-215. See also Lyons, *Linguistic Semantics,* pp. 46-130.

83. Lyons, *Semantics,* I, pp. 177-97, 206-15.

84. Although a more sophisticated approach to *symbols* may be seen in Lyons's discussion of *naming* following his treatment of *denotation, reference,* and *sense* (*Semantics,* I, pp. 215-23).

85. As mentioned, this description of *lexical semantics* is necessarily simplified, and I do not wish to suggest that semantic analysis is this simple or that there is complete agreement among linguists concerning the meaning of 'semantics' generally and 'lexical semantics' specifically. For further detail, see the works by Lyons mentioned above. For an approach by a linguist to the New Testament, see Johannes P. Louw, *Semantics of New Testament Greek* (SemeiaSt; Atlanta: Scholars Press, 1982), esp. pp. 47-54.

something, but it does not carry any meaning itself. The symbols *perro* and *Hund* are symbols in Spanish and German respectively for the four-legged friendly house pet English speakers label with the symbol *dog*. The Greek symbol κύριος itself does not carry meaning. It represents meaning. The meaning represented by the symbol is the *sense*. This is one aspect of lexical semantics that is similar to what I have defined above as 'semantics'. *Sense* is the mental content represented by the symbol—often commonly referred to as 'the meaning' of the word: *dog* means 'hairy four-legged creature'. *Κύριος* generally means 'one in authority'.[86] Finally, *reference* involves what entity can be represented by the symbol. It is the real-world item to which the label refers. For example, the referent of a specific *dog* is 'Spot'. *Κύριος* can have a number of referents such as a leader, a slave owner, the living emperor, and Christ. It is likely that in many treatments of *lexical semantics*, some of what was labelled pragmatics is also involved in both *sense* and *reference*. Although this study will not pursue any formal *lexical semantics*, much of it can be viewed through this theory. I will explore the meaning of the term κύριος in the first century and consider what types of referents the term may have. Essentially, a more powerful theory of pragmatics is necessary to be able to determine when a certain referent such as Christ may be a direct challenge to another potential referent such as Caesar.

(3) *Linguistic Method.* First, a traditional semantic study will be presented for κύριος in order to establish the word's general meaning, usage, and possible interpretations in various contexts with an emphasis on Pauline usage. At this stage I will focus on the basic meaning of the term. From this, I will also discuss the term's relational nature, potential referents, and implications of these observations of our study. This approach is derived from a *lexical semantic* approach as just described. It will be valuable to present an extensive synchronic word study of κύριος to understand the full range of meaning available for the term during the first century (Chapter 4). In addition, I will analyse the implicit relational nature of the term κύριος and the significance of the observations (also in Chapter 4). After a synchronic word study, I will focus not on the term κύριος but on a more abstract superlative concept expressed by the term (more on this below; this will also be developed extensively in Chapter 4).

After establishing important basic aspects of the cognitive environment and the meaning and potential usages for the term κύριος, I will attempt to determine whether the readers would hear a polemic against the emperor in some Pauline passages using the term κύριος (Chapter 5). This transitional stage of our project is most delicate. There is a danger of committing seri-

---

86. The meaning of κύριος will be refined in Chapter 4.

ous exegetical errors[87] including *parallelomania*.[88] This is one reason the approach here will be conceptual rather than simply the more traditional lexical approach.

It is incorrect to assume that these errors *will* occur in the traditional approach, which focuses merely on the occurrence of a term. My approach is more linguistically complex, and it is acknowledged that it may lead to other exegetical problems. However, it seems that the traditional approach is more prone to errors such as those mentioned above. The weakness of my approach is that it appears that the starting point is an inaccessible *concept*. It would seem to be preferable to begin with something we can actually analyse as part of the text, namely, the surface structure word (expression) κύριος; however, as we will see, this concept's existence is undeniable. A more exhaustive treatment of this subject will include significant pre-liminary work in the area of word analysis to help establish the role of our meaning within the pragmatic distribution of usages.

I will begin with a traditional synchronic word analysis. Although this will be a foundational step, this approach will be inadequate to fulfil our desired purposes. A means of looking beyond a simple word meaning/usage description is necessary. This is merely a descriptive analysis giving options on usage based on the range of meaning and usage found in the texts under consideration. This study must go beyond this and provide a measure of probability that a polemical meaning exists in certain contexts. In order to make our leap from the Graeco-Roman world to Paul's letters and then to polemical conclusions, I will utilize further insights from modern linguistics. This is phase 2 of our linguistic analysis.

The linguistic (or communication) theory, *relevance theory*,[89] will provide observations that will be utilized for our purposes.[90] *Relevance theory*,

---

87. Potential errors include a *careless appeal to background material* (D.A. Carson, *Exegetical Fallacies* [Grand Rapids: Baker Book House, 2nd edn, 1996], pp. 41-43) and to some extent the *word–idea fallacy* (Bock, 'Word Analysis', p. 111).

88. See the warning by Samuel Sandmel in his 1961 President Address to the Society of Biblical Literature (Samuel Sandmel, 'Parallelomania', *JBL* 81 [1962], pp. 1-13). See also Carson, *Exegetical Fallacies*, pp. 43-44; and Bock, 'Word Analysis', p. 112.

89. Though *relevance theory* is properly considered a 'communication theory', it is used by linguists for many of the same purposes as other linguistic theories (or sub-linguistic theories such as pragmatics). Owing to this and the close relationship between communication and language, I will also consider it loosely a linguistic theory.

90. Most authoritatively presented in Sperber and Wilson, *Relevance*; the first edition was published in 1986. In general, the theory is unchanged from 1986; however, some refinements (one will be noted below) were added and some clarification was made in a postscript (pp. 255-79) that was added to the unchanged body of the text (the main text has the same pagination: pp. 1-254).

Our discussion here of relevance theory will necessarily be minimal. For a brief introduction to relevance theory, see Deirdre Wilson and Dan Sperber, 'An Outline of Relevance Theory', *NotesLin* 39 (1987), pp. 4-24; Ernst-August Gutt, 'Unravelling

like most linguistic theories, is focused primarily on spoken utterances. However, it has been successfully applied to texts.[91] Considering our reconstructed historical picture and the conclusions of our lexical analysis, this powerful pragmatic theory will help us make explicit the implied non-linguistic detail that would be understood by the original readers.[92] This theory was developed by Dan Sperber and Deirdre Wilson in the late 1970s and early to mid 1980s.[93] It is built on a fundamental observation that commu-

Meaning: An Introduction to Relevance Theory', *NotesTrans* 112 (1986), pp. 10-20; Gutt, *Relevance Theory: A Guide to Successful Communication in Translation* (Dallas: Summer Institute of Linguistics; New York: United Bible Societies, 1992); Gutt, *Translation and Relevance: Cognition and Context* (Manchester: St Jerome, 2nd edn, 2000), pp. 24-46; Blakemore, *Utterances*; Blakemore, *Relevance*, pp. 59-88. For examples of relevance theory used in biblical exegesis, see Gutt, 'Unravelling Meaning', pp. 13-20; Gutt, *Relevance Theory*, pp. 15-17. For a critique of the theory's usefulness for Bible translation (especially as presented by Gutt), see Ernst R. Wendland, 'On the Relevance of "Relevance Theory" for Bible Translation', *BT* 47 (1996), pp. 126-37. For an extensive bibliography of relevance theory, see the Web site maintained and frequently updated by Francisco Yus at http://www.ua.es/personal/francisco.yus/rt.html. In addition, Dan Sperber, cofounder of the theory, maintains his own Web site, which includes many of his articles (published and unpublished) on relevance theory and other topics at http://www.dan.sperber.com.

Finally, there is precedence for using relevance theory for scholarly purposes in New Testament studies. At least three recent theses have used the theory as a basis for research: Marlon Domingo Winedt, *A Relevance-Theoretic Approach to Translation and Discourse Markers: With Special Reference to the Greek Text of the Gospel of Luke* (PhD diss., Free University Amsterdam, 1999); Kevin Gary Smith, *Bible Translation and Relevance Theory: The Translation of Titus* (Unpublished DLitt diss., University of Stellenbosch, 2000); and Stephen Pattemore, *The People of God in the Apocalypse: A Relevance-Theoretic Study* (Unpublished PhD thesis, University of Otago, 2000). A revision of the latter work has been recently published in the Society for New Testament Studies Monograph Series entitled *The People of God in the Apocalypse: Discourse, Structure, and Exegesis* (SNTSMS, 128; Cambridge: Cambridge University Press, 2004). Additionally, since 2003 the International Meetings of the Society of Biblical Literature have included sessions on relevance theory and biblical interpretation.

91. An important work in this area is Anne Furlong, *Relevance Theory and Literary Interpretation* (Unpublished PhD thesis, University College London, 1995). Furlong treats literary interpretation as a 'subset of general communication' (p. 2). Another example is Seiji Uchida, 'Text and Relevance', in Robyn Carston and Seiji Uchida (eds.), *Relevance Theory: Applications and Implications* (P&Bns, 37; Amsterdam: John Benjamins, 1997), pp. 161-78. Also helpful is Ian MacKenzie, *Paradigms of Reading: Relevance Theory and Deconstruction* (Basingstoke, UK: Palgrave Macmillan, 2002).

92. Our notion of the *cognitive environment* introduced earlier is indebted to *relevance theory*.

93. It is probably best to date the formal introduction of relevance theory as a theory of pragmatics to 1986 with the publication of the first edition of Dan Sperber and Deirdre Wilson, *Relevance: Communication and Cognition* (Oxford: Basil Blackwell, 1986); see the preface (p. ix) in Carston and Uchida, *Relevance Theory*. However, as

nication operates through *inference*, as was suggested by Grice.[94] Among other things and recognizing cohesion in a communication situation, Grice suggested that communicators producing a communicative offering generally 'make [their] conversational contribution such as is required, at the stage at which it occurs, by the accepted purpose or direction of the talk exchange in which [they] are engaged'.[95] Given this general principle, called the *cooperative principle*, Grice further suggests four categories with maxims and sub-maxims which are more specific and 'which will, in general, yield results in accordance with the Cooperative Principle'.[96] First, a communicative offering should be as informative as necessary (no more, no less) to add the desired content to the communication situation (category of *quantity*). Second, a communicative offering should contain only propositions (etc.) believed by the communicator to be true and for which adequate evidence exists (*quality*). Third, a communicative offering should be relevant (*relation*). Finally, a communicative offering should be clear and brief (*manner*).[97] Basically, the cooperative principle and categories are based on

with most theories, significant development occurred before the initial publication of the foundational work. In November 1985 at the University of Minho Portugal the authors delivered a paper published in 1987 as 'An Outline of Relevance Theory', in which they conclude by stating, 'we briefly sketched an explanatory pragmatic theory based on a single principle of relevance.' These words seem to imply a newness of the theory. In addition, as early as 1979, the authors wrote an article in which they discuss the '*axiome de pertinence*', which is an earlier version of the *principle of relevance* (Deirdre Wilson and Dan Sperber, 'Remarques sur l'interprétation des énoncés selon Paul Grice', *Communications* 30 [1979], pp. 80-94). Therefore, by 1979 the theory was in a preliminary form, which suggests that the basic theory was in development (at least) slightly earlier. In 1981, a longer English version of the aforementioned article appeared in which the phrase *principle of relevance* was used (Deirdre Wilson and Dan Sperber, 'On Grice's Theory of Conversation', in Paul Werth [ed.], *Conversation and Discourse: Structure and Interpretation* [London: Croom Helm, 1981], pp. 61-131; see also Dan Sperber and Deirdre Wilson, 'Mutual Knowledge and Relevance in Theories of Comprehension', in N.V. Smith [ed.], *Mutual Knowledge* [London: Academic Press, 1982], pp. 155-78).

94. H. Paul Grice, 'Logic and Conversation', in P. Cole and J. Morgan (eds.), *Syntax and Semantics. III. Speech Acts* (New York: Academic Press, 1975), pp. 41-58. This article is a published excerpt of Grice's William James Lectures delivered at Harvard in 1967. This influential lecture built upon important observations about *recognition* and especially *intention* in meaning published ten years previously ('Meaning', pp. 377-88). A collection of Grice's most important articles (including the lecture series) appeared in 1989 (*Studies in the Way of Words* [Cambridge, MA: Harvard University Press, 1989]). However, all references to Grice's work in this book are to the original articles.

95. Grice, 'Logic and Conversation', p. 45.

96. Grice, 'Logic and Conversation', p. 45.

97. Grice, 'Logic and Conversation', pp. 45-48. My words here summarize Grice's four formal categories and nine maxims. His work should be consulted for a

an *ideal* communication situation. In other words, they suggest how communicators *ideally* should communicate and what they *ideally* expect from
their communication partners.[98]

The influence of Grice's theory cannot be exaggerated, and this justifies
our brief statement of his position. Further, his observation about the inferential nature of communication is clearly superior to a simple code model
of communication.[99] However, even our simple exposition reveals serious
problems with Grice's model. First, it is difficult to use effectively a model
of communication based on and so dependent on an *ideal* communication
situation. It does not take one long to produce or witness a communicative
offering that does not adhere to one of Grice's categories, such as quantity.
Second, Grice's categories and maxims seem random. Why does he include
his maxims about clarity and brevity (within his *manner* category) but not
include a maxim such as 'be polite'? Grice is not unaware of these problems. He acknowledges that not all maxims are adhered to in a communicative offering, that other maxims exist, and that he understands the idealized
situation demanded by his theory.[100] Nevertheless, such problems seem too
serious to ignore.

Proponents of relevance theory ultimately view Grice's theory (including developments by others) with its cooperative principle and maxims as
insufficient to account for the act of communication.[101] Therefore, although
relevance theory has roots in Grice (and probably would not exist without
his work), it is neither a simple development nor a summary of Grice's
maxims. It is an independent communication theory.

In essence, relevance theory maintains that communication is generally
driven by the notion of *relevance*. In other words, for a communicative
offering to be relevant, it (both its explicit statements and what is implied)
should include new information and have a connection to context. In this

---

more detailed explanation. Grice's aforementioned article is the first published list and
exposition of the cooperative principle and categories with maxims. These have been
stated and restated in many works on pragmatics and communication, both agreeing and
disagreeing with Grice. See, e.g., Levinson, *Pragmatics*, pp. 100-18; Leech, *Pragmatics*,
pp. 7-10; Sperber and Wilson, *Relevance*, pp. 33-38.

98. For further development of Grice's theory excerpted from the same lecture
series, see H. Paul Grice, 'Further Notes on Logic and Conversation', in P. Cole (ed.),
Syntax and Semantics. IX. Pragmatics (New York: Academic Press, 1978), pp. 113-27.

99. Sperber and Wilson, *Relevance*, pp. 1-24. For an inductive demonstration for a
non-linguistic audience of the superiority of an inferential communication model and
the approach of relevance theory (which will be developed below), see Fantin, *Greek
Imperative Mood*, pp. 43-60.

100. Grice, 'Logic and Conversation', pp. 46-47.

101. Sperber and Wilson, *Relevance*, pp. 161-63; Wilson and Sperber, 'On Grice's
Theory', pp. 155-78.

way it furthers the communication event.[102] Based on this observation, communicators generally follow two *principles of relevance*:

1. Human cognition tends to be geared to the maximization of relevance.
2. Every act of ostensive communication communicates a presumption of its own optimal relevance.[103]

Given these principles, the most probable interpretation of an utterance can best be determined by which interpretation is most relevant to the communication situation. Thus, both explicit and inferred communicative elements are considered.

In this work, two important observations from relevance theory will provide the foundation for our discussion. First, the second principle of relevance suggests that included in a communicative act will be the presumption of its own optimal relevance (the first principle will be assumed here). Second, communication is *efficient*.[104] In other words, communication generally uses only the words/sentences needed to communicate the information desired in a given context.[105] The first observation is a formal principle of the theory. The second supports this principle. However, for the purposes of this work, these will function as complementary principles. A more detailed discussion of these principles awaits development in Chapter 5 when they will be used. For the purposes here, with our other linguistic and historical-critical findings, it will be determined whether a polemic against Caesar in some of Paul's usages of κύριος for Christ is a *relevant* implied aspect of the interpretation of the passage.

102. For a detailed discussion of relevance, see Sperber and Wilson, *Relevance*, pp. 118-55. For a more simplified explanation, see Gutt, *Relevance Theory*, pp. 21-24; Blakemore, *Utterances*, pp. 24-32; Wilson and Sperber, 'Outline', pp. 10-13.

103. In the first edition of Sperber and Wilson's *Relevance* (1986), only the second principle was considered 'the' principle of relevance. After further consideration, the authors refined their presentation to make two explicit principles of relevance (Sperber and Wilson, *Relevance*, pp. 260-61). For further discussion of the principle(s) of relevance, see Sperber and Wilson, *Relevance*, pp. 155-63, 260-79; Gutt, *Translation and Relevance*, pp. 30-32. Although noting Sperber and Wilson's development of two principles, Gutt's discussion interacts only with the original principle (the second cited here). For a less detailed discussion (and only of the original principle), see Wilson and Sperber, 'Outline', pp. 13-16; Blakemore, *Utterances*, pp. 32-37; Gutt, *Relevance Theory*, pp. 24-34.

104. Sperber and Wilson, *Relevance*, pp. 46-50.

105. These are general principles and cannot be assumed to be without exception. Sperber and Wilson acknowledge this (*Relevance*, pp. 158-60). In addition, language is always evolving and is never 'clean' (i.e. without exception or without redundancy).

Relevance theory is not without its critics.[106] Compared to those maintaining an affinity with the work of Grice, relevance theory can claim only a minority of proponents as a pragmatic theory. However, it is a significant theory on the landscape of pragmatics.[107] Also, the newness of the theory suggests that it will be further refined (a valid concern about many linguistic theories).[108] Nevertheless, I am applying only two principles from this theory, which, if taken as general principles and not assumed to be without exception, seem to stand up to scrutiny and are verified through observation of the communication process.

Using these principles as a point of departure and the superlative concept that will be developed, I (will) propose that the superlative lordly relational concept may be expressed in a surface structure (text or utterance) by different words or phrases depending on the referent of the label itself. Specifically, the social status and relationship between the referent and the speaker and what the speaker wishes to communicate about the referent will result in different types of expression for different individuals. As for the first, the following contextual factors will contribute to the choice of expression: (1) The relationship of the referent to the individual using the label. (2) The social status of the referent with respect to the individual using the label. (3) The social status and relationship of the referent to the local community to which the individual using the label belongs. (4) The social status and relationship of the referent to the wider cultural context (e.g. the [known] world or the total sphere of influence). These factors will help to determine whether the superlative concept is expressed in the surface structure by the term κύριος when applied to the emperor. It will then be determined whether a challenge to this position is presented by Paul in his writings. The principles of *relevance* and *efficiency* will provide insights into the communication process that will contribute throughout this study.

The linguistic discussion here has emphasized theory. Further refinement of the method will take place in subsequent chapters where additional lin-

---

106. See, e.g., Stephen C. Levinson, review of *Relevance: Communication and Cognition* (Oxford: Basil Blackwell, 1986), by Dan Sperber and Deirdre Wilson, in *JLin* 25 (1989), pp. 455-72; Mey, *Pragmatics*, pp. 80-82; Lawrence D. Roberts, 'Relevance as an Explanation of Communication', *LinPhil* 14 (1991), pp. 453-72.

107. The significant publisher of scholarly linguistic books, John Benjamins (Amsterdam), has included volumes in its important series, Pragmatics & Beyond (New Series), which are devoted to and from the perspective of relevance theory. See, e.g., Carston and Uchida, *Relevance Theory*; Villy Rouchota and Andreas H. Jucker (eds.), *Current Issues in Relevance Theory* (P&Bns 58; Amsterdam: John Benjamins, 1998); and Elly Ifantidou, *Evidentials and Relevance* (P&Bns 86; Amsterdam: John Benjamins, 2001).

108. In the postscript to their second edition of *Relevance*, Sperber and Wilson acknowledge that the theory is still under development (pp. 278-79).

guistic methodology will be introduced to make specific points. The linguistic observations will be either very specific or needed only for very restricted purposes. For these reasons it seems best to introduce them when they contribute directly to the discussion.

To summarize, my method will be both historical-critical and linguistic. First, a historical method will help provide the context and general cognitive environment in which the proposed polemic operates. Second, more traditional linguistic analysis will provide insights about the meaning and usage of the term κύριος. This will include relational aspects about the term and potential referents. Finally, relevance theory will provide principles observed from the practice of communication to make explicit the (implied) connection between the historical and lexical research and a possible Pauline polemic against the emperor. In addition, this process will reveal contextual clues necessary to make the polemic probable.

5. *Limitations of the Study*

This study should be thought of as a tree. It is not a forest but only one among many trees within a forest. It is not an unimportant tree but a tree nonetheless. There will be many areas of interest that cannot be addressed here. Essentially, we are looking at one word representing a concept and attempting to determine if there is a polemic in its range of usage. If a polemic exists, it is not suggested that it is a primary purpose for Paul either in his overall message or even in the specific passages that I will be addressing. However, I believe that it is an important part of the message, an aspect usually not mentioned in the discussion of Pauline theology. Thus, there is great value in such a study. It contributes to the overall fabric of the message of Paul.

It must be stressed that, although my focus in this study is on the Graeco-Roman contribution to the biblical use of κύριος, this does not necessarily mean that other influences may not be involved, or may even be more prominent. The Septuagint usage of the term cannot be ignored and will be discussed in Chapter 4. This work is not meant to overturn the conclusions of other important studies on this subject. However, it is believed that many works on κύριος are deficient in their understanding of the term. This study will contribute to the richness of Pauline usage of κύριος by examining the term in its Graeco-Roman imperial context.

My focus is upon only one word and the impact that an understanding of its Graeco-Roman context will have on exegesis. However, as noted in the final paragraphs of the introductory section of this chapter above, this work cannot develop the exegetical implications in detail. For such studies, this work can serve as a foundation.

Additionally, the reader may question whether other terms such as σωτήρ should also be considered. Such studies would be fruitful, but space does not permit development of this and similar areas beyond their direct contribution to our main focus. However, the method presented here as well as much of the background work could be used in such a study. Also, in Chapter 5, a limited number of passages will be discussed. One might wish to have seen more or different passages considered to determine whether they include a polemic against the emperor. The choice of passages is intended to represent a wide range within the Pauline corpus. Given the discussion in future chapters, these seem to be among the most likely candidates to contain a polemic. This selection is not meant to be a comprehensive list of possible polemical κύριος passages. Further work may yield other important contributions.

Finally, although I will present conclusions that seem probable from my perspective, I acknowledge that this is an area of some uncertainty. There is one problem that I cannot dismiss when considering this topic. If an anti-emperor polemic was involved in the Pauline corpus when imperial cults were in their infancy and growing rapidly, why do we not see more discussion of this issue in later church writings about the Pauline passages (when the conflict was clearly evident)? As quoted above, the explicit reference in the *Martyrdom of Polycarp* 8.2 (also 9.2–10.1) is a bold example of the conflict between Caesar and Christ. We also see a brief discussion in Tertullian and elsewhere but little more. Should we expect more? Many reasons can be suggested for the lack of explicit discussion of imperial cults; most prominent would be the danger such discussion might bring to the author and recipients of such works. Further, it is possible that this problem subsided as the church grew and in some ways became more accepting of Rome; thus, this aspect of the message was lost (see the next section). Even Polycarp gives a positive response to a Roman official concerning his authority (*Martyrdom of Polycarp* 10.2; this could be influenced by teachings such as Rom. 13.1-7; see below). I am not however suggesting that the second-century (and later) church would have accepted or compromised with emperor worship in any way. The view that the New Testament includes an anti-imperial message is supported by the Apocalypse, which includes what seem to be undeniable references to imperialism and imperial cults; however, the book's imperial imagery is couched in cryptic apocalyptic language. Would the author have dared to say these things in a noncryptic manner? In the end, I must be thankful for the references available and, despite confidence in my conclusions, maintain a level of caution.

6. *Paul and Politics*

There is presently a movement in Pauline studies that seeks to emphasize a political message within the Pauline corpus.[109] Labelling this a 'movement' probably suggests more unity than exists, and I am uncertain whether those involved would see themselves as such. I am using this label only for convenience.[110] The extent to which Paul's message is viewed as a direct challenge to the Roman imperial system varies among proponents but nevertheless is considered by all to be a significant aspect of Paul's purpose. A significant platform for the development of this and related theses is the Society of Biblical Literature's Paul and Politics seminar. This seminar's sessions at annual meetings have thus far resulted in three edited volumes.[111] Additionally, many participants (and others) have published independent

109. A political (or anti-imperial) reading of biblical books is not unique to Paul. The approach is most clearly (and most convincingly) seen with Revelation. It is common and generally accepted to describe this book against the background of the Roman imperial system (e.g. in addition to the many commentaries and works on Revelation, see Friesen, *Imperial Cults;* and J. Nelson Kraybill, *Imperial Cult and Commerce in John's Apocalypse* [JSNTSup, 132; Sheffield: Sheffield Academic Press, 1996]). Additionally, there are considerable efforts to explore this emphasis in other New Testament books. For Mark, see Ched Myers, *Binding the Strong Man: A Political Reading of Mark's Story of Jesus* (Maryknoll, NY: Orbis Books, 1988). For Matthew, see the considerable output by Warren Carter including 'Toward an Imperial-Critical Reading of Matthew's Gospel' (SBLSP, 37; Atlanta: Scholars Press, 1998), pp. 296-324; Carter, 'Contested Claims: Roman Imperial Theology and Matthew's Gospel', *BTB* 29 (1999), pp. 56-67; Carter, *Matthew and the Margins: A Sociopolitical and Religious Reading* (Maryknoll, NY: Orbis Books, 2000); and Carter, *Matthew and Empire: Initial Explorations* (Harrisburg, PA: Trinity Press International, 2001). *Matthew and the Margins* is a major commentary in which Carter traces his anti-imperial emphasis throughout the entire work. This list is selective, and the extent to which these works are successful in proving their agendas varies and evaluation is beyond the scope of this work. For a discussion of various views of Luke's (Luke–Acts) approach to the Roman empire, an evaluation of these proposals, and a further option, see Walton, 'State', pp. 1-41. None of these proposals would be considered 'anti-imperial' in the sense that we are discussing of Paul having a specific and directed anti-imperial message. Nevertheless, they emphasize the conscious effort of the author to deal with the empire. Finally, for a popular survey of how New Testament authors view the Roman empire, see Richard J. Cassidy, *Christians and Roman Rule in the New Testament: New Perspectives* (Companions to the New Testament; New York: Crossroad, 2001).

110. For another recent critique of the 'Paul and Politics' movement, especially focused on Rome and Thessalonica, see James R. Harrison, *Paul and the Imperial Authorities at Thessalonica and Rome: A Study in the Conflict of Ideology* (WUNT, 273; Tübingen: Mohr Siebeck, 2011), pp. 1-14.

111. Richard A. Horsley (ed.), *Paul and Empire: Religion and Power in Roman Imperial Society* (Harrisburg, PA: Trinity Press International, 1997); Horsley (ed.), *Paul and Politics: Ekklesia, Israel, Imperium, Interpretation. Essays in Honor of Krister*

books fleshing out this and related arguments.[112] The purpose of this brief section is both to claim a measure of affinity with and to distance myself from this movement. To some extent, the present project can be seen as part of this development in Pauline studies. It is important to clarify my position on this issue because positive findings in this work can be used in support of many within this movement.

Although any attempt to describe this movement in a unified manner will be unsuccessful, it is worthwhile to examine the approach of Richard Horsley, one of the chief contributors to the movement. Although Horsley has worked broadly in the New Testament, the focus here is on Paul. Helpful for this purpose is his 'general introduction' to his edited volume *Paul and Empire*.[113] As an introduction to the subject matter and a summary of the volume's contents, this article both describes goals of the movement as Horsley sees them and attempts to place the volume's other contributors into the context of the movement.

Horsley maintains that Christianity 'started as an anti-imperial movement'.[114] He finds it ironic that, by the end of the first century, Christianity 'had begun to emphasize that they were not a serious threat to the established Roman imperial order'.[115] Even apologists and martyrs emphasized that, although they exclusively worshipped one God, they were not a threat to Rome. In fact, they were positive examples of loyalty.[116] Horsley suggests (and the book develops) four areas that this reading contributes to our understanding of Paul. These are not simply additions to traditional approaches but are a 'substantive or procedural shift with regard to previous scholarly understanding in New Testament studies'.[117] The first two are primarily shifts in the understanding of the context of early Christianity. First, scholars need to recognize that Christianity emerged in a context that had an imperial gospel. The Roman leader (and Rome) was a saviour. Much

---

Stendahl (Harrisburg, PA: Trinity Press International, 2000); Horsley (ed.), *Paul and the Roman Imperial Order* (Harrisburg, PA: Trinity Press International, 2004).

112. See, e.g., Richard A. Horsley and Neil Asher Silberman, *The Message and the Kingdom: How Jesus and Paul Ignited a Revolution and Transformed the Ancient World* (New York: Grossett/Putnam, 1997; repr. Minneapolis: Fortress Press, 2002); Stanley K. Stowers, *A Rereading of Romans: Justice, Jews, and Gentiles* (New Haven: Yale University Press, 1994).

113. Richard A. Horsley, 'General Introduction', in Richard A. Horsley (ed), *Paul and Empire: Religion and Power in Roman Imperial Society* (Harrisburg, PA: Trinity Press International, 1997), pp. 1-8. The separate introductions to the four parts of this volume also are helpful for this purpose (pp. 10-24, 88-95, 140-47, 206-14).

114. Horsley, 'General Introduction', p. 1.

115. Horsley, 'General Introduction', p. 1.

116. Horsley, 'General Introduction', p. 1.

117. Horsley, 'General Introduction', p. 3.

terminology applied to Jesus was already used of Caesar before (and during) the emergence of Christianity.[118] Second, scholars need to understand the importance of the Roman patronage (patron–client) system. It was in this context that the early Christians functioned and needed to navigate successfully.[119] The remaining two points are Christian responses to these two changes in understanding. An understanding of the presence of the imperial gospel and the patronage system demands a change in the way one views Paul. Thus, third, Paul's gospel was counter-imperial. This is in contrast to the understanding that Paul's message was primarily one of personal and individual salvation. When seen in its imperial context, Paul's message was a challenge to the authorities. Terminology applied originally to Caesar now is applied to Jesus.[120] Fourth, the church was intended to be an alternate society. It was supposed to be separate from imperial society and provided an option in opposition to the assumed structure based on equality.[121]

In many ways, the present work contributes to this agenda. I agree that it is essential that modern readers understand the imperial and patronage systems. I also agree that Paul's gospel was anti-imperial and provided for an 'alternative' community. In fact, this work contributes to point 3 above. However, I depart from this movement regarding the extent of the imperial impact on Paul's message (besides these brief comments here, this will be more fully discussed below). Where the Paul and Politics movement suggests that Paul's message was *primarily* anti-imperial, I maintain that it is only a *part* of the message, and in many (or even most) cases it is not his primary concern. Regarding this work, as mentioned above, if Paul's use of κύριος includes an anti-imperial polemic, it does not demand that this is the only or even primary point of his use of the title. This will be worked out in detail throughout this work. For now it is sufficient to say that the reader cannot escape Paul's primary influence of Judaism and the Greek Old Testament (this is the main work cited in his letters). Further, the traditional approach is not without merit. There was an interest in individual salvation and the like. Additionally, salvation in the New Testament, as in the Old, goes beyond the temporal. In essence, the salvation of God is larger and more far-reaching than the Paul and Politics movement permits. The emphasis of the Paul and Politics movement is a corrective but should not replace all that has come before.

In addition to our specific interaction with Horsley, other points clarifying our position can be made. First, there is much to commend this recent

---

118. Horsley, 'General Introduction', pp. 3-4. This will be seen also in Chapters 3 and 5.

119. Horsley, 'General Introduction', pp. 4-5.

120. Horsley, 'General Introduction', pp. 5-7.

121. Horsley, 'General Introduction', pp. 7-8.

movement. It has introduced with some force an aspect of Paul's agenda that is often ignored or minimized in favour of other aspects of his message. It seems short-sighted to assume that Paul's message, which was intended to transform the lives of its readers (Rom. 12.2) would not speak about the political climate of the day, especially when the readers' lives were full of claims and reminders of the powerful Roman empire.[122] It seems clear that Paul's actions and choice of terminology must have challenged his readers. Terms like σωτήρ, εὐαγγέλιον, πίστις, εἰρήνη and so on, would have called to mind imperial imagery. The frequent use of these terms in imperial contexts would make this association natural.[123] The imperial presence was felt everywhere. It was continually before the people in many ways. Physically, there was the constant reminder of the imperial presence and vision on the coins people used for daily transactions. These coins in pre-multimedia societies served as a valuable means of propaganda. They were a continual reminder of the presence and accomplishments of the emperor. Their message was simple and entirely controlled by the imperium.[124] Also, most important cities included buildings and cults honouring the emperor and his family.[125] In addition to the physical reminders of the imperium, its

122. See Karl Galinsky, *Augustan Culture: An Interpretive Introduction* (Princeton, NJ: Princeton University Press, 1996) and the primary sources cited there. This point will be developed further (more specific) in later chapters.

123. The following examples are representative: σωτήρ (Pompey: SIG³ 751, 752; Julius Caesar: SIG³ 760; Augustus: IGRR 1.1294 = OGIS 657; Gaius: Philo, *On the Embassy to Gaius* 4.1; Nero: IGRR 1.1124); εὐαγγέλιον (Augustus: IPriene 105 = OGIS 458); πίστις (Augustus: *Res gestae* 32; also the Latin *fides*, including the deity and *fides Augusta*: ILS 2971, 3775, 3778); εἰρήνη (Claudius: OGIS 663; ILS 5883 [Greek within Latin]; also the Latin *pax*, including *pax August(a)*: ILS 3787, 3789; also ILS 5883, noted previously, is the Greek version of this phrase). For further discussion of terminology, see Dieter Georgi, *Theocracy in Paul's Praxis and Theology* (trans. David E. Green; Minneapolis: Fortress Press, 1991), pp. 81-104 (edited version in Dieter Georgi, 'Who Is the True Prophet?', in Richard A. Horsley (ed.), *Paul and Empire: Religion and Power in Roman Imperial Society* [Harrisburg, PA: Trinity Press International, 1997], pp. 148-57); Cuss, *Imperial Cult*, pp. 63-71 (σωτήρ).

124. See Niels Hannestad, *Roman Art and Imperial Policy* (trans. P.J. Crabb; Jutland Archaeological Society Publications, 19; Højbjerg, Denmark: Jutland Archaeological Press, 1986), p. 11 (see also pp. 18, 56-58, 111). It is not universally accepted that coins were a successful means of propaganda. See Hannestad's discussion of propaganda with limited bibliography (p. 11 n. 8 [p. 351]). Although this discussion is valuable, for the purpose of this work, it need only be demonstrated that coins contributed to the prevalent presence of the imperial message. This is indisputable.

125. For example, for the presence of imperial cults in Asia Minor and Greece (especially Corinth), see respectively Price, *Rituals and Power;* and Bruce W. Winter, *After Paul Left Corinth: The Influence of Secular Ethics and Social Change* (Grand Rapids: Eerdmans, 2001), pp. 269-76.

presence was felt in the world of ideas and words. Imperial ideology was prominent in the literature of the day, providing a means of distributing the message (informing, educating, brainwashing?) to the populace in imaginative and creative ways.[126] All of these tools were used by the imperial power to saturate the world(s) that it controlled with its own programme. The physical evidence kept the imperial system always in view. Exciting stories like those found in the *Aeneid* were a means of unifying people in the Roman empire with a common history, providing them with a mutual and purposeful experience for the present, and providing them with a shared, hopeful vision for the future. They were part of something great, and the imperial power had a significant and crucial role in inaugurating and sustaining this 'utopia'.[127]

Of course, not all of the governed people were persuaded by nor bought into the imperial vision for their lives. Even more were unable to benefit from the administration of the system. For these, the imperial system utilized the effective tool of fear, even terror, most vividly illustrated in the cross.[128] Therefore, whether by willing acceptance, fear, or indifference, the imperial vision was an important part of the lives of all within the Roman empire.

This recent movement in Pauline studies correctly acknowledges that the claims of Jesus and Paul were counter-imperial. Paul's gospel and his blueprint for a new community demand a rejection of some of the roles Caesar and the empire claim over their subjects. Additionally, this movement has helped focus on many of the wrongs committed by powerful nations in recent history and today.

Recently, there have been attempts to criticize this movement. Most notable is Seyoon Kim's *Christ and Caesar: The Gospel and the Roman Empire in the Writings of Paul and Luke*.[129] Unfortunately, this book fails

---

126. See, for example, the Augustan poets who praise the emperor and his rule in glorious terms: Ovid, *Fasti* 1.607-16; Horace, *Odes* 3.5.1-4 (the expectation and hope in the emperor); and especially Ovid's *Metamorphoses* and Virgil's *Aeneid*.

127. The brief words here represent only a sample of the discussion that will be forthcoming. The persuasive influence of the imperial system in the cognitive environment of first-century readers will be assumed here. The task in later chapters will ultimately demand more than a reconstruction of the imperial culture.

128. See Martin Hengel, *Crucifixion in the Ancient World and the Folly of the Message of the Cross* (trans. John Bowden; Philadelphia: Fortress Press, 1977), pp. 22-32, 87.

129. Seyoon Kim, *Christ and Caesar: The Gospel and the Roman Empire in the Writings of Paul and Luke* (Grand Rapids: Eerdmans, 2008). Although this volume covers both Luke and Paul, only the Pauline critique is considered here. Another negative critique of this movement is Denny Burk's 'Is Paul's Gospel Counterimperial? Evaluating the Prospects of the "Fresh Perspective" for Evangelical Theology', *JETS*

to interact with the substantial issues. For example, Kim engages a limited sample of proponents of the movement;[130] he devotes fewer than six pages to the very important issue of method;[131] and he does not give a full hearing to counter-arguments on his critiques.[132]

However, as already noted, despite some important contributions, I cannot claim complete agreement with the Paul and Politics movement on one crucial point. I reject the notion that Paul's message was *primarily* anti-imperial.[133] The anti-imperial message was part of the package but was not the only or even necessarily the most important aspect of Paul's thought. Claims that Paul's letters 'reveal a kind of Christianity that existed before Christianity became a religion of an intrinsically sick human nature and its cure'[134] or that '[o]nly a gentile church unaccustomed to that perspective, and more familiar with the sacrificial logic of the blood cults, could have transformed Paul's message into a cult of atonement in Christ's blood (the letter to the Hebrews) and charter of Israel's disfranchisement (the *Letter of Barnabas*)'[135] fail to give proportional weight to passages such as Rom. 1.18–4.25 and 2 Cor. 5.21. It is agreed that Paul's message may have been overinterpreted in these directions, and it is acknowledged that there has

51 (2008), pp. 309-37. This article in part challenges an anti-American attitude among some anti-imperial writers and is more narrowly concerned with implications for evangelical theology. Colin Miller has also challenged this movement (although not named specifically) by arguing against a significant imperial cult presence in the Pauline cities during Paul's ministry ('The Imperial Cult in the Pauline Cities of Asia Minor and Greece', *CBQ* 72 [2010], pp. 314-31). Miller's article is helpful as a discussion of imperial cults proper in Paul's time and as a corrective to some excessive claims; however, he purposely avoids considering the larger imperial presence and thus his minimal approach is of little benefit concerning the question of imperial influence on Paul. For a critique of this article, see Joseph D. Fantin, review of 'The Imperial Cult in the Pauline Cities of Asia Minor and Greece', *CBQ* 72 (2010), pp. 314-31, by Colin Miller, *BSac* (2010), pp. 98-99.

130. Kim, *Christ and Caesar*, pp. 3-27. Those discussed are important but are not necessarily representative of the 'movement'.

131. Kim, *Christ and Caesar*, pp. 28-33.

132. Kim, *Christ and Caesar*, pp. 34-64. For a more detailed evaluation of Kim's work, see Joseph D. Fantin, review of *Christ and Caesar: The Gospel and the Roman Empire in the Writings of Paul and Luke* (Grand Rapids: Eerdmans, 2008), by Seyoon Kim, in *BMCR* (2009) http://bmcr.brynmawr.edu. See also Harrison, *Paul and the Imperial Authorities*, pp. 7-8. For a stronger critique, see Warren Carter's review in *RBL* (2009) http://www.bookreviews.org.

133. This is a general statement about an assumption of the Paul and Politics group. It is unlikely that all involved in this group maintain this position.

134. Stowers, *Romans*, p. 329.

135. Neil Elliott, *Liberating Paul: The Justice of God and the Politics of the Apostle* (Bible and Liberation; Sheffield: Sheffield Academic Press, 1995), p. 139.

been an overemphasis on the personal nature of Paul's message;[136] however, imbalance in one direction is not corrected by imbalance in another. It is preferred to see the anti-imperial message as an important aspect of the Pauline message but also to acknowledge that Paul's message is multifaceted and includes many of the traditional emphases in addition to the anti-imperial message.

There are two further reasons I cannot fully endorse the notion that Paul's message is primarily anti-imperial in focus. First, although the terminology mentioned above is common in imperial contexts, it is also common in the Greek translation(s) of the Old Testament.[137] GRAMCORD reveals that σωτήρ occurs 41 times and εὐαγγέλιον occurs only once; but cognate nouns (εὐαγγέλια and εὐαγγελία) occur 5 times, πίστις occurs 59 times, and εἰρήνη occurs 295 times. Searching for cognates such as verbs would yield more examples. The fact that this terminology is shared by both biblical and imperial contexts suggests that it will have both biblical and imperial meaning and implications. However, since Paul uses the Septuagint consistently and rarely, if ever, cites non-biblical literature, it is likely that Paul's message reveals significant Jewish influences and has significant Jewish aims. However, having noted this, it must be remembered that Paul's audience would not necessarily have this same Jewish influence, and they would certainly hear terminology and evaluate concepts from their own background and experience. Paul would have been aware of this.

Second, although probably not as strong an endorsement for authoritative governmental actions (or any and all forms of government) as often assumed, Rom. 13.1-7[138] is difficult to harmonize with a view that sees an anti-imperial agenda as Paul's *main* purpose. Space does not permit me to discuss in any detail the history of interpretation, exegetical problems, and theological implications of various interpretations of this passage; however, a few observations are necessary to support my position. Although some passages that speak of God's ultimate authority over rulers may have anti-imperial implications (13.1b-c, 4), as a whole the passage endorses a rather positive view of some type of governmental authority. Although there may be different explanations for the passage's setting, the traditional and major-

136. Exposed in Krister Stendahl, 'The Apostle Paul and the Introspective Conscience of the West', in his *Paul among Jews and Gentiles and Other Essays* (Philadelphia: Fortress Press, 1976), pp. 78-96.

137. Proponents of the Paul and Politics movement are aware of Paul's Jewish context and do not deny it. However, it seems to me that conclusions that place an anti-imperial message first, minimize Paul's Jewish context. The question of Paul's influence(s) will be discussed in Chapter 2.

138. Other texts within the Pauline corpus with a similar message include 1 Tim. 2.1-3 and Tit. 3.1-3. See also 1 Pet. 2.13-17.

ity interpretation generally maintains some form of this position.[139] In order to maintain that Paul's main message was anti-imperial, one must deal with this passage in some way. Although unrelated to the historical context, the interpretation of this passage is complicated also by its misuse by those in authority and clergy who support authority.[140] The modern concerns may provide a lens through which one can see in this passage (both pro-government and reactions against its abuse by authorities) issues that were not present in the ancient world. Such concerns may be brought into the interpretive process (either unintentionally or intentionally).

One way to dismiss Rom. 13.1-7 is literally to *explain it away*: in other words, to suggest that it is not original.[141] Although some have noticed a lack of connection between this passage and what it precedes,[142] there is no textual support for this position and others seem to be able to place the text successfully in the flow of the argument of the larger section.[143] A second way to deal with the passage is suggest that it has been applied too broadly and too strongly. The effect is to weaken the nature of the command as it

---

139. See, e.g., Paul J. Achtemeier, *Romans* (IBC; Atlanta: John Knox Press, 1985), pp. 203-206; Matthew Black, *Romans* (NCB; Grand Rapids: Eerdmans, 2nd edn, 1989), p. 179; F.F. Bruce, *Romans* (TNTC; Leicester: Inter-Varsity Press, 2nd edn, 1985), pp. 218-22; Brendan Byrne, *Romans* (SP, 6; Collegeville, MN: Liturgical Press, 1996), pp. 385-90; C.E.B. Cranfield, *A Critical and Exegetical Commentary on the Epistle to the Romans* (ICC; 2 vols.; Edinburgh: T. & T. Clark, 1975, 1979), II, 651-63; C.H. Dodd, *The Epistle of Paul to the Romans* (London: Hodder & Stoughton, 1932; repr. London: Collins, 1959), pp. 203-205; James D.G. Dunn, *Romans 9–16* (WBC, 38b; Dallas: Word Books, 1988), p. 279; Joseph A. Fitzmyer, *Romans: A New Translation with Introduction and Commentary* (AB, 33; New York: Doubleday, 1993), pp. 662-65; Douglas J. Moo, *The Epistle to the Romans* (NICNT; Grand Rapids: Eerdmans, 1996), pp. 747, 790-93; Anders Nygren, *Commentary on Romans* (Philadelphia: Fortress Press, 1949), pp. 426-31.

140. See, e.g., Elliott, *Liberating Paul*, pp. 3-24. Although Elliott's political intentions are rather transparent (he makes them explicit) and his supporting evidence linking his examples to Paul is often quite dubious, his examples support his point that Romans 13 (and other Pauline passages) have been used by some for the purpose of suppression. See also Jan Botha's work, which attempts to provide guidelines and methods for the responsible reading and application of this passage (*Subject to Whose Authority? Multiple Readings of Romans 13* [Emory Studies in Early Christianity 4; Atlanta: Scholars Press, 1994]).

141. James Kallas, 'Romans xiii. 1-7: An Interpolation', *NTS* 11 (1964–65), pp. 365-74; Winsome Munro, 'Romans 13:1-7: Apartheid's Last Biblical Refuge', *BTB* 20 (1990), pp. 161-68.

142. Clinton D. Morrison, *The Powers That Be* (SBT, 29; London: SCM Press, 1960), p. 104 (Morrison does not reject the authenticity of this passage).

143. See, e.g., Bruce W. Winter, 'Roman Law and Society in Romans 12-15', in Peter Oakes (ed.), *Rome in the Bible and the Early Church* (Carlisle: Paternoster Press, 2002), pp. 67-102 (81-84) and many of the commentaries mentioned above.

has been traditionally interpreted. Neil Elliott deals with the passage by suggesting that it is best viewed as a 'conventional prophetic-apocalyptic affirmation that God disposes the rise and fall of empires and gives the power of the sword into the hands of the ruler (13:1, 4)'.[144] The passage, however, does have specific application. It is intended 'to keep members of the ekklesia from making trouble in the streets'.[145] Elliott has some valuable insights. I find his position helpful in many ways. His point that this passage has been applied too broadly and too strongly needs to be taken seriously. He is correct to note that the previous context (12.19-21) emphasizes God's role in judgment and vengeance.[146] However, this is instruction on how the community is to deal with being wronged. It does not follow that it removes the ruling power's role in governing and dispensing justice. Elliott is also helpful in pointing out that Paul's positive language labelling the government as 'servants of God' and the like does not 'constitute his evaluation of government in the abstract or government officials in particular'.[147] However, although this passage does not give sanction to a specific government, the context does suggest that some form of government is set up by God. Whether the type of government in view here is an endorsement of all and any form of government is open to challenge. Moreover, it would be wrong for a specific government to assume that this passage is an endorsement of its policies and its particular existence. Nevertheless, some form of government that is a form of Roman authority is spoken of in a positive manner. It is difficult to dismiss the specific nature of this command in this context. Thus, a *primary* anti-imperial and anti-Roman message in Paul is difficult to sustain even if much of Elliott's thesis is correct.

A further approach is to change the referent of the authorities in question. Although Mark Nanos does not adhere to the anti-imperial position, his thesis about this passage can be used to support such a view. In a detailed discussion, Nanos suggests that the authorities are synagogue leaders.[148] However, despite his attempts at contextual placement and terminology, one is still left with minimal explicit clues in the text to support this position. One must really accept his strongly Jewish reading of the entire letter for this even to be plausible. However, even a strongly Jewish reading could sustain a traditional reading of this text with only slightly more difficulty than the more standard positions.

---

144. Elliott, *Liberating Paul*, p. 224.
145. Elliott, *Liberating Paul*, p. 223.
146. Elliott, *Liberating Paul*, p. 223.
147. Elliott, *Liberating Paul*, p. 223.
148. Mark D. Nanos, *The Mystery of Romans: The Jewish Context of Paul's Letter* (Minneapolis: Fortress Press, 1996), pp. 289-336.

Although other solutions may be proposed,[149] it seems most likely that, despite difficulties with the passage, Rom. 13.1-7 cannot be completely shaken from a rather positive view of some form of governmental authority. Thus, Paul's main purpose is not anti-imperial. It is unfortunate that the passage has been used to support brutal regimes; however, the abuse of a passage should not dictate interpretation.

Having suggested that Rom. 13.1-7 contributes to the unsustainability of an anti-imperial agenda as being Paul's primary purpose, the emphasis of the Paul and Politics movement has given us the opportunity to reconsider this passage in fresh ways. For example, although not necessarily a response to this movement, Stanley Porter's view that this passage instructs obedience to just authorities but permits disobedience to unjust authorities is a helpful solution. This maintains the biblical directive and provides Christians with the ability to respond to unjust rule.[150] This view is driven by Greek, rhetorical, and background considerations. This is one way to approach the passage and avoid abuse.

We will revisit this passage briefly in Chapter 5 and propose arguments based on this study that may contribute to an understanding and a use of this passage today. For our purposes here, what is important is to acknowledge that if an anti-imperial message can be found to be part of Paul's agenda, it cannot be his main thrust.

---

149. See the various options presented in commentaries. For a brief survey of patristic views of the larger question of submission to powers, see Gillian Clark, 'Let Every Soul Be Subject: The Fathers and the Empire', in Loveday Alexander (ed.), *Images of Empire* (JSOTSup, 122; Sheffield: JSOT Press, 1991), pp. 251-75.

150. Stanley E. Porter, 'Romans 13.1-7 as Pauline Political Rhetoric', *FilolNT* 3 (1990), pp. 115-39.

Chapter 2

PAUL AND HIS WORLD: SOURCES AND THEIR USE

The stated purpose of this work is to determine whether there was a polemic against the living Roman emperor in certain occurrences of Paul's use of the title κύριος for Christ. In Chapter 1 a number of general issues of importance were introduced in order to accomplish this task successfully. These included the introduction and defence of some basic methodological principles that will undergird this study. In this chapter this preparational emphasis will continue by introducing our sources and providing some preliminary comments. In some cases, the discussion will be defining and in others the purpose will merely be to provide some general comments about usage.

Our sources fall into two categories. First, there are the select Pauline texts themselves, the main focus of this study, from which an attempt to determine whether a polemic exists will be made. Although not limiting the existence of the polemic elsewhere, I am concerned only with the Pauline letters that contain passages that I will discuss in Chapter 5, namely Romans, 1 Corinthians, Ephesians, and Philippians. The specific passages are chosen because they include a variety of contextual features that seem to make the polemic likely. The discussion of these Epistles will be defining in the sense that it will state and defend the position taken here concerning authorship and date. Two of these letters are disputed. One is disputed with regard to authorship, which has implications for its date. The other is disputed with regard to date only. In addition to the basic issues of authorship and date, I will also briefly discuss the broad influences that may have contributed to Paul's thought. Second, there are non-Pauline texts and other sources that will provide the contextual information, the raw informational and tangible material that will be used to reconstruct the cognitive environment that may result in the necessary conditioning to *hear* or *see* the polemic in the Pauline texts. This conditioning is not artificial but rather an attempt to place the modern reader as much as possible into the world of Paul's original recipients. Thus, given an accurate picture of the cognitive environment (both physically and in the realm of ideas), we will be in a position to determine whether in certain contexts an anti-emperor polemic will be evident. Concerning these sources, I will present in this chapter some basic information and principles for usage.

The Pauline letters are part of the literary record of the first century. The suggested division of sources should not be understood as suggesting otherwise. Rather, as the principal focus of examination, they are set apart for analysis. The other sources are intended to illuminate the Pauline texts. Therefore, Paul's letters demand a more precise level of understanding than other sources. For example, the issue of dating is very important as we consider when certain concepts about the emperors first became evident and then became common in the first century.

As already stated, I am not claiming to be able to reproduce an exact or even a remotely complete cognitive environment; rather, I hope to provide as accurate a picture as possible given the available data. This should be sufficient to prove our case. Future discoveries may add to my reconstruction. Such discoveries may either provide further verification or refute the picture reconstructed here of the first century. However, assuming that scholarship has not completely misunderstood the first century, most discoveries will further enhance our understanding of this period by sharpening our picture through a more precise and detailed view of the first century.

1. *Paul: The Authenticity and Date of the Letters*

The role and office of emperor and imperial cults developed rapidly during the first century. In order to understand this period, one must be sensitive to this development. Therefore, we need to have a relatively precise understanding of the dates of the four Pauline letters that contain the five passages that will be discussed in this work. I will argue that it is best to place these writings during the reign of Nero. For reasons that will become apparent in the following chapter, it will be helpful to divide the reign of Nero into two parts. First, 54–59 CE is often considered a period of responsible government. Second, in contrast, 60–68 CE is considered a period characterized by poor governmental policy. Although this distinction is helpful and will generally be important for this study, it is unwise to make too big a distinction concerning the personality of Nero in these periods. For the purposes of this study, it is not necessary to maintain a precise division between the later and earlier reigns of the emperor.

a. *Romans and 1 Corinthians*

Romans and 1 Corinthians demand little discussion. There is no question of Pauline authorship for these letters, and their dates are also generally agreed upon. Romans is assumed to have been written to the church at Rome from

Corinth between 55 and early 57 CE.[1] There are exceptions, but most commentators date the writing of the letter in the early (pre-60) reign of Nero.[2] Corinth as the place of writing is generally accepted. The information provided in Rom. 15.14–16.23 is best interpreted as providing a Corinthian provenance for the letter.[3]

The letter written to the Corinthian church labelled 1 Corinthians also has a relatively stable date. Again the date range falls within the early reign of Nero, usually within the 54 to 57 CE range,[4] and most likely it was written

---

1. See, e.g., C.K. Barrett, *A Commentary on the Epistle to the Romans* (HNTC; Peabody, MA: Hendrickson, 1957), p. 5; Bruce, *Romans*, p. 18; Cranfield, *Critical and Exegetical Commentary on the Epistle to the Romans*, I, pp. 12, 16; James D.G. Dunn, *Romans 1–8* (WBC, 38a; Dallas: Word Books, 1988), pp. xliii, xliv; Werner Georg Kümmel, *Introduction to the New Testament* (Nashville: Abingdon, rev. edn, 1975), p. 311; Lee Martin McDonald and Stanley E. Porter (eds.), *Early Christianity and its Sacred Literature* (Peabody, MA: Hendrickson, 2000), p. 451; Leon Morris, *The Epistle to the Romans* (PNTC; Grand Rapids: Eerdmans, 1988), pp. 6-7; John A.T. Robinson, *Redating the New Testament* (Philadelphia: Westminster Press, 1976), p. 54; Peter Stuhlmacher, *Paul's Letter to the Romans* (trans. S.J. Hafemann; Edinburgh: T. & T. Clark, 1994), p. 5. See these works for a discussion of the reconstruction of Paul's ministry at the point of composition.

2. A few scholars have suggested a slightly later date (Donald Guthrie, *New Testament Introduction* [Downers Grove, IL: InterVarsity Press, 4th edn, 1990], pp. 407-408 [57–59 CE]; Black, *Romans*, p. 5 [58 CE]; Otto Michel, *Der Brief and die Römer* [KEK; Göttingen: Vandenhoeck & Ruprecht, 5th edn, 1978], p. 27 [58 CE]). Exceptions include John Knox, who dated the letter in 53–54 (*Chapters in the Life of Paul* [New York: Abingdon–Cokesbury Press, 1950], p. 86); and, depending on the date of the crucifixion, the results of Gerd Luedemann's reconstruction of Pauline chronology may place the letter as early as 51–52 (*Paul, Apostle to the Gentiles: Studies in Chronology* [trans. F. Stanley Jones; Philadelphia: Fortress Press, 1984], conclusion on p. 263). However, if the crucifixion can be dated late, Luedemann's date is still early but is within Nero's reign (54–55).

3. See Loveday Alexander, 'Chronology of Paul', *DPL*, pp. 115-23 (118); Cranfield, *Romans*, I, p. 12.

4. See, e.g., C.K. Barrett, *A Commentary on the First Epistle to the Corinthians* (HNTC; Peabody, MA: Hendrickson, 1968), p. 5 (early 54 but possibly late 53); Hans Conzelmann, *1 Corinthians: A Commentary on the First Epistle to the Corinthians* (ed. G.W. MacRae; trans. J.W. Leitch; Hermeneia; Philadelphia: Fortress Press, 1975), p. 4 n. 31; Gordon D. Fee, *The First Epistle to the Corinthians* (NICNT; Grand Rapids: Eerdmans, 1987), pp. 4-5; Guthrie, *New Testament Introduction*, p. 458; Robert Jewett, *Dating Paul's Life* (London: SCM Press, 1979), p. 104; Kümmel, *Introduction*, p. 279 (spring 54 or 55); Robinson, *Redating*, p. 54; Anthony C. Thiselton, *The First Epistle to the Corinthians: A Commentary on the Greek Text* (NIGTC; Grand Rapids: Eerdmans, 2000), p. 32 (spring 54). Again Luedemann's reconstruction suggests a different conclusion. Depending on the date of the crucifixion, he suggests that the letter may be written as early as 49 (or 52) (*Paul, Apostle to the Gentiles*, conclusion on p. 263). Additionally, see Knox, *Chapters*, p. 86 (51–53 CE).

before Romans.[5] The letter itself names its place of composition, Ephesus (1 Cor. 16.8). Of importance for our study is that both Romans and 1 Corinthians were written during the early reign of Nero.

b. *Philippians*

Paul's authorship of the letter written to the Philippians is also undisputed. However, its date is less certain. The date of the letter is generally linked to the place of composition. It was clearly written from prison (1.7, 13, 14, 17); however, the identification of this prison has been disputed. The traditional view has claimed Rome as the origin of this epistle,[6] but this view has been questioned primarily because the number and distance of journeys recorded in the letter are difficult to place within the time frame available (see 2.19-30; 4.18). Therefore, Ephesus[7] and, to a lesser extent, Caesarea[8] have been suggested as alternatives. Although not without problems, there does not seem to be a persuasive reason to reject Roman provenance. The appendix in this work will explore this issue in a little more detail. It is enough to note here that, although not exclusive to a Roman context, references to πραιτωρίῳ ('Praetorium' 1.13) and Καίσαρος οἰκίας ('Caesar's household' 4.22) are best understood in a Roman context. The distance of Caesarea to Philippi is approximately the same as Rome to Philippi. Therefore, the most problematic aspect of the Roman imprisonment theory is not resolved by a Caesarean imprisonment. Finally, there is no early evidence that Paul ever was imprisoned in Ephesus.

Therefore, it is likely that Philippians should be dated during Paul's Roman imprisonment, for which Acts 28 is the only source. This is usually dated between 60 and 62 CE (or 61–63). This is the early part of the second part of Nero's reign. There is nothing in the epistle that can allow us to be any more specific than this.[9]

There are two other issues relating to Philippians that need attention. Again, only brief comments will be offered here; additional observations appear in the appendix. First, there is some question whether Philippians is

---

5. Raymond E. Brown, *Introduction to the New Testament* (New York: Doubleday, 1996), p. 434; Michel, *Römer*, pp. 27-28.

6. For a well-balanced defence of a Roman imprisonment, see McDonald and Porter, *Early Christianity*, pp. 373-74, 470.

7. For a detailed defence of an Ephesian provenance for all of the prison epistles, see George S. Duncan, *St Paul's Ephesian Ministry: A Reconstruction with Special Reference to the Ephesian Origin of the Imprisonment Epistles* (London: Hodder & Stoughton, 1929).

8. See Gerald F. Hawthorne, *Philippians* (WBC, 43; Waco, TX: WordBooks, 1983), pp. xxxvi-xliv.

9. If Ephesians is the place of origin, the date would probably be 54–56 CE; if Caesarea, 58–60 CE.

a unified letter.[10] However, with no manuscript evidence for anything other than a unified epistle, a composite of different portions of letters now in the form of Philippians is difficult to prove. In addition, the form and contents are best explained if Philippians is viewed as a single letter.[11] Second, Phil. 2.11 will be discussed in Chapter 5. There is debate over whether the poem/hymn of which this passage is a part originated with Paul or was an earlier piece used by Paul.[12] Although there are good reasons to maintain that Paul wrote this passage specifically for the letter (as will be defended in Appendix 1), the important and unquestionable point is that Paul used the passage for his purpose(s) in the letter. Even if an anti-imperial polemic did not exist in an original pre-Pauline poem/hymn (and it could have), this says nothing of whether or not Paul used it in this way. The existence of an anti-imperial polemic must be determined by its use in the letter in light of the social context in which it was utilized.

c. *Ephesians*

Establishing the authorship and dating of Ephesians poses more difficulty than for the three previous letters that have been considered. Many scholars maintain that this letter was written after Paul had died. I approach Ephesians primarily as an authentic letter of the apostle Paul. Specifically, I maintain that Ephesians was written from prison (3.1; 6.20) and is a circular letter written to churches in Asia Minor. It was probably written during the same Roman imprisonment during which the apostle wrote Philippians; to some extent it shares some of the same problems with provenance as that letter. The arguments for a Roman provenance for Philippians will suffice for Ephesians as well. Ephesians does not evidence the same 'Roman' vocabulary as Philippians, but the theology seems developed in areas such as the universal church beyond that which is found in Romans and Galatians. Thus, it is less problematic to date Ephesians in the early sixties (or later). The words ἐν ᾽Εφέσῳ (1.1) are best considered an addition (see

10. See the discussions in favour of unity in Loveday Alexander, 'Hellenistic Letter-Forms and the Structure of Philippians', *JSNT* 37 (1989), pp. 87-101; McDonald and Porter, *Early Christianity*, pp. 465-67; Peter T. O'Brien, *The Epistle to the Philippians: A Commentary on the Greek Text* (NIGTC; Grand Rapids: Eerdmans, 1991), pp. 10-18; F.W. Beare, *A Commentary on the Epistle to the Philippians* (HNTC; Peabody, MA: Hendrickson, 1959), pp. 1-5.

11. For example, Jeffrey T. Reed finds support for unity from the structure of the letter and also concludes that the contents can be easily explained without resorting to multi-letter theories (*Discourse Analysis of Philippians*).

12. See, e.g., R.P. Martin, *Hymn to Christ: Philippians 2:5-11 in Recent Interpretation and in the Setting of Early Christian Worship* (Cambridge: Cambridge University Press, 1967; repr. Downers Grove, IL: InterVarsity Press, 1997), pp. 42-62; O'Brien, *Philippians*, pp. 186-202.

appendix), making it likely that this was a circular letter. This designation also provides an explanation for the lack of personal greeting in the book. Thus, it is suggested that Ephesians, like Philippians, was written during the second part of Nero's reign.

I am not unaware of the difficulty of this position. Much of the appendix is devoted to defending the position taken here. It is enough to say here that arguments about vocabulary, theology and so on, do not seem to be devastating to Pauline authorship. Harold Hoehner has demonstrated that, even in modern times, there has been nearly a 50-50 split concerning authorship of Ephesians among scholars writing on the issue.[13]

This position on Pauline authorship of Ephesians is not essential to this study. For this reason and because many scholars disagree with the positions stated here, I will also consider implications of a later dating. Those who do not maintain Pauline authorship date Ephesians anywhere from 60 to 100 CE,[14] although it seems that the later part of this period is generally preferred. Thus, in addition to the position that Ephesians was written in the sixties, I will also consider the implications if the book was written in the late first century.

As will be clear in subsequent chapters, the notion of an anti-imperial use of the term κύριος grows more likely as the century progresses. This is due to the role of the emperor, the development of imperial cults, and especially to the expanded use of terms for 'lord' as titles for emperors. What was beginning to increase in usage under Nero (54–68) was common for the following dynasty. Therefore, if a polemic can be successfully defended as present in Ephesians dated in Paul's lifetime, the polemic will be nearly certain for the later dating.

The addressees of Romans, 1 Corinthians, and Philippians are clearly the church(es) in the cities that are named in the openings of the letters and from which the title of each letter is derived. However, it has been noted that Ephesians is a circular letter. Therefore, although the Ephesian church is included among the addressees, it is most accurate to consider the addressees to be churches in Asia Minor (and even possibly elsewhere). It is impossible to be more specific on this.[15] If the reconstruction above is accurate concerning the possible role of the Ephesian church in the distribution of the letter, it is possible that the Ephesians were the most important addressees.

---

13. Harold W. Hoehner, *Ephesians: An Exegetical Commentary* (Grand Rapids: Baker Book House, 2002), pp. 9-20. Hoehner himself takes the position that Ephesians was written by Paul (pp. 2-61).

14. Ernest Best, *A Critical and Exegetical Commentary on Ephesians* (ICC; Edinburgh: T. & T. Clark, 1998; repr. London: T. & T. Clark, 2004), p. 45 (80–90 CE); however, if Paul was the author, Best suggests that a date in the early sixties from Rome would be most probable.

15. We do not know if the addressees were limited to certain Pauline churches, all churches in Asia Minor and so on.

d. *Summary*

A summary of our conclusions concerning our Pauline database can be stated as follows. Of the five passages that will be discussed in detail, four are unquestionably the work of Paul (Rom. 10.9; 1 Cor. 8.5-6; 12.3; Phil. 2.11[16]). Another passage will be considered Pauline (Eph. 4.3), but I am aware of problems with this view. Three of the passages were very likely to have been written during Nero's early reign (Rom. 10.9; 1 Cor. 8.5-6; 12.3). The reconstruction here will place the other two in Nero's later reign (Phil. 2.11; Eph. 4.3). Again I acknowledge that this dating is not universally accepted. Philippians is the most solid example from the later period, but even this is disputed (some date this during the early reign of Nero). The passage from Ephesians is often assumed to have been written during the Flavian dynasty, which followed Nero and the year-long civil war. I wish to accommodate those who differ on this issue. Indeed, a later date for Ephesians will make the case for an anti-imperial polemic easier to defend. As we will see, the use of κύριος for emperors after Nero is much more common than before him. What can be proven with difficulty for 60–62 CE will be almost assumed for 90 CE. Therefore, implications of a later date for this study will periodically be mentioned. I will not purposefully accommodate an early date for Philippians. Nevertheless, the historical reconstruction should result in a convincing argument for those who maintain an earlier date for the letter as a whole or the poem/hymn in 2.6-11. Our conclusions can be summarized as follows:

Letter	Date	Addressees	Alternate Date
1 Corinthians	54–57 CE	church at Corinth	
Romans	55–57 CE	church at Rome	
Philippians	60–62 CE	church at Philippi	
Ephesians	60–62 CE	churches in Asia Minor	late first century

2. *Paul's Thought: From Bousset to Engberg-Pedersen*

What is the primary influence on Paul and his thought? This question is essential for understanding Paul's message. Concerning this, no scholar is more important than Martin Hengel, whose volume *Judaism and Hellenism*[17] argued successfully that we can no longer look at Judaism and Hellenism during the first century as completely distinct conceptual thought worlds.

---

16. Note the discussion above. Although there is debate over whether or not Phil. 2.6-11 is pre-Pauline, it is not questioned that Paul used the hymn for his own purposes.

17. Martin Hengel, *Judaism and Hellenism: Studies in their Encounter in Palestine during the Early Hellenistic Period* (trans. J. Bowden; London: SCM Press, 1974; repr. London: Xpress Reprints [SCM Press], 1996).

Rather, there are relationships between these areas that make a clear break impossible. The issue is much more complex than has often been assumed.

Despite the work of Hengel, until recently (both pre- and post-Hengel), the debate concerning whether Paul's influence was primarily Hellenistic or Jewish was rather simplistic. The framing of the debate seemed to demand an either/or solution. In the brief treatment below, I will discuss three phases of this debate. These three phases are not entirely distinct; rather, they are emphases and are not necessarily mutually exclusive. In many cases, scholars mentioned in one phase may not disagree with those in other phases. Further, although the title of this section suggests a chronological sequence between the positions represented by Bousset and Engberg-Pedersen, there is only a very loose chronology. Finally, both Bousset and Engberg-Pedersen are important representatives of positions and not the exclusive spokespersons of the views they represent. What follows is brief. Nevertheless, it will provide a background for my approach to this issue.

The first phase is the emphasis on the Hellenistic context of Paul. Early in the twentieth century, the *religionsgeschichtliche Schule* was influential. Within this movement, Wilhelm Bousset published his classic work, *Kyrios Christos*.[18] This book attempted to account for a history of the church's belief in Christ from the earliest Christian community to Irenaeus. Bousset's thesis was that the early Palestinian Christian community was highly Jewish but shortly thereafter became Hellenistic. The use of κύριος as a title for Christ did not occur until the hellenization of the church had taken place. Paul's ministry was Hellenistic, and thus he was a Hellenistic thinker and explicitly *not* a Jewish thinker. What distinguishes this phase from later scholars who emphasize a Hellenistic context for Paul is the notion of *derivation*. The belief was that Paul's thought was *derived* from or influenced by Hellenism in contrast to Judaism.

However, despite influential proponents such as Rudolf Bultmann,[19] this position no longer maintains a prominent role in the field. The historical reconstruction of the *religionsgeschichtliche Schule* was unsustainable.[20] Much of the ancient material relied on by supporters was (in some cases

18. The standard English translation is Wilhelm Bousset, *Kyrios Christos* (trans. John E. Steely; Nashville: Abingdon, 5th edn, 1970).

19. Rudolf Bultmann, *Theology of the New Testament,* vol. 1 (trans. Kendrick Grobel; New York: Charles Scribner's Sons, 1951), pp. 187-89. Bultmann himself was not part of the *religionsgeschichtliche Schule*; however, he was strongly indebted to it, as his comments to his introduction (1964) to Bousset's fifth edition of *Kyrios Christos* make clear (Bousset, *Kyrios Christos*, pp. 7-9). For a critique of Bousset's influence, see Larry W. Hurtado, 'New Testament Christology: A Critique of Bousset's Influence', *TS* 40 (1979), pp. 306-17.

20. See the discussion in Dale B. Martin, 'Paul and the Judaism/Hellenism Dichotomy: Toward a Social History of the Question', in Troels Engberg-Pedersen (ed.),

much) later than the New Testament. To conclude *influence* on such grounds has been problematic. A reaction to this movement resulted in a shift of emphasis from Hellenistic to Jewish influences on Paul (see Phase 2). The reaction was so strong that a neglect of Hellenistic influence resulted.[21]

With a decline in the influence of the *religionsgeschichtliche Schule*, the study of Jewish backgrounds became a very fruitful area of investigation for scholars. This is the second phase in the search for Paul's influence. This phase maintains that Paul's thought was derived from Judaism. For example, Albert Schweitzer, against many of his time, proposed that Paul was strongly Jewish in orientation and that his theology was particularly eschatological.[22] Although with a different emphasis, W.D. Davies also argued that Paul was essentially Jewish and should be classified as rabbinic (although sensitive to anachronistic problems with the term).[23] Despite a decline and near extinction of the *religionsgeschichtliche Schule*, voices such as Schweitzer, Davies and others did not have a significant impact on Pauline studies. Possibly because of its radical nature and far-reaching consequences that resonate throughout Pauline studies, it was the work of E.P. Sanders that really drove home the notions of Paul's Jewishness.[24] Sanders's work is significant for a number of reasons, not least of which is its contribution to this debate. Sanders is responsible for directing Pauline studies toward what has been labelled the *new perspective on Paul*. Much of what he has done is still being discussed, critiqued and refined.[25] However, because of Sanders, few question the Jewish nature of Paul's thought.

Paul beyond the Judaism/Hellenism Divide (Louisville, KY: Westminster/John Knox Press, 2001), pp. 29-61 (50-54) (although he is not emphasizing *reaction*).

21. However, the *religionsgeschichtliche Schule* has provided some helpful insights. See Dieter Zeller, 'New Testament Christology in its Hellenistic Reception', *NTS* 46 (2001), pp. 312-33.

22. Albert Schweitzer, *The Mysticism of Paul the Apostle* (trans. William Montgomery; London: A. & C. Black, 2nd edn, 1953), esp. pp. 26-40 (the first draft goes back to 1906 [p. xxiii]).

23. W.D. Davies, *Paul and Rabbinic Judaism: Some Rabbinic Elements in Pauline Theology* (Philadelphia: Fortress Press, 4th edn, 1980).

24. E.P. Sanders, *Paul and Palestinian Judaism* (Minneapolis: Fortress Press, 1977), followed by his *Paul, the Law, and the Jewish People* (Minneapolis: Fortress Press, 1983). See also Wright, *What Saint Paul Really Said*, pp. 11-23 (explained) and applied through the rest of the book.

25. There has been much discussion concerning the *new perspective*. See, e.g., the generally critical appraisal from many of the articles in D.A. Carson, Peter T. O'Brien and Mark A. Seifrid (eds.), *Justification and Variegated Nomism* (2 vols.; Tübingen: Mohr Siebeck, 2001–2004). For a recent positive response, see Donald B. Garlington, 'The New Perspective on Paul: An Appraisal Two Decades Later', *CTR* NS 2 (2005), pp. 17-38. An annotated biography is provided by Jay E. Smith, 'The New Perspective on Paul: A Select and Annotated Bibliography', *CTR* NS 2 (2005), pp. 91-111.

It appears that because of the strong reaction to the *religionsgeschichtliche Schule* and influential scholars such as Sanders, the shift seems to have gone to the other extreme. Phase 2 was important to demonstrate Paul's Jewish influence. However, it still seems to maintain the dualism between Judaism and Hellenism and did not really deal with New Testament texts that seem to be Hellenistic, texts that caused scholars in the first phase to emphasize Hellenism. In Phase 2, sources without a specifically Jewish connection are not often considered as valuable as those which do. Craig Evans's helpful introduction to primary sources for New Testament study begins with this comment, '[The book] is an introduction to the diverse bodies of literature that are in various ways cognate to biblical literature.'[26] However, he devotes only sixteen pages to Graeco-Roman writers in a chapter entitled 'Other Writings'.[27]

Paul was clearly a Jewish thinker; however, Paul's Hellenism cannot be denied. In the midst of an emphasis on the Jewish context of Paul, some argued for a Hellenistic influence as well. For the most part these scholars are emphasizing the Hellenistic background while avoiding some of the dogmatic and extreme assertions of the earlier scholars. John White, whose work was noted in Chapter 1, Dieter Georgi, and Troels Engberg-Pedersen have all produced strongly 'Hellenistic' studies of Paul.[28] These works do not reject a Jewish Paul but do not see a significant distinction between Hellenistic Jewish and simply Hellenistic thought. Engberg-Pedersen states concerning his work *Paul and the Stoics*,

> In brief, the present work argues for similarity of ideas between Paul and the Stoics right across the board and fundamentally questions the widespread view that in the end there remains a basic, intrinsic difference between the perspectives of Paul the (Hellenistic) Jew and the ethical tradition of the Greeks.[29]

Although many may not agree with Engberg-Pedersen's conclusions, his understanding of Paul's influence is clear. He does not dismiss Jewish background; he simply does not see it as distinct. Nevertheless, his position is stated too strongly and seems to obliterate any uniqueness of Hellenistic Judaism within the larger Hellenistic world. Georgi's position is preferable,

---

26. Craig A. Evans, *Ancient Texts for New Testament Studies: A Guide to the Background Literature* (Peabody, MA: Hendrickson, 2005), p. xi.

27. Evans, *Ancient Texts*, pp. 287-302. This is an improvement over the first edition (Craig A. Evans, *Noncanonical Writings and New Testament Interpretation* [Peabody, MA: Hendrickson, 1992], pp. 169-73, 77).

28. White, *Apostle of God*; Georgi, *Theocracy in Paul's Praxis and Theology*; Troels Engberg-Pedersen, *Paul and the Stoics* (Louisville, KY: Westminster/John Knox Press, 2000).

29. Engberg-Pedersen, *Paul and the Stoics*, p. 11.

> Neither is the Judaism from which Paul springs and with which he grap-
> ples a ghetto phenomenon. On the contrary: it is in active dialogue and
> exchange with the pagan world of Hellenism. Whatever the local varie-
> ties of diaspora Judaism may have been, they all consciously reflect the
> universal problems of their contemporary culture and society. They do not
> do so, however, at the expense of their Judaism, which they understand
> as the truest representation of what they held to be the core of Hellenistic
> civilization.[30]

It does not seem wise to suggest that Jews saw their own experience as
'the core of Hellenistic civilization'. However, a more balanced understanding of Hellenistic contexts is emerging. The reaction against the *religionsgeschichtliche Schule* continues but is subsiding. Despite past abuses, it is
difficult to deny a Hellenistic influence on Paul. This has resulted in a third
phase.

As mentioned above, Martin Hengel's 1974 volume *Judaism and Hellenism* was influential in breaking down some of the barriers between Judaism
and Hellenism and between Palestinian and Diaspora Judaism. Although
the third phase would not really take off for many years, it seems appropriate to view this work as the impetus of this phase. However, Hengel does
not seem to have gone far enough. Among other criticism, John Collins
maintains that Hengel has not entirely shed a negative view of Judaism and
that at times he has presented a more unified picture of ancient Judaism than
the sources permit.[31] Nevertheless despite some problems, Hengel's work
presents a persuasive argument for a generally hellenized Judaism in the
first century.

This mature third phase can be represented by two conferences held in
Denmark in 1991 and 1997 with edited volumes appearing shortly after-
wards.[32] The driving force behind these conferences was Troels Engberg-
Pedersen, and the conferences (especially the second) wrestled with the
question of whether the idea of a *division* between Judaism and Hellenism
is helpful for understanding Paul.[33]

---

30. Georgi, *Theocracy in Paul's Praxis and Theology*, p. 79.

31. See the criticism of John J. Collins, 'Judaism as *Praeparatio Evangelica* in the
Work of Martin Hengel', *RelSRev* 15 (1989), pp. 226-28.

32. Troels Engberg-Pedersen (ed.), *Paul in his Hellenistic Context* (Minneapolis:
Fortress Press, 1995); Engberg-Pedersen (ed.), *Paul beyond the Judaism/Hellenism
Divide*.

33. This question is discussed in similar ways with different emphases in the
introduction and the first three articles of the second book: Troels Engberg-Pedersen,
'Introduction: Paul beyond the Judaism/Hellenism Divide', in Engberg-Pedersen (ed.),
Paul beyond the Judaism/Hellenism Divide (Louisville, KY: Westminster/John Knox
Press, 2001), pp. 1-16; and, in the same volume, Wayne A. Meeks, 'Judaism, Hellenism,
and the Birth of Christianity', pp. 17-27; Martin, 'Judaism/Hellenism Dichotomy',

The problem of whether Paul was a Jewish or Hellenistic thinker may essentially be a problem with the question itself. There are significant difficulties with the Jewish and Hellenistic distinction. These difficulties lead to the conclusion that the question itself does not represent a choice of adequate options. Essentially, the choice is too simplistic and does not represent the world of which the apostle Paul was a part. Additionally, it is questionable whether the terms 'Jewish' and 'Hellenistic' as used in this debate have any correspondence to first-century realities.

First, the terms are historically and ideologically charged. Their roots appear to be from the early nineteenth century (although some earlier examples exist). 'Judaism' was set against 'Hellenism' as contrasting spheres of influence upon the church.[34] These terms also represent today more than an ethnic identity. For example, Dale Martin notes that, among other things, Hellenism represents universalism, freedom, culture and so on, and Judaism represents particularism, communalism, legalism and the like.[35] Martin's detailed list is interesting and includes contradictory terms within a category (e.g. Judaism has represented both nationalism and anti-nationalism, asceticism and non-asceticism, historicity and non-historicity; Hellenism has represented nationalism and anti-nationalism) and identical terms across categories (e.g. both Hellenism and Judaism have represented nationalism, anti-nationalism, asceticism, freedom, and dynamism).[36] This illustrates that at issue in this debate is not necessarily the descriptions of first-century cultures, but the terms 'Hellenism' and 'Judaism' are representative labels for certain contemporary issues. Hellenism and Judaism are set against each other. Interestingly, the label representing the positive and negative may differ. For some nineteenth-century German theologians, Hellenism was positive and represented liberal Protestantism. Judaism was the enemy and not only represented Judaism but also Roman Catholicism.[37] However, recently it is not uncommon to find Judaism as the pure influence and Hellenism as corrupting.[38] This contrast reflects modern politics more

---

pp. 29-61; and Philip S. Alexander, 'Hellenism and Hellenization as Problematic Historiographical Categories', pp. 63-80. Much of the following discussion is based on these articles.

34. Martin, 'Judaism/Hellenism Dichotomy', pp. 32-44; Anders Gerdmar, *Rethinking the Judaism–Hellenism Dichotomy: A Historiographical Case Study of Second Peter and Jude* (ConBNT, 36; Stockholm: Almqvist & Wiksell International, 2001), pp. 15-18. Although Gerdmar's work focuses on 2 Peter and Jude, his introduction surveys the general question of Judaism versus Hellenism.

35. Martin, 'Judaism/Hellenism Dichotomy', pp. 58-59.

36. Martin, 'Judaism/Hellenism Dichotomy', pp. 58-59.

37. Martin, 'Judaism/Hellenism Dichotomy', p. 34. This emphasis is found in the *religionsgeschichtliche Schule* (Meeks, 'Judaism, Hellenism', pp. 20-21).

38. Floyd V. Filson, *The New Testament against its Environment: The Gospel of*

than the ancient historical reality. It is not being suggested that interest in contemporary issues is negative. However, it is not helpful to understand the Pauline corpus using terms that are essentially charged with modern contemporary notions, often at odds with one another.

Second, as already noted, the Hellenistic/Judaism debate was based on an either/or choice. This is unsustainable because the comparison is not between mutually exclusive equals. Hellenism permeated the entire Eastern Mediterranean and elsewhere in the Roman empire (and beyond). Hellenism is a larger, more encompassing entity than Judaism. Hellenism as a movement can be described as,

> the comprehensive cultural melting pot that one finds in the lands first con-
> quered and held by Alexander the Great and his successors and then by the
> Romans. This mixture was sufficiently similar across times and places for
> the culture to count as a single, comprehensive entity. Within the mixture
> there certainly were differences in different times and places, reflecting the
> use of different languages. Such differences might also result from differ-
> ent traditions with roots before the Hellenistic period proper.[39]

Judaism, on the other hand, is one of the 'differences' noted in this description that has roots and traditions that precede Hellenism and carry these differences (including religious rites and language) into Hellenism. Judaism was just one such group. Other groups had similar experiences: Egyptians, Persians, Lydians and others also brought traditions with them into Hellenism. These peoples differed with one another because of their ancient pre-Hellenistic culture, but all shared a similar experience as Hellenistic people.[40] Hellenism as a movement could transcend smaller cultural boundaries (so it was thought by Greeks and other educated people).[41] Although it was possible for Jews to create a dualism between their culture and Hellenism, this dualism would overlook important Hellenistic influences already accepted in the culture (language, trade, viewpoints and the like). Most importantly, the events in the early second century BCE (culminating in 167 BCE) leading to the Maccabaean revolt demonstrate that there was a resistance to Hellenism in Israel (1 Macc. 1.10-15, 20-28, 54-61). However, a reaction against the extreme measures taken by a vengeful Antiochus Epiphanes should not be taken as a rejection of all Hellenism. In fact, there appears to be some initiative taken on the part of Jews to embrace Hellenism (1 Macc. 1.1-13; see also 2 Macc. 4.10-13[42]), which resulted in

Christ the Risen Lord (SBT, 3; Chicago: Henry Regnery, 1950), pp. 24-40. See also Meeks, 'Judaism, Hellenism', p. 21.

  39. Engberg-Pedersen, 'Introduction: Judaism/Hellenism Divide', p. 2 (a description that emerged from the 1991 conference).
  40. Martin, 'Judaism/Hellenism Dichotomy', p. 30.
  41. Martin, 'Judaism/Hellenism Dichotomy', p. 30.
  42. These passages portray this initiative as negative. It is not my purpose here to

some of Antiochus's hellenization programme (1 Macc. 1.14-15). The picture drawn by 1 Maccabees is quite negative. However, it probably is not representative of all Jewish people. It clearly reflects the bias of the pro-Maccabaean writer. Even with a pro-Maccabaean bias, the writer of 2 Maccabees states that the response of the rebels was due to extreme Hellenism and excessive adoption of foreign customs (ἀκμή τις ῾Ελληνισμοῦ καὶ πρόσβασις ἀλλοφυλισμοῦ) because of its wicked (ἀσεβοῦς) high priest (2 Macc. 4.13). Although it is likely that there were individuals and groups strongly opposed to anything they perceived as Hellenistic, this does not demand that the entire nation shared this belief. Two further points can be made. First, the rebellion was a reaction to certain acts such as the prohibition of circumcision. These acts focused on forbidding those things that made Jews distinct. This is not the same as Hellenism. Although it can be seen or framed as a Jewish reaction against Hellenism, in reality it was a Jewish reaction against policies within Hellenism that attempted to obliterate this Jewish distinction. The Jews could be distinct within Hellenism and they were. Second, since Hellenism was present in Israel for more than one hundred years, it is likely that it had Hellenistic influences whether acknowledged or not. By the time of Paul, the Romans had controlled Israel for more than one hundred years. Other Hellenistic influences (even in a period of independence) had been present for almost two hundred years previously. It is interesting to note that 2 Maccabees, a book with strong words against Hellenism, was written in Greek. To propose a strict dualism for the first century is simply 'bad history'.[43]

Our emphasis has been on general Hellenization; however, it is worth noting the recent contribution of Seth Schwartz, which focuses on social integration. Considering Ben Sira, Josephus, and the Talmud, Schwartz argues that the Jews participated in the important Roman social areas such as honor and benefaction.[44] Schwartz's work further supports our contention that a strict division between Judaism and Hellenism should be abandoned.

In addition to the general context, it is worth noting that Paul himself was not originally from Israel. Rather, he was from the Greek city in Cilicia, Tarsus (Acts 9.11; 21.39; 22.3). Although Jews lived in Tarsus, this was a Greek city known for its intellectual life and education.[45] It is uncertain how

---

discuss and evaluate bias in the Maccabees texts. The point here is that some Jews were embracing Hellenism.

43. Martin, 'Judaism/Hellenism Dichotomy', p. 31.

44. Seth Schwartz, *Were the Jews a Mediterranean Society? Reciprocity and Solidarity in Ancient Judaism* (Princeton, NJ: Princeton University Press, 2010).

45. Strabo, 14.5.13; see also W. Ward Gasque, 'Tarsus', in David Noel Freedman (ed.), *The Anchor Bible Dictionary* (6 vols.; New York: Doubleday, 1992), VI, pp. 333-34.

much of Paul's development took place here; however, it is unlikely that he was untouched by his early surroundings.[46]

To an extent the picture is somewhat complicated by the existence of different types of Judaism in the first century. It must be acknowledged that some groups emphasized their Jewish identity more than others. This certainly affected the early church. Acts, Romans, Galatians, and Philippians demonstrate that some Jewish Christians were more likely to reject Gentiles than others (e.g. Acts 15.1-33; Rom. 9–11; Gal. 2.1-21; Phil. 3.2-8). Although these differences are not unimportant, I do not wish to create a new dualism, one between types of Judaism. Philip Alexander notes similarities between rabbinic Judaism in Palestine and Hellenism but does not conclude influence. He notes that certain important questions must be first answered.[47] If this is the case for one of the more identity-conscious Jewish groups, Paul as a Jew from the Diaspora would be much more likely to be hellenized. However, if (part of) first-century Judaism in Israel was able to avoid hellenization, how was (the hellenized) Paul able to make sense of it?[48]

The three phases of Pauline influence are instructive. In the first, an emphasis on the Hellenistic context resulted in the belief that Paul *derived* his theology from Hellenism. The second phase reacted strongly against the first and emphasized the Jewish nature of Paul. This phase argued that Paul *derived* his theology from Judaism. This position was somewhat accurate but still had two problems. First, it maintained the dualism between Hellenism and Judaism, which is not sustainable. Second, it is unable to account for any passages that seem to be influenced by Hellenism, and therefore it either minimizes or even ignores these. It seems that much of New Testament scholarship remains in Phase 2. Phase 3 attempts to get a more accurate picture of Hellenism and Judaism and to understand Paul in this context. Many scholars who could be classified within this phase differ on specifics and points of emphasis. However, there is a common belief emerging that it is no longer helpful to maintain a dualism between Hellenism and Judaism. The picture is more complex. There is an acknowledgment of differences within Hellenism and to some extent differences within Judaism of the first century. At this point I will present in more detail the approach taken here from within the third phase.

3. *Paul's Thought: My Approach*

I am arguing for a more complex use of the sources. The Judaism/Hellenism divide is neither accurate nor helpful. All sources need to be critically evalu-

---

46. For a summary of the issues involved in the debate about where Paul was educated, see Martin Hengel in collaboration with Roland Deines, *The Pre-Christian Paul* (trans. J. Bowden; London: SCM Press, 1991), pp.18-39.

47. Alexander, 'Hellenism and Hellenization', pp. 72-79.

48. Alexander, 'Hellenism and Hellenization', p. 80.

ated and used appropriately. Some sources will be more valuable to illuminate certain areas than other areas. Essentially, any source that potentially can aid in the interpretive process must be carefully utilized in the task. Questions concerning the likelihood of direct knowledge by Paul or general cultural and societal concepts must be asked. Only concepts of which there is some probability that Paul was aware can be utilized with any confidence. In this section I will highlight a number of aspects of Paul and his world and suggest a manner to proceed when concepts seem to come from different contexts within Hellenism.

a. *What Is Known about Paul*

Our primary source for understanding Paul is his letters. Although there is debate concerning the authenticity of a number of his letters (see above), the information in this section is drawn only from the undisputed Paulines.[49] There is sufficient material here for our purposes. Additionally, the book of Acts is considered an important secondary source for the life of Paul; however, for our purposes it will be used minimally. The task here is primarily to determine Paul's influences. There are a number of things that can be gleaned from the sources. The information can be grouped into two categories: *descriptive* and *implied*. *Descriptive* information involves statements that are made about Paul or that he has made about himself. This information must be used with what we know about his time (including the discussion about Hellenism and Judaism above). Probably more important for this study is *implied* information. This information is discovered from an examination of Paul's words to determine his influences. This study will necessarily be brief and will focus on the most evident influences.

There are four main areas of *descriptive* information to discuss. First, Paul considered himself to be thoroughly Jewish (in light of the discussion above). He was from an important tribe (Benjamin); he was a Pharisee; and he took his role and faith seriously, demonstrated by his persecution of the church (Gal. 1.13-14; Phil. 3.5-6). Second, according to Luke, Paul was a Diaspora Jew from Tarsus, an important Greek city (Acts 9.11; 21.39; 22.3), who moved to Jerusalem to study Judaism with the famous rabbi Gamaliel (Acts 22.3). This description is compatible with the picture presented in the epistles. Third, despite his Jewish lineage, he took his role as a Christian even more seriously (Phil. 3.7-8). Concerning Paul's influences, his Jewish upbringing probably provided the substantive theological development. However, it seems reasonable to assume that when Paul committed his allegiance to Christ, his views on some of his tradition had changed. Just how much is a matter of debate. Alan Segal argues that

---

49. The undisputed letters of Paul are Romans, 1 Corinthians, 2 Corinthians, Galatians, Philippians, 1 Thessalonians and Philemon.

Paul's 'conversion' had a significant impact on Paul's exegesis.[50] Mogens Müller's words concerning New Testament writers are appropriate, 'New Testament writings are the result of a biblical theology whose scripture had been the Old Testament but whose theological universe was determined by faith in Jesus Christ.'[51] I assume that Paul re-evaluated his beliefs, worldview and so on, in light of his belief in Christ. This is certainly evident in Phil. 3.5-10. Finally, although Acts is a secondary source for our particular issue, it is worth noting that, according to Luke, Paul was a Roman citizen (Acts 22.25-29).

The picture developed here is of a complex individual with the ability to understand both the Jewish culture and the more general Graeco-Roman culture. He seemed at home throughout the Roman empire. His letters reflect knowledge of Graeco-Roman letter writing conventions and, given the addressees, demonstrate the ability to communicate to the larger Graeco-Roman world.[52] Although there is debate over the accuracy of Luke's account on many issues, his broad description of Paul's ability to function in the broader society is likely to be accurate. Paul's vast writing ministry supports this notion. It is likely that Paul actually was imprisoned in Rome and the Lukan record of Paul's Roman citizenship provides a plausible reason for this (as discussed in Acts 25.11-12, 21; 26.32; 27.24; 28.19).

More important for our purposes is *implied* information. Here Paul's influences become more evident. First, Paul was clearly fluent in Greek. Although there were times when Paul used a secretary (e.g. Rom. 16.22), this common practice does not suggest Paul that did not know the Greek language.[53] Further, there were times when Paul wrote himself (Gal. 6.11). Paul communicated with people throughout the empire, and there is no evidence of a translator. It may be an obvious point that Paul wrote in Greek, but this should not be taken lightly. This is one further piece of evidence demonstrating a level of hellenization for Paul specifically and New Testament writers generally. Second, Paul demonstrates knowledge of Graeco-Roman literature or at least common proverbs (1 Cor. 15.33 is attributed to Menander, but in Paul's time it may have been a common proverb).[54] However, this is minimal and one really wonders why

---

50. Alan F. Segal, *Paul the Convert: The Apostolate and Apostasy of Saul the Pharisee* (New Haven: Yale University Press, 1990), pp. 117-49.

51. Mogens Müller, *The First Bible of the Church: A Plea for the Septuagint* (JSOTSup, 206; Sheffield: Sheffield Academic Press, 1996), p. 142.

52. M. Luther Stirewalt, Jr, *Paul, the Letter Writer* (Grand Rapids: Eerdmans, 2002).

53. Concerning secretaries in the ancient world with a discussion of implications, see E. Randolph Richards, *The Secretary in the Letters in Paul* (WUNT, 2.42; Tübingen: Mohr Siebeck, 1991).

54. Although among the disputed Paulines, see also Tit. 1.12.

one does not find quotations and/or allusions to Homer and others. Third, some have seen influence or at least similarities between Paul and philosophers of his day.[55] It is even probable that to some outside observers Paul's churches resembled philosophical schools.[56] There is debate whether Paul was influenced by philosophy specifically (even among those cited above). This debate will not be entered into here. However, the studies do at least demonstrate that there are significant parallels between Paul and the philosophy of his day. Paul and the Graeco-Roman philosophers were a part of the same world of ideas. Fourth, although Luke mentioned that Paul was educated under Gamaliel (Acts 22.3), this does not mean necessarily that he had no Greek education. As noted, Paul was from Tarsus, an important Greek city, and there is evidence in his letters of a Greek education.[57] Fifth, Paul was clearly influenced by first-century Jewish theology. Many of his discussions are based on Old Testament stories, ethics and theology (e.g. Abraham [Romans 4; Galatians 3; 4.21-31], Adam [Rom. 5.12-21; 1 Cor. 15.21-22, 45-49[58]], sexual ethics [Rom. 1.22-27; 1 Cor. 6.9; 2 Cor. 12.21; Gal. 5.19], theology [e.g. monotheism: 1 Cor. 8.4-6; Gal. 3.20; election: Rom. 8.29-30]). Finally, by far the most explicit literary influence on Paul is the Greek Bible (Old Testament). According to a chart compiled by Moisés Silva, in the undisputed Pauline letters, there are 41 citations of passages where the quotation agrees with the LXX[59]

55. See, e.g., David E. Aune, 'Human Nature and Ethics in Hellenistic Philosophical Traditions and Paul: Some Issues and Problems', in Troels Engberg-Pedersen (ed.), *Paul in his Hellenistic Context* (Minneapolis: Fortress Press, 1995), pp. 291-312; Norman Wentworth DeWitt, *St Paul and Epicurus* (Minneapolis: University of Minnesota Press, 1954); Troels Engberg-Pedersen, 'Stoicism in Philippians', in Engberg-Pedersen (ed.), *Paul in his Hellenistic Context* (Minneapolis: Fortress Press, 1995), pp. 256-90; Engberg-Pedersen, *Paul and the Stoics*; Philip F. Esler, 'Paul and Stoicism: Romans 12 as a Test Case', *NTS* 50 (2004), pp. 106-24; Abraham J. Malherbe, 'Determinism and Free Will in Paul: The Argument of 1 Corinthians 8 and 9', in Engberg-Pedersen (ed.), *Paul in his Hellenistic Context*, pp. 231-55; Stanley K. Stowers, 'Does Pauline Christianity Resemble a Hellenistic Philosophy?', in Troels Engberg Pedersen (ed.), *Paul beyond the Judaism/ Hellenism Divide* (Louisville, KY: Westminster/John Knox Press, 2001), pp. 81-102.

56. Loveday Alexander, 'Paul and the Hellenistic Schools: The Evidence of Galen', in Engberg-Pedersen (ed.), *Paul in his Hellenistic Context*, pp. 60-83.

57. R.F. Hock, 'Paul and Greco-Roman Education', in J.P. Sampley (ed.), *Paul in the Greco-Roman World: A Handbook* (Harrisburg, PA: Trinity Press International, 2003), pp. 208-17.

58. See also in the disputed Paulines, 1 Tim. 2.13-15.

59. A brief comment will be made in Chapter 4 describing the difficulties associated with the Greek Old Testament. The Septuagint (LXX) is not a unified literary work. However, what is important for our purposes is only that Paul used a Greek Old Testament. I prefer not to use the term 'Septuagint' or its abbreviation (LXX); however, I will use these when discussing works (such as Silva's here) that use them.

and the Hebrew Old Testament (MT) and 17 citations that agree with the LXX but not the MT. There are only six that agree with the MT but not the LXX and 28 that agree with neither.[60] Based on Paul's literary output, the Greek Bible is his most influential source.[61]

With an emphasis on the *implied* information above, the following can be concluded. Our Jewish Paul was clearly Hellenistic. Extant examples of use of language, his ministry and so on demonstrate that he functions naturally in the Greek-speaking Roman empire. His concepts are strongly Jewish. I use the term 'Jewish' here as described above, without making a distinction between hellenized and Palestinian Judaism. Nevertheless, variations within Judaism and concepts unique to Judaism within Hellenism are acknowledged. The theological and ethical concepts generally are drawn from Judaism.

To return briefly to the definition of Hellenism above, after noting the universal characteristics, Engberg-Pedersen states, 'Within the mixture there certainly were differences in different times and places, reflecting the use of different languages. Such differences might also result from different traditions with roots before the Hellenistic period proper.'[62] Concerning Judaism, ancient traditions produced within its community unique concepts, customs and so on. These are unique in the sense that they are particular within Judaism of the Hellenistic age. However, since they also developed within Hellenism, they are somewhat Hellenistic. The consequences of this development are threefold. First, concepts developed within Judaism may not be immediately comprehensible to non-Jews. Second, although non-Jews may not immediately understand Jewish concepts, the shared Hellenism will make comprehension easier. The ease and ability with which peoples of another culture were able to understand Judaism (or any other Hellenistic culture for that matter) depended on how close their cultures were to Judaism and how uniquely Jewish a specific concept was. The more diverse culturally and the more uniquely Jewish a concept, the more difficult it would be for comprehension to occur. However, the potential of understanding is great.

Third, concepts from different Hellenistic cultures may be expressed with similar or identical surface structures (i.e. the actual words that label a phenomenon or concept). This will not necessarily derail the communication process. Such confusion is usually remedied automatically. A communicator is able to understand the culture in which he/she is presently

---

60. Moisés Silva, 'Old Testament in Paul', *DPL,* pp. 630-42 (631).

61. The Greek Bible as an influence on the entire New Testament cannot be overstated. See Mogens Müller's monograph, in which he argues that the LXX should be considered the Bible of the early church (Müller, *First Bible*).

62. Engberg-Pedersen, 'Introduction: Judaism/Hellenism Divide', p. 2.

functioning, even if this is not his/her native culture. For example, as an American living in England, if I had been asked to play football, I never would have brought a football helmet. Additionally, when on holiday in Florida, if asked the same question, I would not have brought a round ball. The mental switch between 'football' of the European and American varieties was automatic because I was aware of my context.[63] The situation is more difficult when one looks at ancient cultures, and it is likely that scholars have wrongly applied cultural-specific ideas where unwarranted. Therefore, we must proceed carefully in such instances.

The phenomenon of similar concepts using identical labels is important for this study. Terms such as εὐαγγέλιον and titles such as σωτήρ, [ὁ] υἱὸς [τοῦ] θεοῦ (*divi filius*), θεός, and our object of analysis, κύριος, have both Jewish and imperial contexts. For Pauline usage, this poses two problems. First, it must be determined what is the primary background of the terms. Second, such terms might cause a level of confusion among people unaware of the other context. In order to clarify these issues and make them usable for this study, it is helpful to distinguish between what influenced Paul and how he expressed his message to his audience.

b. *Derivation and Contextualization*

In order to determine whether Paul intended an anti-imperial polemic in his writings, it is important to make a distinction between *derivation* and *contextualization*. *Derivation* is the primary root of a concept. It is an external factor that for some reason helped shape an individual's thoughts and conceptual world. This is often drawn naturally from one's native social and community experience. However, it also may be purposefully learned. It is possible for one consciously to allow later learned factors to be the source of one's views on a subject or source of new conceptual matter. This can be the case when one accepts a certain *philosophy* or *theology*. It is one's influence. Above, it was noted that Wilhelm Bousset and the *religionsgeschichtliche Schule* maintained that Paul *derived* his theology from Hellenism as opposed to Judaism. Others maintained that Paul's theology was *derived* from Judaism without reference to Hellenism. The position here, based on what has been discussed above about the nature of Hellenism and Judaism, Paul's religious and cultural background, the overwhelming explicit influence of the Greek Bible and so on, is that Paul's theology and concepts were *derived* from Judaism within Hellenism. To this influence Paul's transforming knowledge of and devotion to Christ can be added. After Paul's experi-

---

63. This of course may be more complicated. For example, if asked the question by an American in England, I might need to think temporarily what is meant. However, such confusion is usually very quickly resolved.

ence with Christ, he appears to have rethought much from his background, and Christ became central (see immediately below).

Contextualization is communicating a concept cross-culturally. This is the linguistic (and other) packaging that a communicator uses to make one's somewhat foreign message comprehensible to one's target audience. An astute communicator may utilize linguistic elements of the target culture to help communicate the message. In some cases, elements of the other culture may actually enhance the message. Thus, if similar or identical terms exist, potential confusion may result in a more forceful message. If a polemic exists in Paul, it is in the realm of contextualization. From Paul's (Hellenistic) Jewish background, he derived his view of God, the Messiah and lordship. From later Christian experiences, he modified his view of lordship to include Jesus as the primary referent.[64] In the remaining chapters of this work, it will be demonstrated that there was a popular non-Jewish notion of *imperial lordship*. Paul would likely have been aware of this. Once this is established, I will determine whether one purpose (not the only purpose) of Paul's christological message using similar terminology drawn from Judaism but with different referents in imperial ideology intentionally challenged this notion in the wider Roman world.

Dieter Zeller provides an insight that will help us to avoid seeing the distinction between derivation and contextualization too simplistically. He points out that the Graeco-Roman environment (including terminology such as κύριος) 'does not simply play a negative role in the reception of the gospel'.[65] Rather, in some places it can 'activate cultural models' that can help the message to be grasped by those from a 'pagan' context.[66] For example, the belief that a historical person can come from heaven in order to perform deeds of salvation helps readers with such knowledge to understand the ministry of Jesus more easily.[67] This helps to reveal the relationship between contextualization and derivation. Although Paul's influence was primarily Jewish from within Hellenism, he was influenced in some ways

64. N.T. Wright suggests that Paul has 'redirected', 'redefined', 'rethought' and 'reimagined' a number of points from Judaism in light of his Christian experience (most recently see *Paul: In Fresh Perspective* [Minneapolis: Fortress Press, 2005], pp. 83-153).

65. Zeller, 'New Testament Christology', p. 333.

66. Zeller, 'New Testament Christology', p. 333. The term 'pagan' is used by Zeller. For the purposes of this work, I prefer to avoid this label, as it implies a negative nuance usually from a Christian perspective. The method used here for understanding both the Roman world generally and Roman religious experience specifically is to attempt to understand them on their own terms.

67. Zeller, 'New Testament Christology', p. 333. Zeller's example is more complex than what is presented here. Nevertheless, this example illustrates the point sufficiently for the purposes of this study.

by the larger Hellenistic world. This influence however is not specifically core content but rather helps to make the contextualization process simpler and more accessible. It helps to shape the content but is not foundational as the central point of derivation.[68]

c. *Summary*

Paul was a thoroughly Jewish thinker. However, this Judaism was not an isolated phenomenon but rather part of the larger hellenized world. Paul's theology was essentially part of this Jewish worldview. However, as Paul lived and functioned in the larger Roman world he understood similarities and differences. Did Paul use similar terminology from both Judaism (modified through his Christian experience) and Roman imperial ideology to challenge his readers to choose Christ over the living emperor as lord? To this question I will return after further preliminary considerations.

4. *Sources and their Use*

The importance of the Greek Bible has been noted above. This appears to be the most important literary source from which Paul *derived* his theological construct(s). This source was not used by Paul in a timeless and objective manner void of context. In addition to his Hellenistic environment, there was his life-changing contact with the risen Christ, which impacted everything he thought and did. However, the Greek Bible and Christian experience can contribute little or nothing to understanding the phenomenon of emperor worship and the emperor's role as lord in the Roman empire. In order to understand this, we must attempt to recreate the cognitive environment of the first-century eastern Roman empire in which Paul and his readers lived and interacted. Any suggestion that this can be achieved in any complete manner is an illusion. The twenty-first-century reader is too far removed from the concepts and events to get a complete (or near-complete) picture. Nevertheless, there is a plethora of available sources on which a modern researcher can draw in order to attempt to understand the period. The reconstruction will be neither complete nor final. New evidence and methodologies will be contributing to an ever-developing picture of the ancient world.

It was mentioned in the previous chapter that historical methodology will be an important aspect of this reconstruction. There are many available sources, and essential to the task is a responsible use of these sources. The remainder of this chapter will briefly introduce the broad categories of

---

68. It is possible that Zeller would go further towards *derivation* than I am prepared to go. Nevertheless, his discussion reveals that neither *derivation* nor *contextualization* can be approached as simple aspects of the *understanding* and *communication* processes.

sources available and include a few guidelines for their use in this project. No attempt here will be made to provide a comprehensive list of rules that, if followed, will produce an accurate picture of the first century (this would be both impossible and hopelessly foolish). Rather, a few guidelines appropriate to the specific goals and purposes of this work will be discussed. The work of a historian is as much *art* as it is *science*. The historian, like the artist, has many materials available to create his or her work. Responsible use of material will often yield specific desired results. Both artists and historians must be masters of their tools and materials. Use, non-use and emphases of materials will result in different finished products. Unlike artists, whose products are often the result of their own concepts and creative processes, historians are attempting to recreate a picture that was not developed by themselves. Although differing from artists in this respect, historians are much like scientists, desiring to discover and accurately describe a phenomenon that they may not have experienced themselves. This goal of the artist is to create something from within. The goal of the historian is to describe something from without.

The sources available include both literary and non-literary sources. Non-literary sources include linguistic (inscriptions, papyri and ostraca), non-linguistic (archaeology, art), and coins, which may be classified as both linguistic (legends) and non-linguistic (pictures). Each type, subtype and individual source must be used in a responsible manner with sensitivity to the uniqueness of each.

a. *Primary and Other Sources: Defined*

Before describing the sources, it is helpful to clarify some terminology. Arthur Marwick, in the revised edition of his classic work on history describes *primary sources* as 'sources which were generated within the period being studied'.[69] They are 'relics and traces of past societies' and they 'form the "raw material" of history'.[70] *Secondary sources* are the 'articles and books written up later by historians, drawing upon these primary sources, converting the raw material into history'.[71] Marwick distinguishes between various types of secondary sources ranging from high-quality, research-based work using primary sources to more popular works.[72] These latter works, which often summarize secondary sources may be labelled *tertiary* sources.[73]

---

69. Arthur Marwick, *The New Nature of History: Knowledge, Evidence, Language* (Chicago: Lyceum, 2001), p. 156.

70. Marwick, *New Nature*, p. 26.

71. Marwick, *New Nature*, p. 26; see also p. 156.

72. Marwick, *New Nature*, p. 27.

73. I am indebted to Professor Loveday Alexander for both the concept and label.

Marwick's classifications are clear and concise; however, his work best applies to general historians attempting to understand a specific period of time. For him, older secondary sources often have little value, as more recent and better quality secondary sources become available.[74] This is generally true. New Testament histories (secondary sources) written a generation ago may maintain value, but newer New Testament histories provide the authoritative voices today. This will be evident also in Chapter 3, when scholarship on imperial cults is surveyed.

This project includes sources that do not quite fit Marwick's categories. For example, if one desires to pursue a study of the later portion of Augustus's reign, sources such as inscriptions and Augustus's own *Res gestae divi Augusti* are primary sources. A.H.M. Jones's biography of the emperor[75] is a secondary source. However, the *History* of Cassius Dio is difficult to classify. It is an ancient source and used by Jones. Is it a primary source? Marwick's description of primary sources suggests that they were created in the period under examination. However, Cassius Dio wrote about two hundred years after the events. This is comparable to a modern historian writing about George Washington or King George III. Is it a secondary source? Cassius Dio used primary sources but not in the way Marwick describes for historians today.[76] If it is secondary (which it really must be based on Marwick's classification), it cannot be classified with Jones's work. There are too many differences between the two. Cassius Dio is an important source because he was much closer to the events and had access to sources (primary and secondary) now lost.[77]

Using Marwick's classification as a point of departure, it is suggested that secondary sources will be divided into *ancient* and *modern* secondary sources. This division is intended only for ancient historical pursuits. Ancient secondary sources, although distant from the events, are still rather distant from today. These ancient secondary sources used primary sources unavailable to modern writers. Because of the obvious difference between ancient and modern secondary sources (e.g. Cassius Dio and A.H.M. Jones), both can simply be labelled *secondary* but the distinction made here is implied throughout this work.

The distinction between primary sources and ancient secondary sources is often based on the object of inquiry of the modern historian. If the histo-

74. Marwick, *New Nature*, p. 157.

75. A.H.M. Jones, *Augustus* (ed. M.I. Finley; Ancient Culture and Society; London: Chatto & Windus, 1970).

76. Marwick, *New Nature*, p. 27.

77. Marwick seems to be aware of this problem as he discusses secondary sources (*New Nature*, pp. 27-28, 157). However, his interest is not restricted to ancient material and does not make further terminological distinctions.

rian is interested in Augustus's reign, Cassius Dio is an *(ancient) secondary* source. However, if the modern historian is interested in later ancient views of Augustus's reign, Cassius Dio is a *primary* source.

This classification is helpful with reference to the discussion above of Paul's thought. His letters are the only primary source for this subject. Acts is a secondary source.[78]

Although primary sources are essential to one's historical pursuit, the difference between primary and secondary sources is not necessarily one of accuracy. It is possible that a primary source is incorrect and a secondary source, through further analysis, is able to correct the primary source. Marwick emphasizes the importance of multiple primary sources[79] and the value of good secondary sources. He states, 'a good secondary source relating to that [historical] topic is far more useful than any single primary source'.[80] Nevertheless, primary sources have pride of place in inquiry. They are the raw material with which secondary sources must work.

b. *Sources and their Use*

This work demands several types of sources. These range from highly literary to completely non-literary. This section will briefly describe the sources and their use. Additionally, it will discuss the role that they play in this project.[81]

In a way, there are two tasks before us in which sources will be used. First, there is the background or contextual task of recreating the cognitive environment of the first-century world. Second, once this is established, the focus will be on the use of the word κύριος against this context.

Owing to the nature of ancient sources, to some extent examples must be representative. Douglas Edwards suggests that there is a relationship between specific examples and general patterns. He states, 'Well-chosen examples illuminate general patterns even though they offer at best marginal glimpses.'[82]

---

78. To reiterate the previous point, it is the object of inquiry that distinguishes between primary and ancient secondary sources. Although a secondary source for Paul's thought, Acts or parts of Acts may be a primary source for understanding first-century Christianity.

79. Concerning a single primary source, Marwick states, 'one will not learn very much from a single source' (*New Nature*, p. 26).

80. Marwick, *New Nature*, p. 157.

81. For a brief discussion of sources and some guidelines for use, see Joseph D. Fantin, 'Background Studies: Grounding the Text in Reality', in Darrell L. Bock and Buist M. Fanning (eds.), *Interpreting the New Testament Text: Introduction to the Art and Science of Exegesis* (Wheaton, IL: Crossway, 2006), pp. 167-96.

82. Douglas R. Edwards, *Religion and Power: Pagans, Jews, and Christians in the Greek East* (Oxford: Oxford University Press, 1996), pp. 9-10.

(1) *Literary Sources.* Since this project is an attempt to reconstruct the cognitive environment of the first century, literary works will be important.[83] Two types of literary sources will be used. First, there are later historians who have written about our period. Second, there are works written during the period that share the cognitive environment with Paul and his readers. Historians must be challenged for biases. In addition, the time of composition is important. What factors in the historian's world, social status, religion and so on will colour the view of previous events? For what purpose is the work intended? For whom is it written? Late material is not without value for the study of a previous age (for this is the case with most *historical* writing); however, the time must be considered when evaluating the weight placed upon such evidence.

The most important historians for this project are Tacitus (early second century), Suetonius (early second century) and Cassius Dio (early third century). All of these historians were from the upper-class Roman aristocracy and must be read with this in mind. Tacitus especially shows anti-imperial bias but nevertheless is essential for understanding the times.[84] Suetonius is not producing a history as such but rather provides 'biographies' of the emperors. His work often appears to be like a modern tabloid emphasizing the sensational and reporting rumour and gossip that cannot be verified. Finally, Cassius Dio provides important information about the first century in his history of Rome from its beginning to his time.[85] However, much of his work is lost, and we rely on later summaries to fill in the gaps.[86] Moreover, he is far removed from the events of our period.

---

83. For a helpful survey and bibliography of the use of this type of literature for the reconstruction of history, see Emilio Gabba, 'Literature', in Michael Crawford (ed.), *Sources for Ancient History: Studies in the Use of Historical Evidence* (Cambridge: Cambridge University Press, 1983), pp. 1-79. Gabba provides helpful information on many specific authors.

84. For helpful discussions about Tacitus, see Ronald Syme, *Tacitus* (2 vols.; Oxford: Oxford University Press, 1958); Ronald Martin, *Tacitus* (London: Batsford, 1981), pp. 13-38;

85. On Cassius Dio, see Fergus Millar, *A Study of Cassius Dio* (Oxford: Oxford University Press, 1964).

86. The present state of Cassius Dio's *Roman History* is rather complex. Only Books 36–54 (68–10 BCE) survive intact. Books 55–60 (9 BCE–46 CE) survive in fragments. Part of Books 79–80 (death of Caracalla to the middle of the reign of Elagabal) survive as a section. The contents of the remainder of the work must be taken from later excerpts and epitomes written in the tenth and eleventh century. Thus, the value of this work is diminished somewhat for the period under consideration here. Nevertheless, the work is often helpful, since in many cases these sources actually preserve the words of the original. For a helpful introduction to this problem, see Millar, *Cassius Dio*, pp. 1-4.

In addition to later historians, there are many authors who wrote during the first century who shared much with the writers and readers of the New Testament. Authors such as Philo, Josephus (who could also be discussed as a historian), Virgil, Horace, Seneca and others help us to get a glimpse of the first century. The drawback of this material is that it is often on subjects not related to ours.

One problem with the use of literature as a source for New Testament contexts is the difficulty in proving that writers such as Cicero ever influenced writers such as Paul. However, it is not necessary to prove direct influence. Gerald Downing has demonstrated that Cicero and others reflected ideas common in the context of the day.[87] In this way, their literature is of great value to helping recreate the cognitive environment.

Although literature is important, it will not be our most important group of sources. This study is primarily interested in the use of a specific title for a living emperor. Simon Price points out that literary sources do not explain imperial cults and that non-literary sources must play an important role in our understanding.[88]

(2) *Non-literary Sources.* The main sources for our project are from the period itself. Most of these are non-literary. These provide examples of the title κύριος used for the emperor during his lifetime.

(a) *Inscriptions.* The value of inscriptions cannot be overstated. These documents often include official statements about an issue from the time in which the statements were to be put into effect. Unlike histories (owing to later writing and/or the process of copying), they bring the modern reader to the actual time of the ancient writers and recipients. These artifacts were inscribed and read by the people of interest to the modern researcher. These documents may have contributed to the creation of policy. However, by their official nature, they are prone to be used for explicit propaganda purposes and it is difficult to reconstruct the actual response of the people to an inscription. Nevertheless, these are common and very important to the present study. The material used for inscriptions (e.g. stone) and their placement (prominent walls, tombs, etc.) reveals the intention of the inscriber for the message to be of high value and of lasting importance.[89]

---

87. F. Gerald Downing, 'A bas les aristos: The Relevance of Higher Literature for the Understanding of the Earliest Christian Writing', *NovT* 30 (1988), pp. 212-30.

88. Price, *Rituals and Power*, pp. 2-7.

89. For discussion of types of inscriptions, see John Edwin Sandys, *Latin Epigraphy: An Introduction to the Study of Latin Inscriptions* (Cambridge: Cambridge University Press, 2nd edn, 1927; repr. Chicago: Ares, n.d.), pp. 59-188. For an overview of the use of inscriptions in the historical task, see Fergus Millar, 'Epigraphy', in Michael

(b) *Papyri and Ostraca.* Two other types of sources that actually allow the modern researcher to *touch* the ancient world are papyri and ostraca.[90] These fragile documents permit us to glimpse all types of people in the ancient world. They include content ranging from classical works to receipts and personal letters. The value of these materials is immeasurable; however, they need to be handled with care. Accurate dating is essential.[91] Fortunately, most of the time the title appears in these documents; it is used as part of the dating formula. In addition, the content of this material may be idiosyncratic. For example, in a personal letter, one may get only a single view on a subject and it cannot be assumed to represent the society at large. It may represent the community, but this cannot be taken for granted. Concerning papyri, because of their fragile nature, all of the extant examples have been found in Egypt (and surrounding deserts). Therefore, the picture received from the papyri may represent only the Egyptian community. However, this reconstruction may be too simple. Though most papyri have been found in Egypt, it does not necessarily follow that all originated there. For example, a letter found in Egypt may have been sent from anywhere in the empire. Travel was common in the ancient world, and papyri were light and easy to carry. The picture from the papyri may be more representative than it may seem at first.[92]

(c) *Coins.* Coins were a constant reminder of the imperial presence and vision in the first century. Coins in pre-multimedia societies could serve as valuable means of propaganda.[93] However, I am unaware of a coin with the

Crawford (ed.), *Sources for Ancient History: Studies in the Use of Historical Evidence* (Cambridge: Cambridge University Press, 1983), pp. 80-136. Millar includes a helpful discussion of important inscription collections and sources for keeping up with recent discoveries.

90. On papyri, see especially E.G. Turner, *Greek Papyri: An Introduction* (Oxford: Oxford University Press, 2nd edn, 1980).

91. For papyri dating, see Roger S. Bagnall, *Reading Papyri, Writing Ancient History* (Approaching the Ancient World; London: Routledge, 1995), pp. 55-72.

92. Concerning the transmission of the New Testament text, Eldon Jay Epp argues convincingly that papyri represent more than a single locality ('The Significance of the Papyri for Determining the Nature of the New Testament Text in the Second Century: A Dynamic View of Textual Transmission', in Eldon Jay Epp and Gordon D. Fee [eds.], *Studies in the Theory and Method of New Testament Textual Criticism* [Grand Rapids: Eerdmans, 1993], pp. 274-97). It seems likely that the more important the document, the more travel potential it would have. Religious texts, classical literature and the like are more likely to be carried by travellers than less-enduring types of writing. See also Turner, *Greek Papyri*, pp. 42-53.

93. Hannestad, *Roman Art and Imperial Policy*, p. 111.

title κύριος for any Julio-Claudian emperor. Therefore, their use here will be restricted to recreating the cognitive environment of the first century.[94]

(d) *Archaeology and Architecture*. In addition to verbal and partially verbal (i.e. coins) means of communicating, physical layouts of towns and buildings communicate much to people who are exposed to them. Most important cities in the empire included buildings and cults honouring the emperor and his family.[95] The size and prominence of such temples revealed the importance of the emperor in that city.[96]

(3) *The Importance of Perception*. The use of sources is intended to recreate a picture of the first-century world that reflects what Paul and the original readers of his letters knew and experienced. Although historical accuracy is valued, it is not essential for this purpose. Rumours and gossip cannot be dismissed because such content could have been common knowledge among the people. The main concern here is to reconstruct the cognitive environment. Rumour and gossip play an important role in this. Thus, although for much of this reconstruction I will strive for historical accuracy to the level the sources permit, a place will be allotted to rumour and gossip. What is essential is to understand what the writers and recipients of the New Testament experienced, understood and believed in their own context, not necessarily historical accuracy.

(4) *Use of Sources Summary*. A variety of sources will be used in this project. Both literary and non-literary sources will be used to reconstruct the cognitive environment of Paul and his readers. However, when it comes to the specific use of the title κύριος for living emperors, the most important sources will be papyri, ostraca and, to a lesser extent, inscriptions. These are the sources that reflect the common people's knowledge most directly. These are the sources that were produced while the emperors were alive and when the relevant New Testament letters were penned.

94. See Michael Grant, *Roman History from Coins: Some Uses of the Imperial Coinage to the Historian* (Cambridge: Cambridge University Press, 1958); Michael Crawford, 'Numismatics', in Crawford (ed.), *Sources for Ancient History: Studies in the Use of Historical Evidence* (Cambridge: Cambridge University Press, 1983), pp. 185-233; Christopher Howgego, *Ancient History from Coins* (Approaching the Ancient World; London: Routledge, 1995).

95. For example, for the presence of the imperial cult in Asia Minor, see Price, *Rituals and Power*; for temples to Augustus, see Heidi Hänlein-Schäfer, *VENERATIO AUGUSTI: Eine Studie zu den Tempeln des ersten römischen Kaisers* (Archaeologica 39; Rome: Giorgio Bretschneider, 1985).

96. On Archaeology, see Anthony Snodgrass, 'Archaeology', in Michael Crawford (ed.), *Sources for Ancient History: Studies in the Use of Historical Evidence* (Cambridge: Cambridge University Press, 1983), pp. 137-84.

Chapter 3

Imperial Cults and Emperors:
The Presence of Caesar

In the preceding chapters we have covered preliminary matters essential to recreating the appropriate cognitive environment for this study. We covered methodological issues as well as introducing, and in some cases discussing, the available sources. The purpose of this chapter is provide the general framework of the cognitive environment specifically related to the emperor. What role did the living emperor play in the lives of first-century people of the empire? In other words, I will attempt to determine what place in the cognitive environment the emperor held. How pervasive was he in the day-to-day lives of the people? The focus of this chapter will be to re-create as much of the relevant cognitive environment as sources permit. This includes a survey of imperial cults and a description of the presence and roles of the emperor in the Roman world. Our re-creation will be limited to what is relevant for demonstrating the lordship role of the living emperor. A detailed development of the meaning and implications of *lordship* and the role of *lord* awaits Chapter 4.

Although it is suggested that this is a limited discussion, a significant amount of detail must be presented in order to re-create the cognitive environment sufficiently. Words for 'lord' have a wide range of meaning. Describing the living emperor's role as 'lord' must go beyond lexical study alone. Therefore, I will provide a brief sketch of the history and development of imperial cults in the context of Roman religion and the office of the emperor through the late first century. I will attempt to describe these in the context of the Roman world, explicitly attempting to avoid description from the standpoint of Christian experience. I do not think we can shed the impact of our Christian worldview so simply. We are continually discovering just how much we are influenced by our heritage. Nevertheless, I will consciously attempt to view this period in its own context, always being aware that biases contributing to our view exist. Additionally, I will focus on important areas that have been misunderstood in the study of imperial cults and the like, in both the classical and New Testament disciplines (often owing to our Christianized presuppositions).

This chapter will also contribute substantively to the argument by providing the general framework for the reconstruction of the cognitive environment of Paul and the first-century addressees of Romans, 1 Corinthians, Philippians, and Ephesians. I will reconstruct the general picture of the role of the emperor and imperial cults in the minds and lives of the communities of interest. Once this is established, we have the context in which we can begin to understand the use of the term κύριος for the living emperor and for Christ.

1. *Imperial Cults: History of Research*

Prior to discussing the history of research of emperor worship, we need to revisit the issues surrounding the label 'imperial cult' once more. In Chapter 1 I stated that I will avoid the singular (imperial cult) unless discussing a specific local realization of the cult. Instead, I am following Steven Friesen, who argues that emperor worship was a diverse practice that had many distinct realizations and thus he prefers the plural, imperial cults. This is worth revisiting here to avoid the impression that emperor worship was a single entity (albeit with some diversity). As early as 1972 (published 1973), Elias Bickerman made the bold statement that 'a universal cult of the ruler did not exist in the Roman Empire'.[1] Rather, the concept of an 'imperial cult' for the Roman empire is a modern notion. Bickerman notes in a response to a question about his paper, 'there was not "the *Imperial* worship", but a numberless variety of cults which modern scholars for their convenience, but wrongly, class together as "the worship of emperors"'.[2] He continues by noting that different types of worship such as offerings to *divus* Augustus or to Nero Asclepius would be understood as having different religious meaning and thus, 'Our common denomination "ruler worship" would be unintelligible to the Ancients.'[3] This clarification is important and is followed by informed researchers in imperial cults.[4] This does not demand that there are no similarities and that one should not discuss in some man-

---

1. Elias Bickerman, 'Consecratio', in Willem den Boer (ed.), *Le culte des souverains dans l'empire romain* (Geneva: Fondation Hardt, 1973), pp. 1-37 (specifically, p. 9).

2. Bickerman, 'Consecratio', p. 26 (emphasis in the original).

3. Bickerman, 'Consecratio', p. 26.

4. See, e.g., Fernando Lozano, 'The Creation of Imperial Gods: Not Only Imposition versus Spontaneity," in P. Iossif (ed.), *Royal Cult and Emperor Worship* (Athens: forthcoming), n. 66 (I am thankful to the author for providing me with a copy of this article prior to its publication. Unfortunately, page numbers will not correspond to the original. The footnote only is recorded here).

ner emperor worship on an empire-wide scale.[5] Although it is uncertain if Bickerman would grant this, his words are helpful, 'In practice, virtually every emperor was worshipped everywhere, but this coincidence does not negate the fundamental diversity of cults honoring the emperor.'[6] Bickerman's use of the term 'coincidence' is certainly too weak. The fact that 'emperors were worshipped everywhere' is more than mere coincidence. Nevertheless, I must grant that my notion of the *imperial cult* is essentially modern. Failure to understand the local and diverse nature of emperor worship will result in a simplistic understanding and in incorrect interpretations of the available data. The diverse and local nature of imperial cults will be assumed throughout this discussion, as reflected by the use of the plural in most instances.

As one reviews the history of the study of emperor worship, a number of trends seem to appear. I will organize the data in three ways, and each of the three contributes to the present understanding of the phenomena. These approaches occur somewhat simultaneously; nevertheless, it is helpful to isolate the three aspects in order to understand how we have arrived at our present understanding. First, the history of research can be described in terms of the level of acknowledgment of the emperor worship as a *real* religion. This involves an acknowledgment of and an attempt to shed a Christian view of religion. Second, a shift in the emphasis on which type of sources inform our picture has made a difference. Finally, there has been a shift from studying the cult as a general phenomenon to emphasizing local expressions of emperor worship. In addition, this section will conclude with a discussion of imperial cults in New Testament study.

a. *Imperial Cults as Religion*
Previously, the importance of attempting to shed Christian bias when analysing and describing ancient religion was emphasized. Directly related to this acknowledgment has been a change in the understanding of emperor worship. Until the late twentieth century, modern scholarship had generally classified emperor worship as an aberration, a practice unworthy to be considered *ancient religion*. It was often seen merely as a form of flattery

---

5. For example, in a further question to Bickerman about the modern invention of empire-wide emperor worship, G.W. Bowersock, in general agreement with Bickerman, wonders if he has gone too far and mentions a calendar and recurring festivals to show that there was some official organization taking place. Bickerman replies that the calendar mentioned and others are usually specific to certain groups. He reiterates his point, 'But there was no worship of the emperor common to the population of the Empire as a whole' (Bickerman, 'Consecratio', pp. 26-27). There is no recorded follow-up by Bowersock.

6. Bickerman, 'Consecratio', p. 9.

devoid of any significant religious content.[7] It was thought that it was better classified as politics than as religion. Although not the first, Simon Price's 1984 book *Rituals and Power*[8] persuaded the scholarly community that the practice of emperor worship was indeed a legitimate ancient religion. This book revolutionized the study of emperor worship to such an extent that early works can be used with value only when considered with Price.[9] Price's contribution was made possible because he attempted to view the phenomenon within Roman religion and without a Christian notion of what religion should be like. This latter point is important. Older scholars such as A.D. Nock (cited above) produced excellent work; however, their view of religion was shaped from a Christian perspective.

b. *Shift in Source Emphasis: A More Balanced Approach*

Before Simon Price, the understanding of imperial cults was primarily determined by literary sources. The elevation of importance of non-literary sources provided the groundwork for a more balanced understanding of emperor worship. Inscriptions, papyri, ostraca, coins, archaeology and art have always been used; however, recently with the focus on very specific locations, these nonliterary materials are being used more often. The result is that the literary sources are no longer as dominant. When in conflict with non-literary sources, literary sources are subjected to closer scrutiny. Again, this process has been ongoing; however, there has been a progressive shifting of balance taking place. Price used this material extensively. For more recent scholars (influenced by Price), non-literary sources seem to be becoming even more impor-

---

7. Duncan Fishwick, 'The Development of Provincial Ruler Worship in the Western Roman Empire', in *ANRW*, II.16.2 (Berlin: W. de Gruyter, 1979), pp. 1201-53 (1252-53); Arthur Darby Nock, 'Religious Developments from the Close of the Republic to the Death of Nero', in S.A. Cook, F.E. Adcock and M.P. Charlesworth (eds.), *The Augustan Empire: 44 B.C.–A.D. 70* (vol. X of *CAH*; Cambridge: Cambridge University Press, 1934), pp. 481-82; Ronald Mellor, *ΘΕΑ ΡΩΜΗ: The Worship of the Goddess Roma in the Greek World* (Hypomnemata, 42; Göttingen: Vandenhoeck & Ruprecht, 1975), pp. 20-22 n. 50; Lily Ross Taylor, *The Divinity of the Roman Emperor* (American Philological Association Monographs, 1; Middletown, CT: American Philological Association, 1931; repr. New York: Arno Press, 1975), pp. 237-38; G.W. Bowersock, *Augustus and the Greek World* (Oxford: Clarendon Press, 1965), pp. 112-21; however, Bowersock has retracted this position based on the work of Simon Price mentioned below (Bowersock, 'Divine Might: Review of Price, *Rituals and Power* and Lambert, *Beloved and God*', *New Republic* [11 February 1985], pp. 35-38).

8. Simon R.F. Price, *Rituals and Power: The Roman Imperial Cult in Asia Minor* (Cambridge: Cambridge University Press, 1984).

9. The old view is not entirely without adherents; see Eleanor G. Huzar, 'Emperor Worship in Julio-Claudian Egypt', in *ANRW*, II.18.5 (Berlin: W. de Gruyter, 1995), pp. 3092-143 (3110-11).

tant. Steven Friesen's use of non-literary sources is impressive.[10] Ittai Gradel as well produced an excellent work with an emphasis on non-literary sources.[11] Duncan Fishwick's work must also be mentioned. His work on imperial cults in the West predates Price and is continuing. Fishwick's impressive use of non-literary sources seems to be an exception to the discussion here.[12] Finally, a very helpful article by Richard DeMaris, a New Testament scholar, illustrates this point well. He argues that religion in Roman Corinth has been incorrectly viewed because of an emphasis on literary sources such as Strabo. In the late first century Strabo described ancient Greek (pre-Roman) Corinth as a city of sexual debauchery, Aphrodite's temple employing one thousand prostitutes, and so on. However, such views of the city cannot be sustained when other factors are considered.[13] The emphasis on non-literary sources will be continued in this work. As will be discussed below, some common assumptions about emperor worship will be found to be insufficient, and thus our picture of this phenomenon will be adjusted accordingly.

c. *General versus Specific Approaches*

Many problems arise when one attempts to describe the phenomena of imperial cults. A number of directions may be pursued. Excluding brief (and not so brief) specialized studies,[14] one may wish to describe diachroni-

---

10. Steven J. Friesen, *Twice Neokoros: Ephesus, Asia, and the Cult of the Flavian Imperial Family* (RGRW, 116; Leiden: E.J. Brill, 1993).

11. Gradel, *Emperor Worship and Roman Religion*.

12. Fishwick's large contribution to this area is being brought together in the ongoing work *ICLW*.

13. Richard DeMaris, 'Cults and the Imperial Cult in Early Roman Corinth: Literary versus Material Record', in Michael Labahn and Jürgen Zangenberg (eds.), *Zwischen den Reichen: Neues Testament und römische Herrschaft. Vorträge auf der ersten Konferenz der European Association for Biblical Studies* (TANZ, 36. Tübingen: Francke, 2002), pp. 73-91. DeMaris is not the first to question the literary record. For example, Jerome Murphy-O'Connor clearly articulated this position in 1983 (in his *St Paul's Corinth: Texts and Archeology* [GNS, 6; Wilmington, DE: Michael Glazier, 1983], pp. 55-56; 3rd edn, Collegeville, MN: Liturgical Press, 2002, pp. 56-57).

14. Specialized studies are those that focus on a small aspect of imperial religion. These studies are not interested in describing imperial religion and its practice in any comprehensive manner (even at a local level). Rather they attempt to analyse a very specific aspect of imperial cults such as temples, buildings and the like or their presence in literature. Such studies are of use for those who desire to construct a more comprehensive picture of the cults. See, e.g., Marion Altman, 'Ruler Cult in Seneca', *CP* 33 (1938), pp. 198-204; John Dobbins, 'The Imperial Cult Building in the Forum at Pompeii', in Alistair Small (ed.), *Subject and Ruler: The Cult of the Ruling Power in Classical Antiquity. Papers Presented at a Conference Held in the University of Alberta on April 13–15, 1994, to Celebrate the 65th Anniversary of Duncan Fishwick* (Ann Arbor: Journal of Roman Archaeology, 1996), pp. 99-114; U. Monneret de Villard,

cally the empire-wide movement of worshipping the emperors. This was an approach among many older (although not exclusively older) works on the subject.[15] Still maintaining a general diachronic framework, others may wish to focus on emperor worship in a particular location.[16] Some may

'The Temple of the Imperial Cult at Luxor', *Archaeologia* 95 (1953), pp. 85-105; Pedro Mateos Cruz (ed.), *El 'Foro Provincial' de Augusta Emerita: un conjunto monumental de culto imperial* (Anejos de Archivo Español de Arqueología, 42; Madrid: Instituto de Arqueología de Mérida, 2006); José Miguel Noguera Celdrán (ed.), *Foro Hispaniae: paisaje urbano, arquitectura, programas decorativos y culto imperial en los foros de las ciudades hispanorramanas* (Monografías del Museo Arqueológico de Murcia, 3; Murcia, Spain: Museo Arqueológico de Murcia, 2009 [this work is broader than imperial cults]); D.M. Pippidi, *Recherches sur le culte impériale* (Institut roumain d'études latines collection scientifique; Paris: Les Belles Lettres, n.d. but most likely 1939 [Pippidi's treatment is not comprehensive; it discusses the *Numen Augusti* and a few specific texts]); Christopher Ratté, Thomas N. Howe and Clive Foss, 'An Early Imperial Pseudodipteral Temple at Sardis', *AJA* 90 (1986), pp. 45-68; Sara Karz Reid, *The Small Temple: A Roman Imperial Cult Building in Petra, Jordan* (Gorgias Dissertations, 20; Near Eastern Studies, 7; Piscataway, NJ: Gorgias Press, 2005); Franz Sauter, *Der römische Kaiserkult bei Martial und Statius* (Tübinger Beiträge zur Altertumswissenschaft, 21; Stuttgart: W. Kohlhammer, 1934); Fikret Kutlu Yegül, 'A Study in Architectural Iconography: *Kaiseraal* and the Imperial Cult', *Art Bulletin* 64 (1982), pp. 7-31; etc. The study of Jürgen Süss on imperial cult buildings in city planning is worth noting here: 'Kaiserkult und Urbanistik: Kultbezirke für römische Kaiser in kleinasiatischen Städten', in H. Cancik and K. Hitzl (eds.), *Die Praxis der Herrscherverehrung in Rom und seinen Provinzen* (Tübingen: Mohr Siebeck, 2003), pp. 249-81. See also the following study on women in imperial cults: María Dolores Mirón Pérez, *Mujeres, religión y poder: el culto imperial en el occidente mediterráneo* (Granada: University of Granada, 1996). Mirón Pérez's work is broader than many others cited in this note. Other more specific studies could be cited here; some will be noted elsewhere in this chapter.

15. See, e.g., E. Beurlier, *Le culte impérial: Son histoire et son organisation depuis Auguste jusqu'à Justinien* (Paris: Ernest Thorin, 1891); L. Cerfaux and J. Tondriau, *Le cult des souverains dans la civilization gréco-romaine* (Bibliothèque de théologie, série III, 5; Paris: Desclée de Brouwer, 1957); Louis Matthews Sweet, *Roman Emperor Worship* (Boston: Richard G. Badger, 1919); Fritz Taeger, *Charisma: Studien zur Geschichte des antiken Herrscherkultes*. II. (Stuttgart: W. Kohlhammer, 1960). Although more complex than those above, Manfred Clauss may be best listed here (*Kaiser und Gott: Herrscherkult im römischen Reich* [1999; repr. Munich: K.G. Saur, 2001]).

16. See, e.g., Price, *Rituals and Power*; Aline L. Abaecherli, 'The Institution of the Imperial Cult in the Western Provinces of the Roman Empire', *SMSR* 11 (1935), pp. 153-86; a number of articles in Hubert Cancik and Konrad Hitzl's (eds.), *Die Praxis der Herrscherverehrung in Rom und seinen Provinzen* (Tübingen: Mohr Siebeck, 2003); Robert Étienne, *Le culte impérial dans la Péninsule Ibérique d'Auguste à Dioclétien* (BEFAR, 191; Paris: Editions E. de Boccard, 1958); Fishwick, *ICLW;* also Fishwick's 'The Imperial Cult in Roman Britain', *Phoenix* 15 (1961), pp. 159-73; and 'The Imperial Cult in Roman Britain (cont.)', *Phoenix* 15 (1961), pp. 213-29; José A. Garriguet Mata, *El culto imperial en la Córdoba romana: una aproximación arqueológica* (Córdoba: Diputación de Córdoba, 2002); Gradel, *Emperor Worship*; Uta-Maria Liertz, *Kult und*

focus on a specific period of time or dynasty without restricting the study to a specific place.[17] Finally, one may wish to be very specific and describe the cult in a specific location at a specific time.[18] Each of these approaches has advantages and disadvantages. The more general approaches suggest that the practice of emperor worship was rather uniform, even if allowing for regional differences. This may give the incorrect impression that emperor worship was a uniform religion analogous to modern identifiable religions such as Christianity, Judaism or Islam. In other words, it is *the imperial cult.* The more specific approaches highlighting local influences and uniqueness solve this problem but fail to emphasize any unifying factors the practice may bring to the empire.

In addition to these approaches, one may classify works on imperial cults in another manner.[19] On the one hand, some studies are primarily *descriptive.* This seems to be the case with a number of studies focusing on imperial cults in the West.[20] On the other hand, some approaches are more focused on *interpretation.*[21] To some extent, this appears to parallel to our statements above regarding older works that concentrate on diachronics, with interpre-

---

Kaiser: Studien zu Kaiserkult und Kaiserverehrung in den germanischen Provinzen und in Gallia Belgica zur römischen Kaiserzeit (Acta Instituti Romani Finlandiae, 20; Rome: Institutum Romanum Finlandiae, 1998); Trinidad Nogales Basarrate and Julián González (eds.), *'Culto imperial: política y poder'. Actas del congreso international* (Hispania Antiqua, Serie Arqueológica, 1; Rome: L'Erma di Bretschneider, 2007); Stefan Pfeiffer, *Der römische Kaiser und das Land am Nil: Kaiserverehrung und Kaiserkult in Alexandria und Ägypten von Augustus bis Caracalla (30 v. Chr.–217 n. Chr.)* (Historia–Einzelschrift, 212; Stuttgart: Franz Steiner, 2010); Benjamin B. Rubin, *(Re)presenting Empire: The Roman Imperial Cult in Asia Minor, 31 BC–AD 68* (PhD diss., University of Michigan, 2008); Thomas Witulski, *Kaiserkult in Kleinasien: die Entwicklung der kultischreligiösen Kaiserverehrung in der römischen Provinz Asia von Augustus bis Antoninus Pius* (NTOA/StUNT, 63; Göttingen: Vandenhoeck & Ruprecht, 2007).

17. Though Lily Ross Taylor's work is quite general in approach, it would be best to classify it here since it focuses primarily on Augustus (*Divinity*). See also Kenneth Scott, *The Imperial Cult under the Flavians* (Ancient Religion and Mythology; Stuttgart: W. Kohlhammer, 1936; repr. New York: Arno Press, 1975).

18. See, e.g., Monika Bernett, *Der Kaiserkult in Judäa unter den Herodiern und Römern* (WUNT, 203; Tübingen: Mohr Siebeck, 2007); Friesen, *Twice Neokoros;* Maria Kantiréa, *Les dieux et les dieux Augustes: Le culte impérial en Grèce sous les Julio-claudiens et les Flaviens: études épigraphiques et archéologiques* (Meletemata, 50; Athens: Centre de recherches de l'antique grecque et romaine, 2007); and Fernando Lozano, *La religión del poder: el culto imperial en Atenas en época de Augusto y los emperadores Julio-Claudios* (British Archaeological Reports, International Series, 1087; Oxford: John and Erica Hedges, 2002).

19. I am indebted to Fernando Lozano of the University of Seville for the following distinction. He described it to me in an e-mail correspondence late in 2009.

20. For example, Fishwick, *ICLW.*

21. Most importantly, Price, *Rituals and Power.*

tative works being written more recently. However, there still are significant *descriptive* works being produced today. Both approaches are necessary. There is a need to catalogue and describe all available data. There is also a need for this data to be interpreted.

Perhaps no single approach is sufficient. However, given the incredibly diverse nature of our sources, the somewhat autonomous nature of provinces, local differences in religious practices, and the diversity of emperor worship that is known, specific approaches should take priority.

d. *Imperial Cults in New Testament Research*
In general, New Testament scholarship has responded well to insights about imperial cults that have been published by classical scholars such as Price and Fishwick.[22] New Testament researchers have not always agreed on the particulars of how this information should be used. Nevertheless, they have engaged the information in a productive manner.

The openness of New Testament studies to these developments is most dramatically evident in the inclusion of a portion of Price's seminal work, *Rituals and Power*, in a collection of essays edited by Richard Horsley in association with the Paul and Politics group of the Society of Biblical Literature (as mentioned in Chapter 1).[23] This same group was also partially responsible for bringing Price to the 2000 annual meeting of the SBL as a guest lecturer.[24] His lecture was not devoted to imperial cults specifically, but his presence demonstrates the desire to understand Roman religion as accurately as possible. In addition to the lecture, Price also responded to papers at the Paul and Politics session devoted to the topic 'Paul and the Roman Imperial Order'.[25]

Works from classical studies will be the most important secondary sources for an understanding of the Roman world generally and imperial cults and the emperor specifically. However, works from the field of New

---

22. For examples of earlier New Testament works that utilized research on imperial cults, see H.A.A. Kennedy, 'Apostolic Preaching and Emperor Worship', *Exp* 7 (April 1909), pp. 289-307; Deissmann, *Light from the Ancient East*, pp. 338-83.

23. Simon R.F. Price, 'Rituals and Power', in Richard A. Horsley (ed.), *Paul and Empire: Religion and Power in Roman Imperial Society* (Harrisburg, PA: Trinity Press International, 1997), pp. 47-71.

24. Simon R.F. Price, 'Religious Pluralism in the Roman World: Pagans, Jews, and Christians' (Paper delivered at the Annual Meeting of the Society of Biblical Literature, 2000). In addition to the Paul and Politics group, both the Wisdom and Apocalypticism group and the Archaeology and Early Judaism and Early Christianity group were responsible for bringing Price to Nashville.

25. The response is published as Simon R.F. Price, 'Response', in Richard A. Horsley (ed.), *Paul and the Roman Imperial Order* (Harrisburg, PA: Trinity Press International, 2004), pp. 175-83.

Testament studies will also contribute in important ways. Concerning imperial cults, one of the most important from a New Testament scholar is Steven Friesen's (already mentioned) monograph *Twice Neokoros*,[26] the published version of his Harvard PhD dissertation. This work not only utilizes the best in classical studies on imperial cults, but it also makes a contribution to the understanding of imperial cults by discussing in detail the temple of the Sebastoi in Ephesus.

In addition to Friesen, other New Testament scholars have demonstrated the mature use of recent classical scholarship on imperial cults.[27] The importance of this subject is evident also in the devotion of the 2001 Social

26. See n. 10 above.

27. See, e.g., Justin K. Hardin, *Galatians and the Imperial Cult: A Critical Analysis of the First-Century Social Context of Paul's Letter* (WUNT, 2.237; Tübingen: Mohr Siebeck, 2008); Philip A. Harland, *Associations, Synagogues, and Congregations: Claiming a Place in Ancient Mediterranean Society* (Minneapolis: Fortress Press, 2003); Harrison, *Paul and the Imperial Authorities*; Oakes, *Philippians*; Joan E. Taylor, 'Pontius Pilate and the Imperial Cult in Roman Judaea', *NTS* 52 (2006), pp. 555-82; Lance Byron Richey, *Roman Imperial Ideology and the Gospel of John* (CBQMS, 43; Washington, DC: Catholic Biblical Association of America, 2007); Bruce W. Winter, 'The Imperial Cult and the Early Christians in Roman Galatia (Acts XIII 13-50 and Galatians VI 11-18)', in Thomas Drew-Bear *et al.* (eds.), *Actes du Ier congres international sur Antioche de Pisidie* (Lyon: Université Lumière-Lyon 2, 2002), pp. 67-75 (and other works by Winter). Steven Friesen's more popularly aimed volume is one of many good works related to the book of Revelation (*Imperial Cults and the Apocalypse of John*); also Hans-Georg Gradl, 'Kaisertum und Kaiserkult: Ein Vergleich zwischen Philos *Legatio ad Gaium* und der Offenbarung des Johannes', *NTS* 56 (2010), pp. 116-38; and Kraybill, *Imperial Cult and Commerce in John's Apocalypse* (see also Kraybill's popular volume, *Apocalypse and Allegiance: Worship, Politics, and Devotion in the Book of Revelation* [Grand Rapids: Brazos, 2010]). See also Rüdiger Beile, *Zwischenruf aus Patmos: Eine neue Gesamteinschätzung der Apokalypse des Johannes von Ephesus* (Göttingen: V&R unipress, 2005). Beile lacks important secondary literature in his study; Martin Ebner and Elisabeth Esch-Wermling (eds.), *Kaiserkult, Wirtschaft und Spectacula: Zum politischen und gesellschaftlichen Umfeld der Offenbarung* (NTOA/StUNT, 72; Göttingen: Vandenhoeck & Ruprecht, 2011). For a survey of recent scholarship on imperial cults and revelation, see Michael Naylor, 'The Roman Imperial Cult and Revelation', *CBR* 8 (2010), pp. 207-39. There are also helpful studies outside of the field of New Testament studies specifically; see, e.g., Christoph Auffarth, 'Herrscherkult und Christuskult', in Cancik and Hitzl (eds.), *Praxis der Herrscherverehrung*, pp. 282-317. Additionally, some works discuss imperial cults in a broader manner in relation to Christianity; see Allen Brent, *The Imperial Cult and the Development of Church Order: Concepts and Images of Authority in Paganism and Early Christianity before the Age of Cyprian* (VCSup, 45; Leiden: E.J. Brill, 1999); and for an example of a study of imperial cults and Christian emperors, see Pedro Barceló, 'Beobachtungen zur Verehrung des christlichen Kaisers in der Spätantike', in Cancik and Hitzl (eds.), *Praxis der Herrscherverehrung*, pp. 319-39. The works mentioned in this footnote are selective, and others will be introduced throughout this work. Finally,

World Seminar to this topic.[28] Further, a recent issue of *JSNT* (vol. 27, no. 3, March 2005) was also devoted to imperial cults.[29] Scholars vary in their views concerning the role imperial cults played in the formation of early Christianity. For example, Leonard Thompson sees minimal impact[30] while Adela Yarbro Collins suggests that emperor worship was one of a number factors that "led to the worship of Jesus."[31] Nevertheless, such scholars use recent research in a responsible manner.

In light of this positive state of scholarship, it is surprising to read the words of P.J.J. Botha written in 2004:

> Among New Testament scholars a sort of consensus has formed which, by and large, depicts the imperial cult as disguised politics, a conglomeration of abhorrent rituals, an expression of personal megalomania by cruel dictators and blatant flattery by opportunistic and unscrupulous subjects. New Testament scholars tend to underplay the significance of the emperors within the actual everyday experience of provincials in the Roman empire, and especially to deny the religious nature and significance of the imperial cults or worship of the emperors.[32]

This is simply not the case. Botha's support for this statement includes ten works, only one of which was published after Price's *Rituals and Power,* and that book (Carson, Moo and Morris's *Introduction*) is a general New Testament introduction.[33] Other statements are often made about general

---

see the works associated with the Paul and Politics group mentioned in Chapter 1. These works exhibit varying degrees of mature use of imperial cult scholarship.

28. This seminar was part of the annual meeting of the British New Testament Society (Manchester). It was chaired by David Horrell.

29. David G. Horrell, 'Introduction', *JSNT* 27 (2005), pp. 251-55; and, in the same issue, James S. McLaren, 'The Jews and the Imperial Cult: From Augustus to Domitian', pp. 257-78; C. Kavin Rowe, 'Luke–Acts and the Imperial Cult: A Way through the Conundrum?', pp. 279-300; Peter Oakes, 'Re-Mapping the Universe: Paul and the Emperor in 1 Thessalonians and Philippians', pp. 301-22; Harry O. Maier, 'A Sly Civility: Colossians and Empire', pp. 323-49; and Steven J. Friesen, 'Satan's Throne, Imperial Cults and the Social Settings of Revelation', pp. 351-73.

30. See, e.g., Leonard L. Thompson, *The Book of Revelation: Apocalypse and Empire* (New York: Oxford University Press, 1990), pp. 158-64.

31. Adela Yarbro Collins, 'The Worship of Jesus and the Imperial Cult', in Carey C. Newman, James R. Davila and Gladys S. Lewis (eds.), *The Jewish Roots of Monotheism: Papers from the St Andrews Conference of the Historical Origins of the Worship of Jesus* (Journal for the Study of Judaism Supplement, 63; Leiden: E.J. Brill, 1999), pp. 234-57 (251).

32. P.J.J. Botha, 'Assessing Representations of the Imperial Cult in New Testament Studies', *VerbEccl* 25 (2004), pp. 14-45 (15-16).

33. D.A. Carson, Douglas J. Moo and Leon Morris, *An Introduction to the New Testament* (Grand Rapids: Zondervan, 1992).

introductions.[34] It is not these types of works where one would expect the integration of the most recent research work, and these cannot make up a "consensus." Botha does not even mention the work of Friesen. Nevertheless, his discussion of imperial cults is very good and is an example of a New Testament scholar understanding imperial cults quite well.

Some New Testament works still exhibit an uninformed view of recent work in this area. However, these do not appear to be writings in which imperial cults are a significant factor. For example, Everett Ferguson's very helpful work *Backgrounds of Early Christianity* (now in its third edition), includes a fairly helpful section on emperor worship. However, despite important works noted in the bibliography (including Price's work discussed above), for the most part this section could have been written in 1950. There is little acknowledgment of advances made by Price and others.[35]

New Testament scholarship has used recent classical scholarship on imperial cults in a positive way. Nevertheless, there is still a lot of work to be done on understanding the cults themselves and applying this to the New Testament text.

2. *Imperial Cults and Roman Religious Experience*

The religious experience of the Roman people is a complex phenomenon. It is inaccurate even to describe it as *a religion*. Unlike Judaism and Christianity, the religious experience of the Romans evidenced little homogeneity.[36] There was no specific set of dogmatic tenets associated with much of the practice. In R.M. Ogilvie's discussion of Roman religious experience he states, 'It would be quite wrong to suppose that a substantial body of Romans would have shared the outline in this book: some might have held some of them.'[37] Although there is no such thing as *Roman religion* per se,

---

34. See, e.g., Botha, "Assessing Representations," p. 17 n. 3.

35. Everett Ferguson, *Backgrounds of Early Christianity* (Grand Rapids: Eerdmans, 3rd edn, 2003), pp. 199-212. Ferguson studied under Nock at Harvard (Ferguson, *Backgrounds*, p. xvi). The first edition was published in 1987 and thus should have been able to incorporate Price. However, even in the third edition, only three works cited are from the 1970s. Everything else is earlier.

36. R.M. Ogilvie, *The Romans and their Gods* (London: Chatto & Windus, 1969; repr. London: Pimlico, n.d.), pp. 2-3; Mary Beard, John A. North and Simon R.F. Price, *Religions of Rome*. I. *A History* (Cambridge: Cambridge University Press, 1998), pp. 301-4. This statement, of course, is relative; there was some measure of uniformity in Roman religious experience (pp. 301-4), and neither Judaism nor Christianity was monolithic. For a recent survey of scholarly development in understanding the Roman religious experience, see James B. Rives, 'Graeco-Roman Religion in the Roman Empire: Old Assumptions and New Approaches', *CBR* 8 (2010), pp. 240-99.

37. Ogilvie, *Romans*, p. 2.

in the sense that it is analogous to Judaism, Christianity and so on, the label will occasionally be used, but its meaning is as described here, namely, the religious experience of the Roman people. The study of this experience is really a complete field in itself. In this section I will briefly survey aspects of Roman religious experience that are helpful for understanding imperial cults in their own context. Often this will result in points being emphasized here that may not have been of much concern to the Romans themselves. Our religious and cultural conditioning has resulted in the rise of certain questions (e.g. was the emperor divine?). Therefore, it will be necessary to address these. However, it must be kept in mind that these may not be the same concerns as those of the original participants in the various aspects Roman religion. Further, much discussion of Roman religion is centred on the city of Rome itself. Rome certainly was influential, but it is important to realize that significant differences existed.[38] In addition to locality, time is also a factor in the study of this phenomenon. Religion developed during the republic and was "reformed" under Augustus. Sensitivity to both time and location is necessary. Ideally, we would like to focus on first-century Roman religious experience in the areas that correspond to the Pauline texts. However, the sources do not provide this. Nevertheless, given the vast spatial area of Paul's ministry and the nature of religion, which does not change very rapidly, we must draw from a wide range of sources. Proportional weight must be given to sources as critically discerned.

No attempt will be made here to define religion generally or Roman religious experience specifically beyond a few introductory comments. We are not using the term to describe a certain set of religious concepts, actions and the like. Such a specific concept of *religion* seems anachronistic when applied to the first century. The Latin term *religio* basically referred to reverence or honours paid to deities by the state.[39] Although it may apply more generally, Gradel states, '*Religio* meant reverence, conscientiousness, and diligence towards superiors, commonly but not exclusively the gods.'[40] The modern use of the term, which includes specific beliefs, ritual, philosophy, theology and so on, developed in late antiquity with reference to Christianity.[41] The concept of *religion* is not without problems. Nevertheless, when the term is used in this work, it will essentially describe a relationship between human beings and some concept of the divine.[42] Early Imperial

---

38. On religion outside the city of Rome, see Beard, North and Price, *Religions of Rome*, I, pp. 320-39.

39. Beard, North and Price, *Religions of Rome*, I, p. 216.

40. Gradel, *Emperor Worship*, p. 4.

41. Gradel, *Emperor Worship*, p. 4.

42. Gradel's definition is similar. He states, 'The most useful definition, in my view, interprets the concept of "religion" as defined by action of dialogue—sacrifice, prayer,

Roman religion is a people-specific and time-specific manifestation of this relationship.[43] Again, I emphasize that I wish to consider Roman religion on its own terms. As a world religion among other world religions, Roman religion was a valid option for its people. There is no attempt here to dismiss the religious experience of the Romans as a cold or decadent religion.[44]

a. *The Holistic Nature of Roman Religious Experience*

A study of Roman religion reveals that the Romans, like other ancient peoples, were very religious. Religion saturated all aspects of life. There was no distinction between religion and politics analogous to the modern distinction. Simon Price points out that this distinction is a product of the early church's (third to eighth/ninth century) debate concerning the role of religious images.[45] This fits well into a modern worldview that desires to categorize things as either sacred or secular (this difference may be made by both secular politicians [and others] and religious proponents, often for quite different reasons). In light of the importance of various priesthoods and posts in the Roman republic and imperial periods, it is surprising that the distinction between the political and the religious has been maintained for so long. The most profound example was the cherished lifetime post of *pontifex maximus*. This position, which included significant religious duties, was held by Julius Caesar, Augustus and future emperors. It illustrates that

or other forms of establishing and constructing dialogue—between humans and what they perceive as "another world", opposed to and different from the everyday sphere in which men function' (Gradel, *Emperor Worship*, p. 5).

43. For further discussion of religion in the context of Rome, see John Scheid, *An Introduction to Roman Religion* (trans. Janet Lloyd; Edinburgh: Edinburgh University Press, 2003), pp. 18-29; Gradel, *Emperor Worship*, pp. 4-8. We are fortunate to have some excellent recent books on the subject of Roman religion. In addition to Scheid's work noted above, see also Robert Turcan, *The Gods of Ancient Rome: Religion in Everyday Life from Archaic to Imperial Times* (trans. Antonia Nevill; Edinburgh: University of Edinburgh Press, 2000). The excellent work by Mary Beard, John North and Simon Price is the present standard in English on Roman religion (*Religions of Rome.* I). There is also a companion source book, Mary Beard, John North and Simon Price (eds.), *Religions of Rome. II. A Sourcebook* (Cambridge: Cambridge University Press, 1998). Older works are still of value but need to be read with later studies in mind. See, e.g., Ogilvie, *Romans;* and J.H.W.G. Liebeschuetz, *Continuity and Change in Roman Religion* (Oxford: Clarendon Press, 1979). For an introduction from a New Testament scholar, see Hans-Josef Klauck, *The Religious Context of Early Christianity: A Guide to Graeco-Roman Religions* (trans. Brian McNeil; Studies of the New Testament and its World; Edinburgh: T. & T. Clark, 2000).

44. Scheid, *Roman Religion*, p. 17. One explicit purpose of Scheid's book is to challenge this assumption.

45. Price, *Rituals and Power*, pp. 15-16.

the boundary between the religious and the political was not as clear as our modern perspective might assume.

In addition to the incorrect distinction between the political and the religious, the division between the sacred and the secular cannot be applied to the ancient Roman world. Very little of significance was done without religious input. The importance of religion in the daily life of Romans can be seen in a number of ways. First, the boundaries (the *pomerium*) of the city of Rome itself were sacred. Livy, writing during the early reign of Augustus, records the early-fourth-century BCE discussion about the possibility of relocating away from Rome. However, this is rejected because of the religious significance of the city itself (5.52).[46] The calendar was essentially religious. It provided a fixed system to assure honouring all the necessary gods.[47] I have already mentioned the importance of priesthoods. These were very important positions. Rome is one of the rare peoples who did not have an actual priestly profession. Rather, priestly positions were held by prominent political people.[48] There were four major colleges with approximately sixty major priesthood positions which could be held for life. From 180 BCE on, a person could hold only one priesthood. However, Julius Caesar and later emperors were members of all four.[49] There were two hundred to four hundred public persons who would like to have held these positions.[50] Additionally, the cities themselves were peppered with temples and altars to various gods.[51] Finally, even athletic competitions were religious activities.[52] One could not walk through a Roman city without being continually confronted with religious symbolism and activity. Everything was part of the existence of the people with the divine. Beard, North and Price's summary of the situation for Rome is applicable to the empire during the first century CE,

46. See also Beard, North and Price, *Religions of Rome*, I, pp. 167-68, 177-81.

47. Ogilvie, *Romans*, pp. 70-72.

48. Ogilvie, *Romans*, p. 106.

49. Richard Gordon, 'From Republic to Principate: Priesthood, Religion and Ideology', in Beard and North (eds.), *Pagan Priests*, pp. 177-98 (182-83) (mentions Caesar and Augustus). On the priesthood during the republic, see Mary Beard, 'Priesthood in the Roman Republic', in Beard and North (eds.), *Pagan Priests*, pp. 19-48. On the priesthood during the transition from republic to empire and the participation of the emperor, see Gordon, "From Republic to Principate," pp. 179-98. Concerning aspects of the emperor as priest, see Ruth Stepper, 'Der Kaiser als Priester: Schwerpunkte und Reichweite seines oberpontifikalen Handelns', in Cancik and Hitzl (eds.), *Praxis der Herrscherverehrung*, pp. 157-87.

50. Ogilvie, *Romans*, p. 106.

51. On the importance of temple building during the early principate, see Beard, North and Price, *Religions of Rome*, I, pp. 196-201.

52. Beard, North and Price, *Religions of Rome*, I, pp. 201-206.

When we look, therefore, at the way in which religion and society interacted, we do not find special institutions and activities, set aside from
everyday life and designed to pursue religious objectives; but rather a
situation in which religion and its associated rituals were embedded in all
institutions and activities.[53]

b. *Polytheism and Non-Exclusivity*

Roman religious experience, like most ancient religion, was polytheistic. Romans worshipped many gods and acknowledged even more. They
believed that the world was filled with gods, some known to them but some
unknown as well.[54] Richard Gordon states, 'no one has ever succeeded in
counting the number of divinities worshipped in the Roman Empire'.[55] The
most important gods were the Capitoline triad, Jupiter, Juno and Minerva.
These were the state gods of Rome who were worshipped in a prominent
place in the city, the Capitoline Hill. They assured the success of Rome. In
addition, other gods were important, and many needed attention throughout
the year.[56]

The relationship between the divine and the human realms was somewhat
mutual. Humans honoured, worshipped, and sacrificed to gods who could
help them. In turn, it was believed that the honoured god might indeed help
the worshipper.[57] This process did not imply that gods not worshipped were
less important. The focus however, was on the gods who were believed to
be able to affect an outcome for the worshipper. In many ways, this practice
mirrored the patronage and benefaction system in place for Roman society.[58]

Roman religious practice was also not exclusive.[59] Devotees of one god
could equally honour other gods as desired. It was even possible for one to
join a number of mystery cults.[60] The non-exclusivity of Roman religion
made it very flexible and fluid. There was little problem of incorporating
other gods into the religious life of Rome as necessary. Soldiers brought

---

53. Beard, North and Price, *Religions of Rome,* I, p. 43.

54. Scheid, *Roman Religion,* p. 154.

55. Richard Gordon, 'The Veil of Power: Emperors, Sacrificers and Benefactors', in
Beard and North (eds.), *Pagan Priests,* pp. 199-231 (201).

56. For a helpful chart of some of the important deities, see Scheid, *Roman Religion,*
pp. 155-57.

57. Liebeschuetz, *Continuity,* p. 37 (discussion of Varro); Gradel, *Emperor Worship,*
p. 15.

58. See the discussion in Gradel, *Emperor Worship,* pp. 49-53. On the patronage
system in the ancient world, see the helpful collection of articles, Andrew Wallace-
Hadrill (ed.), *Patronage in Ancient Society* (London: Routledge, 1989).

59. Ogilvie, *Romans,* pp. 2-3; see also the helpful discussion in Beard, North and
Price, *Religions of Rome,* I, pp. 301-11.

60. Ogilvie, *Romans,* p. 3. On mystery religions, see below.

their gods and cults with them throughout the empire.[61] Foreigners could become part of the Roman empire without needing to abandon their religious heritage. Often, their gods and practices became part of the fabric of Roman religious life.[62] Syncretism went both ways. Generally, adherents of cults must also acknowledge important Roman deities.[63] There were exceptions to this for political expediency. For example, at times the Jewish nation was not required to participate in aspects of Roman religion in order to keep peace in Judaea.[64] Nevertheless, the Roman state took its religion seriously and demanded that the gods that helped them were to be honoured. They believed that neglect of this duty could bring ruin upon the state.[65]

c. *Practice (Ritual and Sacrifice) and Belief*

Roman religion was a religion of *doing*.[66] There was no set dogma that needed to be adhered to.[67] Ritual and sacrifice were the most important aspects of the religion. It was through these activities that people honoured their gods. Belief, on the other hand, was not unimportant but was not necessarily essential for successful religion. It did not have a 'particularly privileged role in defining an individual's actions, behaviour or sense of identity'.[68] Simon Price has suggested that 'belief' itself is a Christian assumption: 'it was forged out of the experience which the Apostles and Saint Paul had of the Risen Lord. The emphasis which "belief" gives to spiritual commitment has no necessary place in the analysis of other cultures'.[69] Price's point is not necessarily that Romans did not believe anything about their religion. He is merely stating that it may not have been a priority as it is in Christianity. This is difficult for modern Christians, especially those of

61. Note the example of Mithras: Manfred Clauss, *The Roman Cult of Mithras: The God and his Mysteries* (trans. Richard Gordon; New York: Routledge, 2000), pp. 21-22.

62. Turcan, *Gods of Ancient Rome*, pp. 106-31.

63. This is especially true for Roman citizens (Beard, North and Price, *Religions of Rome*, I, p. 317).

64. Michael Grant, *The Jews in the Roman World* (London: Weidenfeld & Nicolson, 1973; repr. London: Phoenix Press, 1999), pp. 59-60; Beard, North and Price, *Religions of Rome*, I, p. 361. For a detailed history of Roman and Jewish relations, see E. Mary Smallwood, *The Jews under Roman Rule from Pompey to Diocletian: A Study in Political Relations* (SJLA, 20; Leiden: E.J. Brill, 2nd edn, 1981; repr. 2001).

65. This is the argument that Augustine countered in his work *The City of God*. Some were blaming the problems of Rome on the abandonment of the ancestral gods.

66. See the discussion in Beard, North and Price, *Religions of Rome*, I, pp. 42-43; Price, *Rituals and Power*, pp. 7-11 (ritual); Gradel, *Emperor Worship*, pp. 1-4.

67. Ogilvie, *Romans*, pp. 2-3.

68. Beard, North and Price, *Religions of Rome*, I, p. 42.

69. Price, *Rituals and Power*, p. 11. The context of Price's words are a discussion of whether or not Romans believed that their emperors were gods. Nevertheless, his remarks apply more broadly to religion in general.

many of the Protestant varieties, to understand. Religion is often seen today as *what one believes*. *Practice* is important, but unless it come from accurate belief, it is not valid. This was not the case in ancient Rome.

Emotion is also less prominent or even non-essential to the Roman religious experience.[70] As already noted, there were many gods and many days devoted to these gods. It was important that these gods be honoured, but it was not necessarily important that they be honoured with masses of devotees who had an emotional attachment to the deities. Of course, it is possible that such worship could happen, but it was not necessary. What was important to the success of Roman religion was that all deities were honoured with appropriate ritual and sacrifice. This could be accomplished by a few whose activity was unknown by most. What was important to the Roman state was that specific ritual was carried out. It was less important that people attended all rituals. For example, based on literary discussions, the Arval brothers seemed to go about their business for centuries without attracting too much attention.[71] Additionally, one of the purposes of the calendar was to ensure that all the important deities were attended to annually.[72]

Simon Price describes ritual as the way the ancients *conceptualised* their world.[73] Sacrifice was a display of religious honour. It clearly marked the distinction between god and man, indicating the one receiving the sacrifice was superior.[74] It was through these activities that the Romans related to the divine. Certainly some notion of belief is involved. The Romans believed what they were doing was of value; otherwise they would not have done it. However, this was not a unique belief in contrast with other beliefs. It was the worldview of the empire. It simply was the state of affairs. There was

---

70. Price, *Rituals and Power*, pp. 9-11.

71. The most important works on this college are John Scheid, *Romulus et ses frères: Le collège des Frères Arvales, modèle du culte public dans la Rome des empereurs* (BEFAR, 265; Rome: École Française de Rome, 1990); and Scheid, *Commentarii Fratrum Arvalium qui supersunt: Les copies épigraphiques des protocoles annuels de la Confrérie Arvale (21 AV.–31 AP. J.-C.)* (Roma Antica, 4; Rome: École Française de Rome, Soprintendenza Archeologica di Roma, 1998) [abbreviated CFA]. The former discusses the group in detail, and the latter is a collection of inscriptions describing their activities. Gradel provides a helpful summary of the group and cautions concerning the use of their inscriptions (*Emperor Worship*, pp. 18-22). See also Beard, North and Price, *Religions of Rome*, I, pp. 194-96.

72. Ogilvie, *Romans*, p. 70.

73. Price, *Rituals and Power*, p. 7. On emperor sacrifices, see also Simon R.F. Price, 'Between Man and God: Sacrifice in the Roman Imperial Cult', *JRS* 70 (1980), pp. 28-43.

74. Scheid, *Roman Religion*, pp. 93-94; Gradel, *Emperor Worship*, p. 15. See also Beard, North and Price, *Religions of Rome*, I, pp. 36-37.

no defending this, arguing about it, etc. It was assumed. This may be too simplistic; there were some thinking about such issues[75] but for the average person, given the very limited evidence we have, it appears to be part of the fabric of life. In contrast Christian belief both in ancient Rome and in the modern world is a belief against a backdrop of other beliefs. Christianity is presented as a choice.

Therefore, to understand Roman religion, we must shed any Christian commitment to religion as primarily belief or emotion. Roman religion was *activity* based.

d. *The Nature of the Gods*

In a world dominated by the major monotheistic religions of Christianity, Judaism, and Islam, one may not think twice about the notion of *god*. However, failing to ask about the meaning of god in Roman religion could lead to misleading assumptions resulting in incorrect conclusions. Although Jupiter was a supreme deity, had titles such as *Jupiter Optimus Maximus* or *Jupiter Omnipotens*, and even was considered a creator god,[76] he was nothing like the all-powerful God of monotheistic religions. Jupiter was much more human-like and was limited in his abilities. He is very positively portrayed in Virgil's *Aeneid*; nevertheless, he is persuaded to act by other gods at times (see book 12). He seems more like an earthly monarch or even a modern-day business owner than a supreme deity.

The divinity in the major monotheistic religions mentioned above is unpredictable, because humankind is unable to comprehend his ways but his actions are presumed to be always good. Jupiter is unpredictable because one does not know how he will respond. One hopes that he will repay devotion positively, but one cannot be sure. Additionally, the God of these monotheistic religions is all-knowing, can do no wrong and so on. Jupiter, on the other hand, has limited knowledge and can be impulsive, resulting in actions that may not be just. Essentially, the God of monotheistic religions

---

75. See, e.g., Cicero's *Nature of the Gods*.

76. Cicero, *Nature of the Gods* 2.4 (= 2.2). See also *The Martyrdom of Pionius the Presbyter and his Companions* 19.11-13 (Herbert Musurillo [ed.], *Acts of the Christian Martyrs: Introduction, Texts and Translations* [OECT; Oxford: Oxford University Press, 1972], pp. 162-63). Written probably in the late third century (Musurillo [ed.], *Christian Martyrs*, p. xxix) and describing an event from the Decian persecution in the middle of the same century, this passage includes a discussion between Pionius and a Roman official in which the latter states that Zeus (the Greek Jupiter) created the world. Despite the date and possible historical problems, this passage likely reflects a shared belief in the Roman world. However, Gradel points out that this belief has no support in any texts or philosophical school (*Emperor Worship*, p. 2). Its presence here in this distinctly Christian account suggests that it was a belief in the culture that early Christians needed to reject.

is completely above and separate from humankind (although he may be very personal). Jupiter and the other gods are more like glorified and powerful people. Indeed, the stories of the Greeks and the Romans have gods who get injured in battle (*Iliad* 5.343-422). However, despite this observation, ancient worship often emphasized the status gap between the devotees and the object of their worship.[77] Thus, Jupiter, for example, is worshipped because of his status in relation to the worshippers, not simply because he was a God.[78] Gradel suggests that "divine status," not "divinity" should be used to describe the worshipped.[79] This emphasizes the relative nature of the relationship between the participants in the worship activity.[80] Additionally, unlike the God of modern monotheistic religions, neither Zeus nor any other god created all things. The world and the rest of creation were in existence before the gods came to power.[81]

Images (statues) were very important in Roman religion. Although, it appears that a statue only represents a god, it is possible that some actually believed that statues were gods. Whatever the *belief*, the importance of these items is clear. They were very important in the worship process.

Finally, the Roman religious system is very complex. Some discussed a supreme deity behind all deities. However, this was usually more like a force than a personal God believed in by the monotheistic religions of today. Further, when describing Roman religion in general, care must be taken when using philosophical works such as Cicero's *Nature of the Gods*. Gradel's highly detailed work on emperor worship ignores such works entirely.[82] This is essentially the approach taken here. Philosophical works are not representative of the average religious experience. It is only in works such as this that the question What is a god? in an absolute sense is ever asked.[83] In addition, it appears that this type of question was not encouraged in Augustan time. Arnaldo Momigliano states, 'The Augustan restoration discouraged philosophical speculation about the nature of the gods.'[84]

---

77. Gradel, *Emperor Worship*, p. 29.

78. Gradel, *Emperor Worship*, p. 29.

79. Gradel, *Emperor Worship*, p. 29.

80. Gradel, *Emperor Worship*, pp. 29-30.

81. H.J. Rose, *The Gods and Heroes of the Greeks: An Introduction to Greek Mythology* (New York: World, 1958), p. 13.

82. Gradel, *Emperor Worship*, p. 3.

83. Gradel, *Emperor Worship*, p. 28. Although not necessarily pertaining to this point, Price's discussion of θεός is helpful (Simon R.F. Price, 'Gods and Emperors: The Greek Language of the Roman Imperial Cult', *JHS* 104 [1984], pp. 79-85).

84. Arnaldo Momigliano, 'Roman Religion: The Imperial Period', in *On Pagans, Jews, and Christians* (Middletown, CT: Wesleyan University Press, 1987), p. 181.

Thus, for our purposes the observation is important: in Roman religious experience divinity is a *relative* status between participants in worship and the worshipped.

e. *Mystery Religions*

Before concluding our section on Roman religion, it is worth noting the popularity of mystery religions. Unfortunately, we know little about these religions because they were very secretive. One could participate only by becoming initiated. Mystery religions included both oriental cults that came into the Greek and Roman world and certain older Greek cults coming under the influence of Hellenism.[85] The most prominent of these were the Eleusinian mysteries, in which Demeter and her daughter Persephone were honoured. The story behind the mystery is Demeter's search for her daughter after she is abducted by Hades. Persephone returns to her mother for part of the year and then returns to Hades. This follows a harvest cycle. Other important mysteries honour Bacchus, Magna Mater, Isis and Mithras.[86] Many comparisons have been made between mysteries and Christianity.[87] This will not be discussed here. What is important is that these mysteries were popular and did provide an aspect of *personal* religion for participants. Some have suggested that the rise of these cults is a sign of the failure of Roman religion. However, it seems that this conclusion is based on a Christian assumption that personal religious experiences are preferable. This assumption suggests that Roman religion was not satisfying and mysteries were able to help satisfy hungry spiritual seekers. Christianity then was able ultimately and completely to satisfy this need. Again, my point here is not to make a moral judgment concerning Christianity's role as the most valid religion. I merely wish to describe Roman religion in its own terms. Certainly some Romans may have felt this way. However, there is no reason to assume that the mysteries were *preferable* to traditional religion because they were personal. Mysteries were *part* of the religious world. They had their place within the larger structure of Roman religion. Initiates in the mysteries also participated in more traditional religious practices. Additionally, traditional gods were present in worship. For example, a number of statues of traditional (and other) gods have been found in sanc-

---

85. Antonia Tripolitis, *Religions of the Hellenistic-Roman Age* (Grand Rapids: Eerdmans, 2002), p. 16.

86. See Walter Burkert, *Ancient Mystery Cults* (Cambridge, MA: Harvard University Press, 1987); Tripolitis, *Religions*, pp. 9-36, 47-59; Klauck, *Religious Context*, pp. 81-152.

87. See the discussions in Klauck, *Religious Context*, pp. 151-52; and Clauss, *Mithras*, pp. 168-72. Scheid strongly dismisses any similarities (*Roman Religion*, p. 188).

tuaries of mithraic worship.[88] This is most vividly illustrated by Augustus himself. Augustus was a great champion of traditional religion evidenced by religious reforms. Nevertheless, he was initiated into the Eleusinian mysteries (Dio Cassius 54.9.10). It seems best to view the mysteries as one piece of the larger religious picture rather than as an emerging phenomenon in competition with other aspects of the religious world. As noted above, it was possible for one to join a number of mystery religions.[89]

f. *Imperial Cults in the Context of Roman Religious Experience*

This survey of the religious experience of the Roman people is important for understanding imperial cults. To describe emperor worship outside of this context is problematic. Imperial cults were an important part of the fabric of religion in the Roman empire. It would be too simplistic to compare their importance with other aspects of the Roman religious experience (whether gods, rituals, etc.). The imperial worship was an important part of this experience.[90] Emphases in the religious experience would vary depending on time, place, present needs and so on. Each aspect of the Roman religious experience described above provides important contextual information for understanding emperor worship. Before describing imperial cults specifically, I will look at each of these characteristics and note how emperor worship fits into the context of the larger picture of Roman religion. Some of these points will be addressed further as we describe the cults in more detail.

Romans took their religion seriously. The already packed religious calendar added days for emperors. Often these occurred after the emperor died (see the discussion of the *divus* emperor below). The importance of the emperor is seen further in his role as priest. It was extremely rare for any one man to hold more than one major priesthood among the four major colleges. Julius Caesar however was *pontifex maximus* and held one other major priesthood (auger). However, the emperor could be a member in all four colleges (Augustus, *Res Gestae* 7.3).[91] Additionally, emperor worship was visually present just about everywhere. Temples and altars to emperors and their families were common[92] and these buildings were displayed on coins.[93]

---

88. Clauss, *Mithras*, pp. 146-67.

89. Ogilvie, *Romans*, p. 3.

90. Philip Harland demonstrates that imperial worship was comparible with other types of worship in associations in the Greek East ('Imperial Cults within Local Cultural Life: Associations in Roman Asia', *AHB* 17 [2003], pp. 85-107). It is likely safe to apply his finding wider than associations.

91. Ogilvie, *Romans*, pp. 106-7.

92. See the impressive study of temples and altars devoted to Augustus, Heidi Hänlein-Schäfer, *VENERATIO AUGUSTI*.

93. See, e.g., BMCRE, *Augustus*, 705; 706; BMCRE, *Claudius*, 228 (all from

Because Roman religion was holistic, polytheistic, and not exclusive, emperor worship did not need to satisfy all religious needs. After describing his reconstruction of imperial cults, Steven Friesen states that imperial cults were

> one aspect of an evolving polytheistic system. Imperial cults did not compose an independent, mythic world view; they were a distinguishable part of their broader, polytheistic cultural context. As such, they did not need to shoulder the whole burden for the religious life of the communities in which they were practiced. Rather, the worship of the imperial families and institutions constituted an identifiable feature of the larger symbolic world of Greco-Roman polytheism.[94]

The importance of this observation cannot be overstated. Emperor worship was only one part of an ongoing religious system. It was not a new religion that set itself up against other religions and competed for converts. It fit well within the religious framework of the period. Adding the emperor to one's religious life was simple and did not disrupt one's already established worldview. Indeed, even aspects of the mystery religions occurred in some imperial worship.[95]

The notion of whether or not participants in the imperial cult believed that the emperor (living or divinized) was a god is probably a modern question. I will address this in more detail later in the chapter. However, our overview of Roman religion provides some insights worth discussing briefly here. First, since specific belief and emotion are not the crucial aspect of Roman religion, belief in an emperor's deity would not be essential to the successful practice of the cults. Of course, from a modern perspective such an understanding would be helpful. Second, the notion of *god* is not necessarily the same as the concept in the great modern monotheistic religions. The Roman gods were much more human-like. Worship of specific gods was partially intended to develop a reciprocal relationship whereby the gods would help the participant, the participant would give thanks to the god, and so on. The Roman emperor, as the most powerful person known to the empire, could substantively help (or hurt) the individual citizens of the empire.

Finally, the first emperor was interested in religion. Augustus made religious reform a priority. He repaired, rebuilt, and built many temples (Augustus, *Res Gestae* 19-21) and attempted to restore many of the ancient rites that had suffered neglect. Imperial religion was part of this reform.

Ephesus mint; reverse: temple of Roma and Augustus); BMCRE, *Augustus*, 565; BMCRE, *Tiberius*, 62; BMCRE, *Claudius*, 227 (all from Lugdunum mint; reverse: altar of Roma and Augustus; granted, the Lugdunum mint is in the West, Gaul).

94. Friesen, *Imperial Cults*, p. 122.

95. H.W. Pleket, 'An Aspect of the Emperor Cult: Imperial Mysteries', *HTR* 58 (1965), pp. 331-47.

It was not a completely new religion but rather (as will be seen below) was built on traditions of the past. The increasing focus however, was on the emperor himself.[96] In many ways this was the genius of Augustus. His success as emperor was largely due to his ability to create a fiction that presented the Roman world as returning to a now long gone republican past. This glorified past never really existed, at least not since before the social upheaval of the Gracchi in the late second century BCE. Nevertheless, the Romans bought what Augustus was selling. They may have sincerely believed Augustus; they may have realized that they were incapable of ruling without him; or they may simply have been tired of constant civil war (or any combination of the three). The result was the Roman empire with one man at its head. Included in this was a reformed and restructured religious environment that now included the worship of the imperial family.

3. *Imperial Cults and Emperor Worship: A Survey*

The more discovered about emperor worship the more complex it appears. Developments in the history of research noted above concerning the *actual religious nature* of the phenomenon has resulted in a blossoming of understanding about many aspects of the practice. However, the vast increase in understanding has also opened up many previously unknown areas of inquiry that will keep scholars busy for years to come. In this section, imperial cults will be discussed in order to provide the cultic context of the emperor.[97]

a. *Background and Influences of Imperial Cults*

Emperor worship did not occur in a vacuum. The people of the Roman empire were not the first to worship their rulers. Greeks, Egyptians, Babylonians, Persians, Chinese and Japanese all had ancient practices of ruler worship.[98] Ruler cults in places quite distant from Rome and lacking any significant cultural connections such as China and Japan are unlikely to have any relationship to Roman ruler worship.[99] Ancient Near Eastern prac-

---

96. Beard, North and Price, *Religions of Rome*, I, p. 169.

97. For a helpful introduction to imperial cults, see Friesen, *Imperial Cults*, pp. 23-151. More detailed discussion can be found in Price, *Rituals and Power*; Fishwick, *ICLW*; Gradel, *Emperor Worship*. See also the works cited throughout this section.

98. See Sweet, *Roman Emperor Worship*, pp. 15-36. Concerning Persian and later Parthian influence on the art and archaeology of imperial cult building in certain cities in Asia Minor, see Rubin's PhD dissertation, *(Re)presenting Empire*.

99. Similarities appear to exist. Two articles (prepared for one volume) seek to compare Japanese emperor worship with Roman (including Byzantine) in order to help Japanese Catholics (Louis Bréhier and Pierre Batiffol, *Les survivances du culte impérial romain: A propos des rites shintoïstes* [Paris: Auguste Picard, 1920], see pp. 5-6 for purpose).

tices may have some connection through Alexander and his successors who conquered and ruled that territory.[100] Egypt and the cult of Alexander were important influences for Roman development. However, most important for imperial cults as they appear in the first century are Julius Caesar, Roman tradition and the developments made under the early principate.

The focus of this section is on influences that may have contributed to the practice of emperor worship. As has been discussed above, emperor worship became part of the religious environment throughout the Roman empire. It was not essentially a new religion intruding into and against the sphere of other cults. Rather, it was integrated into the fabric of religious life. Therefore, the notion of *influence* being discussed here does not necessarily end with the inauguration of imperial religious activities. Often imperial ritual and the like was added to established practice. This has at least two implications. First, every local area probably contributed to the practice of imperial religious experience. In other words, every local area *influenced* its particular manifestation of emperor worship. This is far too complex to pursue here beyond noting this influence. Each local area could be the subject of its own study. Second, the actual imperial religious practice would maintain some of this earlier influence. In order to be sensitive to these issues and yet keep the focus of this section on *influence,* the following principles will be followed. First, the focus here will be on more universal influences on emperor worship. In other words, the selected topics are of more importance than merely local significance. Second, imperial-period developments will be noted when it helps to illuminate the influence under discussion. For example, Augustus in a pharaonic role will be introduced here. However, some later developments based on the areas discussed here will be developed below in sections concerning emperor worship itself. For example, Julius Caesar's influence is crucial but yet developed further in the imperial period. These developments will be noted here and, where applicable, below.

Before these potential influences are discussed, one further distinction in cults that may be dedicated to humans must be addressed.

(1) *Ruler and Hero Cults.* In addition to ruler cults, hero cults also functioned as a means of honouring mortal individuals. Although there was significant development of hero cults,[101] it basically was a means of honouring someone

---

100. Concerning earlier Mesopotamia and although focusing on theocracy and not ruler worship specifically, Lanier Burns has explored the role of kingship in such cultures (*Aspects of Babylonian Theocracy as Background for the Biblical Polemic* [ThD diss., Dallas Theological Seminary, 1979]). Burns's study also discusses Old Testament polemic against this system.

101. Price, *Rituals and Power*, pp. 32-40. For developments in the study of hero cults, see J.N. Coldstream, 'Hero-Cults in the Age of Homer', *JHS* 96 (1976), pp. 8-17;

after death who had done something great during his or her lifetime.[102] This included war heroes (e.g. Marathon victors),[103] healers (e.g. Asklepios),[104] doers of great acts (e.g. Hercules),[105] poets,[106] and city founders.[107] The latter, when quite local, may simply be an ancestor cult. Although both hero and ancestor cults focus on the past, they are distinct. Carla Antonaccio suggests that they present competing versions of the past.[108] Hero cults are universally important on account of great deeds and/or virtue; however, ancestor cults are usually restricted to a locality in which a person's actions are of only local significance.[109] Heroic honours were not restricted to men. Women heroine cults were also common. The reasons for which women were honoured often differed from those for men. Some warriors were honoured (e.g. Amazons);[110] some were honoured with male relatives;[111] but the most famous were victims.[112] With hero cults it is sometimes difficult to distinguish between historical individuals[113] and myth (e.g. Hercules);[114] however, the vast archaeological evidence of burial makes the mortal ele-

Roy Kenneth Hack, 'Homer and the Cult of Heroes', *TAPA* 60 (1929), pp. 57-74; and especially Carla M. Antonaccio, 'Contesting the Past: Hero Cult, Tomb Cult, and Epic in Early Greece', *AJA* 98 (1994), pp. 389-410. Antonaccio highlights the shift from Homer toward archaeological evidence in understanding this phenomenon. For evidence of hero cults reflected in the writing of Pindar, see Bruno Currie, *Pindar and the Cult of Heroes* (Oxford Classical Monographs; Oxford: Oxford University Press, 2005).

102. For a general discussion of heroes and the process of making a hero ('heroization'), see Christopher P. Jones, *New Heroes in Antiquity: From Achilles to Antinoos* (Revealing Antiquity; Cambridge, MA: Harvard University Press, 2010).

103. Lewis Richard Farnell, *Greek Hero Cults and Ideas of Immortality* (Gifford Lectures 1920; Oxford: Clarendon Press, 1921; repr. Chicago: Ares, 1995), pp. 361-64.

104. Farnell, *Greek Hero Cults*, pp. 234-79.

105. Farnell, *Greek Hero Cults*, pp. 95-174. Both Hercules and the aforementioned Asklepios are considered demigods or 'heroes' in the sense being half man and half god. It is possible that these were actual historical individuals. Thus, they could be men who because of their great deeds became immortalized in myth and legend; however, any such connection to historical figures is now lost.

106. Diskin Clay, *Archilochos Heros: The Cult of Poets in the Greek Polis* (Hellenic Studies, 6; Cambridge, MA: Harvard University Press, 2004).

107. Carla M. Antonaccio, *An Archaeology of Ancestors: Tomb Cult and Hero Cult in Early Greece* (Lanham, MD: Rowman & Littlefield, 1995), pp. 267-68.

108. Antonaccio, 'Contesting the Past', pp. 389, 404.

109. Farnell, *Greek Hero Cults*, p. 343.

110. Jennifer Larson, *Greek Heroine Cults* (Madison: University of Wisconsin Press, 1995), pp. 110-16.

111. Larson, *Greek Heroine Cults*, pp. 78-100.

112. Larson, *Greek Heroine Cults*, p. 101.

113. Farnell, *Greek Hero Cults*, pp. 361-72.

114. Farnell, *Greek Hero Cults*, pp. 95-342; Antonaccio, *Archaeology of Ancestors*, pp. 145-97.

ment of this practice clear.[115] Additionally, although some semidivine people were subjects of hero cults, there seems to have been a clear distinction between heroes and gods.[116]

Although there are similarities between the ancient ruler and hero cults, the two are to be distinguished. Most importantly, hero cults are usually inaugurated after the death of the hero. It is likely that early Greek ruler cults were an extension of hero cults, giving the honours to a surviving hero that would have been given if the person had died in the heroic act.[117] However, hero-cult honours are not really appropriate for rulers. Heroic honours would emphasize the hero's mortality, and this is not something a ruler would wish to celebrate.[118] The discussion below will focus on ruler cults unless explicitly noted otherwise.

(2) *Egypt.* The pharaoh was believed to be the divine son of the sun god Ra. This tradition is ancient and continued for leaders such as Alexander and his Ptolemaic successors. Cleopatra VII, the final Ptolemaic ruler, presented herself as the goddess Isis. Essentially, the ruler of Egypt fulfilled the role of a divine being among the people. The importance of the role of leader overshadows any lineage claims. The leader had a specific relationship with the people, which was manifested in divine honours for the one with absolute power.

Since this is the way people in Egypt had related to their leaders, when Alexander, Ptolemy, his successors and finally the Roman emperors ruled this land, it was natural for them also to assume divine honours. These foreign rulers used a tradition that had been in place for centuries as a foundation for their rule. The influence of ancient Egypt was important for the development of the Roman ruler worship. However, this influence is mediated through Alexander, the Ptolemies and Julius Caesar. These will merit attention in their respective sections below.

(3) *Pre-classical and Classical Greece.* The ruler cult in the Greek-speaking world really took off with Alexander (see below). As noted above, worship of heroes and ancestors was common. Homer and other writers praise heroes for great deeds, and they are worshipped in cult settings.[119]

---

115. Antonaccio, *Archaeology of Ancestors*, pp. 11-143.
116. Farnell, *Greek Hero Cults*, p. 370.
117. M.P. Charlesworth, 'Some Observations of Ruler-Cult, Especially in Rome', *HTR* 28 (1935), p. 11. See the discussion below.
118. Price, *Rituals and Power*, pp. 34-35.
119. See above, 'Ruler and Hero Cults'.

The first living Greek to be worshipped was probably the great Spartan general Lysander (died 395 BCE), who was given cult in Samos while alive.[120] Other cults are difficult to find. It appears that the people of Thasos honoured the Spartan leader Agesilaus (died 359) with divine honours, but he mocks this.[121] Additionally, when Dion (died 353 BCE) "liberated" Syracuse, he was given divine (hero) honours in gratitude.[122]

Despite the distinction drawn above between ruler and hero cults, one point of connection is clear in this period. Heroic honours are given for doing great deeds. The logic follows that if a person does something great that would result in heroic honours if death occurred while performing the action, why not give the same honours to one who survives the great deed?[123] These cults bear no resemblance to dynastic ruler cults in which one is born divine.[124]

(4) *Alexander and the Hellenistic Kingdoms.* Philip II of Macedon (382–336 BCE) conquered the city-states of Greece and had aspirations to invade Persia. His plans for a Persian war were never acted upon owing to his assassination. He did have divine honours, but there were no important innovations to discuss.[125] It is with his son and heir, Alexander, that the ruler cult began to become universally important.

(a) *Alexander.* The question of whether Alexander instituted his own ruler cult during his lifetime is debated. Concerning the establishment of the official ruler cult, some of this discussion in the early twentieth century revolved around the meaning and implications of προσκύνησις in an event recorded in Arrian, *Anabasis* 12, and Plutarch, *Alexander* 54-55.[126] At Bactra, a number of individuals bow (προσκύνησις) to Alexander; however, one individual, Callisthenes, refuses and angers Alexander. Among other points, Lily Ross Taylor, emphasizing the Persian background, has argued

120. Plutarch, *Lysander* 18.3-4. See the discussion in Christian Habicht, *Gottmenschentum und griechische Städte* (Zetemata, 14; Munich: Beck, 2nd edn, 1970), pp. 3-6.

121. Charlesworth, "Observations," p. 12.

122. Diodorus 16.20.6. See also Habicht, *Gottmenschentum*, pp. 8-10; and Charlesworth, "Observations," p. 12.

123. Charlesworth, "Observations," p. 11.

124. For two unlikely cults to living people (Lysander in Ionia and Alcibiades in Athens), see Habicht, *Gottmenschentum*, pp. 6-8.

125. For a discussion of cults for Philip, see Habicht, *Gottmenschentum*, pp. 12-16.

126. For a very helpful discussion of προσκύνησις in this context and its Persian background, see J.P.V.D. Balsdon, 'The "Divinity" of Alexander', *Historia* 1 (1950), pp. 373-82.

that Alexander himself started the ruler cult.[127] Others, such as W.W. Tarn, have suggested that there was no cultic implication in the προσκύνησις and the ruler cult was started after Alexander's death.[128]

There is evidence that at least some ruler cult institutions were in place during Alexander's lifetime. For example, E. Fredricksmeyer argues that the Alexander cult in Megalopolis mentioned by Pausanias (8.32.1) must have begun while Alexander was alive.[129]

Whether the ruler cult was established by Alexander or during his lifetime by others is important but not essential to the development of later ruler cults. Four things are certain. First, Alexander was influenced by the Persian ruler cult.[130] In order for him to be taken seriously by his Persian subordinates, he must take on the role of the divine Persian king. Failure to do so would suggest that there was something wrong with him, that the conqueror of the Persians was not a real king.[131] It is through Alexander that Persian influence is brought into later Roman practices. However, this influence is clearly hellenized. Second, there does not appear to be any question about whether Alexander saw himself as divine. He was believed to be a second Hercules.[132] Alexander also viewed himself as the divine son of Zeus. This is most vividly confirmed by his treacherous journey in January 331 BCE to the temple of Ammon in Siwa, North Africa, to consult the god's oracle about his future. Ammon was considered Zeus by the Greeks, and his oracle proclaimed Alexander to be god's son.[133] Although he took up his divine role with many of his subjects, he restrained his divine role among

---

127. Lily Ross Taylor, 'The Proskynesis and the Hellenistic Ruler Cult', *JHS* 47 (1927), pp. 53-62; Taylor, *Divinity*, pp. 247-66 (two appendixes entitled 'The Worship of the Persian King' [pp. 247-55] and 'Alexander and the *Proskynesis*' [pp. 256-66]).

128. W.W. Tarn, 'The Hellenistic Ruler Cult and the Daemon', *JHS* 48 (1928), pp. 206-19 (this is a direct response to Taylor's work).

129. E. Fredricksmeyer, 'Three Notes on Alexander's Deification', *AJAH* 4 (1979), p. 1.

130. Taylor, *Divinity*, pp. 247-55. See also E. Badian, 'Alexander the Great between Two Thrones and Heaven: Variations on an Old Theme," in Alastair Small (ed.), *Subject and Ruler: The Cult of the Ruling Power in Classical Antiquity. Papers Presented at a Conference Held in the University of Alberta on April 13–15, 1994, to Celebrate the 65th Anniversary of Duncan Fishwick* (Ann Arbor: Journal of Roman Archaeology, 1996), pp. 11, 15-17. Badian admits to not previously giving sufficient attention to Persian influence and uses this article to correct some of his earlier work.

131. Balsdon, 'Alexander', p. 376. This statement is in the context of accepting προσκύνησις but applicable to the entire treatment of the Persian king.

132. Balsdon, 'Alexander', p. 377.

133. Plutarch, *Alexander* 27. A specific identification of Alexander with Dionysus is probably slightly later than Alexander's death (Arthur Darby Nock, 'Notes on Ruler-Cult, I–IV', *JHS* 48 [1928], pp. 21-30).

Greeks and Macedonians.[134] Nevertheless, it appears that Alexander desired the Siwa experience to be known throughout the Greek world.[135] Additionally, Alexander may have sent a letter to Greece requesting divine honours in 324–323 BCE.[136] There is no record of the reply. Third, Alexander was given divine honours while he was alive. Even Greeks sent an embassy and honoured him as a god.[137] Fourth, after the death of Alexander, there can be no doubt that official cults were established in his honour throughout his kingdom. It is with Alexander, whether while alive or after his death, that large-scale official ruler worship became part of the religious landscape of the part of the ancient world that would influence Roman emperor worship.

The importance of Alexander in antiquity cannot be overestimated. His contribution to the ruler cult is also important. He was the paradigmatic conqueror and thus leader. A young Julius Caesar, after seeing a statue of Alexander in Spain, was so discouraged because when Alexander was Caesar's age he had already conquered the world. Caesar departed in order to seek opportunity for great deeds.[138] Three hundred years later, even Octavian after defeating Antony and Cleopatra and conquering Egypt is said to have visited the shrine of Alexander and paid him homage.[139]

(b) *Alexander's Successors: Ptolemies and Egypt.* After Alexander's death in 323 BCE, a struggle for control of his vast empire finally resulted in a four-part division. In 301 BCE the kingdom was divided between Ptolemy (Egypt and Palestine to Sidon), Seleucus (Babylon and Syria to north of Sidon), Cassander (Macedonia) and Lysimachus (Thrace and Bithynia). Each of these rulers saw himself as the heir of Alexander. All continued a version of Alexander's cult, and all incorporated themselves into it.

When Ptolemy became ruler of Egypt, he inherited a long-established tradition of ruler worship. He was the heir of the pharaohs; however, his worship was not restricted to Egypt. He also claimed that his dynasty began with Alexander; he thus inherited Alexander's legacy in Egypt. Before the formal division of the kingdom, Ptolemy 'liberated' the island of Rhodes (c. 304 BCE). He was given the title *Sōtēr* (saviour) and received divine honours.[140] Under his successor, Ptolemy II (Philadelphus) divine honours

---

134. Plutarch, *Alexander* 28.

135. Fredricksmeyer, 'Alexander's Deification', p. 1.

136. But see the discussion in Balsdon, 'Alexander', pp. 383-88.

137. Arrian, *Anabasis* 23.2. For a discussion of the Alexander cult in Greece and Macedonia, see Habicht, *Gottmenschentum*, pp. 17-36.

138. Suetonius, *Julius* 7.1-2.

139. Suetonius, *Augustus* 18.1.

140. Edwyn Robert Bevan, 'The Deification of Kings in the Greek Cities', *English Historical Review* 16 (1901), p. 627; see also Sweet, *Roman Emperor Worship*, p. 26.

increased greatly. Ptolemy II's wife Arsinoë was also considered divine.[141] Thus, from that time on, the Ptolemaic Egyptian king and his wife were considered to be divine. However, whether for political tact and/or not to impose on Alexander's status, the early Ptolemies did not generally propagate their own divinity. They did not oppose others who wished to so honour them. Despite clear divine honours for the first four Ptolemaic rulers, the term 'god' (θεός) was not used officially (except in dating a document) until Ptolemy V. A dedication of a temple in honour of Asklepios at Philae (186–180 BCE) reads as follows: Βασιλεὺς Πτολεμαῖος καὶ βασίλισσα Κλεοπάτρα θεοὶ Ἐπιφανεῖς, καὶ Πτολεμαῖος ὁ υἱὸς Ἀσκληπιῶι ('King Ptolemy and Queen Cleopatra, gods manifest, and their son Ptolemy, to Asklepios [dedicate this temple]').[142]

Concerning Roman ruler worship during the empire, it is likely that the influence of Cleopatra VII, the final Ptolemaic ruler (died 30 BCE), is not insignificant. This is not usually considered but worth noting here.[143] Embodied in her was the tradition of the ancient pharaohs, Alexander and her own family. She was considered the goddess Isis and ruled Egypt as a divine monarch. She was close to Julius Caesar and, although we do not know the extent to which she may have contributed to any divine aspirations he had at Rome, it is probably more than a coincidence that his relationship to her coincided with many of the divine honours he was receiving. It is likely that Caesar would have sought and/or been offered these honours if he had never met Cleopatra; however, one wonders if things would have progressed differently under different circumstances.

Cleopatra also influenced Octavian, although not in the way she influenced Caesar. Octavian was at war with Antony and Cleopatra. His propaganda against the two included their positions as divine monarchs. Octavian probably knew the Egyptian ruler cult well. Whether he had any desire to assume such a position is unknown. Two facts are clear. First, he learned from Caesar that the acceptance of too many outward honours could prove fatal. In order to rule effectively, he needed support and did not need to anger leaders in Rome unnecessarily. Second, after defeating Antony and Cleopatra and annexing Egypt for Rome, he now assumed the position of divine monarch to the people of Egypt. This was not optional. It came with the victory. To reject this position among the Egyptians would have placed

---

However, this has been questioned; see R. Hazzard, 'Did Ptolemy I Get his Surname from the Rhodians in 304 B.C.?' *ZPE* 93 (1992), pp. 52-56.

141. Sweet, *Roman Emperor Worship*, p. 27.

142. OGIS 98. The implications of this inscription for the Ptolemaic ruler cult are discussed by Carl Garth Johnson, '*OGIS* 98 and the Divination of the Ptolemies', *Historia* 51 (2002), pp. 112-16.

143. However, it is mentioned by Fishwick, *ICLW,* I.1, p. 67.

him in the same position in which Alexander would have found himself if he had rejected the Persian honours. Fortunately for Octavian, he was in a position that permitted different types of responses to the ruler depending on locality. The Egyptian response to Octavian was less important to Romans than his relationship to them. He never hinted at a desire for Romans to treat him as the Egyptians (or any other conquered people) did. Additionally, Octavian's presentation of himself as ruler of Egypt appears to be more through Alexander than through the Ptolemies. Octavian, like Alexander, was more than an Egyptian pharaoh.[144]

The traditions of Egypt and influence of Cleopatra on Caesar and Octavian must not be taken too far. Certainly there was influence, but, as we will see below, under Octavian major innovations were made in the Roman ruler cult. This is true in Egypt as well. While retaining much of its local flavour, much of the Ptolemaic organization was replaced by Roman.[145]

(c) *Alexander's Successors: Other Successors.* The other three successors of Alexander followed a similar pattern to what took place in Egypt. All claimed to be the heirs of Alexander, continued his cult, and incorporated themselves into it. The Seleucid ruler cult was empire-wide but had local, decentralized provincial administration.[146] Despite significant differences between Hellenistic ruler cults (significant enough to be considered different cults), Alexander is both a beginning and unifying factor in these cults. Each had its own local influences as well. None of the traditions was as ancient as those of Egypt. Nevertheless, their development is complex, and all (including Egypt) probably influenced one another.[147]

(d) *Summary.* The Hellenistic ruler cults are complex phenomena. The local expressions of these cults provided the basis for local expressions of emperor worship. In many ways, the emperors merely took over the roles held by previous leaders. Of course development continued, and emperor worship was much grander and provided a means of connection between diverse peoples. The Alexander influence is important because it provides a unifying beginning to the cults that are again brought together under the emperors. Additionally, although difficult to prove with any certainty,

144. Gregory S. Dundas, 'Augustus and the Kingship of Egypt', *Historia* 51 (2002), pp. 433-48.

145. Gregory S. Dundas, *Pharaoh, Basileus and Imperator: The Roman Imperial Cult in Egypt* (Unpublished PhD diss., University of California, Los Angeles, 1994), pp. 97-177.

146. Fishwick, *ICLW,* I.1, p. 16.

147. For a discussion of these cults, see Habicht, *Gottmenschentum*, pp. 37-41, 82-108; Fishwick, *ICLW,* I.1, pp. 15-20.

it seems likely that Cleopatra VII influenced the emperor cults directly through the emperors' predecessor Julius Caesar. However, as we will see, this influence must be seen in light of major developments by the early emperors themselves.

(5) *Julius Caesar.* In many ways Julius Caesar is the figure who brings together the background elements that contribute to the creation of Roman emperor worship. Caesar was familiar with Hellenistic divine-kingships. He greatly admired Alexander and spent significant time with Cleopatra in Egypt.[148] Nevertheless, Caesar made (or permitted) significant innovations in his ruler cult. As a result, his influence must be viewed as a contributing factor to the background of emperor worship. Victor Ehrenberg says that his aim was to be '[a] deified ruler, not a Hellenistic or Roman king, but an imperial one'.[149]

It seems likely that Caesar was given divine honours in his lifetime.[150] Gradel notes three events that make this identification clear. In 46 BCE, after the battle of Thapsus, the senate granted Caesar a chariot and a statue to be placed on the Capitol with an inscription calling Caesar a ἡμίθεος (demigod).The Greek term is a translation of an original Latin. It is likely that the Latin was the name of a specific demigod such as Romulus.[151] In 45 BCE, after the battle of Munda, Caesar's statue was placed in the temple of Quirinus with an inscription calling him Θεῷ ἀνικήτῳ (unconquered god).[152] Finally, in the months before his death in 44 BCE he was granted honours similar to those of the state gods: the title *Divus Julius*, a state priest, a state temple, and a sacred couch for his image.[153] The title *Divus* would later be given to deified emperors.

---

148. Fishwick, *ICLW* I.1, p. 67.

149. Victor Ehrenberg, 'Caesar's Final Aims', in Ehrenberg, *Man, State and Deity: Essays in Ancient History* (London: Methuen, 1974), pp. 127-42 (142) (originally published in *Harvard Studies in Classical Philology* 68 [1964], pp. 149-61).

150. Most importantly, see Cicero, *Philippics* 2.43.110. See also Cassius Dio 44.4-8; Appian, *Civil Wars* 2.106; Suetonius, *Julius* 76.1; 84.2. Additionally, see Fishwick, *ICLW* I.1, pp. 56-67; Gradel, *Emperor Worship*, pp. 54-61. For an extensive discussion of the primary sources, see Stefan Weinstock, *Divus Julius* (Oxford: Clarendon Press, 1971). For an impressive bibliography concerning Caesar to the mid-1970s, see Helga Gesche, *Caesar* (Erträge der Forschung, 51; Darmstadt: Wissenschaftliche Buchgesellschaft, 1976), pp. 207-325 (for this topic, specifically pp. 300-304).

151. Fishwick, *ICLW* I.1, p. 57.

152. Cassius Dio 43.45.3 (again the original would have been in Latin).

153. Gradel, *Emperor Worship*, pp. 54-55 (and see the primary sources already noted in this section).

Some do not agree that Caesar was deified before his death. Plutarch may be understood to suggest that divine honours followed Caesar's death,[154] but this event, unique to Plutarch, is either an error (in light of the primary evidence cited above) or is intended to suggest that divine honours were confirmed after his death.[155] Helga Gesche takes a mediating position suggesting that divine honours were agreed upon while Caesar was living but not intended to be inaugurated until after his death.[156] However, the ancient evidence discussed here seems to be best understood as indicating that divine honours were granted during Caesar's lifetime.

Julius Caesar's influence on the development of later emperor worship may be more indirect than might first be supposed. Despite the similarities between the deification of Julius and later emperors and the establishment of temples, priests and so on for both, a number of differences in both expression and purpose can be noted. First, Julius's deification was important for the legitimacy of his successors (those who desired to continue his programmes, e.g. especially Octavian and Antony). This is a similar purpose for later deification; however, later emperors honoured and built upon the deeds of 'good' emperors. Caesar's heirs had him deified in the midst of a divided empire. Second, Julius's image and cult underwent revisions under Augustus. Imperial cults really began with Augustus, after the Julius cult was established. Interestingly, there is little extant evidence of Julius's cult today. Third, a very important influence of Caesar on the establishment of imperial cults is negative. Julius's situation served as an example of what not to do.[157] Augustus was careful to avoid Julius's mistakes. It is not certain that Julius directly sought divine honours—or at least how much he sought them.[158] It is possible that such honours were primarily a response of the Senate as they attempted to define the relationship between the state and the absolute ruler.[159] Nevertheless, to many, Caesar appeared a threat, and the honours played a role in this discontent. Augustus learned from this.

154. Plutarch, *Caesar* 67.4.

155. Fishwick, *ICLW* I.1, pp. 65-66.

156. Helga Gesche, *Die Vergottung Caesars* (Frankfurter althistorische Studien, 1; Kallmünz/Opf.: Michael Lassleben, 1968), esp. pp. 47-50.

157. This is also the conclusion of Fishwick, *ICLW* I.1, p. 72.

158. With the exception of encouraging Julius's cult, Augustus generally attempted to dissociate himself from Caesar (Edwin S. Ramage, 'Augustus' Treatment of Julius Caesar', *Historia* 34 [1985], pp. 223-45; Peter White, 'Julius Caesar in Augustan Rome', *Phoenix* 42 [1988], pp. 334-56).

159. Gradel, *Emperor Worship*, p. 58; Fishwick states, 'On the whole it seems best to believe that the driving force was not Caesar himself. At the urging of the senate he agreed—unwisely—to honours that even included deification and trappings that could look monarchical" (Fishwick, *ICLW* I.1, p. 71). I find it difficult to concede however that Caesar himself did not take interest in this process.

Once monarchical rule was solidified in Rome (much later than Augustus), a more explicit public cult would be accepted. However, as will be discussed below, in the beginning Octavian had to be very careful to walk a line between the explicit and the implicit. It cannot be doubted that Augustus's cult was incredibly extensive. It helped to establish firmly his presence throughout the empire. However, this was done through careful diplomacy and the contribution and participation of many individuals, cities, provinces and imperial influences.

There is one further important contribution that Caesar made to the development of the ruler cult, or more broadly, to the rule of Augustus. Caesar essentially put an end to the republic. In Caesar, Rome had an absolute ruler. Whatever, this ruler was to be called, in practice he was a king. A brief ideological act of resistance in the form of Caesar's assassination was doomed to failure. The second Brutus could not repeat his ancestor's success. Rome was unable to return to republican rule. Caesar completed the groundwork for a single ruler. A single absolute ruler would have a certain relationship with the rest of the empire that could be best expressed in imperial cults.

(6) *Roman Tradition*. It has often been argued that ruler worship in Rome either was the result of the disintegration of traditional Roman religion[160] and/or could not have seriously taken hold in Rome at all. This view may be due largely to Cassius Dio's description of the establishment of imperial cult temples in Asia and Bithynia. Concerning temples to living emperors Cassius Dio says, 'For in the capital [Rome] itself and in Italy generally no emperor, however worthy of renown he has been, has dared to do this.'[161] Additionally, this view may be influenced by modern Western assumptions about religion concerning which I cautioned in Chapter 1.

Cassius Dio's statement needs to be understood in its historical context. The passage from which this quotation is taken will be discussed in detail below. When imperial cults are described more thoroughly, the passage may be viewed differently. The purpose here is to demonstrate that divine honours for human beings are not antithetical to Roman tradition. There is sufficient evidence for this conclusion.

Even with the various influences noted above and the developments introduced by Julius Caesar, Roman imperial worship would not have been able to take hold without some precedence in Roman tradition. This is especially true for its practice in the West (including Rome) but it is true also for its growth in the East. I am not suggesting that it would not have been

---

160. Taylor, *Divinity*, p. 54. Although this is an accurate representation of Taylor's view, her position is more nuanced than this simple statement may imply. See also Sweet, *Roman Emperor Worship*, pp. 99-104, 111-23.

161. Cassius Dio 51.20.8 (trans. Cary, LCL).

practised in the East without Roman tradition, but rather that its acceptance among Romans both in the East and in Rome would have been difficult without some precedent. Interestingly, the young Octavian accused Antony of Eastern ruler cult practices in his successful propaganda war against the older general. How Octavian managed to do successfully what contributed to Antony's downfall will be explained further below in a section devoted to the cults' development under Augustus. Here the focus will be on Roman tradition.

It may have seemed preferable to place this section before the discussion of Julius Caesar. However, I will argue in the section on the development of the cults that, despite the essential nature of the figure of Caesar, emperor worship is not a direct continuation of the Caesar cult. Other factors are more directly responsible than Caesar's cult.

First, the Republican government of Rome had no ruler with absolute power. Therefore, one could not expect a *ruler* cult in the style of Egypt or the East. Thus, Rome had no ruler cult because it had no ruler![162] We cannot say with certainty, therefore, whether a ruler with absolute power would have been given divine honours. However, there are many observations that may support the notion. First, absolute rulers received divine honours throughout the ancient world. Rome was not isolated, and it is likely that Roman practices would have followed patterns similar to other communities with similar rulers. Second, Rome honoured their gods, especially Jupiter, as rulers. Thus, although the Romans had no formal human king, Jupiter may have been seen as their king.[163] For Jupiter's worship to be seen as similar *in kind* to ruler worship, it is essential to break down the anachronistic distinction between politics and religion already discussed.[164] However, the thoroughgoing republican repulsion of monarchy suggests that Jupiter's role may not be so narrowly defined. It seems difficult to view Rome as adopting such a role for Jupiter. Nevertheless, it is possible that, in practice, Jupiter functioned this way without official republican recognition.

Second, Romulus, the (mythical?) founder of Rome, is considered a god in Roman tradition. Romulus is said to have been the son of Mars, taken to heaven and ultimately worshipped as the god Quirinus.[165] Livy describes in some detail how Romulus becomes a god.[166] Romulus is not the only ruler

---

162. Gradel, *Emperor Worship*, p. 27.

163. Gradel, *Emperor Worship*, p. 30.

164. Gradel, *Emperor Worship*, p. 27.

165. Greg Woolf, 'Divinity and Power in Ancient Rome', in Nicole Brisch (ed.), *Religion and Power: Divine Kingship in the Ancient World and Beyond* (Oriental Institute Seminars, 4. Chicago: University of Chicago Press, 2008), p. 243.

166. Livy 1.16.

to have such an honour.[167] Further, many aristocratic families traced their lineage back to a deity (e.g. the Julians considered themselves descended from Venus).[168] Additionally, many believed that the gods had human origins.[169]

Third, a discussion of Roman ruler worship during the republican period usually focuses on state cult. This limitation demands the conclusion that Romans did not give divine honours to humans. There was no absolute ruler until Julius Caesar. However, the private sphere of religion is more accommodating to divine honours for people. Unfortunately, the nature of the sources is such that official state cults are easier to understand. The private sphere provides only limited and fragmented data. Nevertheless, enough evidence is extant to provide important insight into the practices of divine honours for people. The most important individual for such honours was the *paterfamilias*, the head of the family. Unlike the republican system of government, the household had an absolute, king-like ruler. The relationship differed to some extent between the *paterfamilias* and his wife, children, freedmen and slaves, but essentially he was the ruler and everyone was dependent on him. Gradel compiles literary evidence from Plautus as well as non-literary evidence from Pompeii to demonstrate that the cult of the *paterfamilias'* Genius goes back at least into republican times.[170] The Genius is a difficult concept for the modern student to understand. It was some type of life force, a divine aspect of an individual, possibly even a protective spirit. In any case, it is tied to the individual.[171] Every person has a Genius (a woman's is called a Juno). However, it seems that only the Genius of the *paterfamilias* was worshipped in the household cult.[172] Additionally, each god and goddess had his or her own Genius or Juno.[173] This is an interesting similarity between humans and gods.

In addition to the Genius of an individual, families had Lares and Penates. There was originally a single Lar, but this developed into a pair around the time of the Augustus.[174] These were attached to families and were expected to be honoured. They were some type of household spirits related to the particular family. Descriptions seem to slightly differ. Turcan describes the Lar as 'a kind of demon of the ancestors and of the continuity of the tribe

167. Liebeschuetz, *Continuity*, 269. see also Fishwick, *ICLW* I.1, pp. 45-55.
168. Woolf, 'Divinity and Power', p. 244.
169. Liebeschuetz, *Continuity*, p. 33.
170. Gradel, *Emperor Worship*, pp. 36-49.
171. Gradel, *Emperor Worship*, p. 37; Turcan, *Gods of Ancient Rome*, p. 16.
172. Gradel, *Emperor Worship*, p. 37.
173. Scheid, *Roman Religion*, p. 166.
174. Scheid, *Roman Religion*, p. 165.

as well as being the familiar spirit of the household'.[175] I doubt that the term 'demon' would be appropriate from the Roman's point of view. Ogilvie describes them as 'the deified spirits of dead ancestors, who still took an interest in the family . . . .[176] The Lares had the potential to bless those who attended to them.[177] The importance of Lares is clear; all Roman households had a Lararium, a shrine to make offerings to the Lares.[178] If there is a tie here to actual ancestors, this may be further evidence of attributing to people that which is often reserved for the divine. This further supports the observations described above about the importance of status and the relative nature of divinity. Penates may have been spirits who watched over the food supply;[179] however, their functions are not entirely certain. Although they may originally have been distinct from the Lares, they do not seem to have differed much from them later.[180]

These private practices would become public with Augustus. As will be discussed below, the worship of his Genius, Lares, and his Numen will play an important role in the early development of imperial religion. These developments move out of the sphere of private and into official public religious forum.

In summary, republican Rome did not have an absolute ruler. Therefore, the notion of a republican ruler cult would make little sense. However, there is ample evidence from Roman tradition, such as previous divine rulers and the worship of human Genius and possibly Lares, that not only makes a ruler cult plausible under the right circumstances but may actually have influenced the establishment of such a cult.

(7) *Summary.* It is clear that Roman emperor worship had many influences. Alexander's memory was important, since his figure loomed large in the late republic and early imperial periods. His influence brought with it Greek and other Eastern aspects of ruler worship. Many of his successors continued the cult of Alexander and incorporated their own families into the practice of religion in their kingdoms. Julius Caesar may either have desired to be proclaimed god while alive or was making arrangements for his deification after death. After his assassination, the heirs of Caesar's power were able to have him officially deified. This turned out to be especially convenient for Octavian, the adopted son of Caesar, who now could claim the position of *divus filius*, son of god. Finally, Roman tradition itself provided influences. All of

175. Turcan, *Gods of Ancient Rome*, p. 15.
176. Ogilvie, *Romans*, p. 101.
177. Turcan, *Gods of Ancient Rome*, p. 16; Ogilvie, *Romans*, p. 101.
178. Ogilvie, *Romans*, p. 101.
179. Ogilvie, *Romans*, p. 102.
180. Gradel, *Emperor Worship*, p. 38.

this is important for the emergence of imperial worship. However, Roman emperor worship is more than just large-scale ruler worship. It is a phenomenon uniquely developed during and for the needs of the Roman empire.

b. *Roman Imperial Cults: Preliminary Matters*

Before a survey of the development of imperial cults in the first century is undertaken, a few explanatory comments must be made. The early portion of this section may also have been included in the description of Roman religious experience; however, it is introduced here because of its appropriateness to understanding emperor worship.

(1) *Honour and Worship in Ancient Rome.* It has been common for modern students of Roman history to understand Roman emperor worship as a symptom of a significant decline in Roman religion. As discussed above, this is due in part to our heritage, which includes specific beliefs about what religion is supposed to be. A modern student asks, How could the ancients worship a man? The answer must be that their religion had degenerated so far as to be nearly meaningless.

What has been discussed thus far about Roman religious experience and ruler cults should challenge these beliefs. In this section a focus will be on the act of honouring and worshipping itself. Additionally, a discussion of official deification for dead emperors will be described. Finally, the section will conclude by answering the question, Was the emperor divine?

(a) *Human Honours and Divine Worship: A Distinction of* Kind *or* Degree? In order to understand Roman ruler worship, it is essential to understand the nature and role of honours in Roman society. I have argued that a distinction between political and religious spheres is anachronistic; and, once this is understood, a more accurate picture of honours can be described.

An honour is given by one party to another. It usually is granted for some act or deed that the honouree has accomplished, and/or it is given because of the person's abilities to provide something to/for those honouring him or her. This act demonstrates an important relational statement about the parties involved. It makes explicit a social gap between the two parties.[181] The larger the honour bestowed, the larger the gap between parties. The highest honours one can give are divine honours.[182] Such honours may include statues, priests and ritual. These honours reveal the largest gap between honourers and the honouree.

---

181. Gradel, *Emperor Worship*, p. 29.
182. Gradel, *Emperor Worship*, p. 29.

There does not appear to be a specific line where human honours end and divine honours begin. At least there does not seem to be such a line provided in the ancient evidence. In other words, the distinction between human honour and divine worship is really one of *degree*, not *kind*.[183] Gradel makes this point convincingly. He demonstrates that the gods were not worshipped simply because they were gods.[184] This is in contrast to modern monotheistic religions, where God is worshipped because of who God is. If deity was the primary requirement for worship, it would seem that Romans would be required to worship every deity. This is not the case. They worshipped Jupiter because he was their chief god, the most powerful and the one responsible for the prosperity of Rome.[185] They worshipped many other gods who could provide assistance in many ways.

Given this perspective, divine honours or worship for an absolute ruler is logical. During the republic, Romans honoured men for various reasons. However, their highest honours were reserved for those who could do more than republican generals and temporary leaders had done, namely, the gods. With Caesar came a new class of human ruler, perceived to be absolute in power. How were such rulers to be honoured? How was the social gap between the ruler and people to be expressed? It was more appropriate to grant them honours that had heretofore been granted only to gods. These honours were not in a special class. They were simply greater than what had been granted to people before.

Jason Davies goes further. Discussing Tacitus's treatment of this issue, he suggests that the honours granted to the emperor by the senate were a means by which this body was attempting to 'locate itself' in its relationship to the emperor.[186]

(b) *Honours in a Patronage System.* Roman imperial bureaucracy was relatively small and could not hope to micro-manage its vast territory.[187] Local authorities were relied upon to govern their own areas.[188] One important feature of Roman society that contributed to order was its system of relationships often referred to as *patronage*.[189] Every Roman had a place

183. Gradel, *Emperor Worship*, p. 29.

184. Gradel, *Emperor Worship*, p. 28.

185. Gradel, *Emperor Worship*, p. 28.

186. Jason P. Davies, *Rome's Religious History: Livy, Tacitus and Ammianus on their Gods* (Cambridge: Cambridge University Press, 2004), p. 183.

187. Peter Garnsey and Richard P. Saller, *The Roman Empire: Economy, Society and Culture* (Berkeley: University of California Press, 1987), pp. 20-40.

188. Garnsey and Saller, *Roman Empire*, p. 26.

189. For both positive and negative aspects of this system for running the republic and empire, see David Braund, 'Function and Dysfunction: Personal Patronage in Roman Imperialism', in Andrew Wallace-Hadrill (ed.), *Patronage in Ancient Society* (London:

in this web of relationships.[190] In this system some individuals (patrons, benefactors) were responsible for various degrees of care of others (clients).[191] Most obvious is the role of the *paterfamilias* in the family.[192] However, others served in this way as well.[193]

Within this system, the one of higher status would provide something for the lower-status individual. Societal expectations resulted in a reciprocal relationship (*reciprocity*). The receiver is in some way bound to the giver. This process adds cohesion to a society.[194] In theory, the 'ideal benefactor was supposed to act without thought of what was due to him, but this was unrealistic'.[195] Seneca suggested that, in giving, the benefactor was storing up future treasure (as long as the recipient is alive; *On Benefits* 6.43.2-3). Cicero notes that a good man repays favours done to him (*On Duties* [*De officiis*] 1.48 = 1.15). Return need not be material but could involve political support, allegiance or other non-tangible commodity.

Patronage can be seen within the honour system that was entrenched also in Roman society. Honours reflected a two-way relationship. When honours were accepted, responsibilities were also implied.[196] If an honouree did not wish to assume the responsibilities attached to the honour, it should be rejected. This is the ideal situation, and it is acknowledged that abuse may occur. Nevertheless, this is the expectation placed on the activity by society.

Routledge, 1989), pp. 137-52. For how this system affected the poor, see Peter Garnsey and Greg Woolf, 'Patronage of the Rural Poor in the Roman World', in Andrew Wallace-Hadrill (ed.), *Patronage in Ancient Society* (London: Routledge, 1989), pp. 153-70.

190. Garnsey and Saller, *Roman Empire*, p. 148.

191. Géza Alföldy, *The Social History of Rome* (trans. David Braund and Frank Pollock;Totowa, NJ: Barnes & Noble, 1985), pp. 98-101. On patronage, see the articles in Wallace-Hadrill, *Patronage* (some of which are cited in this section). See also the many relationships discussed in Fergus Millar, *The Emperor in the Roman World (31 BC–AD 337)* (London: Duckworth, 1977).

192. L. Casson, *Everyday Life in Ancient Rome* (Baltimore: Johns Hopkins University Press, rev. and exp. edn, 1998), pp. 10-11. However, Casson's focus is on the rights rather than the responsibilities of the *paterfamilias*.

193. For a more theoretical approach to the subject, see Terry Johnson and Christopher Dandeker, 'Patronage: Relation and System', in Andrew Wallace-Hadrill (ed.), *Patronage in Ancient Society* (London: Routledge, 1989), pp. 219-41.

194. See Seneca, *On Benefits* 1.4 (N.B. the essay is not to be confused with *Epistle 81*, often with the same English title. Only the essay is referred to in this section). See also the discussion in Andrew Wallace-Hadrill, 'Patronage in Roman Society: From Republic to Empire', in Andrew Wallace-Hadrill (ed.), *Patronage in Ancient Society* (London: Routledge, 1989), pp. 71-78.

195. Garnsey and Saller, *Roman Empire*, p. 148.

196. See the discussion in Bruce J. Malina, *The New Testament World: Insights from Cultural Anthropology* (Louisville, KY: Westminster/John Knox Press, 3rd rev. and exp. edn, 2001), pp. 94-97.

From the point of view of those granting honours, they honoured those who could help them. This is why ancients honoured gods. They believed that the gods were able to help in war, with crops, with fertility and so on. This belief is why specific Romans worshipped certain gods and not others.

(c) *Apotheosis and the Dead Emperor* (Divus). Julius Caesar was given the Latin title *divus* during his lifetime. There is debate on the meaning of this term and its relationship to *deus*. It has been suggested that *divus* is something less than *deus*. Thus, the Latin *deus* is equivalent to the Greek θεός (god); *divus* corresponds to θεῖος (divine, from the gods). This distinction may be too simplistic and may be the result of modern attempts to understand how to relate people to gods. Whether the emperor was considered a god will be addressed in the next section.[197] Here the focus will be on the Roman act of official deification.

When an emperor deemed good by the senate died, he could undergo apotheosis (deification, elevation to divine status). He was granted official state status by being given the title *divus* and receiving the paraphernalia of a cult. It is incorrect to see this process as *making* the emperor a god. Rather, it granted divine status and honour to an individual *in relation to* the worshippers.[198] After Julius Caesar, the term was no longer used of a living ruler but became more of a technical title for the dead deified ruler (including Julius). Ancient writers who lived after the ruler often used this title with the name when mentioned.[199] Official apotheosis was very important, as is evident from the massive extant archaeological artistic remains. The cult of the emperors was present throughout the landscape of the Roman world. Our focus here however is upon its contribution to the living emperor's position.[200]

---

197. For a discussion of the terminology (including θεός, *divus* and *deus*), see Price, 'Gods and Emperors', pp. 79-95.

198. Gradel, *Emperor Worship*, pp. 29-30.

199. For example concerning Julius Caesar: Augustus, *Res Gestae* 19; Suetonius, *Augustus* 2.1, 15; 17.5; 100.3; for Augustus: Tacitus, *Annals* 1.9 (Tiberius of Augustus at his funeral); Suetonius, *Augustus* 31.1-2; Velleius Paterculus, 2.124.4.

200. For a detailed discussion of the role of deceased deified emperors through their funerary monuments, see Penelope J.E. Davies, *Death and the Emperor: Roman Imperial Funerary Monuments from Augustus to Marcus Aurelius* (Cambridge: Cambridge University Press, 2000; rcpr. Austin: University of Texas Press, 2004). Additionally, important discussions on this issue are provided by Simon R.F. Price, 'From Noble Funerals to Divine Cult: The Consecration of Roman Emperors', in David Cannadine and Simon R.F. Price (eds.), *Rituals of Royalty: Power and Ceremonial in Traditional Societies* (Cambridge: Cambridge University Press, 1987), pp. 56-105; and Bickerman, 'Consecratio', pp. 1-25; plus further discussion, pp. 26-37. For a discussion of apotheosis in Luke–Acts in the context of the ancient world, see Ilze Kezbere,

An extant inscription from 183 CE mentions that there are sixteen individuals who have received *divus* status.[201] In addition to Julius this number would include five women associated with the imperial family. A later list from 224 CE adds four to account for the emperors who ruled after the previous list was compiled.[202] These inscriptions omit some minor deified non-emperors. In total, between Augustus and Constantine (died 337 CE), 36 of 60 emperors were deified, and 27 people from imperial families were deified.[203] Of importance to our period, there are four emperors listed for the Julio-Claudian (31 BCE–68 CE) and Flavian (69–96 CE) dynasties: Augustus, Claudius, Vespasian, and Titus. In discussing these lists, James Oliver notes that it seems likely that Vespasian when reorganizing the official cult, omitted Livia, Augustus's wife, who was deified by Claudius.[204] Thus, she does not appear on these lists.[205] The exclusion of Julius Caesar from these lists supports our contention that imperial cults began with Augustus.

As our discussion of honours has demonstrated and as will be discussed further below, it is wrong to assume that only at this point was an emperor considered a god. The apotheosis is important, but its primary importance is in the official state realm. Although I do not wish to minimize the importance of this action to the Roman's religious experience, it appears that the

Umstrittener Monotheismus: Wahre und falsche Apotheose im lukanischen Doppelwerk (NTOA/StUNT, 60; Göttingen: Vandenhoeck & Ruprecht, 2007). For a discussion of apotheosis in art, see Eugenia Sellers Strong, 'Lecture I: Divus Augustus: The Influence of the Imperial Apotheosis on Antique Design', in *Apotheosis and After Life: Three Lectures on Certain Phases of Art and Religion in the Roman Empire* (Freeport, NY: Books for Libraries Press, 1969), pp. 30-111. For a discussion of the posthumous deification of some imperial individuals in Tacitus, see J.P. Davies, *Rome's Religious History*, pp. 176-85.

201. CIL, VI, 2099.2.5-6, 2.14 (= CFA 94.2.5-6, 2.14).

202. CIL, VI, 2107.13 (= CFA 105b.13).

203. Price, 'Noble Funerals', p. 57.

204. Cassius Dio 60.5.2. During Augustus's life Livia increasingly shared honours with Augustus (Gertrude Grether, 'Livia and the Roman Imperial Cult', *AJP* 67 [1946], pp. 223-28 [this article provides a good overview of honours given to Livia]). However, many in his family shared in his honours. It would be natural for his wife to have an elevated position. In Augustus's will she was adopted into the Julian clan and given the Augustan name (Tacitus, *Annals* 1.8; however, Cassius Dio suggests that she already had the name [56.46.1]). Also, Livia appears to have been considered divine in places prior to formal deification (Fernando Lozano, '*Thea Livia* in Athens: Redating *IG* II² 3242', *ZPE* 148 [2004], pp. 177-80). For inscription and coin evidence concerning the women of the imperial house, see Ulrike Hahn, *Die Frauen römischen Kaiserhauses und ihre Ehrungen im griechischen Osten anhand epigraphischer und numismatischer Zeugnisse von Livia bis Sabina* (Saarbrücker Studien zur Archäologie und alten Geschichte, 8; n.p.: Saarländische Druckerei und Verlag, 1994).

205. James H. Oliver, 'The Divi of the Hadrianic Period', *HTR* 42 (1949), pp. 35-40 (36).

act of deification does not assure that the emperor will be remembered in any significant way. Augustus was remembered for what he did for the empire, not because he was granted a state cult. Claudius's cult was neglected and reinstated by Vespasian.[206] At the same time, a provincial cult to Tiberius in Smyrna, an emperor not officially deified,[207] appears to have been active long after the emperor's death.[208]

The relationship between the Roman process of deification and the worship of the living emperor is complex. To some extent this is dependent on the local religious activity. Fernando Lozano argues that 'the absence of a policy of imposing from the centre a homogeneous practice regarding emperor worship allowed significant variety and divergence in provincial innovations'.[209] He further suggests that, although the two phenomena are closely related, they are not equivalent.[210] This is most easily demonstrated by the fact that the list of *divi* and the list of those worshipped while living are not identical.[211] Again, the worship of the living emperor is our main concern as we develop our arguments below.

Additionally, official deification could be an important propaganda tool for a ruling emperor. In order to establish legitimacy, it is helpful to be related to the divine. This seems especially important for the deification of women. Of the six women in the deification lists cited above, four were deified by Hadrian, who had questionable claims to the throne.[212]

Therefore, official deification was important, especially on the state level and for the purposes of the religious calendar. It also was a power tool for the reigning emperor. However, the deified emperor does not supersede the ruling emperor's role in the empire. If anything, it enhanced it.

206. Oliver, 'Divi', p. 36.

207. There is confusion over a line in Seneca's *Pumpkinification* (or *Apocolocyntosis*) 1.2 which states, '. . . et divum Augustum et Tiberium Caesarem ad deos isse' ('both the divine Augustus and Tiberius Caesar went to the gods'; Latin LCL; trans. mine). However, this clause does not have to be interpreted as attributing deity to Tiberius. Only Augustus is called 'divine' (*divum*). Tiberius is simply called 'Caesar'. For a discussion of this issue, see Steven J. Green, 'Undeifying Tiberius: A Reconsideration of Seneca, *Apocolocyntosis* 1.2', *Classical Quarterly* 60 (2010), pp. 274-76.

208. See the discussion below.

209. Fernando Lozano, '*Divi Augusti* and *Theoi Sebastoi*: Roman Initiatives and Greek Answers', *CQ* 57 (2007), pp. 139-52 (139).

210. Lozano, '*Divi Augusti* and *Theoi Sebastoi*', p. 139.

211. Lozano, '*Divi Augusti* and *Theoi Sebastoi*', p. 139.

212. Davies, *Death and the Emperor*, pp. 118-19; Oliver, 'Divi', pp. 36-39. Hadrian also deified his young lover Antinous after death. This was a questionable use of this practice. See also Royston Lambert, *Beloved and God: The Story of Hadrian and Antinous* (Secaucus, NJ: Meadowland, 1984).

(d) *Was the Living Emperor Divine?* Was the living emperor divine? This question, expanded to include the emperors who died and were deified (*divus*) is probably the most common one asked by modern students of emperor worship.[213] It is a decidedly modern question and does not appear to have troubled the ancients, at least not in the manner that it troubles us. Some ancients were concerned with the position the ruler held but not necessarily whether he was a god.

The answer to the question is somewhat dependent on one's meaning of 'divine'. If by this word we intended to place the emperor in a position like the God of modern monotheistic religions, the answer would probably be negative. However, such a god was not an option for the vast majority of people living under Roman rule in the first century. However, if 'divine' means that the emperor is comparable to the traditionally worshipped deities in Roman religion, the answer may be different.

Much of what has been discussed above already has reconstructed the cognitive environment for this question to be answered. Modern distinctions between religion and politics and between secular honours and divine worship are anachronistic. Honour and worship differ in *degree, not kind*. Roman religious experience included many gods. Romans worshipped those deities who could help them. It has also been suggested that divinity was relative. This will be explored more here. Additionally, the discussion of deified emperors above has demonstrated that apotheosis was not *making* a god but rather granting divine status in an official manner. Further discussion below will also add important information to this cognitive environment. However, it seems best to address the present issue here in order to be able to proceed with maximum benefit.

First, we must revise the question to reflect discussion to this point: Did Romans approach their living emperor in a manner similar to their gods? Even this is not satisfactory. The word 'approach' seems to weaken the question considerably. One might wish to use the word 'believe' in its place. In light of the above discussion of the role of belief in Roman religious experience, it would be inappropriate here. Nevertheless, I do not intend to weaken the question too much. The key point in this anachronistic question is whether the worshippers saw the emperor as divine. Even the emperor's own opinion, which varied from emperor to emperor, is really not important.[214] Addition-

---

213. See, e.g., Matthias Peppel, 'Gott oder Mensch? Kaiserverehrung und Herrschaftskontrolle', in Cancik and Hitzl (eds.), *Praxis der Herrscherverehrung*, pp. 69-95.

214. On the emperor's self-understanding, see Christian Habicht, 'Die augusteische Zeit und das erste Jahrhundert nach Christi Geburt', in Willem den Boer (ed.), *Le culte des souverains dans l'empire romain* (Geneva: Fondation Hardt, 1973), pp. 76-85. Pliny clearly rejects divinity for Trajan (*Panegyricus* 2). See the discussion in Daniel N. Schowalter, *The Emperor and the Gods: Images from the Time of Trajan* (HDR, 28; Minneapolis: Fortress Press, 1993), pp. 71-75. Pliny survived Domitian's reign (who

ally, although the phrase 'similar to the gods' may be misleading, it seems acceptable here in that it expresses the point of the modern question.

Second, as has already been introduced, the Roman concept of divinity was relative. The notion of deity in an absolute sense appears to be foreign to Roman religious practice. Price grants that emperors were treated as gods.[215] However, he also argues that the ritual and language of emperor worship were less than for full deities. He gives four pieces of evidence: first, emperor statues have subordinate positions in traditional temples;[216] second, sacrificial practice towards the emperor is more restrained; third, the use of εὐσέβεια (reverence, piety) for emperors is ambiguous since it could refer to gods or people; fourth, prayers are offered both *for* and *to* the emperor.[217] Price suggests that the ambiguity concerning deity is a way to explain the inclusion of emperors in worship. They were somehow between gods and people.[218]

On the larger, more theoretical issue, Gradel disagrees with Price and suggests that it is significant that only philosophical sources (the sources Price uses for his point) ask the question What is a god? in absolute terms.[219] These sources seem unimportant to the cultic practice (as argued above concerning the role of faith and belief in Roman religious experience). Instead, Gradel argues that gods such as Jupiter were worshipped because of their power and position over the worshippers.[220] As already noted, Jupiter was not worshipped mainly because he was a god. There were many gods, and, if deity was the crucial element demanding worship in Roman society, all should be worshipped. Divine honours were the highest possible honours one could pay. The emperor's position in relation to his subjects was comparable only to what had in the past been the position of gods. Therefore, the emperor had divine status among his worshippers. This is relative, not absolute, divinity.

Friesen also disagrees with Price. He believes that Price has created an artificial tension that supports his conclusions. Friesen answers each of the four pieces of evidence that Price uses to argue that the emperor was less than the gods. First, it should be expected that statues of emperors would be in subordinate positions in traditional temples. Price's discussion involves

may have had divine tendencies) and wrote to a subsequent emperor who desired to distance himself from Domitian. This section of the *Panegyricus* is contrasting the new (Trajan) with the old. This nobleman's view can hardly represent a common first-century view of the emperor.

215. Price, *Rituals and Power*, pp. 231-32.
216. Price, *Rituals and Power*, pp. 146-56, 232-33.
217. Price, *Rituals and Power*, pp. 207-20, 232-33.
218. Price, *Rituals and Power*, p. 233.
219. Gradel, *Emperor Worship*, p. 28. See also Friesen, *Twice Neokoros*, p. 152. In addition to Gradel and Friesen, a brief but helpful discussion of this issue is Pfeiffer, *Der römische Kaiser und das Land am Nil*, pp. 27-29.
220. Gradel, *Emperor Worship*, pp. 28-29.

the emperors' statues *in* temples of other gods. Friesen shows that in the Flavian temple in Ephesus, the statues of traditional gods are subordinate to statues of the emperor.[221] Thus, the god to whom a temple is dedicated is likely to be dominant. Other gods in the temple would take a less prominent position. Concerning the final three points, Friesen demonstrates that tension does not arise from sacrificial practice. Sacrifice does not indicate who is divine or human.[222] The use of εὐσέβεια does not imply an intermediate status between god and the emperor. It describes the relationship between emperors and worshippers in terms of the benefaction system.[223] Finally, the existence of both prayers *for* and *to* an emperor should not be viewed as a means of minimizing the emperor's status. It reflects his position in the cultic system: he is not independent of other gods. The emperor does the work of the other gods as well as being protected by other gods. These facts do not weaken his position.[224] The literary evidence is strong. For example, after the death of Augustus, Tacitus states 'Versae inde ad Tiberium preces' ('Then all prayers were directed toward Tiberius').[225]

Generally, Romans appealed to gods who could do something for them. From the perspective of the people, in many ways the emperors seemed to control more of the areas of importance than many of the gods. The emperors could bless in very tangible ways. Therefore, it was appropriate to worship these individuals with the highest possible honours.

To this evidence we can add two points in favour of the divine status of the living emperor. First, it is acknowledged that Romans worshipped the emperor's Genius. This officially occurred around 12 BCE (see discussion below). It would be wrong to assume that this is somewhat less than worship.[226] Tacitus states that Augustus 'had left no small room for the worship of heaven, when he claimed himself adorned in temples and in the image of godhead by flamens and priests!'[227] Second, after receiving a letter from the Parthians, it was arranged that Augustus's name be included in their hymns as equal to the gods (Cassius Dio 51.20.1).

When sacrifices, honours, and the divine are viewed in the context of the Roman religious experience, divine emperors fit nicely into the system. This conclusion will be strengthened as we proceed. Further dis-

---

221. Friesen, *Twice Neokoros*, pp. 74-75, 147-48. Friesen's evidence is all from one provincial temple from the late first century. However, given that provincial temples were often more restrained than other expressions of the cult (see below), it seems probable that his arguments are applicable to other and earlier forms of the practice.

222. Friesen, *Twice Neokoros*, p. 150.

223. Friesen, *Twice Neokoros*, p. 150.

224. Friesen, *Twice Neokoros*, pp. 150-52.

225. Tacitus, *Annals* 11.1 (trans. Jackson, LCL).

226. See the discussion in Taylor, *Divinity*, pp. 193-94.

227. Tacitus, *Annals* 1.10 (trans. Jackson, LCL).

cussion of the diversity of cults and their development (especially under Augustus) will provide additional evidence for a divine emperor. In cultic practice, inscriptions, etc., the emperor was honoured in the same manner as the gods. This is made explicit by an inscription from Eresos: Τὸν εἴρεα καὶ ἀρχείρεα τῶν Σεβάστων καὶ τῶν ἄλλων θέων πάντων καὶ παίσαν διὰ βίω ('The priest and high priest of the Sebastoi and all of the other gods and goddesses for life').[228]

Therefore, the worship of the Roman ruler was not the final result of a fatally declining religious system. It was a natural response to absolute leadership in that period. As already stated, Rome's lack of a ruler cult in republican times was not because of its republican religious tradition. It was because they had no human figure who served as absolute ruler.

(2) *Classification of Imperial Cults.* Two types of classifications are often suggested when describing imperial cults. First, a geographical distinction is made. Second, an administrative distinction is made based on whom the cult primarily serves.

(a) *Geographic Distinctions: East, West and Italy.* When describing emperor worship, it is common to make a two- or three-way geographic distinction: (1) the Eastern provinces; (2) the Western provinces; and (3) Italy and the city of Rome. The two-way distinction is simply East versus West. The East with its tradition of ruler worship is seen as the most fruitful for worship of emperors, both living and dead. Emperor worship took root and grew rapidly, almost welcomed by the people. The West, without much tradition, is understood to have had emperor worship imposed on it by the governing authorities. It was successful, but its form is not as extreme as that of the East. Finally, it is argued that Italy and the city of Rome itself (which is seen as part of the West in the two-way distinction) had cults to deified dead emperors but did not worship living emperors. This distinction is based partially on Cassius Dio's discussion of the inauguration of some of Augustus's provincial cults.[229] To some extent this division is valid; however, the descriptions of the three areas are too simplistic and misleading to be very helpful. Imperial cults took on the flavour of their locality. This is certain. The local influences are more important than whether the cult is in the East, the West, or Italy.[230]

---

228. IGRR 4.18.

228. Cassius Dio 51.20.6-8. This passage will be discussed below under the development of emperor worship under Augustus.

230. We are fortunate to have helpful sources on these three areas. Although focusing on Asia Minor, Price's work is representative for the East (*Rituals and Power*); Fishwick's in-process work describes the West (*ICLW*). Gradel's work focuses on

Fernando Lozano has demonstrated conclusively that the distinction between Eastern *spontaneity* and Western *imposition* is false. He cites numerous examples that do not fit this paradigm. Instead, Lozano suggests that emperor worship developed throughout the empire within a larger religious and cultural transformation. Imposition and spontaneity were both involved but were not restricted to the West and East specifically. These were part of a larger process.[231]

For convenience, the three-way distinction will be maintained here, and my focus will be on the Eastern and Italian (especially Rome) expressions of emperor worship. However, the descriptions of the areas will be abandoned. I will develop my own understanding of what the cults were like.

(b) *Types of Administration: Provincial, Municipal and Private.* Although strict distinctions between types of imperial cults are not possible, three general categories of administration based on who is being served may be noted. First, *provincial* cults were imperial cults that were officially granted from Rome and served an entire province. They appear to have been initiated by the provinces but could not proceed without confirmation from Rome. Our best evidence for these cults are for the province of Asia. In the early first century only Augustus and Tiberius had lasting provincial cults initiated during their lifetimes in Asia (Gaius Caligula's ended with his death).[232] Later in the first century, the Flavian dynasty also had a provincial cult in Asia established during the reign of Domitian. Provincial cults were also built in other provinces as well including Bithynia (see Cassius Dio 51.20.6-8 discussed below with Augustus [3.3.3.1]). Also, it appears this type of temple was built in Britain and Greece (Achaia).[233]

Possibly because of their official status and connection to Rome, they seemed to have been restrained in their honours for the emperor. Most vividly, the term θεός was not used. However, beyond this, at least in the Flavian cult, the worship was the same as that of the traditional deities.[234] Both Augustus and Tiberius were included with others. Augustus and Roma were worshipped in his cults,[235] and Tiberius, Livia and the senate were worshipped in at least one provincial temple.[236]

Rome (*Emperor Worship*). All of these works are helpful beyond their areas but their concentrations must always be considered.

231. Lozano, 'Creation of Imperial Gods', pp. 1-31. As mentioned above, the author provided this article prior to publication. I do not have the specific page numbers for this article.

232. For the possibility of a cult for Nero, see below, pp. 132-33, on Nero.

233. See below in the discussion of Claudius, pp. 131-32.

234. Friesen, *Twice Neokoros*, p. 147.

235. Cassius Dio 51.20.6-8. See further discussion below.

236. Tacitus, *Annals* 4.15. See further discussion below.

In the case of Augustus and Tiberius, the historical literature provides the most extensive discussions of these types of cults, and thus it is possible to confuse provincial imperial cults with the entire phenomenon of emperor worship. There is no literary evidence for the Flavian provincial cult; however, the temple has been located and there is ample inscriptional evidence.[237]

Individual cities also could set up their own versions of emperor worship. *Municipal* cults were set up to meet the needs of the cities. These cults were widespread, and both temples and isolated altars (without a temple) were common.[238] They probably varied quite a bit and reflected local concerns.[239] They included imperial mythology and other points of connection between the imperial family and their subjects. The imperial family played a larger role in these cults.[240] Important for our interests, they were less retrained than the provincial cults in their language toward the imperial family. For example, unlike in provincial cults, θεός was commonly applied to emperors.[241] It is likely that these cults played a significant role in the life of a city.[242]

Finally, there must have been countless private cults where emperors were honoured both in various associations and in the home. Association could both contribute to and benefit from imperial participation.[243] Additionally, it is clear that emperor honours were part of household worship. In Miletos so many altars dedicated to Hadrian have been found that is has been speculated that an altar to Hadrian was in every home in the city.[244] This is later than our period, and, because altars to other emperors were not found, it is likely that these were from a special event.[245] Nevertheless, the presence of these altars makes it clear that emperor worship could easily be incorporated into family devotion.

237. For a detailed introduction to provincial cults, see Friesen, *Imperial Cults*, pp. 25-55. Concerning the West but still appropriate, see Fishwick, *ICLW* III.

238. Friesen, *Imperial Cults*, p. 65. See also the maps in Price, *Rituals and Power*, pp. xxii-xxvi.

239. Friesen, *Imperial Cults*, p. 76.

240. Friesen, *Imperial Cults*, p. 75. See the example of Aphrodisias (Friesen, *Imperial Cults*, pp. 77-95).

241. Habicht, 'Die augusteische Zeit', pp. 83-84. Habicht provides a number of examples from the East.

242. For a detailed introduction to municipal cults, see Friesen, *Imperial Cults*, pp. 56-103. Fishwick's massive discussion of imperial cults in the West plans to devote volume IV to this task.

243. Philip A. Harland, 'Honouring the Emperor or Assailing the Beast: Participation in Civic Life among Associations (Jewish, Christian and Other) in Asia Minor and the Apocalypse of John', *JSNT* 77 (2000), pp. 99-121 (111). For Ephesus specifically, see Philip A. Harland, 'Honours and Worship: Emperors, Imperial Cults and Associations at Ephesus (First to Third Centuries C.E.)', *SR* 25 (1996), pp. 319-34.

244. Friesen, *Imperial Cults*, p. 117.

245. Friesen, *Imperial Cults*, p. 117.

Although distinctions between types of imperial cults are not always clear, all are valid expressions of emperor worship. It would be an error to emphasize a certain type as more valid than others. Because of strong literary evidence, it is tempting to view provincial cults as most important. However, this would really provide an unbalanced view of the phenomenon. In fact, I would argue that provincial cults would have less influence in the lives of average Romans than other types of emperor worship. Municipal and private cults provide far more opportunities for involvement and participation than the few scattered provincial temples in the first century. One exception to this would probably be the impact of provincial cults on the cities in which they were located. These certainly would have brought many outsiders to the city and involved many locals.

c. *Roman Imperial Cults: Development in the First Century*
In this section, a brief sketch of the development of imperial cults will be presented. The main focus will be on the Julio-Claudian rulers, but it will conclude with observations about the Flavian dynasty as well. This survey will essentially cover more than one hundred years, from the end of the first century BCE to the end of the first century CE. The purpose is to continue to develop the role of the emperor in the cognitive environment of the recipients of Paul's letters.[246]

(1) *Augustus (31 BCE–14 CE).* David Cannadine has said, 'Power is like wind: we cannot see it, but we feel its force. Ceremonial is like the snow: an insubstantial pageant, soon melted into thin air.'[247] Octavian (later Augustus) understood this well. He created a position that concentrated more power in himself than any Roman before him. After defeating Antony at Actium in 31 BCE, Octavian stood as the sole leader without rival for supremacy in the Roman empire. He reigned over forty years (31/27 BCE–14 CE[248]).

It was under Octavian that official provincial imperial cults got their start. In a passage already noted above, Cassius Dio describes the establishment of the first provincial cult temples devoted to the emperor,

> Caesar [Octavian] . . . gave permission for the dedication of sacred precincts in Ephesus and in Nicaea to Rome and to Caesar, his father, whom

246. For a helpful survey of the development of imperial cults, see Friesen, *Imperial Cults*, pp. 25-53. For the Julio-Claudians, see Friesen, *Twice Neokoros*, pp. 7-27.

247. David Cannadine, "Introduction: Divine Rites of Kings', in David Cannadine and Simon R.F. Price (eds.), *Rituals of Royalty: Power and Ceremonial in Traditional Societies* (Cambridge: Cambridge University Press, 1987), p. 1.

248. The two dates for the beginning of Augustus's reign reflect his victory at Actium, when he functionally became the ruler of the empire (31 CE) and the date he was granted (confirmed in) his position by the senate (27 CE).

he named the hero Julius. These cities had at that time attained chief place in Asia and Bithynia respectively. He commanded that the Romans resident in these cities should pay honour to these two divinities; but he permitted the aliens, whom he styled Hellenes, to consecrate precincts to himself, the Asians to have theirs in Pergamum and the Bithynians theirs in Nicomedia. This practice, beginning under him, has been continued under other emperors, not only in the case of the Hellenic nations but also in that of all the others, in so far as they are subject to the Romans. For in the capital itself and in Italy generally no emperor, however worthy of renown he has been, has dared to do this; still even there various divine honours are bestowed after their death upon such emperors as have ruled uprightly, and, in facts, shrines are built to them (51.20.6-8; trans. Cary, LCL).

This event took place early in Octavian's reign (29 BCE) before he even received the name Augustus and included the goddess Roma as an object of worship as well. The inclusion of Roma is certain because of extant coins and inscriptions.[249] Cassius Dio's omission of Roma probably reveals that the goddess was not important and thus nearly forgotten. However, the inclusion of Roma fits the Augustan model of (relative) modesty.

Cassius Dio's words reveal a number of things about imperial cults. First, a distinction was made between a hero-type cult to the city of Rome and Julius Caesar for provincial Romans, cults to the living emperor in the provinces for non-Romans, and special practices for the people of Rome. Second, the cult of the city of Rome and Julius Caesar was separate from the cult of the emperor himself. It was intended to serve a specific purpose different from that of the cult for the living emperor. This cult appears not to have lasted very long. There is no other evidence of its existence.[250] Third, the provincial cults served the entire province. Fourth, these temples appear to have been initiated from the provinces themselves. Although this seems to be the best way to read Cassius Dio, there is not enough detail to know for sure. However, this is clearly the case with Tiberius, and he is claiming to be following Augustus's example (see below). Whether the inclusion of Roma was the request of the provinces or Augustus's addition is uncertain. Thus, this is not a command from Augustus. In fact, his reply reflects a measure of restraint by making the distinction between his cult and that of Julius. Only the latter was aimed at Romans.

---

249. See, e.g., RIC, *Augustus*, 505 (19–18 BCE, minted in Pergamum). The reverse of this coin includes a temple with 'ROM ET AVGVST' inscribed on the top of the temple; OGIS 470.12-13 (= IGRR 4.1611.b5-6; 2 BCE–14 CE, from Hypaepis); For date and connection to the temple, see Friesen, *Imperial Cults*, pp. 229-30 n. 7. For further discussion, see Friesen, *Imperial Cults*, pp. 27-28.

250. Friesen, *Imperial Cults*, p. 26. Although Friesen admits that there is a possible site of a double altar or temple in Ephesus for two deities, it is yet to be identified conclusively as the Julius and Roma temple (Friesen, *Imperial Cults*, p. 26).

Although this event is a foundational moment for imperial cults, it would be misleading to see it as the most important development during this period. History is not as neat as Cassius Dio suggests. Our interest is not primarily in official state religion but rather in lower-level participation in emperor worship. It is likely that the municipal and other, more localized expressions of emperor worship were more influential in daily life. This is supported by the abundant evidence of the existence of temples and altars devoted to the emperor.[251]

Also, Cassius Dio's remark that 'in the capital itself and in Italy generally no emperor, however worthy of renown he has been, has dared to do this' (trans. Cary, LCL) seems at odds with Tacitus who states, 'He [Augustus] left small room for the worship of heaven, when he claimed to be himself adored in temples and in the image of godhead by flamens and priests!' (*Annals* 1.10; trans. Jackson, LCL). Tacitus is a much harsher critic of Augustus's role in the Roman religious experience. Lily Ross Taylor argues that the diverse statements of these two historians should be read in light of the worship of Augustus's Genius.[252] In the city of Rome and throughout Italy, the emperor was not officially worshipped. Nevertheless, there is significant evidence from inscriptions of priests and temples for Augustus during his lifetime.[253] Worship was directed to his Genius and Numen,[254] and this obtained an official status in Italy.[255] This was part of the emperor's fiction that pacified resistance to his position and programme.[256] It appears to have worked. Augustus reigned successfully and established a dynasty. Even Cassius Dio over two centuries later still bought it. However, this was a semantic game that essentially meant worship of the emperor himself. Tacitus, the more astute historian, understood this.

Other developments especially under Augustus support the notion that the emperor was divine. The name 'Augustus' itself seems to imply divinity when granted to Octavian in 27 BCE.[257]

---

251. Taylor, *Divinity*, p. 205.

252. Lily Ross Taylor, 'The Worship of Augustus in Italy during his Lifetime', *TAPA* 51 (1920), pp. 116-33.

253. Taylor, "Worship of Augustus," pp. 116-17.

254. The worship of the Numen did not occur until late in Augustus's reign (Fishwick, *ICLW,* III.1, p. 5).

255. Taylor, *Divinity*, pp. 190-91.

256. There is no compelling evidence to support Manfred Clauss's claim that Augustus was an *official* state god during his lifetime ('*Deus praesens:* Der römischer Kaiser als Gott', *Klio* 78 [1996], pp. 400-433; Clauss, *Kaiser und Gott*, p. 60 [and throughout]). Although Clauss is correct in understanding the practical divinity of the emperor, his position fails to allow for the careful nuancing of Augustus's position.

257. Kenneth Scott, 'Tiberius' Refusal of the Title "Augustus"', *CP* 27 (1932), pp. 43-50.

It was under Augustus that emperor worship began. He was able to control the provincial practice to some extent, but it would be impossible to control the local expressions of the cult. As Simon Price notes, in the East, emperor worship was a means for the people to relate to their distant ruler.[258]

(2) *Tiberius (14–37 CE)*. Tiberius may have been the most conservative emperor with respect to divine honours. Nevertheless, he granted Asia its request to build a temple to the senate, his mother Livia, and himself. Like the previous temple in Asia to Augustus at Pergamum, the impetus came from the province itself. After favourable verdicts in two court cases against Roman officials in the province, in 23 CE the province voted the honours, '. . . the Asiatic cities decreed a temple to Tiberius, his mother, and the senate. Leave to build was granted' (Tacitus, *Annals* 4.15; trans. Jackson, LCL). Friesen argues that the act of the province here establishes a connection between the Asian elite and the capital (and emperor) that could be used as leverage against local Roman officials.[259]

The Asia temple was granted, but it took further discussion and debate to decide on a location. Eleven cities argued that their city would be an appropriate place for the temple. Finally, in 26 CE it was decided that the temple would be built in Smyrna (Tacitus, *Annals* 4.55).

After the granting of the Asian temple but before settling on its final location, some criticized Tiberius for permitting the temple (Tacitus, *Annals* 4.37-38). When a Spanish province made the same request of Tiberius as the Asians, he rejected the request and defended his previous decision based on the precedent of Augustus (Tacitus, *Annals* 4.37-38).[260] This decision appears to be important. With the exception of a failed attempt by Caligula to establish his own provincial cult in Asia (see below), no further provincial cult was set up during an emperor's lifetime in Asia for almost 60 years. When the temple for the cult of the Sebastoi was established in Ephesus by Domitian for the Flavian emperors, it was different in some ways from the earlier models. Despite the lack of construction of further provincial temples, the cults dedicated to Augustus and Tiberius functioned well past the close of the first century CE.[261]

---

258. Price, *Rituals and Power*.

259. Friesen, *Imperial Cults*, p. 37.

260. For the rejection of divine honours, see also Suetonius, *Tiberius* 26.1.

261. Tiberius's temple in Smyrna functioned at least into the third century (Barbara Burrell, *Neokoroi: Greek Cities and Roman Emperors* [CCS, NS 9; Leiden: E.J. Brill, 2004], p. 61). There is evidence of Augustus's temple functioning in the early second century (IGRR 4.353; see Friesen, *Twice Neokoros*, p. 15). It probably functioned much longer than this given his importance relative to Tiberius.

The role of both Augustus and Tiberius in the promoting of emperor worship was rather minimal. They did not initiate anything official but rather reacted to requests by provinces. Both permitted limited official imperial worship. As discussed above, this worship was rather restrained in both language and practice. Nevertheless, it was during the reigns of these two emperors that official imperial cults began and were firmly established. Augustus's reign was a break with the chaos of the past. But uncertainty still existed because succession was still unassured (among other things).[262] This was when the foundation of emperor worship was laid. Thus, as far as the development and innovation of the cults are concerned, this was the most innovative and important time.[263] This may seem surprising because of the nature of these two emperors compared to others who were far more focused on the outward trappings of rule (e.g. Caligula, Nero, Domitian). Indeed, such emperors did contribute to some development of imperial cults, including making the emperor's role more outward and visible.[264] Nevertheless, the most significant development in imperial cults occurred during this period.

(3) *Caligula (37–41 CE)*. During the first year of Caligula's reign, he forbade sacrifice to his Numen.[265] This was more modest than either Augustus or Tiberius. However, before long he broke with this practice and participated in excesses far beyond the relative modesty of the previous emperors. Cassius Dio states,

> Gaius ordered that a sacred precinct should be set apart for his worship at Miletus in the province of Asia. The reason he gave for choosing this city was that Diana had pre-empted Ephesus, Augustus Pergamum, and Tiberius Smyrna; but the truth of the matter was that he desired to appropriate to his own use the large and exceedingly beautiful temple which the Milesians were building to Apollo. Thereupon he went to still greater lengths, and actually built in Rome itself two temples of his own, one that had been granted him by vote of the senate and another at his own expense on the Palatine (59.28.1-2; trans. Cary, LCL).

There is no record of Asians requesting the honour of building a temple to Caligula. Rather, he ordered the temple to be constructed at Miletos.

---

262. Friesen, *Imperial Cults*, p. 148.

263. Friesen, *Imperial Cults*, pp. 148-50; see also Price, *Rituals and Power*, p. 54.

264. See Adela Yarbro Collins, *Crisis and Catharsis: The Power of the Apocalypse* (Philadelphia: Westminster Press, 1984), pp. 71-72.

265. C.J. Simpson, 'Caligula's Cult: Immolation, Immortality Intent', in Alastair Small (ed.), *Subject and Ruler: The Cult of the Ruling Power in Classical Antiquity. Papers Presented at a Conference Held in the University of Alberta on April 13–15, 1994, to Celebrate the 65th Anniversary of Duncan Fishwick* (Ann Arbor: Journal of Roman Archaeology, 1996), p. 63.

Unlike Augustan and Tiberian motives for placing their temples in strate-
gic cites, it appears that Caligula chose Miletos because that city was in
the process of building a grand temple to Apollo. Whether he intended to
replace the deity or to be enshrined together is not known.[266] In some ways,
there are similarities between this act and his desire to put his own image
in the temple in Jerusalem.[267] However, the Miletos population would have
been much less offended by the project and may have even welcomed it.
Also, we see the explicit temple placement in Rome.

In addition, he broke from the established model by using bolder language. A second piece of evidence for Caligula's provincial cult is an
inscription that refers to Caligula as θεὸν Σεβαστόν (god Sebastos).[268]
One reason for Caligula's practice may have been an expression of power
over the senate and people.[269] However, it is also likely that he, like many
Romans, believed in his role as a god. C.J. Simpson states, 'There can be
little doubt, then, that, in the popular conception at least, the ruling emperor
was equated with the gods.'[270]

Caligula's excesses and assassination resulted in the discontinuation of
his cult before his temple in Miletos was ever completed.[271]

(4) *Claudius (41–54 CE).*[272] Claudius returned to the modesty of Augustus
and Tiberius. There is no evidence of a provincial cult in Asia for Claudi-

266. See the discussion in Friesen, *Imperial Cults*, pp. 40-41, and the literature cited
there.
267. It seems uncertain whether Caligula's desire to place an image in the Jerusalem temple was part of his program for his own worship or an angry response to
Jewish actions. It probably was both and is an example of the flexibility of emperor
worship. However, the temple in Jerusalem does not appear to have been intended as a
provincial temple. For a discussion of this event, see Josephus, *Antiquities,* 18.257-309;
Jewish War, 2.184-203; Philo, *On the Embassy to Gaius;* Anthony A. Barrett, *Caligula:
The Corruption of Power* (New Haven: Yale University Press, 1989), pp. 143, 188-91;
Auffarth, 'Herrscherkult und Christuskult', 287-91 (includes implications for Caligula's
status as divine).
268. Louis Robert, 'Le culte de Caligula à Milet et la province d'Asie', *Hellenica* 7
(1949), pp. 206-38 (206).
269. Simpson, 'Caligula's Cult', pp. 70-71.
270. C.J. Simpson, 'The Cult of Emperor Gaius', *Latomus* 40 (1981), pp. 489-511
(509).
271. For a detailed survey of Caligula's cults, see Simpson, 'Emperor Gaius', pp.
489-511. For Egypt specifically, see Ernst Köberlein, *Caligula und die ägyptischen
Kulte* (Beiträge zur klassischen Philologie, 3; Meisenheim am Glan, Germany: Verlag
Anton Hain, 1962). On divine honours for Caligula, see Barrett, *Caligula,* pp. 140-53.
272. For a highly detailed study of the religious environment during the reign of
Claudius, see David Alvarez Cineira, *Die Religionspolitik des Kaisers Claudius und
die paulinische Mission* (Herders Biblische Studien, 19; Leiden, Brill, 1999). This thor-

us.[273] There were cults dedicated to him at various cities such as Philippi.[274] In the West however there is evidence of provincial cult activity. It appears that a temple was built in Britain for Claudius during his lifetime. Since Claudius was the emperor responsible for making Britain into a province, worship of him there would seem fairly natural. Tacitus mentions a temple in reference to the revolt of Boudicca in 60 CE (*Annals* 14.31), and Seneca mentions a temple in his satire of Claudius (*Pumpkinification* 8). However, Fishwick, who has probably done more work in this area than anyone, maintains that any temple would have been completed after Claudius's death.[275] There appears to be a provincial temple for Greece (Achaia) in Corinth built during the end of Claudius's reign. However, this does not appear to have been built for Claudius exclusively but rather for the entire Julio-Claudian family.[276]

(5) *Nero (54–68 CE)*. Although there was much controversy during Nero's rule because of his own actions, his reign saw little development of emperor worship. Nero had his adopted father Claudius deified (Suetonius, *Nero* 9.1).[277] However, Tacitus mentions that at one point Nero himself rejected divine honours (*Annals* 15.74).[278]

There is no specific record of a provincial cult temple being built for Nero. However, based on a piece of numismatic evidence in which Ephesus

ough study of Roman religious experience and Paul's ministry during Claudius's reign includes discussions of imperial cults (pp. 55-89) and possible connections between Christianity and imperial cults (pp. 89-97). Although Cineira mentions titles used in common of the Caesar and Christ (including κύριος) (p. 89), this is not developed in any detailed manner.

273. Friesen, *Twice Neokoros*, p. 27.

274. Chaido Koukouli-Chrysantaki, 'Colonia Iulia Augusta Philippensis', in Charalambos Bakirtzis and Helmut Koester (eds.), *Philippi at the Time of Paul and after his Death* (Harrisburg, PA: Trinity Press International, 1998), pp. 25-26.

275. Duncan Fishwick, 'Studies in Roman Imperial History', unpublished work (1977), pp. 89-91; Fishwick, *ICLW*, II.1, pp. 137-41; Fishwick, 'The Temple of Divus Claudius at Camulodunum', *Britannia* 26 (1995), pp. 11-27; Fishwick, *ICLW*, III.1, pp. 75-89.

276. See the section on Corinth below, pp. 142-44.

277. See also Seneca's satire of this incident (*The Pumpkinification of Claudius*). Although a satire, the positive portrayal of Augustus in this book suggests that Seneca may not be mocking emperor worship but only Claudius, whom he does not see as deserving of the honour (Spencer Cole, 'Elite Scepticism in the *Apocolocyntosis*: Further Qualifications', in K. Volk and G.D. Williams [eds.], *Seeing Seneca Whole: Perspectives on Philosophy, Poetry and Politics* [Leiden: Brill, 2006], pp. 175-82).

278. See also a papyrus (document #62.1-4) edited and translated in Robert K. Sherk, *The Roman Empire: Augustus to Hadrian* (Translated Documents of Greece and Rome, 6; Cambridge: Cambridge University Press, 1988), p. 103.

is called νεωκόρος (temple warden; see the following section) in 65/66 CE, Barbara Burrell suggests that there may have been plans for a provincial cult for Nero in this city.[279] She suggests that, after the failed attempt of the Ephesians to get the Tiberius provincial temple (Tacitus, *Annals* 4.55), they may have finally been granted one late in Nero's reign.[280] However, before work could progress Nero lost power and the project ceased.[281] However, this is far from certain. Ephesus was the νεωκόρος for the temple of Artemis[282] (see Acts 19.35).[283] Also, if this title is used for a city with a provincial imperial cult temple, it would be the earliest such usage by over 20 years. Steven Friesen suggests that the title is not used in an official manner for cities until the cult of the Sebastoi for the Flavian dynasty.[284] If a provincial cult was granted to Ephesus for Nero, it is lost to history. Unless further discoveries are made to validate the existence of this temple, we must proceed as if it did not exist.

Nero was fascinated with Greek culture and was identified with the New Sun.[285] Additionally, he was identified with deities such as *Agathos Daimon* (POxy 1021.8-9 [54 CE]; Alexandria) and Zeus Eleutherios (SIG³ 814.51-52 [67 CE]; Greece). However, as Miriam Griffin suggests, these actions are more likely "eastern habits" than imperial religious activities.[286] Nero probably saw himself more and more as an Eastern king than as a *princeps*.[287]

Nero's contribution to this study is more in his role as emperor (see below, *The Emperor in the Roman World*) than his contribution to imperial cults. He appreciated flattery and certainly was self-promoting. Imperial cults could be one mode for this expression; however, as we will discuss below, Nero was not restricted to this sphere of activity for the defining of himself.

279. Burrell, *Neokoroi*, pp. 60-61.

280. Burrell, *Neokoroi*, p. 61.

281. Burrell, *Neokoroi*, p. 61.

282. The numismatic evidence probably refers to Artemis's temple (Josef Keil, 'Die erste Kaiserneokorie von Ephesos', *Numismatische Zeitschrift* NF 12 [1919], pp. 115-20). In addition to rejecting a provincial temple for Nero, Keil also rejects one for Claudius.

283. Friesen sees the coin and Acts usages as "unofficial" (*Twice Neokoros*, p. 53). It is later with the temple for the Sebastoi under the Flavians that the title is an official city title (Friesen, *Twice Neokoros*, p. 57).

284. Friesen, *Twice Neokoros*, p. 50. Note Friesen's comments (p. 50 n.1) about Burrell's use of the term in her 1980 PhD dissertation, *Neokoroi: Greek Cities of the Roman East* (Harvard University, 1980), of which the work cited above is a revision.

285. Miriam T. Griffin, *Nero: The End of a Dynasty* (New Haven: Yale University Press, 1984), p. 217.

286. Griffin, *Nero*, p. 217

287. See Griffin, *Nero*, pp. 218-19.

(6) The Flavian Dynasty (69–96 CE). The death of Nero on 9 June 68 CE was followed by a civil war that saw three emperors (Galba [to 15 January 69],[288] Otho [15 January–16 April 69], Vitellius [2 January–20 December 69]) rise and fall before Vespasian finally established himself as the ruling emperor. Vespasian ruled approximately ten years (69–79) and was succeeded by his sons, Titus (79–81) and Domitian (81–96). When Domitian was assassinated at age 45 on 18 September 96, the Flavian dynasty came to an end.

Vespasian lacked any credentials by birth to be emperor. It is likely that he used anything at his disposal to legitimize his rule. Stories of him during the civil war and early reign include miracles, positive heavenly signs and so on (Suetonius, *Vespasian* 7.2-3). However, once his rule was secure such stories became rare.[289] It is likely that imperial cults served Vespasian's need for this as well. In religious matters, Vespasian essentially followed the example of Augustus.[290] This would be prudent policy. Vespasian's position needed to reach back to this founder, and through similar policies he was able to establish this connection. Early in his reign, one relevant act was to restore and complete the temple to the deified Claudius (Suetonius, *Vespasian* 9.1).

When Vespasian died (79 CE), he was deified by his son and successor, Titus. After Titus's untimely early death (81 CE), the same was done for him by his brother Domitian. It is under Domitian that a third provincial cult is added in Asia dedicated in 89–90 CE to his entire family (at least to his father, brother, himself, and probably his wife).[291] This temple differs from the Augustan and Tiberius model in at least three ways. First, it is devoted not to a single emperor but to the dynasty. Second, there are no other objects of worship such as Roma (in Pergamum with Augustus) and Livia and the senate (in Smyrna with Tiberius). Third, the term νεωκόρος (temple warden) is used for the first time in an official manner for a city that has a provincial cult.[292] Nevertheless, the modest language of these cults is maintained. For example, the living emperor Domitian is not called "god."

Despite the significant addition of the provincial cult temple in Ephesus and the new use of νεωκόρος in this context, there is little innovation in emperor worship compared to the activities under Augustus and Tiberius. Certainly it was an important tool for Vespasian to establish stable con-

---

288. The civil war actual preceded Nero's death. In March 68 CE, Vindex in Gaul appealed for help in a revolt against Nero. On 2 April, following a meeting at Carthage Nova, Galba sided with Vindex and called himself the general and representative of the senate and people of Rome. Vindex was defeated in May, but the senate proclaimed Nero an enemy of the state and, with the praetorian guard, supported Galba.

289. Scott, *Imperial Cult*, p. 17.

290. Scott, *Imperial Cult*, p. 25.

291. For a comprehensive discussion of this temple, see Friesen, *Twice Neokoros*.

292. For the significance of this, see Friesen, *Twice Neokoros*, pp. 50-59.

trol of the empire, but in many ways he was simply doing what Augustus had done a century earlier. It sometimes is suggested that abuses of imperial religion and persecution by Nero and Domitian account for the strong anti-imperial imagery of the book of Revelation.[293] However, with reference to imperial cults, we have seen that these emperors were no more offensive than others. The negative picture of Domitian is based primarily on sources such as Suetonius and Tacitus, in whose interest it was to support the present regimes through a negative portrayal of Domitian.[294] There may be some truth to the negative portrayal of Domitian's character;[295] however, it is also likely to be exaggerated. Additionally, recent scholarship has suggested that there is little evidence for a major persecution under Domitian.[296] Rather, Revelation is responding to the normal development of the imperial cults.

(7) *Summary and Observations.* This survey of imperial cult development has noticeably focused on provincial cults. This is primarily due to the nature of the literary sources. However, this should not minimize the importance of lower-level cults. Compared to other expressions of emperor worship, provincial cults were rare.[297] The provincial cult is important because this is the result of official Roman policy. As was noted above, there is not always a clear distinction between the role of a province and the role of a city in a specific location of worship. Additionally, it is important to emphasize that the provincial cults were rather restrained in their practice as a result of their official ties with Rome. Such restrictions were not present for other forms of emperor worship. Cities and individuals were free to make any positive claims for the emperor they wished.

One significant observation from this survey is that the most innovative and important developments in emperor worship occurred during the reigns of Augustus and Tiberius. Often one considers Caligula, Nero, and Domitian as emperors who abused the cult for their own purposes. The excesses of Caligula were rejected. Nero does not appear to have been overly interested in official provincial cults and did not have one. Domitian was honoured in Ephesus with a provincial cult, but this cult reflects the restrained language of previous cults of this type. Additionally, it appears to have been a cult for his entire dynasty. Although figures such as the goddess Roma or the senate

---

293. Donald L. Jones, 'Christianity and the Roman Imperial Cult', in *ANRW*, II.23.2 (Berlin: W. de Gruyter, 1980), p. 1033.

294. See also Eusebius, *Ecclesiastical History*, 3.17-20.

295. See Hamilton Moore and Philip McCormick, 'Domitian (Part i)', *IBS* 25 (2003), pp. 74-101; Hamilton Moore and Philip McCormick, 'Domitian (Part ii)', *IBS* 25 (2003), pp. 121-45.

296. Collins, *Crisis and Catharsis*, pp. 69-73.

297. Friesen, *Imperial Cults*, p. 54.

are missing, it does not appear to have been intended as a temple devoted to Domitian alone. There is no evidence that he was attempting anything like Caligula had tried. Essentially, emperor worship had been practised as normal during his reign.

This is important for our study because it demands that we broaden our cognitive environment beyond the impact of emperor worship itself. There are many aspects of emperors that are not directly associated with emperor worship. Further, although there is some conceptual overlap, the emperor as κύριος does not appear to be a significant factor in the cults. Emperor worship plays an important role in this study. It helps to define the role of the emperor in the cognitive environment of the first century. However, other facts also are present.

4. The Emperor in the Roman World

The bulk of this chapter has been devoted to a description of relevant aspects of imperial cults for this topic. However, the emperor's role as a recipient of divine honours is only part of his presence in the cognitive environment. We are in complete agreement with Peter Oakes, who, after citing Ernst Lohmeyer's contrast between Jesus the Christ cult with the emperor and the imperial cult, states,

> Why need Lohmeyer's final sentence have the term 'cult' in it? The Emperor was not σωτήρ or κύριος simply in the Emperor-cult: he was these things in the life of the whole Empire. . . . If Christ relativises the Emperor in every way, then this clearly does undermine the Emperor-cult, but it also has far wider ramifications for society and politics—and hence for NT study.[298]

Imperial cults are only one (albeit important) aspect of the emperor in the Roman world. Fergus Millar has produced a massive study looking at many of the ways in which the emperor functioned in the Roman empire. Little of this work is devoted to the role that we would consider religious today.[299]

The purpose of this section is to broaden our picture of the emperor. We will not provide a comprehensive view of his role in the empire (see Millar for this). Our focus will be on relevant aspects of his presence that will contribute to this study. We will conclude this section with a brief look at Nero, the emperor in power under whom most of Paul's letters were written.

When one considers the rule of Augustus and later emperors, one is impressed with the shear amount of direct evidence pointing to the emperor

---

298. Oakes, *Philippians*, p. 130 (discussing a citation from Ernst Lohmeyer, *Christkult und Kaiserkult* [Tübingen: J.C.B. Mohr (Paul Siebeck), 1919], p. 28).

299. Millar, *Emperor*.

encountered in the daily lives of Romans. The emperor was everywhere. Statues filled important places. Buildings (including emperor-worship facilities) were devoted to the emperor. Important civic projects were sponsored by the emperor. Coins changed hands and with them pictures and messages of the emperor and his deeds.[300] The literature of the period often carried messages of the greatness of the emperor and his rule (e.g. Virgil, Horace).[301] Additionally, the ruler even made it into the private sphere. Under Augustus, people were instructed to pour out libations to the emperor's Genius.[302]

The physical and verbal messages were not merely random images arbitrarily thrown at the public. But, as Paul Zanker has shown, there was a conscious effort from the imperial house to present specific messages for common consumption.[303] The emperor was a great benevolent ruler whose existence was tied to the welfare of the everyone.

A well-known example of the imperial message is the so-called calendar inscription that was posted throughout Asia. The best copy comes from the city of Priene, not far from Ephesus,

> [30] Decree of the Greek Assembly in the province of Asia, on motion of the High Priest Apolionios, son of Menophilos, of Aizanoi- **WHEREAS** Providence that orders all our lives has in her display of concern and generosity in our behalf adorned our lives with the highest good: **Augustus**, whom she has filled with arete for the benefit of humanity, [35] and has in her beneficence granted us and those who will come after us [a Savior (σωτῆρα)] who has made war to cease and who shall put everything [in peaceful] order; and whereas Caesar, [when he was manifest], transcended the expectations of [all who had anticipated the good news], not only by surpassing the benefits conferred by his predecessors but by leaving no expectation of surpassing him to those who would come after him, [40] with the result that the birthday of our God (τοῦ θεοῦ) signalled the beginning of Good News (εὐαγγελί[ων]) for the world because of him; . . . [47] . . . (proconsul Paul Fabius Maximus) has discovered a way to honor Augustus that was hitherto unknown among the Greeks, namely to reckon time from the date of his nativity; therefore, with the blessings of Good Fortune and for their own welfare, [50] the Greeks in Asia **Decreed** that the New Year begin for all the cities on September 23, which is the birth-

---

300. See Larry J. Kreitzer, *Striking New Images: Roman Imperial Coinage and the New Testament World* (JSNTSup, 134; Sheffield: Sheffield Academic Press, 1996).

301. For a discussion of imperial ideology in Virgil's *Aeneid*, see John Dominic Crossan, 'Roman Imperial Theology', in Richard A. Horsley (ed.), *In the Shadow of Empire: Reclaiming the Bible as a History of Faithful Resistance* (Louisville, KY: Westminster/John Knox Press, 2008), pp. 59-73 (62-63).

302. See Cassius Dio 51.19.7. How common this practice was and how long it lasted are unknown.

303. Paul Zanker, *The Power of Images in the Age of Augustus* (trans. Alan Shapiro; Ann Arbor: University of Michigan Press, 1988).

day of Augustus; and, to ensure that the dates coincide in every city, all documents are to carry both the Roman and the Greek date, and the first month shall, in accordance with the decree, be observed as the Month of Caesar, [55] beginning with 23 September, the birthday of Caesar.[304]

This inscription illustrates the prominent place of the emperor in official Roman policy, describing the results of a contest to see who could think up the highest possible honour for Augustus. Lofty language such as 'god', 'saviour' and 'good news' ('gospel') describe the emperor. The honour chosen as the best is essentially to organize the calendar around the emperor. Thus, the goal is to make the emperor central to even the notion of time in the Roman experience.

As already noted, the Roman system relied heavily on patronage. Essential to this system is *reciprocity*. We have seen that, if one accepts a gift, one is bound to repay it in some way. Granting honours also implied a response. If one did not wish to accept the responsibility associated with the honour, it was rejected. This probably accounts for some of the rejection of honours by various emperors.[305]

At the top of the patronage system was the emperor. He was the benefactor and patron of the empire.[306] This is partially reflected in the imperial title 'father of the country'.[307] The importance of the benefactor role for the emperor in the Roman world is most vividly seen in Augustus's *Res Gestae*, in which he spends much time discussing all the benefits he has given to the Roman people. The emperor was the benefactor of all Romans including the lowest classes.[308] He was supposed to be a protector, even a saviour.[309] The emperor was not the only benefactor, but he was the top benefactor. His activities in this role could help enable others to be benefactors on smaller scales.[310]

---

304. IPriene 105.30-56 = OGIS 458.30-56; trans. Frederick W. Danker, *Benefactor: Epigraphic Study of a Graeco-Roman and New Testament Semantic Field* (St Louis: Clayton Publishing House, 1982), p. 217 (emphasis added by Danker). For Danker's complete translation and discussion of this inscription, see pp. 215-22.

305. See, e.g., Suetonius, *Augustus* 52.

306. James Harrison suggests that some literature of the time describes the emperor as a 'cosmic benefactor', especially Augustus and Nero (Harrison, *Paul and the Imperial Authorities*, pp. 123-37). See also Harrison's discussion of the role of the 'dishonoured benefactor' in this context as well (pp. 165-99).

307. For Augustus this title was granted in 2 BCE (Suetonius, *Augustus* 58). See also Pliny's description of Trajan (*Panegyricus* 21).

308. Garnsey and Saller, *Roman Empire*, pp. 149-50; Miriam T. Griffin, 'Urbs Roma, Plebs and Princeps', in Loveday Alexander (ed.), *Images of Empire* (Sheffield: JSOT Press, 1991), pp. 19-46.

309. See Jean Béranger, *Recherches sur l'aspect idéologique du Principat* (SBAlt, 6; Basel: Reinhardt, 1953), pp. 252-78.

310. Garnsey and Saller, *Roman Empire*, p. 150.

One other factor is worth exploring before proceeding. The emperor and imperial policy did not achieve their place in society by accident or in a random manner. Rather, imperial propaganda permeated all aspects of society. Not only was it present, but it successfully claimed the allegiance of the people. The Priene calendar inscription cited above is but one example. Clifford Ando has demonstrated in detail the effectiveness of the imperial propaganda machine.[311] Following the lead of Edward Gibbons, Ando is not asking the question, Why did the Roman empire fail? Rather, he wishes to answer, Why did the Roman empire last so long?[312] This question is important; the Roman empire was a massive collection of peoples with every imaginable difference. The answer pursued by Ando is of significance to this study. Four of his arguments, all part of imperial propaganda, are worth noting. First, Rome was able to persuade people of its legitimacy to rule. Ando states, 'Acquiescence and, ultimately, loyalty to Rome thus required recognition that the Roman construction of society, in relations between provinces, cities, individuals, emperors and empire, adequately mapped the collective value commitments of its residents.'[313] By getting the people to believe that Rome's rule was legitimate, the ability for Rome to 'control' its people was made much easier. If Roman rule is assumed, challenges to the emperor and his rule are generally seen as counter to what is natural. Thus, at some point Rome began to rule mainly through its subjects' good will, not through coercion.[314] Ando acknowledges that this view was not unanimous.[315] Rome preferred to rule through faithful locals.[316] However, unanimity is not demanded. Rome needs only to be seen as legitimate as the assumed main position in the cognitive environment of the empire. Legitimacy was achieved in many ways. For emperors, a link to both tradition[317] and past emperors was important.[318] Second, the emperor and his empire were able to provide stability and peace to the people of which adoption and secure succession were a part.[319] Third, people felt a part of the empire through Rome's policy that helped make its subjects *Roman*.[320] Finally, in part as a result of the policy, Rome was able to secure the loyalty (often through what

311. Clifford Ando, *Imperial Ideology and Provincial Loyalty in the Roman Empire* (Classics and Contemporary Thought, 6; Berkeley: University of California Press, 2000).

312. Ando, *Imperial Ideology*, pp. 1-2.

313. Ando, *Imperial Ideology*, p. 5.

314. Ando, *Imperial Ideology*, p. 19.

315. Ando, *Imperial Ideology*, p. 19.

316. Ando, *Imperial Ideology*, pp. 362-68.

317. Ando, *Imperial Ideology*, pp. 29-33.

318. Ando, *Imperial Ideology*, pp. 36-39.

319. Ando, *Imperial Ideology*, pp. 34-35.

320. Ando, *Imperial Ideology*, pp. 49-70.

Ando calls 'consensus') of most of its subjects.[321] Of course, the role of a massive imperial propaganda campaign helped cement this strategy. Rome devoted significant resources to communicating with its people.[322] Imperial cults function within this sphere to contribute to the message of loyalty.[323]

It is interesting to note that Ando's treatment of this subject and his use of terms such as 'consensus' suggest that the Romans took an approach to their rule in some ways similar to my approach in this book. The Romans were attempting to construct a cognitive environment in which they could control both the content and their subjects. This study is attempting to reconstruct that cognitive environment in order to understand how Paul's words would be received in that context.[324]

In the next chapter we will discuss the term κύριος in detail. It is important to recognize that roles of *lordship* are much wider than spheres of activity that we today consider religious. Lordship covers all aspects of life.

Before concluding this section, we will briefly consider the reign of Nero. It is often suggested that Nero's reign can be divided into two segments: positive and negative. The positive or responsible reign is approximately the first half, in which Seneca and Burrus essentially ruled for the young emperor. During the second half of his reign these men lost influence and finally died (Burrus in 62 and Seneca in 65). Without the advice and restraint of these men, Nero reigned as a tyrant. A source for this common assumption is a saying attributed to the emperor Trajan in which he suggests that the first five years of Nero's reign were the best of any emperor. However, this statement is not without difficulty, and it is debated just *how positive* Nero's first part of his reign was.[325]

When one looks at the reign of Nero, there seems to be a relatively positive rule in the beginning. However, more important for our purpose than how the empire was run is the character of Nero and whether he was promoted in such a way that can be identified as lordly.

First, when one considers the ancient sources, one finds that they describe Nero negatively throughout his reign. For example, Cassius Dio states of Nero in 55 CE,

---

321. Ando, *Imperial Ideology*, p. 5; Ando's development of this is complex (pp. 131-74). Here I am mainly concerned with the more general result of loyalty and the particulars of how it was gained.

322. Ando, *Imperial Ideology*, pp. 73-272.

323. Ando, *Imperial Ideology*, pp. 385-98.

324. Concerning the role of the emperor and imperial ideology explicitly with reference to Paul, see Harrison, *Paul and the Imperial Authorities*, pp. 47-323.

325. See J.G.C. Anderson, 'Trajan on the Quinquennium Neronis', *JRS* 1 (1911), pp. 173-78; F. Haverfield, 'Note on the Above by Prof. F. Haverfield', *JRS* 1 (1911), pp. 178-79.

He indulged in many licentious deeds both at home and throughout the city, by night and by day alike, though he made some attempt at conceal-ment. . . . And Nero not only failed to restrain them [troublemakers], even by words, but actually incited them the more; for he delighted in their behaviour and used to be secretly conveyed in a litter into the theatre, where, unseen by the rest, he could watch what was going on. (61.1-2; trans. Cary, LCL).

Second, and most important, is how Nero was portrayed throughout his reign. It was in the interest of the empire (no matter who was running it) to have Nero perceived as no less than his predecessors. In fact, at the begin-ning of his reign he was declared *Agathos Daimon* in Alexandria (POxy 1021.8-9)[326]

Thus, no matter who was in charge in Rome, Nero was the emperor. He was the subject of the imperial propaganda. He was the figure who was larger than life throughout his reign.[327]

5. *Cities*

There are many aspects of Roman life that were somewhat uniform through-out the empire. A measure of peace and stability provided inhabitants with opportunities to participate in various activities and to advance socially in their communities. Of course, the communities also varied widely. Cities with the rich Greek tradition of the East were very different from western cities that had their own histories. Also, among other potential differences, issues of size, primary type of commerce (e.g. agriculture, shipping port, etc.), relationship to Rome (colony, non-colony, etc.), and population com-position all make various cities somewhat unique. The purpose of this chap-ter's final section is to provide further content for the cognitive environ-ment through an understanding of city life. The complexity of this subject demands that we focus only on those aspects that contribute information that will help determine the existence of a polemic. First, it will highlight certain aspects of the particular cities to which some of Paul's letters were directed. Passages that will be looked at in Chapter 5 dictate that Rome, Corinth, Ephesus and Philippi will be described. Second, the more general subject of city rivalry will be addressed.

326. For the significance of this title, see Deissmann, *Light from the Ancient East*, p. 345 n. 4.

327. On Nero, see Griffin, *Nero*; Edward Champlin, *Nero* (Cambridge, MA: Harvard University Press, 2003); Jürgen Malitz, *Nero* (trans. Allison Brown; Malden, MA: Blackwell, 2005).

a. *Rome*

The city of Rome is different from all of the other cities described in this section. First, as the capital, it was not involved in rivalries with other cities for attention and benefits. Second, its devotion to the living emperor was more restrained than the Greek East. Third, it had a republican (and anti-monarchy) history that made it reluctant to acknowledge (at least explicitly) a supreme ruler. These are all aspects of other cities that provide fertile soil for very elevated language about the emperor.

However, Rome did share a number of things with the entire empire. First, it was as much an object of imperial messages of propaganda as anywhere. Second, although the honour of the living emperor was restrained, this was generally an official policy. The common people could do as they pleased (including worshipping the emperor).

Additionally, Rome had certain unique features that actually enhanced the emperor's presence. First, the official deified emperors were all honoured there. Of course this happened throughout the empire, but here is where the official worship began. It was from Rome that instruction was sent concerning this and other matters. Second, this is the only place that most emperors were consistently physically present. They were at shows, feasts and the like. Their bodyguards were probably visible. Where most of the empire relied on statues and coins for their visual picture of the emperor, the people of the city could see him in person. Of course, this could be negative if the ruler did not act in a dignified manner. Third, the emperor's role as benefactor was very evident in Rome. He often provided food, games and other benefits for the city.[328]

One clarification is in order. We do not intend to suggest too uniform a view of the city (this is true of all the cities discussed below as well). It is likely that groups such as Jews, Christians and others would see things differently.[329] However, much of this difference would be in their subjective values and opinions of the city. Our main interest here is in what Romans would be exposed to. Our concern is not in what they thought about what they were exposed to. There is some measure of consistency in the former.

b. *Corinth*

In the introduction to Ross Saunders's brief essay 'Paul and the Imperial Cult', the author describes a discussion he had with Charles Williams III, the director of the US archaeologists in Corinth. Saunders states, '[Williams] told me he believed that Paul's greatest enemy in Corinth was the

---

328. See Millar, *Emperor*, pp. 368-75. Also relevant is Gradel, *Emperor Worship*.

329. See Peter Oakes, 'Christian Attitudes to Rome at the Time of Paul's Letter', *RevExp* 100 (2003), pp. 103-11.

Imperial Cult.'[330] The validity of this statement is difficult to prove conclusively; however, the emperor and imperial cults were a significant part of city life.

In the classical period, Corinth was an important Greek city. However, after leading an uprising of Greek cities against Rome, it was sacked, the men were killed and women and children were sold into slavery. Corinth essentially ceased to function as a Greek city. In 44 BCE the city was refounded by Julius Caesar as a Roman colony, thus establishing important ties to both Rome and Caesar.

The city was successful and served as the capital of the province of Achaia during Paul's time.[331] It had a rich religious climate including temples to Apollo, Asklepius, Demeter and Sarapis.[332] In Paul's time there was a temple to Aphrodite, but common notions of excessive sexual activity including over a thousand temple prostitutes (based on Strabo's work) are both anachronistic and extremely excessive.[333] Within this environment was a

---

330. Ross Saunders, 'Paul and the Imperial Cult', in Stanley E. Porter (ed.), *Paul and His Opponents* (Pauline Studies, 2; Leiden: E.J. Brill, 2005), pp. 227-37 (specifically, p. 227). Saunders considers 64 CE the important year of the beginning of imperial cult influence for the growth of Christianity. Saunders suggests that it was during this year that Christianity lost its 'imagined protection' as a Jewish sect in the persecution of Nero (p. 227). However, the imperial cult was likely very important earlier. First, Nero's persecution was probably restricted to Rome. Thus, this date is probably of little relevance in Corinth. Additionally, it seems difficult to see this as the key year for the distinction between Christian and Jew in Rome let alone throughout the empire (where this distinction may have broken down at different times). Second, elsewhere in Saunders's article he treats imperial cults as important during the writing of letters earlier than 64 CE (e.g. Corinth; pp. 233-34).

331. On the history of the city, see James Wiseman, 'Corinth and Rome I: 228 B.C.–A.D. 267', in *ANRW,* II.7.1 (Berlin: W. de Gruyter, 1979), pp. 438-548; G.D.R. Sanders, 'Urban Corinth: An Introduction', in Daniel N. Schowalter and Steven J. Friesen (eds.), *Urban Religion in Roman Corinth: Interdisciplinary Approaches* (HTS, 53. Cambridge, MA: Harvard University Press, 2005), pp. 11-24; Donald Engels, *Roman Corinth: An Alternate Model for the Classical City* (Chicago: University of Chicago Press, 1990); Henry S. Robinson, *Corinth: A Brief History of the City and a Guide to the Excavations* (Athens: American School of Classical Studies, 1964) (very brief with a focus on archaeology). Also, for a discussion of relevant ancient texts and archaeology, see Murphy-O'Connor, *St Paul's Corinth.*

332. See Nancy Bookidis, 'Religion in Corinth: 146 B.C.E. to 100 C.E.', in Daniel N. Schowalter and Steven J. Friesen (eds.), *Urban Religion in Roman Corinth: Interdisciplinary Approaches* (HTS, 53. Cambridge, MA: Harvard University Press, 2005), pp. 141-64; John Fotopoulos, *Food Offered to Idols in Roman Corinth: A Social-Rhetorical Reconsideration of 1 Corinthians 8:1–11:1* (WUNT, 2.151; Tübingen: Mohr Siebeck, 2003), pp. 49-155.

333. Strabo, *Geography* 8.6.20c. Strabo, who wrote in the late first century BCE, is referring to pre-146 BCE Corinth. On his visit in 29 BCE, there was only a small temple

temple dedicated to Octavia or, more likely, the imperial family (temple E).[334] This temple is in a prominent location in the city, which emphasizes its importance. It may have been built near the end of the reign Claudius (approximately 54 CE),[335] in which case it would have been a new and significant addition to the landscape of the city. It is possible that this was a provincial-type cult such as we have seen in Asia (Pergamum and Smyrna).[336]

Although there has been some debate over the identification of the temple, what is clear is that imperial religion played a prominent role in the city. Based on inscriptions with references to priesthood (20 of 31 refer to priests of imperial religion), Donald Engels describes the Corinthian upper class's participation in the cult as 'devotion' or 'obsession'.[337] Given the nature of a Roman colony, the importance of emperors in its recent history, the significant imperial temple, and the prominent role of emperor worship, it seems clear that the emperor would hold a prominent place in the cognitive environment of Corinth at the time of Paul.

c. *Ephesus (and Asia Minor)*

Much of the above discussion has been focused on Asia Minor and specifically Ephesus. There were official provincial cults established for Augustus (Pergamum) and Tiberius (Smyrna) that were functioning during the ministry of Paul. Although a provincial cult temple for an emperor was unlikely in Ephesus before the Flavian dynasty, Augustus did establish a cult for

to the goddess (8.6.21b). Additionally, there appears to be no evidence to support these claims for the earlier city. On this issue, see Murphy-O'Connor, *St Paul's Corinth*, pp. 55-57 (see also pp. 144-47 on Athenaeus's similar but later account); John R. Lanci, 'The Stones Don't Speak and the Texts Tell Lies: Sacred Sex at Corinth', in Daniel N. Schowalter and Steven J. Friesen (eds.), *Urban Religion in Roman Corinth: Interdisciplinary Approaches* (HTS, 53. Cambridge, MA: Harvard University Press, 2005), pp. 205-20; DeMaris, 'Cults', pp. 73-91.

334. This identification is debated but seems to be the best option. See Charles K. Williams II, 'A Re-Evaluation of Temple E and the West End of the Forum of Corinth', in Susan Walker and Averil Cameron (eds.), *The Greek Renaissance in the Roman Empire: Papers from the Tenth British Museum Classical Colloquium* (London: University of London Institute for Classical Studies, 1989), pp. 156-62. See also Engels, *Roman Corinth*, pp. 101-102; Winter, *After Paul Left Corinth*, pp. 271-80.

335. Mark T. Finney, 'Christ Crucified and the Inversion of Roman Imperial Ideology in 1 Corinthians', *BTB* 35 (2005), pp. 20-33 (26).

336. Antony J.S. Spawforth, 'Corinth, Argos and the Imperial Cult: Pseudo-Julian, *Letters* 198', *Hesperia* 63 (1994), pp. 211-32; with a revised extract, Spawforth, 'The Achaean Federal Cult Part I: Pseudo-Julian, Letters 198', *TynBul* 46 (1995), pp. 151-68. See also Bruce W. Winter, "The Achaean Federal Imperial Cult II: The Corinthian Church," *TynBul* 46 (1995), pp. 168-78 (this builds off of the previous article).

337. Engels, *Roman Corinth*, p. 102.

Julius Caesar at Ephesus. Emperor worship was prevalent throughout the region.[338]

Ephesus was a city of great importance during the first century. It had a distinguished history (whether myth or fact)[339] and was well known for its temple of the goddess Artemis.[340] The prominence of Ephesus in the region and the strong imperial presence both in the city specifically and in the region generally suggest that the emperor would have been a significant part of the cognitive environment of the first-century inhabitants and visitors of the region.[341]

The Flavian temple for the cult of the Sebastoi was dedicated in 89–90 CE, so it is too late to have been part of the cognitive environment of Paul and his original readers. However, we acknowledge that many consider Ephesians to be post-Pauline. If this book was written late in the first century, this temple would have been a significant part of the readers' cognitive environment.[342] Additionally, the temple would not have been awarded unless the city had been favoured by Rome. Such favour must be acquired over time. This further supports the claims above about the imperial presence during the middle of the first century CE.

d. *Philippi*

Philippi, like Corinth, was a Roman colony. Founded originally by Trasians as Krenides in 360 BCE, it became part of Philip II's kingdom and was renamed Philippi in 356 BCE. It came under Roman control in 148 BCE and was the site of the decisive battle in which Octavian and Antony defeated Brutus and Cassius (42 BCE). It was this event that made it an important city

338. Price, *Rituals and Power*. For Ephesus specifically, see Paul Trebilco, *The Early Christians in Ephesus from Paul to Ignatius* (WUNT, 166; Tübingen: Mohr Siebeck, 2004), pp. 31-37.

339. Peter Scherrer, 'The City of Ephesos from the Roman Period to Late Antiquity', in Helmut Koester (ed.), *Ephesos: Metropolis of Asia: An Interdisciplinary Approach to its Archaeology, Religion, and Culture* (ed. Helmut Koester; HTS, 41. Valley Forge, PA: Trinity Press International, 1995), pp. 1-25; Trebilco, *Early Christians*, pp. 11-18; Guy Rogers, *The Sacred Identity of Ephesos: Foundation Myths of a Roman City* (London: Routledge, 1991).

340. Lily Ross Taylor, 'Artemis of Ephesus', in F.J. Foakes Jackson and Kirsopp Lake (eds.), *The Beginnings of Christianity*. Part I. *The Acts of the Apostles*. V (London: Macmillan, 1933), pp. 251-56; Trebilco, *Early Christians*, pp. 22-30.

341. For a discussion of Eph. 2.11-22 and the Roman peace, see Eberhard Faust, *Pax Christi et Pax Caesaris: Religionsgeschichtliche, traditionsgeschichtliche und sozialsgeschichtliche Studien zum Epheserbrief* (NTOA, 24; Göttingen: Vandenhoeck & Ruprecht, 1993).

342. See above, pp. 133-35 (*The Flavian Dynasty*). On the early second century (specifically Trajan), see Richard Oster, 'Christianity and Emperor Veneration in Ephesus: Iconography of a Conflict', *ResQ* 25 (1982), pp. 143-49.

for Rome. After this battle the victors settled veterans there and made it into a Roman colony.[343]

However, unlike Corinth, Philippi was much smaller (approximately twenty thousand inhabitants), primarily agricultural, and had a strong Roman presence.[344] Approximately one-third of the city and one-third of the community founded by Paul were probably Romans.[345] Peter Oakes suggests, 'No other city in which Paul founded a church is likely to have had this many Romans.'[346] In addition to many of the traditional Greek and Roman cults, Philippi had important cults dedicated to Augustus and Livia as well as to Claudius.[347] The imperial temples were erected in important places in the city.[348] The Roman presence in Philippi may have somewhat tempered the worship of the living emperor;[349] however, as already noted, even if it was comparable to Italy and Rome, as in those cities, emperor worship was likely to have been practised. For the issues raised in this work, what may be more important is the commitment of the city to imperial ideology. Oakes suggests that this is 'unquestioned'.[350] Nevertheless, a measure of caution is necessary. Oakes also notes that even though the imperial cult temple was in an important place, the extant inscriptions collected in Pilhofer's collection reveal only minor influence.[351]

---

343. Koukouli-Chrysantaki, 'Colonia', pp. 5-8. For a detailed history of the city, see Paul Collart, *Philippes, ville de Macédoine: Depuis ses origines jusqu'à la fin de l'époque romaine* (2 vols.; Travaux et Mémoires, 5; Paris: Ecole Française d'Athènes, 1937) (volume II is a helpful collection of loose plates and maps). For a discussion of Macedonia, especially Philippi and Thessalonica, including their relationship to Rome, see Ekaterini Tsalampouni [Αικατερινη Τσαλαμπουνη], *Η Μακεδονια στην Εποχη της Καινης Διαθηκης* [Macedonia during the Period of the New Testament] (Βιβλικη Βιβλιοθηκη, 23; Thessaloniki: Pournaras Press, 2002).

344. Oakes, *Philippians*, pp. 71-76.

345. Oakes, *Philippians*, p. 76.

346. Oakes, *Philippians*, p. 76.

347. Koukouli-Chrysantaki, 'Colonia', pp. 25-26. For more on imperial cults in Philippi, see Lukas Bormann, *Philippi: Stadt und Christengemeinde zur Zeit des Paulus* (NovTSup, 78; Leiden: E.J. Brill, 1995), pp. 32-67; and Joseph H. Hellerman, *Reconstructing Honor in Roman Philippi: Carmen Christi as Cursus Pudorum* (SNTSMS, 132; Cambridge: Cambridge University Press, 2005), pp. 80-87.

348. M. Séve and P. Weber, 'Un monument honorifique au forum de Philippes', *BCH* 112 (1988), pp. 467-79.

349. Hellerman, *Reconstructing Honor*, p. 188 n. 65.

350. Oakes, 'Re-mapping the Universe', p. 308.

351. Oakes, 'Re-mapping the Universe', p. 313. The inscriptions are found in Peter Pilhofer, *Philippi. II. Katalog der Inschriften von Philippi* (WUNT, 119; Tübingen: Mohr Siebeck, 2000) Since Oakes's article was published, a second edition of Pilhofer has been made available (2009).

e. *City Rivalries*

As with individuals, cities also desire recognition and status in relation to others. Rivalry is often a contributing factor in wars. In the Greek East, this was true of the Peloponnesian War, in which Sparta defeated Athens after a long, drawn-out conflict. Rivalry also contributed to the constant warfare between city-states in Greece before Philip of Macedonia established his rule over the region. When the Romans exerted their control over the area, city rivalries continued, but both the nature of the conflicts and the means of settling them changed.

The city of Rome, as capital and seat of power, served as a great benefactor; its relationship to other cities was similar to benefactors over their supporters or even as to the emperor over all people. As the social status of individuals may be dependent on service, the same is true for the position of cities among their peers. Cities that could attain honours from Rome would be set apart from other cities. The granting of imperial buildings and other imperial activities would provide prestige as well as possible economic benefits. Thus, where in the past, rivalries might be for land and might be settled through war, now they would be fought for imperial favour and would be settled by Rome.

City rivalries were common.[352] Here we will recall one conflict already introduced above. In the cases of granting provincial cults, Tiberius permitted Asia the right to erect a temple to the senate, his mother, and himself (Tacitus, *Annals* 4.15). This resulted in rivalries among eleven cities in these provinces for the right to have the temple in their cities (Tacitus, *Annals* 4.55). The benefits of having such a temple were great. It gave the city a specific position among its peers. As inscriptions from the cult of the Sebastoi in Ephesus reveal, other cities came to Ephesus and contributed to the temple. The cities attempted to use language that would minimize the importance of Ephesus.[353] However, this strategy was not successful.[354] This temple was larger than an ordinary city temple.

Thus, under Roman domination, cities competed for Roman attention. With Roman recognition came great benefits. This atmosphere would certainly affect the way the people of a city would view the emperor and view others who did not share their same goals.

f. *Further Considerations, Summary and Implications*

In order to determine whether a polemic is possible in certain Pauline letters, three further factors must be briefly considered as we reconstruct the

---

352. Although most are later than our period, see the discussions in Burrell, *Neokoroi*, pp. 46, 58, 75, (and throughout).

353. Friesen, *Twice Neokoros*, pp. 39-40.

354. Friesen, *Imperial Cults*, pp. 47-50.

cognitive environment of the period. First, the relationship between Rome and other cities of the empire was one of subordination. Rome had the power to grant or take away status, economic benefits, and so on. Second, the cities' relationships to Rome and to each other resulted in rivalries that could be settled only by Rome. This led to attempts to please Rome. One important aspect of a city's plan to find favour in Rome's eyes would have been through honouring the emperor. The presence of important imperial buildings and rituals would draw the attention of Rome as well as of surrounding cities. Finally, each city had its own unique expression of its relationship to Rome.

We have seen that, although different, the cities discussed here all shared a strong imperial presence. The emperor's presence was prevalent in many ways and in many facets of daily life. Whether through history, temples, coins or other imperial propaganda, the emperor made his mark and could not be avoided. Given what could be gained, cities also competed for imperial recognition and the benefits that could come from such attention. Thus, the imperial message was strong, and many eagerly accepted it for a connection to Rome and the potential advantages that could be gained from this relationship.

This situation contributes to a cognitive environment that was highly focused on the emperor, that would value participation in imperial ritual and that would pursue honouring of the emperor in as many ways as possible. In such a climate, it would even be likely that local officials might go beyond Rome's own desires in this area.

6. Conclusion

This chapter has served to re-create some of the important aspects of the cognitive environment relevant to understanding whether a polemic was likely to be heard in certain passages in Paul. Much discussion was devoted to imperial cults and their role in the empire. However, these alone are really part of a larger picture, namely that of the role and relationship of the Roman emperor to his subjects. Therefore, further discussion was devoted to the Roman emperor himself. Finally, a brief discussion of the cities from which Pauline passages will be discussed was included to bring the more general empire-wide discussion into the more specific.

The results of this discussion demand a conclusion that the living emperor was a prominent part of the cognitive environment of the first readers of Paul's letters. Despite the minimal direct contact the people had with the emperor, he nevertheless loomed large. Rituals devoted to him, building and art made to honour him and propaganda created to praise him all contributed to his unique position in the lives of the people he ruled.

Chapter 4

KYRIOS IN THE FIRST CENTURY:
MEANING, REFERENTS AND RANGE OF USAGE

This project has thus far demonstrated that the emperor and emperor worship were prominent in the contextual environment that the readers of Paul's
letters shared. There was overwhelming evidence for this conclusion. However, although essential to this work, a vital and growing imperial presence
does not demand that Paul's use of κύριος was ever polemical. This task
will demand further support based on the analysis of the meaning and use
of the term itself, an understanding of the roles of the possible referents of
the term with those using it, and relevant aspects of the nature of Paul's
message itself. It is to these tasks that I now turn. The present chapter will
provide a basic understanding of the meaning of κύριος. In addition to the
basic *meaning* of the term, this chapter will describe the range of meaning
and the potential referents associated with the term. Additionally, important
issues that contribute to the study will be highlighted. Conclusions will provide a starting point for understanding the specific usage being suggested in
this work. As Chapter 3 provided the foundational contextual information
to reconstruct the cognitive environment in which a polemic against Caesar
may have been active, this chapter will provide the foundational linguistic
information for this same task. It will provide the broad meaning of κύριος
available to authors and familiar to readers in the first century. It will look
in a general manner at Pauline usage. This will be similar to traditional
approaches such as lexical studies. Conclusions from this approach will be
somewhat limited. The information provided by this means cannot in itself
prove or disprove a polemic. I suggest that the twenty-first-century reader
is too far removed linguistically and culturally from the initial readers for
this approach in itself to determine the existence of a polemic. A polemical usage may be quite subtle and even implicit. Discovery of a polemic
depends more on an understanding of inference and associations of possible
referents than on solid explicit semantic analysis. Further, more complex
linguistic work in conjunction with the non-linguistic contextual reconstructed cognitive environment will be necessary to determine whether a
polemic was available and used by Paul. This will occur in Chapter 5.

1. *Towards the Meaning of* Κύριος *in the First Century: Further Methodological Clarification*

The literature on κύριος, both linguistic and theological, is immense. Although it is difficult to separate precisely the linguistic from the theological, this chapter will focus on the linguistic aspects of the term. This should be the starting point for any theological discussion. The purpose here cannot be a comprehensive linguistic analysis. My focus will necessarily be on the meaning and usage in New Testament times. Some diachronic observations will be made; however, my focus of analysis is synchronic. For extensive discussion of the term κύριος from linguistic (both diachronic and synchronic) and theological perspectives, a useful starting point is Werner Foerster and Gottfried Quell's 1965 *TDNT* article.[1] This article is somewhat dated and does not utilize any modern linguistic methodology; nevertheless, it provides helpful insight into the range of usage of the term. It contains a wealth of references and observations about usage. This chapter, especially the work on the pre-first-century usage of the term, is indebted to this article. In addition to Foerster and Quell, H. Bietenhard's 1976 *NIDNNT* article provides updated material with more accepted methodology for our study.[2] One striking feature of these sources is that, despite their length and the many occurrences cited, the general linguistic meaning (semantics) of κύριος is rather uniform. It may apply to different people at different times and in different places; nevertheless, the meaning it brings to the referent is similar. This observation will be reflected in the discussion later in this chapter.

This study will determine whether κύριος in the New Testament was used as a polemic against the living Roman emperor. In order for this to be done, two distinctions of meaning were made in Chapter 1. First, a distinction between *semantic* and *pragmatic* meaning was developed. *Semantic meaning* was defined as the inherent linguistic meaning encoded and expressed by the use of language in an utterance without reference to non-linguistic factors such as beliefs, social considerations and the like, or other contextual linguistic elements. It is the linguistic meaning directly involved in the linguistic element under discussion. By contrast, *pragmatic meaning* was described as indirect linguistic (contextual) meaning and non-linguistic meaning including factors such as beliefs, social considerations and the like, and its relationship to the communicator. Further, the interaction

---

1. Werner Foerster and Gottfried Quell, 'Κύριος' [and cognates], *TDNT*, III, pp. 1039-98 (original German, 1938). Pages 1039-58 and 1081-98 were written by Foerster and 1058-81 by Quell. This article provides a wealth of material on κύριος and related terms.

2. H. Bietenhard, 'Κύριος', *NIDNTT*, II, pp. 510-20.

of elements of *pragmatic meaning* with the *semantic meaning* results in what was described as *pragmatic implicatures*. In order to demonstrate the existence of a polemic for κύριος, it will have to be proven that pragmatic implicatures exist with this nuance. Second, concerning lexical forms, a distinction was made between *denotation* (symbol), *sense* (generally speaking the *semantic meaning* as described here), and *reference* (the entity that is represented by the symbol). Both *sense* and *reference* will be important areas of analysis in this chapter.

In order to determine the semantic meaning of the term κύριος, it is important to analyse how the word was used in and around the first century CE. The most important analysis involves looking at the specific range of usages and attempting to discern whether an inherent or general meaning emerges. This will involve a brief discussion of previous usages but will focus in and around the first century. In addition, older literature that might still be impacting the usage will be emphasized (e.g. the Greek Old Testament). Essentially, the purpose is to attempt to provide an understanding of the term and its meaning for Paul and his readers (not necessarily the same at all times). Synchronic word analysis will dominate the next section (2. Semantics 1: Internal Considerations and Potential Referents). However, in order to avoid redundancy, this section will also identify the types of referents who may be labelled κύριος and by whom they may be labelled.

Although this method is common for understanding words, its sole focus on the word itself could cause one to miss aspects of meaning that may be illuminated by other means. It is possible that one could overlook meaning without something in which to contrast the term. Therefore, the subsequent section (3. Semantics 2: External Considerations) will look at the word in relation to other similar terms, most importantly, δεσπότης. This section will serve two purposes. First, it will compare κύριος with other terms in order to provide another means of looking at the word and determining its meaning. Second, it will evaluate conclusions about the term from the section that preceded it.

This study will then lead in two directions. First, it will consider the relational nature of the term, and second, it will go beyond the title itself and consider the conceptual level of *lordship*. In addition, this chapter will include discussion of issues such as whether or not κύριος includes the meaning of divinity. Although this could have been treated in the other two sections, its importance demands that it have special attention.

2. Semantics 1: Internal Considerations and Potential Referents

The semantic discussion in this section will focus on the internal nature of the word κύριος. In other words, we will attempt to determine what the word brings to its context and answer the question, Why does an author use the word? This is probably the most important step in determining the *sense* or (semantic) *meaning* of the term. As discussed above in the distinction between symbol, sense, and referent, I am not suggesting that the term's semantic context is some innate feature of the symbol. Rather, it is the meaning determined by common usage of a specific time and place. This meaning represented by a symbol can differ widely over time and place. Fortunately for this project, the use of κύριος does not vary greatly in ancient Greek.

a. *Etymology and the Adjective*

The masculine noun ὁ κύριος is derived from the adjective κύριος,[3] which appears to be derived from the neuter noun τό κῦρος,[4] meaning 'supreme power' or 'authority' (see LSJ, *s.v.* κύριος and the references cited there). For the adjective, the notion of supreme power or authority may be quite subtle and, depending on the substantives modified, may be present more in the sense of *preferable* or even *acceptable* in an *authoritative* or *legitimate* manner. Neither the adjective nor the earlier noun appears in the New Testament.[5] However, the adjective occurs in the Septuagint twice (1 Macc. 8.30; *4 Macc.* 1.19).[6] The superlative adjective in *4 Macc.* 1.19 includes the notion of *supremacy* (κυριωτάτη δὲ πάντων ἡ φρόνησις . . . , 'and insight is most supreme over all [of these]', that is, over the types of wisdom ([σοφία] mentioned in the preceding verse). It is the superlative usage of the adjective that contributes to the nuance of *supremacy* nuance here. The adjective in 1 Macc. 8.30 has more of a nuance of *legal or authoritative acceptability* in the context of a Roman treaty with the Jewish people (καὶ οὗτοι προσθεῖναι ἢ ἀφελεῖν ποιήσονται ἐξ αἱρέσεως αὐτῶν καὶ ὃ ἂν προσθῶσιν ἢ ἀφέλωσιν ἔσται κύρια, 'and these additions and subtractions they will make on their own might be acceptable ["valid" NRSV] additions and subtractions').

3. Unless explicitly noted as an adjective, the form κύριος in this work will always refer to the noun.

4. Foerster, 'Κύριος', p. 1041.

5. Unless otherwise noted, lexical statistics in this work from biblical texts are from GRAMCORD for Windows (morphological search engine 2.4cx and later [Battle Ground, WA: Gramcord Institute, 1999]). An exception to this is the short section below describing the percentages of occurrences per New Testament book (i.e. occurrences per one thousand words). These figures were taken from the older, now unsupported DOS programme because the Windows version is unable to provide this function at this time.

6. Edwin Hatch and Henry A. Redpath, *A Concordance to the Septuagint and Other Greek Versions of the Old Testament (Including the Apocrypha)* (3 vols. in 2; Oxford: Clarendon Press, 1897–1906; repr. Grand Rapids: Baker Book House, 1983). Despite correct tagging in the GRAMCORD database, the current GRAMCORD for Windows search software is unsuccessful when attempting to search for this adjective.

Only the noun occurs in the New Testament. However, prior to the Hellenistic period, the noun was rare.[7] Thus, since it is not always easy to distinguish between the noun and substantival adjective (which often have an identical form and function), as other literature is considered, I will avoid making too strict a distinction between the noun and substantival adjective.

b. *Early and Classical Usage*

The word has a general meaning of 'one having authority over' throughout ancient Greek usage. The classical dramatists' use was not quite distinguishable from the adjective used substantively.[8] Nevertheless, the general meaning and the main types of referents are already evident this early. In Sophocles' play *Oedipus at Colonus* (fifth century BCE), Oedipus is cited by his messenger as referring to King Theseus as ὁ κύριος Θησεύς (1643-44). In Euripides' play *Iphigeneia at Aulis* (fifth century BCE), the author has Agamemnon speak of Aegina's marriage to Zeus and confirms that the one responsible for the girl gave her to him. This individual is called ὁ κύριος (703).[9] Also in Euripides, there is an example of a master of a captured individual being called κύριος. In the process of saving Andromache (the once wife of Hector and now captured concubine), Pelius, the grandfather of her master Neoptolemus, calls Neoptolemus κύριος in relation to her (*Andromache* 558). It is difficult to determine what aspect of the relationship between Andromache and Neoptolemus results in the latter being κύριος. He is the one who captured her; she is a slave; and she is under his authority as a woman. It may be one or all of these relations. It also applies to owners of slaves. In Demosthenes' 37th Oration (*Against Pantaenetus*; mid-fourth century BCE), speaking of his slave in relation to himself, he calls himself a κύριος (*Oration* 37.51). One who is an owner or master of a house or other inanimate objects may also be a κύριος.

The term is used also for rulers. Aristotle in his *Politics* (mid-fourth century BCE) calls those who rule κύριοι (2.6.4 = 1269b.10; plural). Demosthenes says of Philip of Macedonia, ἁπλῶς αὐτὸς δεσπότης, ἡγεμών, κύριος πάντων ('he was sole master, leader, and lord of all' [*Oration* 18.235; *Oration* 18 is entitled *On the Crown*]).[10] Additionally, the term is used for gods. Pindar in the early fifth century states, Ζεὺς ὁ πάντων κύριος ('Zeus [is] the lord of all' [*Isthmean Ode* 5.53]).[11] This type of claim

---

7. Foerster, 'Κύριος', p. 1046.

8. Foerster, 'Κύριος', p. 1042.

9. See also Isaeus 6.32 (early fourth century; Isaeus's *Oration* 6 is called *On the Estate of Philoctemon*).

10. Foerster considers this an example of the adjective ('Κύριος', p. 1044 n. 13).

11. An (adjectival?) usage occurs in Plato (late fifth/early fourth century BCE) referring to the gods in general: *Laws* 966c (book 12).

does not seem too common. It makes strong claims for Zeus similar to those made of Yahweh in the Greek Old Testament. However, during this period, κύριος is always used with a genitive when applied to gods.[12]

In all of these examples, there appears to be a nuance of *authority over*. Given the sociological situation of the ancient world, in which slavery was common and women had few if any rights, and in view of the responsibilities of subjugated people to their rulers, this meaning may be modified slightly to include a nuance of *legitimacy* (as judged by the cultural and legal context). One may wish to make a distinction between *one in authority* in the sense of *master* and *one in authority* in the sense of *owner*. This may be possible. However, in light of what we know about the ancient world (e.g. roles of slaves, women, etc.), this may be anachronistic and may result in an interpretation of the word that was not immediately apparent to the ancients. There may be some evidence of this distinction when we compare κύριος with δεσπότης. However, because κύριος was used freely for both types of related meaning, it seems prudent not to make a significant distinction as we pursue the semantic meaning of the term. Therefore, in the classical period, κύριος can be defined as 'one having legitimate authority over someone or something'. The examples cited in this section reveal a number of types of people who can be referred to as κύριος. These include legal guardians of women, masters/owners of slaves, rulers of subjugated peoples, and gods.

c. Koine *Usage (Excluding the New Testament)*

Although there can be no crisp break with the classical period, the conquests of Alexander the Great resulted in a vast geographical expansion of Greek language usage. With this expansion came changes in the Greek language. This is generally considered the *Koine* period (approximately 330 BCE–330 CE). Although this period of the language had significant variation, it was marked by a simplicity lacking in the literary dialects of the classical period.[13] The Greek Old Testament, New Testament, Josephus, Philo, and the early church fathers all are examples of *Koine* Greek.

---

12. Bietenhard, 'Κύριος', p. 511. Foerster, 'Κύριος', p. 1049. Foerster also includes rulers in this statement. However, the passages from Sophocles (*Oedipus at Colonus*, 1643-44) and Aristotle (*Politics* 2.6.4 = 1269b.10) apply this term without direct modification to rulers. It may be that Foerster is referring to supreme rulers here such as Philip in Demosthenes, *Oration* 18.235. Or in Sophocles it is possible that Theseus is not viewed as a ruler in the strictest sense by the speaker. In Aristotle, Foerster may see implied modification, viewing the article as a possessive pronoun: τοῖς κυρίοις (with their lords). More likely, this passage is not relevant for Foerster's statement because no specific ruler is in view.

13. For a discussion of the development of the Greek language immediately following the classical period, see Geoffrey C. Horrocks, *Greek: A History of the Language and its Speakers* (Longman Linguistic Library; London: Longman, 1997), pp. 32-70.

Concerning the literature of the first century CE alone, the term κύριος was fairly common; however, it was not nearly as common as it is in the Septuagint or later Christian literature. In the first century, the title was familiar enough that one would be aware of it and would have a general idea of what type of people would be the referent of the term and what one's relationship to the referent(s) would be. This is enhanced by the term's use in previous centuries. The use of GRAMCORD and TLG reveals 2,459 occurrences of the term in its various forms during this period. This figure is high because it includes works in the early second century such as Ignatius and Polycarp. However, limitations of the TLG search classifications make this unavoidable (Ignatius and some other church fathers are classified as A.D. 1-2). Additionally, in TLG the forms themselves are searched and therefore some adjectives are to be included.[14] The statistics will become more precise through the discussion here. With the exception of this introductory section in which statistics will be presented, New Testament usage will be discussed in two separate sections (non-Pauline and Pauline usage, pp. 166-70). Additionally, a short post-New Testament Christian section (pp. 170-71) will be used primarily to confirm usage described in previous sections (assuming usage influenced by the New Testament and the LXX). This is for organizational reasons. This study is primarily concerned with Pauline usage and thus Pauline usage will demand more attention.

---

14. For the non-biblical data, TLG searches were constructed to look for all possible forms of the noun; therefore, adjectives with identical forms may be among the number. The date range that was searched was also rather broad. It permitted all works labelled AD 1 and beyond (a. A.D. 1, a. A.D. 1?, a. A.D. 1/2, A.D. 1, A.D. 1?, A.D. 1-2, A.D. 1-2?, A.D. 1-7, A.D. 1/2, A.D. 1/2?, A.D. 1/3, A.D. 1?/6; however, not p. A.D. 1) and any works labeled 1 BC through AD 1 (1 B.C.-A.D. 1, 1 B.C.-A.D. 1?, 1 B.C./A.D. 1, and 1 B.C./A.D. 1?). However, it did not include searches where A.D. 1 fell within a larger range (e.g. 2 B.C.-A.D. 4). This seems the most prudent course to pursue. The difficulty of dating some works has made multiple ranges necessary. However, four of these date ranges accounted for the majority of the works (1 B.C.-A.D. 1, A.D. , A.D. 1?, and A.D. 1-2). These include a significant number of authors who can be dated around the New Testament with some confidence. The remainder of the ranges include fewer examples. Many of the ranges included only one author (e.g. a. A.D. 1?, A.D. 1-7). Therefore, we can be confident that the vast majority of extant literary examples will be identified by these searches. Any legitimate examples missed because A.D. 1 was within a date range excluded (e.g. 2 B.C.-A.D. 4) are likely to be offset by the inclusion of examples from outside A.D. 1 in broad range searches (e.g. A.D. 1-7). Additionally, the older material permitted in the searches would be more likely to contain adjectives than the later. The purpose here was general and the results are primarily illustrative; therefore, more precise searches (period) and analysis of the data (to exclude adjectives) were not necessary. This approach is warranted because as already stated, the use of these statistics is meant to be illustrative and in the case of a number of works there remains a debate over dating. An exact figure is impossible to produce.

Nearly 30 per cent of the literary occurrences during the first century CE are found in the New Testament (717 in 660 verses). There are 1,742 examples of κύριος outside of the New Testament. However, most of these (1,212 of 1,742) are found in Jewish and Christian writings from the period. There remain 530 examples from outside Jewish and Christian literature.

The singular is most important for this study because the polemic involves individual referents. The singular accounts for most of the examples (2,300 total: 703 New Testament; 1,167 Jewish and Christian; 430 other). However, the vocative is less important (the vocative singular κύριε accounts for 121 of 703 New Testament and 147 of 1,597 non-New Testament singular occurrences). There are two reasons for this. First, the vocative κύριε may have a slightly different linguistic history from the other cases. This will be explored briefly below (p. 176). Second, they are rare in Paul's letters. The singular vocative (κύριε) only occurs twice in the entire Pauline corpus (Rom. 10.16; 11.3). Both examples are related to quotations from the Old Testament (Isa. 53.1 and 1 Kgs 19.10, 14 [LXX 3 Kgdms 19.10, 14] respectively[15]). The first is part of the quotation, and the second introduces the quotation. Both address God directly. There are two plural nominative occurrences of κύριος (Eph. 6.9; Col. 4.1), both referring to slave owners. They function like vocatives; however, there are no plural vocatives in the New Testament. These are nominatives used for address.[16]

(1) *Jewish Usage*

(a) *The Greek Old Testament and its Influence on Subsequent Jewish and Christian Writings.* It was noted above that the majority of examples outside of the New Testament were found in early Christian and Jewish literature (1,212 [1,167 singular] of 1,742 [1,597 singular]). The reason for this is twofold. First, for the Christian literature the common New Testament usage was highly influential. Second, for both Jewish and Christian

---

15. The vocative does not occur in 1 Kgs 19.10, 14. Elijah is in conversation with God and the addressee is clear. The Romans passage is abbreviated and direct. The vocative is used as a quick means of directing the statement towards God.

16. Address is a function of both the vocative and nominative cases (Stanley E. Porter, *Idioms of the Greek New Testament* [Biblical Languages: Greek, 2; Sheffield: JSOT Press, 2nd edn, 1994], pp. 86-87). The lack of a plural vocative complicates matters since the author did not have an option other than the nominative. Nevertheless, the morphology demands a nominative classification. The function however is the same, address. D.B. Wallace includes a nominative classification called 'nominative for vocative' (alternate label, 'nominative of address') (*Greek Grammar beyond the Basics*, pp. 56-58). This seems to suggest that the nominative becomes a vocative. Given the morphology and uncertainty over the development of the cases, this may go beyond the evidence. Although it is best to see these simply as nominatives of address, Wallace's approach highlights the closeness of this particular function of both of the cases.

literature (including the New Testament) the influence of the Greek Old Testament was significant.

The Greek Old Testament demands special attention. The translation of the Hebrew Old Testament into Greek probably began in the middle of the third century BCE with the Torah and continued over the next two hundred years. The term κύριος is used an overwhelming 8,543 times (in 6,865 verses) in the Septuagint.[17] It is primarily used where the Hebrew text has the divine name (יהוה)[18] but also can translate the general term for God/god (אל and related; e.g. Job 8.20; 15.4; this is common in Job), and refer to God in books composed in Greek (e.g. 1 Esd. 8.6; Jdt. 6.19; 2 Macc. 2.8; Sir. 3.18).[19] Additionally, it may have a human referent (1 Macc. 2.53; 9.25;[20] Judg. 19.22-23 [2x, translating בעל[21]]).

With human referents, the meaning, usage and potential referents are similar to the classical period (and more general Hellenistic period [see below]). Usages for 'master of a house' (Exod. 22.7), 'one who has authority over a wife or girl' (Gen. 18.12 [Sarah speaking of Abraham]; Gen.

---

17. I am not unaware of the difficulties involved in using the LXX for this study. The LXX is a complex entity (or entities) including different types of Greek, containing significant textual difficulties. In their introductory textbook on the LXX, Karen H. Jobes and Moisés Silva state, 'Strictly speaking, there is really no such thing as *the* Septuagint' (*Invitation to the Septuagint* [Grand Rapids: Baker Book House, 2000], p. 30). When I mention the Septuagint or LXX, there is no intention to minimize this complexity. I prefer the label 'Greek Bible' or 'Greek Old Testament'; however, 'LXX' will be used at times (including when in dialogue with sources using this label). It is merely the most economical means of identifying the Greek translations usually classified as 'Septuagint' in contrast to other Greek versions. This is sufficient for the purposes here. The point being made here is certain, namely that the use of κύριος in the LXX manuscripts available in the first century CE was extensive and influential to Jewish and Christian writers. However, see below for a brief discussion of the debate on whether or not the earliest copies of the LXX had κύριος for the divine name.

18. Bietenhard mentions 6,156 occurrences ('Κύριος', 512). See, e.g., Gen. 2.8; Exod. 3.4; Deut. 5.6; Judg. 4.6; 1 Kgdms 12.24 [MT 1 Sam. 12.24]; 1 Chron. 25.6; Ps. 22.1 [MT Ps. 23.1]; Isa. 7.3; Amos 3.12; Mal. 2.14. For a discussion of the use of κύριος as a translation for the divine name in the Greek Old Testament, see Christiane Zimmermann, *Die Namen des Vaters: Studien zu ausgewählten neutestamentlichen Gottesbezeichnungen vor ihrem frühjüdischen und paganen Sprachhorizont* (Ancient Judaism and Early Christianity, 69; Leiden: E.J. Brill, 2007), pp. 173-87.

19. For a comprehensive discussion of κύριος as name for God, see Wolf W.G. Baudissin, *Kyrios als Gottesname im Judentum und seine Stelle in der Religionsgeschichte* (ed. Otto Eissfeldt; 4 vols.; Giessen: Alfred Töpelmann, 1929). Although this study is broader than the Greek Old Testament, the majority of the work is concerned with the LXX.

20. These are the only two occurrences of the noun κύριος in 1 Maccabees. The first refers to the patriarch Joseph. The second is plural and refers to a group of leaders.

21. Bietenhard mentions that κύριος translates בעל 15x ('Κύριος', p. 511).

31.35 [Rachel of her father Laban—an interesting usage, given that Rachel was married to Jacob]), 'one who is master/owner of a slave' (1 Kgdms [= 1 Sam.] 16.16; Judg. 19.11), and 'one having authority over subject people' (2 Kgdms [= 2 Sam.] 4.8). Again, all of these usages demonstrate a meaning of 'legal authority over someone or something'.

The major use of κύριος in the Greek Old Testament is for God. Paul Kahle has questioned whether the LXX translators actually used κύριος where the Hebrew had the divine name (יהוה). The term 'translation' is avoided here because either κύριος was simply substituted for the divine name or was used as a translation of an oral circumlocution to avoid directly uttering the divine name. It has been argued that the original Jewish translators used some form of Hebrew script for the divine name; thus using the same symbol (יהוה) found in the Hebrew manuscripts from which they were working. The theory suggests that it was Christians who first inserted κύριος into the LXX for the Tetragrammaton.[22] There are a number of points that seem to support this conclusion. The earliest LXX fragments available that were produced by Jews, in which the underlying Hebrew had the Tetragrammaton, retain either a Hebrew-type script or some other convention for the divine name. However, the extant evidence is minimal. There appear to be only eleven or twelve extant manuscripts of Jewish origin that can be dated between the second century BCE and the first century CE (PRyl 458; 4Q127; 4QLXXLev[a]; 4QLXXLev[b]; 4QLXXNum; 4QLXX-Deut; 7QLXXEx; 7QEpJer; PFouad 266; POxy 3522; 8HevXIIgr and possibly POxy 4443).[23] Five of these are relevant for this issue. First and most importantly, Papyrus Fouad 266 (c. 100 BCE; second oldest extant LXX manuscript), containing Deut. 31.28–32.6 has the Hebrew square script for the divine name.[24] Second, POxy 3522 (first century CE) containing Job

22. See esp. Paul Kahle, *The Cairo Geniza* (Oxford: Basil Blackwell, 2nd edn, 1959), p. 222; also pp. 162, 218-19, 224); see also Sydney Jellicoe, *The Septuagint and Modern Study* (Oxford: Clarendon Press, 1968), pp. 271-72.

23. The first ten examples come from Martin Hengel, *The Septuagint as Christian Scripture: Its Prehistory and the Problem of its Canon* (trans. Mark E. Biddle; OTS; Edinburgh: T. & T. Clark, 2002), pp. 41-42 n. 54. Hengel actually states that there are "nine." This may be because he either includes 4QLXXLev[a] and 4QLXXLev[b] as one manuscript (cited as 4QLXXLev[a+b]) or does not include 4Q127, of which he says, 'As far as can be determined given their very fragmentary condition, the eighty fragments of 4Q127 represent a free Greek rendition of Exodus' (Hengel, *Septuagint*, p. 42 n. 54). I assume that he concludes nine because he is combining the two Leviticus fragments. POxy 4443 is the earliest fragment of Esther (E 16-9.3). Hengel dates this as late first or early second century. He appears not to include it in his list. I have noted it here as a possibility.

24. For information about this papyrus fragment, see Ernst Würthwein, *The Text of the Old Testament: An Introduction to the Biblica Hebraica* (trans. Erroll F. Rhodes;

42.11-12 has archaic Hebrew letters.[25] Third, in two places, the Naḥal Ḥever Minor Prophets scrolls (8ḤevXIIgr; turn of the era) include the divine name in ancient Hebrew script in Habakkuk 2–3 and Zechariah 8. Fourth, a fragment from cave 4 of Qumran containing Leviticus 2–5 (4QLXXLev[b]) has the Greek majuscule letters ΙΑΩ for the divine name.[26] Finally, the Rylands Papyrus 458 (mid second century BCE; the oldest extant LXX manuscript), containing fragments from Deuteronomy 23–28, does not contain the divine name but breaks off just before it at Deut. 26.17.[27] Although C.H. Roberts supplies κύριος,[28] Kahle argues that the divine name here was most likely in some type of Hebrew script; he claims that Roberts agreed with him when he pointed this out.[29]

In addition to the early manuscripts, there is some evidence from early Christian writers of this practice among Jewish scribes. Origen's *Hexapla* (230–40 CE), a six-column parallel Old Testament including a Hebrew text, a transliteration of the Hebrew into Greek letters, and four Greek versions (the LXX is the fifth column), appears to render the divine name in the second column (transliteration) with the Hebrew letters and in the Greek columns of Aquila, Symmachus, and LXX with Greek letters ΠΙΠΙ, which seems to be a visual parallel to the Tetragrammaton (יהוה).[30] Unfortunately, very little survives of this work. The most important manuscript is a tenth-century palimpsest discovered by Giovanni Mercati late in the nineteenth century which bears the characteristics described above.[31] Prior to this discovery, scholars were primarily dependent on descriptions from early Christians such as Eusebius, Epiphanius and Jerome concerning this work.[32] Kahle concludes that Origen's rendering of the divine name suggests that

Grand Rapids: Eerdmans, 2nd edn, 1995), pp. 190-91; Kahle, *Cairo Geniza*, pp. 218-20 (also p. 162). Additionally, W.G. Waddell discusses this papyrus in a short note; it appears to be his sole authority for claiming that the LXX in general uses Hebrew (or Aramaic) script for the divine name ('The Tetragrammaton in the LXX', *JTS* 45 [1944], pp. 158-61).

25. See the comments by the editor of the papyrus.

26. For information on this papyrus fragment, see DJD, IX, p. 120 (esp. fragment 20.4, p. 174 [with plate 40], also 168 and fragment 6.12, p. 170 [with plate 39]); Kahle, *Cairo Geniza*, p. 224. N.B. The entire papyrus is in majuscule script, not merely the ΙΑΩ.

27. For information on this papyrus fragment, see Würthwein, *Text*, pp. 188-89; C.H. Roberts, *Two Biblical Papyri in the John Rylands Library Manchester* (Manchester: Manchester University Press, 1936), pp. 9-46; Kahle, *Cairo Geniza*, pp. 220-22.

28. Roberts, *Two Biblical Papyri*, p. 39 (see the top line of the page; line 27 of the papyrus fragment).

29. Kahle, *Cairo Geniza*, p. 222.

30. Waddell, 'Tetragrammaton,' pp. 158-59.

31. Jellicoe, *Septuagint*, p. 127; Jobes and Silva, *Invitation*, pp. 50-51.

32. Jellicoe, *Septuagint*, p. 127.

he used Jewish manuscripts.[33] Additionally, there are a few statements by church fathers that also suggest that the Jews practised this convention concerning the divine name. Jerome states, 'Even today we find the tetragrammaton name of God written in archaic letters in some Greek manuscripts.'[34] Referring to Origen's commentary on Ps. 2.2, de Lacey states, 'Origen also comments on "the most accurate copies" containing the divine name in Hebrew characters "not the current ones, but the most archaic characters."'[35] However, these statements are concerning the Jewish practice of the time. They do not refer to the original translation of the LXX.

Given this evidence, there can be no certain conclusion about the *original* LXX practice of rendering the divine name. Although there are no extant Jewish LXX manuscripts that have κύριος where the Hebrew reads יהוה, the evidence is too limited and too late to contribute much to determining the original. Additionally, the variety of conventions used, such as Hebrew letters, ΠΙΠΙ and others, suggests that there was not a uniform policy regarding the divine name.[36]

Essentially, there are only three examples of a Jewish text using this convention through the first century CE (PFouad 266, 8HevXIIgr [2x], and POxy 3522). This evidence (with limited support from PRyl 458 and 4QLXXLev[b]), with the statements of the church fathers, supports the notion that some Jews practised this convention. However, this evidence is late. PFouad 266 dates from well after the original translation was made. There is simply too little known about the previous one hundred plus years before PFouad 266 was produced. It is even possible that later Jewish writers changed the LXX's κύριος to the Hebrew Tetragrammaton as reflected in the manuscripts discussed above.[37] Reasons for this could be suggested. For example, there may have been a desire to make Greek translations more

33. Kahle, *Cairo Geniza*, pp. 162-63; see also Jellicoe, *Septuagint*, p. 272. The evidence from Origen is not always clear. See D.R. de Lacey, '"One Lord" in Pauline Christology', in Harold H. Rowdon (ed.), *Christ the Lord: Studies in Christology Presented to Donald Guthrie* (Downers Grove, IL: InterVarsity Press, 1982), p. 193 n.14.

34. From Jerome's *Prologus Galeatus* cited by Würthwein, *Text*, p. 190. See also the quotation from Jerome's *Epistle 25 ad Marcellam* cited on the same page.

35. De Lacey, '"One Lord"', p. 192.

36. De Lacey, '"One Lord"', p. 193.

37. This seems to be suggested by Robert Hanhart, 'Introduction: Problems in the History of the LXX Text from its Beginnings to Origen', in *The Septuagint as Christian Scripture: Its Prehistory and the Problem of its Canon,* by Martin Hengel (Edinburgh: T. & T. Clark, 2002), pp. 7-9. See also Würthwein, *Text*, p. 190.

'Palestinian'.[38] This is purely speculative and will not be pursued.[39] However, there is support for the original containing κύριος. First, it is unlikely that the practice of using Hebrew (or related) script occurred for the LXX works written in Greek.[40] The labelling of God as κύριος was already established by Jewish writers. In fact, the use of the term in some of the apocryphal books and even Philo (see below) suggests that this usage was 'too thoroughly accepted and widespread for its legitimation to have been based on anything other than the canonised writings in the LXX'.[41] Second, it is likely that κύριος was the form actually read and discussed orally among Greek speakers[42] as Hebrew speakers used אֲדֹנָי where the Hebrew read יהוה. Finally, and most importantly for this work, there is no evidence that any New Testament author used this practice. It is to this point that we now direct our attention.

We are claiming strong LXX influence on Paul's use of the term κύριος. However, if Paul's LXX texts did not have κύριος for the divine name, and if he cited these texts with some form of Hebrew characters, the LXX influence on Paul for his use of κύριος would be greatly diminished. It is worthwhile briefly to defend Paul's likely original here before proceeding. It is highly probable that Paul's LXX and his original letters used the term κύριος where a quotation from a Hebrew original had the Tetragrammaton. First, there is no manuscript evidence for a single reading with Hebrew script for any New Testament book. It may be argued that all manuscripts are far removed from the originals and have undergone changes. Of course, this is possible but unlikely for a number of reasons. There are some fairly early Pauline manuscripts such as P[46], which is usually dated to approxi-

---

38. Zimmermann suggests that Jewish revisionists may have replaced κύριος with the Tetragrammaton to show the uniqueness (*Einzigartigkeit*) of the divine name (*Die Namen des Vaters*, p. 173).

39. Dismissing this line of argument does not imply that the argument for an original Tetragrammaton in the LXX is any stronger. In fact, as we build the case against the argument we will see that it is just as speculative (and maybe even more so).

40. The LXX has 847 occurrences of the noun. However, some of these may be translations. Four works not officially labelled 'apocrypha' account for 246 of these usages. The *Odes* (118 occurrences) and *Psalms of Solomon* (120) are translations. However, 3 *Maccabees* (6) and 4 *Maccabees* (2) were probably composed in Greek. All references in 3 *Maccabees* refer to God (2.2 [2x]; 5.7, 35; 6.15 [2x]). However, the two occurrences in 4 *Maccabees* both refer to one being *lord* over one's emotions (2.7; 7.23). In the fifteen works (assuming that the Letter of Jeremiah is a separate work from Baruch) classified as apocrypha all written in Greek, nine include the noun κύριος (1 Esdras 137; Tobit 60; Judith 67; Wisdom of Solomon 26; Sirach 201; Baruch 49; Susanna 14; 1 Maccabees 2).

41. Hanhart, 'Introduction', p. 8.

42. Bietenhard, 'Κύριος', 512.

mately 200 CE, without any evidence of a Hebrew Tetragrammaton. Extant manuscripts are from all over the Roman empire do not have anything but κύριος. It would seem likely that the Hebrew would survive in at least some manuscripts if it was original. The analysis of extant copies reveals genealogical relationships among the manuscripts. There are at least three major text-types that seem to have very early archetypes.[43] Within a text-type, manuscripts often share common characteristics that distinguish them from other text-types.[44] It would be difficult to maintain that a change of this magnitude would occur among all text-types without any trace of an original Hebrew script. It is more likely that a change would have had to occur earlier than the development of these text-types, very close to the originals. It would then be difficult to maintain that someone purposely changed what was considered to have been written by an apostle.

Additionally, the principal manuscript of Origen's *Hexapla* is about 750 years removed from the original but appears to keep Origen's original symbols for the divine name. If scribes could be careful for this long period of time, it is not impossible to believe that at least some New Testament manuscripts would survive with the Hebrew script if it ever existed. Also, there is no evidence of any concerted attempt to purge the Hebrew script in any early patristic work. Although it is highly unlikely that all manuscripts with an original Hebrew for the divine name could be changed, if this happened, a major effort would need to be undertaken to purge the documents of the Hebrew. It would seem likely that some record of this effort would be extant. Such a massive undertaking would demand some type of impetus such as an accusation and purging of heresy. There is no indication of this charge, nor is there any indication that the practice would be considered heresy. The second reason to assume an original is contemporary writing such as Paul's fellow Diaspora Jewish writer Philo. Philo is highly influenced by the LXX (see below), but there is no evidence he used Hebrew lettering for the divine name. It can again be argued that Philo has been preserved by Christians and therefore has not maintained the Jewish convention. However, for better or worse, this is the way the writings have survived. It would be helpful to have Jewish copies, but we

---

43. On text-types, see Bruce M. Metzger and Bart D. Ehrman, *The Text of the New Testament: Its Transmission, Corruption, and Restoration* (Oxford: Oxford University Press, 4th edn, 2005), pp. 306-13; Michael W. Holmes, 'New Testament Textual Criticism', in Scot McKnight (ed.), *Introducing New Testament Interpretation* (Grand Rapids: Baker Book House, 1989), pp. 58-60; and Kurt Aland and Barbara Aland, *The Text of the New Testament: An Introduction to the Critical Editions and to the Theory and Practice of Modern Textual Criticism* (trans. Erroll F. Rhodes; Grand Rapids: Eerdmans, 2nd edn, 1989), pp. 49-71.

44. See Holmes, 'Textual Criticism', p. 58.

do not. Additionally, this argument assumes that Christians changed the text. This is a circular argument based on a premise of a weak possibility with little extant manuscript evidence. There simply is no evidence of change taking place by Christian hands. Finally, the evidence of the earliest patristic writers (e.g. Ignatius, Barnabas, Clement; see below for number of occurrences) who were influenced by the LXX, Paul and the rest of the New Testament show no evidence that their manuscripts of these writings had any Hebrew script for the divine name.

Finally, the argument that suggests that Christians changed manuscripts demands an exaggerated distinction between early Christians and Jews. The New Testament was written by Jews. Indeed, if Daniel Boyarin is correct, these groups were much closer for much longer than often assumed.[45]

To summarize the discussion about the divine name in the LXX and Paul, despite some arguments produced here in favour of an original κύριος for the divine name in the LXX (as opposed to the Hebrew), there is not enough evidence to conclude how the original LXX rendered the divine name. It is clear that some Jewish scribes maintained the Hebrew script for the Tetragrammaton. However, it also seems probable that the LXX manuscripts familiar to Paul had κύριος in the passages he quoted that had the Tetragrammaton in the Hebrew. Additionally, all the evidence favours the view that Paul's citations originally had the term κύριος, as the unanimous manuscript tradition maintains. Therefore, we may proceed to consider briefly Greek Old Testament usage of the term with confidence that this would have influenced Paul's use of the term.

As already noted, κύριος occurs more times in the Greek Old Testament than in all extant literature for the first centuries BCE and CE combined. It is used 8,538 times in the Greek Old Testament with the majority of occurrences found in the books translated from Hebrew or Aramaic (7,690).[46] Nevertheless, it is used often in the books composed in Greek (848 total: Sirach [201]; 1 Esdras [137]; *Psalms of Solomon* [121]; *Odes* [118] Judith [67]; Tobit [60]; Baruch [49]; 2 Maccabees [45]; Wisdom [26]; Susanna [14]; *3 Maccabees* [6]; 1 Maccabees and *4 Maccabees* [2 each]).

The usage is consistent. Most books, whether translation or written in Greek, have God as the referent of κύριος. The unique situation of the substitution for יהוה makes it difficult to know for sure whether κύριος is func-

---

45. Daniel Boyarin, *Dying for God: Martyrdom and the Making of Christianity and Judaism* (Figurae: Reading Medieval Culture; Stanford, CA: Stanford University Press, 1999). Even if Boyarin's thesis is not fully vindicated concerning the interaction between Judaism and Christianity for over three centuries, his observations about the emergence of early Judaisms and Christianity (which in its earliest period was one of these emerging "Judaisms") is helpful.

46. This is over twice as often as θεός, which is used 3,944 times.

tioning as a proper name or referential noun maintaining the semantics, as already discussed. Both are probably intended. The Lord is his name, but as *the Lord*, he also has authority over all.

The exception to the above are the four usages in 1 Maccabees and *4 Maccabees*. In 1 Maccabees, Joseph is "lord" over Egypt (2.53) and godless officials are "lords" over (in charge of) the country. In *4 Maccabees* the term is used in reference only to one's *mastery* over emotions (2.7; 7.23). Only in these two books is God not called κύριος. The meaning of the term is consistent with what we have described above.

The study of LXX usage leads to one further point. In 1930, J.A. Smith wrote a short article on the meaning of κύριος in the LXX in which he argued against some common proposals for the meaning of the term (e.g. legal authority over). He especially rejects an emphasis on the term applying to a master of slaves.[47] He acknowledges the use of the term for slave owners but suggests 'that at no time in Greek usage was the δοῦλος necessarily regarded as a chattel of his "master"'.[48] Additionally, he acknowledges the existence of passages where δοῦλος is property, a tool and so on, but he maintains that 'the effect of such passages must not be exaggerated'.[49] He approaches the term as a translation for אדון and emphasizes the relational nature of the term. Further, Smith emphasizes the role and responsibility of the κύριος in this relationship. The κύριος is more of a 'tutor to pupil than that of curator to ward'.[50] He is responsible for protection, care and the like.

These insights certainly seem to be valid for some usages in the LXX, and it is important to highlight the relational nature of the term. However, Smith seems to minimize the unique usage for God and the passages that clearly include nuances of *owner* or *master* (e.g. 1 Kgdms [= 1 Sam.] 16.16). The overwhelming use for God will impact any Greek Old Testament understanding of the word. The meaning, then, is conditioned on one's understanding of God. However, it is difficult to determine the main reasons for the choice of the word for God. Is it a simple substitution of יהוה through the reading of אדני, or was it chosen for its meaning? Or do both apply? When the usages for God are omitted, the range of meaning is similar to other periods under discussion. One could argue that Smith's insights apply to the Pauline view of Christ. However, to focus on this to the neglect of other nuances would ultimately be misleading. In light of the discussion in the previous chapter concerning the role of the emperor and the purposes of high and divine honours bestowed on him, such responsibilities observed by Smith seem likely, at least in ideological theory, to apply to him. He is

47. J.A. Smith, 'The Meaning of Κύριος', *JTS* 31 (1929–30), pp. 155-60 (158-59).
48. Smith, 'Meaning', p. 158.
49. Smith, 'Meaning', p. 159.
50. Smith, 'Meaning', p. 157.

benefactor (εὐεργέτης), saviour (σωτήρ) and so on. Although these terms also have important relational elements, the legal and authoritative aspect of κύριος seems to imply a responsibility on the part of the referent toward those to whom he is κύριος. This is an aspect of κύριος to which we will return.

(b) *Philo and Josephus.* Of the Jewish authors in and around the first century, Philo, who writes on biblical themes, uses the forms frequently (390 total [364 singular]). Josephus's *Antiquities,* in which one might expect κύριος to be frequent for the same reason as Philo, uses it only 30 times (22 are singular).[51] In his other writings, Josephus uses the term only eleven more times (nine are singular).[52]

Philo uses the form κύριος and declensions more than any other writer in the first century. However, given his prolific writing output, it is relatively less (in percentage) than Paul. When used for God, it seems that his usage is generally influenced by the Greek Old Testament. In addition, Philo is early evidence of the title's use for an emperor (e.g. *On the Embassy to Gaius* 286).

Josephus's minimal usage of the title is of interest. Two of Josephus's principal influences used the title extensively. First, as we have seen, the Greek Old Testament uses the title often. Second, it was a title applied to the emperors of the Flavian dynasty (see Chapter 5). Josephus's principal works are closely tied to these. First, he wrote a history of the Jews (*Antiquities*) that is dependent on the Old Testament for much of its content. Second, he wrote the *Jewish War,* in which two of the Flavian emperors played a large part (Vespasian and Titus). There are occurrences referring to both God (e.g. *Antiquities* 13.3.1 §68) and the Flavian emperors (4.6.2 §366). However, given the size of these works, such usage is almost insignificant.

What could account for this minimal usage? Although it is impossible to go far beyond speculation, it could be the importance of the title in these two spheres that resulted in a tension in Josephus. Extensive use for one could result in offence to the other. Therefore Josephus avoided the term. To a lesser extent this may explain Philo's usage as well (also note that the title for the emperor was not as common in Philo's time as in Josephus's).

---

51. Comparative or superlative usages that function in a clearly adjectival manner are omitted from these statistics.

52. Jewish and Christian works in the searches account for 792 occurrences. As already noted, just under half are accounted for by Philo and Josephus (395). The remaining occurrences were found in the *Apocalypse of Elijah, Assumption of Moses, Life of Adam and Eve, Testament of Abraham, Letter of Barnabas,* the letters of Clement, the letters of Ignatius, and the *Letter of Polycarp.*

However, as an argument from silence, such a theory must be given minimal weight in the issues related to this work.

(c) *Other Jewish Usage.* The importance of the Greek Old Testament and its use of κύριος for יהוה clearly impacted the use of the term in other Jewish literature. Although variation existed, works such as those classified as Pseudepigrapha used the term in a manner similar to the Old Testament, probably because the authors wished these works to be viewed as sacred.[53] However, some authors (e.g. those who wrote *3* and *4 Maccabees*, the *Sibylline Oracles* and the *Letter of Aristeas*), whose Hellenism was less acquainted with Judaism, seem to avoid the use of the term, which may not have been clearly understood in its Old Testament sense.[54] Foerster also discusses rabbinic usage.[55] Although this is not unimportant, it contributes little to determining whether a polemic exists in Paul.

(2) *Non-Jewish Usage.* Concerning *Koine* literature without Jewish influence, the meaning, usage and potential referents are similar to those of the classical period (and non-God LXX usages).[56] Usages for 'master of a house' (POxy 288.36 [22–25 CE]; PTebt 5.147 [118 BCE]; plural), 'one who has authority over a wife or girl' (POxy 255.4-5 [48 CE]), 'one who is master/owner of a slave' (Plutarch, *Sayings of Kings and Commanders* 176-77 [= *Agathocles* 2]), 'one having authority over subject people' (OGIS 415.1 [37-4 BCE: Herod the Great]; 186.8 [62 BCE: Ptolemy XIII]; OGIS 418.1 [37-44 CE: Herod Agrippa I]) and gods (see below) are all attested. Again, all of these usages demonstrate a meaning of 'legal authority over someone or something'.

Of importance during this period is the use of the term for the first time of deities and rulers without a genitive modifier (although note our clarification above). Foerster suggests that the first occurrence of an unmodified κύριος for a god is the application of the related feminine word κύρια for Isis in 99 BCE (OGIS 180).[57] Other first-century BCE examples include an application to Kronos (θεὸς Κρόνος κύριος; 'god Kronos lord') in a Syrian inscription (OGIS 606) and the adjective applied to the god Soknopaios

---

53. Foerster, 'Κύριος', p. 1083.

54. Foerster, 'Κύριος', p. 1083.

55. Foerster, 'Κύριος', pp. 1084-85.

56. In the first century (based on the search described above), there are 530 [430 singular] extant usages in literature without direct Jewish or Christian influence.

57. Foerster, 'Κύριος', p. 1049. Foerster cites CIG 4897a and dates the inscription to 99–90 BCE. Here I have referenced a later edition of the same inscription with the dating from that source.

(ὡς θέλει ὁ Σεκνεβτῦ[νις] ὁ κύριος θεός, 'as Soknopaios, the lord god desires' [PTebt 284.5-6; see also OGIS 655]).

For the purposes of this work, the most significant occurrences may be in the context of certain banquet invitations. For example,

Ἐρωτᾷ σε Ἀντώνιο(ς) Πτολεμ(αίου) διπνῆσ(αι)
παρ᾽ αὐτῶι εἰς κλείνην τοῦ κυρίου
Σαράπιδος ἐν τοῖς Κλαυδ(ίου) Σαραπίω(νος)
(POxy 523.1-3 [second century CE])

Antonios [son] of Ptolemaios invites you to dine
with him at the table (couch?) of the lord
Sarapis in the [house] of Claudius Sarapion

The use of κύριος in such documents refers mostly to the god Sarapis;[58] however, the feminine κύρια appears with Isis (POxy 4539.2-3).[59] These are generally dated to the second century CE or later (however, POxy 2592 may be late first or early second century). Other gods appear in invitations, but not usually with the title κύριος (e.g. POxy 1485.3 [Demeter; second to fourth centuries CE]).

d. *New Testament Usage (Non-Pauline)*

The noun κύριος is very common in the New Testament. It occurs 717 times in 660 verses, of which 703 (in 652 verses) are singular. The singular is of most interest to this study and will be referred to here.[60] The Pauline corpus accounts for the most uses (269; see below). Luke uses the singular often (206: 102 in the Gospel and 104 in Acts).[61] Matthew, Mark and John

---

58. See also POxy 110.2-3 (second century CE); 1484.3-4 (second or early third century CE); 1755.4 (second or early third century CE); 2592.2 (late first or early second century CE); 3693.3-4 (second century CE); 4339.2-3 (second–third century CE); 4540.2-3 (third century?). John Fotopoulos also includes POslo 157; PFlor 7; PColl.Youtie 51, 52; PNovio 4; PMil.Vogl 68.57 (*Food Offered to Idols*, pp. 107-9).

59. Fotopoulos also includes PFouad 76 (*Food Offered to Idols*, p. 110).

60. There are fourteen occurrences of the plural. It is most commonly used to refer to masters or owners of slaves (Acts 16.16, 19; Eph. 6.5, 9; Col. 3.22; 4.1; and probably Mt. 6.24 and parallel Lk. 16.13) or beasts (Mt. 15.27; Lk. 19.33). It is once used of Paul and Silas by one who would normally be considered of higher social rank (Acts 16.30); however, in light of miraculous circumstances and Paul and Silas's restraint (by not escaping), the jailer was both in awe and in the debt of the two men. Finally, it is used of groups of lords who are inferior to one lord (1 Cor. 8.5; Rev. 17.14; 19.16).

61. The study of κύριος in the Lukan material is an area of recent interest. See, e.g., Donald L. Jones, 'The Title *Kyrios* in Luke–Acts', in George W. MacRae (ed.), *Society of Biblical Literature 1974 Seminar Papers* (SBLSP, 2; Cambridge, MA: Scholars Press, 1974), pp. 85-101; James D.G. Dunn, 'ΚΥΡΙΟΣ in Acts', in *The Christ and the Spirit: Collected Essays of James D.G. Dunn*. I. *Christology* (Grand Rapids: Eerdmans, 1998; repr. from *Christus als die Mitte der Schrift* [Berlin: W. de Gruyter, 1997]), pp. 241-53;

account for 78, 18 and 52 occurrences, respectively.[62] The Catholic Epistles use the term 59 times; however, it is not used in the three Johannine Epistles.[63] Finally Revelation uses the singular 21 times.

The meaning of the term in the New Testament does not vary from what has already been stated. BDAG, for example, provides two major categories: 'one who is in charge by virtue of possession, *owner*' and 'one who is in a position of authority, *lord, master*'. The former can refer to those who are owners of impersonal items (e.g. a vineyard: Mt. 20.8; Lk. 20.13; a colt: Lk. 19.33; a house: Mk 13.35). The latter accounts for most of the New Testament examples (e.g. Mt. 5.33; Lk. 1.6; etc.). Also included in this classification for BDAG is the term's only use for a husband's relationship to his wife (1 Pet. 3.6). However, this is not a simple description of a husband but demonstrates Sarah's submissive role to Abraham (see Gen. 18.12 mentioned above). Nevertheless, this is presented as a positive example, and it is clear that the author of 1 Peter desires Sarah's example to be followed by the married women among his readership. In addition to these two major categories, the term κύριος is used (often in the vocative) as a simple term of respect. This is especially the case in contexts of addressing another in some type of higher standing. See also the discussion in MM, which is similar to that of BDAG.

Louw and Nida's lexicon is particularly helpful. It is arranged by semantic domains and thus organizes words into various categories. The categories (subdomains) into which they place New Testament occurrences of κύριος are (1) supernatural powers (12.9: 'Lord'; Mt. 1.20; 1 Cor. 1.3[64]), (2) rule,

---

C. Kavin Rowe, *Early Narrative Christology: The Lord in the Gospel of Luke* (BZNW, 139; Berlin: W. de Gruyter, 2006). For a treatment that Dunn ('ΚΥΡΙΟΣ', p. 242) considers a 'starting point' for this study, see Henry J. Cadbury, 'The Titles of Jesus in Acts', in F.J. Foakes Jackson and Kirsopp Lake (eds.), *The Beginnings of Christianity. Part I. The Acts of the Apostles*, V (London: Macmillan, 1933), pp. 359-62.

62. For an article arguing that κύριος plays a more significant role in Mark than it is often afforded, see Daniel Johansson, '*Kyrios* in the Gospel of Mark', *JSNT* 33 (2010), pp. 101-24. Johansson focuses on God and Jesus as referents of κύριος and does not consider the imperial context. For an article on κύριος in material traditionally considered Q, see Marco Frenschkowski, 'Kyrios in Context: Q 6:46, the Emperor as "Lord", and the Political Implications of Christology in Q', in Michael Labahn and Jürgen Zangenberg (eds.), *Zwischen den Reichen: Neues Testament und römische Herrschaft. Vorträge auf der ersten Konferenz der European Association for Biblical Studies* (TANZ, 36. Tübingen: Francke, 2002), pp. 95-118. For a discussion of κύριος in John with sensitivity to the imperial context, see Sjef van Tilborg, *Reading John in Ephesus* (NovTSup, 83; Leiden: E.J. Brill, 1996), pp. 55-56.

63. However, in 2 John 3, κυρίου is added before Ἰησοῦ Χριστοῦ in many important manuscripts, including the original hand and second corrector of ℵ and 33. It is added also in the manuscripts represented by gothic M. However, the omission has equal or better support including A, B, 81 and 1739. The shorter reading is to be preferred.

64. The passages listed in this paragraph are all the verses cited by LN.

govern (37.51: 'ruler'; Mt. 6.24), (3) have, possess, property, owner (57.12: 'owner'; Lk. 19.33; Jn 13.16; Gal. 4.1), (4) high status or rank (including persons of high status) (87.53: 'sir'; Mt. 13.27).[65] As with BDAG, notions of ownership and/or authority are evident in all of these subdomains.

As with any attempt to classify usage too precisely, BDAG's distinction between 'ownership' and 'authority' cannot be easily delineated (as is acknowledged: 'The mng. *owner* easily passes into that of *lord, master*, one who has full control of somth.'). Where does the notion of *owner* end and the notion of *master* begin? If a simple distinction could be made between personal and impersonal, such a classification system could be more helpful. For example, why is the *owner* nuance for κύριος used for slaves and a household (clearly the metaphorical meaning of Mk 13.35) but not a wife? A distinction between items paid for and not paid for is similarly problematic. One may pay for a slave, but one may also receive a slave from a subjugated people (in a war or the like). Is it possible that the modern distinction is anachronistic to the first century? Despite the various relational differences, the essential nuance is *authority over*. One is a κύριος in relation to others. The κύριος has authority over someone/something else. Also in addresses often in the vocative, there is an acknowledgment of authority, even if not necessarily in relation to the speaker. The meaning determined here is confirmed by the standard lexicons such as LSJ, BDAG, LN, and even the more specifically focused MM.

As noted above in a footnote, the Lukan material is of recent interest. However, the works cited do not discuss in any detail the imperial implications of the term. One recent study by C. Kavin Rowe discusses this in detail and concludes, among other things, that in Acts 10.36 an explicit challenge to *all lords* is made. This includes the emperor.[66] Concerning the phrase describing Jesus, οὗτός ἐστιν πάντων κύριος, Rowe points out that πάντων κύριος is used of the emperor (e.g. Epictetus, *Discourses* 4.1.12).[67] More importantly, he rejects the common view that this clause is parenthetical, as it is sometimes translated: 'he is Lord of all' (NRSV).[68] Rowe gives the demonstrative pronoun (οὗτος) its full force, which impacts the entire clause,

---

65. The categories or subdomains are all within larger domains. These are respectively: (1) supernatural beings and powers (12), (2) control rule (37), (3) possess, transfer, exchange (57), (4) status. Additionally, LN includes κύριος as part of two idioms (53.62 [2 Tim. 2.19] and 87.56 [Rom. 14.4]).

66. C. Kavin Rowe, "Luke–Acts and the Imperial Cult: A Way through the Conundrum?" *JSNT* 27 (2005), pp. 279-300 (290-91).

67. Rowe, "Luke–Acts and the Imperial Cult," pp. 292-93. See further discussion on this verse and others in Chapter 5.

68. The RSV and the NASB put the clause in parentheses; the NIV makes it a relative clause: 'who is Lord of all'.

Taken seriously, οὗτός excludes the idea that the sentence is parenthetical in importance and instead points to the dramatic nature of Peter's claim: Jesus Christ, this one, is κύριος πάντων. The underside of the stress that the demonstrative places on this claim is that there are others who are acknowledged as κύριος. Οὗτός thus serves as a countering devise and raises the volume of the πάντων: *this one*—and not someone else—is the κύριος of all.[69]

Thus, the clause is translated, 'this one is lord of all' with an emphasis on Jesus' role as κύριος in contrast to others. Although not denying possible anti-imperial implications of the event described, Rowe concentrates on the original readers of the book, which he dates to the Flavian dynasty.[70]

e. *Pauline Usage*

Κύριος occurs in the singular 269 times in 241 verses (plus 5 in the plural). Most are in the seven undisputed Pauline Epistles (187). The so called 'deutero-Pauline' Epistles (Ephesians, Colossians, and 2 Thessalonians) account for 60, and the Pastorals account for only 22 (none in Titus[71]).

As for relative occurrences within a book compared to other words, the term is most frequent in the two Thessalonian epistles. Based on occurrences per 1000 words, 2 Thessalonians uses κύριος most frequently (26.7 times). First Thessalonians uses it 16.2 times. Philemon (14.9) and 2 Timothy (12.9) also have high percentages.[72] With one exception (2 Thessalonians) these statistics can be explained by the relatively short length of the books. For example, the obligatory mention of the Lord Jesus Christ (or similar appellation) at the beginning and the end accounts for two or three of the uses in Philemon (vv. 3, 5 and 25). Only two more references to Jesus as κύριος in the letter (vv. 16 and 20) and the ratio of the term would be 14.9 times per 1000 words. Compare this to the lengthy books by Luke,

69. Rowe, 'Luke–Acts and the Imperial Cult', p. 291.

70. Rowe, 'Luke–Acts and the Imperial Cult', p. 291, esp. n. 46.

71. However, in Tit. 1.4 κυρίου is added before Ἰησοῦ Χριστοῦ (although Χριστοῦ Ἰησοῦ is likely the original as reflected in NA[27]; see the external evidence for the omission below) in the ninth-century Western tradition (represented by F, G, and the second corrector of D) as well as a majority of manuscripts (mostly late Byzantine minuscules) represented by gothic M in NA[27]. Additionally, although the eleventh-century Alexandrian minuscule 1175 does not explicitly contain this verse, its inclusion in parentheses in NA[27] suggests that there is evidence (probably spacing) that the term was included. However, the case for its omission is convincing. In addition to superior external support, including the fourth-century uncial ℵ, the fifth-century uncials A and C, and the original hand of D (sixth century), there are favourable internal arguments such as the preference for the shorter reading and the difficulty of accounting for its omission.

72. Two other New Testament books have high percentages: Jude (15.2) and 2 Peter (12.7).

which have the most occurrences (102 and 104 respectively) and the frequency per 1000 words is only 5.2 and 5.6 respectively.[73]

The vast majority of usages refer to Jesus (e.g. Rom. 1.4; Phil. 2.19; 1 Thess. 3.11; Phlm 1.16). However, it also refers to God, the Father (often related to Old Testament quotations; e.g. Rom. 4.8).[74] In the singular, κύριος refers to humans only one time: Gal. 4.1 (slave owner). Four of the five plural usages cited above also refer to slave owners. For Paul, then, κύριος is primarily used for Jesus. However, this cannot be taken to suggest that Paul has reserved this term generally for Jesus. The contents of Paul's letters do not provide the same opportunities as narrative to describe various types of authority figures. The use of the word for slave owners (especially Gal. 4.1) suggests that if opportunities arise, Paul would not hesitate to use the term.

f. *Early Post-New Testament Christian Usage*

Here we will consider only the earliest post-New Testament writings usually labelled the Apostolic Fathers, as defined by works such as that of Michael W. Holmes.[75] This is because these works are the closest in time to the New Testament. The literature associated with Clement of Rome accounts for the most occurrences among Christian writers (317 [313 singular]). Ignatius and the *Epistle of Barnabas* also use the term consistently (219 [217 singular] and 105 [104 singular], respectively). The remaining 140 [138 singular] examples occur in other Pseudepigrapha and other patristic literature.[76] As noted, the extensive use of κύριος in this literature is due to the prominence of the term in the Septuagint and the New Testament, which are often the focus, basis, or primary influence of the literature. Nevertheless, despite the high proportion of uses for Jesus (e.g. *1 Clement* 42.1; *2 Clement* 8.5;

---

73. To put this in perspective it is helpful to compare this with a common word such as the conjunction καί. Luke uses this function word ten times more in Acts than κύριος (1,038 times; 56.2/1000 words) and even more in the Gospel (1,379; 70.7/1000). However, Philemon uses it fewer than three times more (14; 41.8/1000) and 2 Thessalonians just over twice as much (45; 54.7/1000).

74. Maximilian Zerwick's suggestion that Paul uses κύριος with the article for Jesus and without for Yahweh is too simplistic and not sustainable (*Biblical Greek Illustrated by Examples* [trans. Joseph Smith; Scripta Pontificii Instituti Biblici, 114. Rome: Editrice Pontificio Istituto Biblico, 1963.], p. 54 [section 169]). His own discussion demonstrates this. He notes that in 2 Cor. 3.17 the article appears with κύριος, but the title here probably refers to God. He identifies the article as anaphoric (which it probably is) (p. 54 [sec. 169]). Nevertheless, this reasoning exposes the failure of this view to account for the evidence. The use of the article is too complex to make simple statements about meaning or referents based on its presence or absence.

75. See, e.g., Michael W. Holmes, ed. and trans., *The Apostolic Fathers*.

76. *Testament of Abraham* (88 [recension A: 50; recension B: 38]); *Life of Adam and Eve* (31); *Epistle of Polycarp* (18 [16 singular]); *Apocalypse of Elijah* (2); *Assumption of Moses* (1).

Martyrdom of Polycarp 22.3; *Didache* 9.5), this literature demonstrates a range of meaning similar to that described above: 'one having lawful authority over a slave' (Hermas, *Similitudes* 105.4; *Barnabas* 19.7 [plural]); 'one having authority over a subject people' (*Martyrdom of Polycarp* 8.2 [this is the passage discussed elsewhere where Caesar is called Lord]) and a similar usage for 'one having authority over creation' (Hermas, *Mandates* 47.3).[77] The nuance of legal authority is an inherent aspect of the meaning for the referents and the roles they take in relation to others. In these examples however the final usage ('authority over subject people') is prominent and is usually associated with a divine being.[78]

g. *Κύριος and Divinity*

Of interest to a study of Pauline Christology is whether the term κύριος includes a nuance of divinity. Adolf Deissmann makes a strong statement after discussing the use of the term for gods and rulers considered divine: 'It may be said with certainty that at the time when Christianity originated "Lord" was a divine predicate intelligible to the whole Eastern world.'[79] This clearly is overstating the case. The fact that it is consistently used of non-divine people makes this clear (see the majority of references cited above from non-biblical literature and New Testament examples such as Eph. 6.9a; 1 Pet. 3.6; etc.). Bietenhard makes a more sober claim concerning the use of κύριος for the emperor: 'In and of itself the title *kyrios* does not call the emperor god; but when he is worshipped as divine, the title Lord also counts as a divine predicate.'[80] This is preferable to Deissmann because it acknowledges that the term does not imply divinity itself. However, the second statement suggests that the term has a divine nuance when applied to gods (or those so worshipped). For an understanding of the meaning of the term κύριος, one wonders whether this is much of an improvement over Deissmann. It basically suggests that κύριος includes the meaning 'divinity' *when* its referent is divine. It may be true that, if the term is commonly applied to divinity, this meaning may become associated with the term or even become part of it. However, in such cases, usage for the non-divine would decrease and possibly even disappear. This is not the case. When considering *Koine*, there has always been a significant proportion of examples in which the referent is not divine. However, it is possible that the word carried this implication in certain contexts (e.g. religious) while not in others.

---

77. The vocative also occurs as a simple address of respect (Hermas, *Mandates* 29.4).

78. There is some variety in the translation of κύριος in the Syriac version of the New Testament, which may reflect theological concerns. See Alain-Georges Martin, "La traduction de κύριος en syriaque," *FilolNT* 12 (1999), pp. 25-54.

79. Deissmann, *Light from the Ancient East*, p. 350.

80. Bietenhard, 'Κύριος', 511.

However, such suggestions must be made with extreme caution. In addition to words like κύριος, it could be argued that other words applied to deity in religious contexts (e.g. σωτήρ[81]) could also imply divinity. In this case, it is the religious context that supplies the divine nuance, not the term. In other words, it is an issue of pragmatics, not semantics as defined in this work.

A simple (and imperfect) analogy may illustrate the point. Consider a table in a religious building used for religious purposes such as sacrifice. Worshippers may consider this table *holy*. In discussion, statements about the table such as 'the sacrifice is on the table', 'do not allow anything common to touch the table', and 'be very careful, the table is in there' suggest that the table is a holy item. However, does the word 'table' itself provide this nuance? No, it is the context. It is unlikely that a worshipper who, in this context when at home, heard a family member say, 'the meal in on the table', would think the meal was on a holy object. The symbol 'table' does not imply holiness. I suggest that the survey of referents above makes it clear that the term κύριος was used for many in the first century. It was fairly common. Even in religious contexts, the term itself does not imply divinity. When one reads ὁ κύριος in the LXX or in the New Testament, the reader will easily identify the referent as יהוה and Jesus (except in most Old Testament quotations), respectively, when intended.[82] However, this identification should not be mistaken for a claim of divinity because of the term used by the writers for these referents. The referents may be divine, but it is not the term κύριος that brings this meaning to the context.

It may be the case that the extensive use of "lord" in English for God and Jesus has caused an anachronistic reading of the *Koine* κύριος. This is probably more true of American English than British, since the latter does use the term to apply to various types of leaders. Few Americans would ever use the term for anyone other than God or Jesus.

In order further to support the position previously suggested, it may be helpful to draw on principles from H. Paul Grice and developed by Mari Olsen to clarify the distinction between the meaning of the term and associated non-inherent meanings (semantics and pragmatics). The question of concern here is whether the term κύριος included the nuance of *divinity* as part of its semantic meaning.

A 1996 dissertation on verbal aspect by Mari Olsen has made a distinction between semantic and pragmatic meaning similar to (but not identical with) that which was made above, where semantic meaning is basically what the term brings to the context. This dissertation was published as *A Semantic*

---

81. See Werner Foerster and Georg Fohrer, 'Σῴζω' [and cognates], *TDNT*, VII, pp. 1003-1005 (this section was written by Foester). See also Cuss, *Imperial Cult*, pp. 63-64.

82. In rare instances when other referents are intended, identification is always clear.

and Pragmatic Model of Lexical and Grammatical Aspect.[83] In this book the distinction between semantics and pragmatics is based on Grice's notion of *cancelability* (and its opposite principle, *redundancy*). This notion was briefly introduced by Grice in his influential William James Lecture series given at Harvard University in 1967.[84] However, since Grice's treatment is brief, I will focus on Olsen's development. Olsen uses these principles for both lexical and grammatical work. I have previously rejected Olsen's theory as a basis for grammatical work because notions such as *cancelability* and the like were too precise, given a cognitive view of language.[85] I acknowledged, however, that it could be helpful for lexical work.[86] Though not perfect, it may be helpful to support the point being made here.

For Olsen, semantic meaning 'cannot be cancelable without contradiction nor reinforced without redundancy'.[87] For a basic description of this principle, Olsen's own lexical example *plod* will be considered.[88] To determine whether the semantic meaning of *plod* includes the meanings *slow* and *tired*, the following sentences may be considered:

1a. Cancelable?:   Elsie plodded along, but not slowly
1b. Reinforcement?:   Elsie plodded along, slowly

2a. Cancelable?:   Elsie plodded along, although she wasn't tired
2b. Reinforcement?:   Elsie plodded along, she was very tired

The meaning 'slow' is part of Olsen's understanding of the semantic meaning of *plod*. The first sentence (1a) is contradictory. The second clause contradicts or cancels the meaning of the first clause. In the second sentence (1b) 'slowly' is redundant (reinforces) the meaning in the first clause. However, concerning 'tired', both sentences (2a and 2b) are acceptable. Its presence in clause two neither cancels the first clause nor is redundant in the second. However, since in a specific context the meaning of *plod* may include the notion of 'tired', tired is a (pragmatic) implicature of *plod*.

In order to apply these principles to the question of whether κύριος includes a divine nuance, we simply need to consider whether the addition

---

83. Mari Broman Olsen, *A Semantic and Pragmatic Model of Lexical and Grammatical Aspect* (Outstanding Dissertations in Linguistics; New York: Garland, 1997).

84. Grice, "Logic and Conversation," p. 57. The notion of *cancelability* is explained further in another paper from the same lecture series, H. Paul Grice, "Further Notes on Logic and Conversation," pp. 115-18. It seems that only the former work was used by Olsen (see her bibliography).

85. Fantin, *Greek Imperative Mood*, pp. 131, 345-46.

86. Fantin, *Greek Imperative Mood*, p. 346.

87. Olsen, *Aspect*, p. 17.

88. Olsen, *Aspect*, p. 17.

of a divine nuance is cancelable and/or provides reinforcement (is redundant) to the meaning of κύριος:

3a. Cancelable?:   He is lord (κύριος), but not divine
3b. Reinforcement?:   He is lord and divine

The first sentence (3a) is acceptable. The denial of divinity does not cancel the nature of lordship for the referent. Additionally, the second sentence (3b) is not redundant. Therefore, we conclude that *divinity* is not part of the semantic meaning of κύριος. To follow through with Olsen's example above, it might be concluded that *divinity* is a pragmatic effect of *lord* in certain contexts. However, it seems preferable to maintain that, given the nature of what we have discussed previously about the meaning of κύριος, a notion of divinity is supplied by other means. *Divinity* is clearly compatible with the meaning of κύριος; however, it is not necessarily brought to the context by the use of the term.[89]

When discussing specific referents of the label κύριος, some may still question whether *divinity* is not really part of the term. Christians may reject this conclusion. I must reiterate that the exercise here is linguistic not theological. By denying the nuance of *divinity* in the meaning of κύριος, I am not denying Paul's belief in Jesus' divinity. In fact, I am not making any statement about this here at all. Such christological conclusions are based on other means. This study may contribute, but it is not the focus. One need only consider the great christological debates throughout early church history, which appealed to Scripture for their views. For example, the Arians did not believe that Jesus was God; however, they did not question whether Jesus was ὁ κύριος.

In summary, it is of crucial importance to avoid assuming that a word used extensively of deity implies divinity. In the case of κύριος, the term is well suited to divinity. This is because its semantic meaning includes nuances of *authority*, *lordship* and so on and suggests a certain relationship between the one called κύριος and the one using the term.

3. *Semantics 2: External Considerations*

In order to understand a term, it is important to consider external factors that can help determine meaning in a more precise manner. In this section I will consider κύριος in its vocative form, compare it with two synonyms, and contrast it with the Latin *dominus*.

---

89. This method also demonstrates that *divinity* does not include *lord* as part of its semantic makeup. Both of the following sentences are acceptable:
4a. Cancelable?:   He is divine but not lord (κύριος)
4b. Reinforcement?:   He is divine and lord

a. *The Vocative*

The vocative has been mentioned above (see pp. 154-56, *Koine Usage,* for statistics). It is used for both emperors (Caligula: Philo, *On the Embassy to Gaius* 356) and Christ (Mt. 8.2). We have minimized its importance throughout. The reason for this is that the vocative seems to have a unique history. In a discussion of Roman politeness, Eleanor Dickey has described the vocatives, κύριε, δέσποτα, and *domine* in detail.[90] Against the traditional view, which suggests that *domine* is a Grecism from κύριε, Dickey believes that κύριε was essentially created in the first century CE to translate *domine*.[91] This is a somewhat peculiar claim, given that the singular vocative is found 720 times (in 630 verses) in the Greek Old Testament.[92] However, she acknowledges a rare usage in Pindar and suggests that the Greek Old Testament usage is essentially due to translation technique.[93] *Domine* was used in our period as a 'courteous but not especially subservient address'.[94] The term can be used to address not only superiors but also family members and equals. In her research of masculine and feminine singular vocatives in first-century CE papyri, Dickey concludes, '[the vocatives] seem to be equally divided between contexts in which distanced respect is plausible and letters to family and friends'.[95]

In the New Testament, the vocative is used in the same manner. Each of the Gospels uses it for Jesus in a way that cannot imply much more than the meaning of 'sir' (Mt. 8.6; Mk 7.28 [only Markan occurrence]; Lk. 7.6; Jn 4.11).

Despite the use of the vocative for the emperor, given its history and that there is no potential polemical usage in the vocative in Paul (used only in Rom. 10.16; 11.3), it is prudent to minimize vocative usages in our discussion.

b. *Synonyms*

There are two terms used in the New Testament that can be considered synonyms of κύριος. First, ἐπιστάτης is found exclusively in Luke (7x) and refers only to Jesus. Three times it is spoken by Peter (5.5; 8.45; 9.33), twice by the disciples as a group (8.24 [2x]; these occurrences are in the same statement right next to each other), once by John (9.49). It is used

---

90. Eleanor Dickey, 'Κύριε, Δέσποτα, *Domine*: Greek Politeness in the Roman Empire', *JHS* 121 (2001), pp. 1-11. This study is highly detailed and includes a diachronic study of the terms noting changes in usage throughout the Roman period. Our focus is on only the first century CE.

91. Dickey, 'Κύριε, Δέσποτα, *Domine*', pp. 10-11.

92. See, e.g., for God: Exod. 5.22; 2 Chron. 1.9; Ps. 3.2; Isa. 63.16; for men: Gen. 31.35. The plural occurs once (Gen. 19.2).

93. Dickey, 'Κύριε, Δέσποτα, *Domine*', p. 5.

94. Dickey, 'Κύριε, Δέσποτα, *Domine*', p. 10.

95. Dickey, 'Κύριε, Δέσποτα, *Domine*', p. 7.

by non-disciples only once—by a groups of lepers (17.13). It is always in the vocative case (ἐπιστάτα). The term is used for general supervisors or overseers in the Greek Old Testament (Exod. 1.11; 5.14; 3Kgdms 2.35h; 5.30 (= 1 Kgs 5.16); 4 Kgdms 25.19; 2 Chron. 2.1; 31.12; 1 Esd. 1.8; Jdt. 2.14; 2 Macc. 5.22; Jer. 36.26; 52.25). Louw and Nida include it in their domain of 'status' within the subdomain of 'high status or rank' (87.50; citing Lk. 5.5 as the only example). Thus, they view this term as similar to κύριος in the same subdomain (87.53). This usage of κύριος is also usually vocative, and both can be translated 'sir' (Mt. 13.27 is the example cited). The meanings given by LN are similar; both are terms of respect. However, ἐπιστάτης includes the meaning of 'leader': 'a person of high status, particularly in view of a role of leadership' (LN, 87.50). This is evident for six of the usages; however, 'leadership' cannot be part of the intended meaning when uttered by the lepers (Lk. 17.13).[96] Κύριος can also be used in this manner, since the example given also includes the referent as a leader (landowner addressed by servants; Mt. 13.27). Nevertheless, ἐπιστάτης is never used by slaves in the New Testament (disciples and in one case healed lepers). Thus, although our database is limited, it seems that ἐπιστάτης has a narrower meaning than κύριος. The latter can be a term of respect used by many, including slaves; the former is used only of free individuals. Although the usage in Lk. 17.13 can only loosely (if at all) be seen as having a nuance of 'leadership', ἐπιστάτης may include this meaning in most cases.

᾽Επιστάτης has the same meaning also outside biblical literature with various referents.[97] Luke may use it as a translation for רַבִּי;[98] however, this cannot be demonstrated beyond speculation based on one parallel: Lk. 9.33 ‖ Mk 9.5 (ῥαββί) (‖Mt. 17.4, κύριε). There are only two other parallels with other Synoptics: Lk. 8.24 [2x] ‖ Mk 4.38 (διδάσκαλε) ‖ Mt. 8.25 (κύριε) and Lk. 9.49 ‖ Mk 9.38 (διδάσκαλε). The other three usages are not paralleled with an address. Luke uses both διδάσκαλε (12x; e.g. 7.20 [from Peter]) and κύριε (27x; e.g. 9.54 [from James and John]) more than ἐπιστάτα. Luke does not use either ῥαββί or the Aramaic ῥαββουνί, which are used by the other Gospel writers (although Matthew does not use the Aramaic form).

In the end, the usage of ἐπιστάτης only by Luke (and only seven total occurrences) minimizes its usefulness for our purposes. I have not seen any usages for the emperor in the first century, nor is it clear how common this term actually was.[99]

---

96. It does not appear that Louw and Nida account for this verse.

97. See MM.

98. MM; Albrecht Oepke, '᾽Επιστάτης', *TDNT*, II, pp. 622-23 (623).

99. Oepke may be overstating his case when he says, 'We have no knowledge

Κύριος shares much of its semantic field with δεσπότης. The same type of referents we have seen with κύριος appear also with δεσπότης: 'master of a house' (Aeschylus, *Persians*, 169 [fifth century BCE]), 'one who is master/owner of a slave' (Aristotle, *Politics* 1.3 = 1253b.3-4 [fourth century BCE]), 'one having authority over subject people' (Herodotus 3.89 [fifth century BCE]), and gods (Xenophon, *Anabasis* 3.2.13 [fifth–fourth century BCE; gods in general]), including Yahweh (Isa. 1.24; 2 Macc. 5.17).

One type of example lacking from these passages is the nuance of 'one who has authority over a wife or girl'. It is possible that this is understood under the 'master of a household' usage. Further, it is difficult to say that this would not have occurred. However, given the lack of extant evidence, it is likely rare at best.

A striking example of δεσπότης occurs in Josephus. At the end of the Jewish War, a number of Sicarii escape to Egypt and attempt to incite the Jew there to fight. Among other things, they encourage the people to make θεὸν . . . μόνον ἡγεῖσθαι δεσπότην ('God alone to be Lord' [*War* 7.10.1 §410]). After the Sicarii are handed over to the Romans, they (including children) refuse to acknowledge Καίσαρα δεσπότην ('Caesar is lord' [7.10.1 §§418, 419]) even under torture. This example is very similar to the Polycarp martyrdom and will be returned to below.

Louw and Nida list δεσπότης in two domains. In both cases the subdomains also include a usage of κύριος. First, in the domain of 'control', subdomain 'rule, govern', define this usage for κύριος as 'one who rules or exercises authority over others' (37.51; citing Mt. 6.24). However, their meaning for δεσπότης is stronger, 'one who holds complete power or authority over another' (37.63). In the verses cited by LN (1 Tim. 6.1; Acts 4.24), this nuance of 'complete' is evident. Both are in the context of honour. In 1 Tim. 6.1, slaves are instructed to honour their masters in order that God will not be blasphemed. The master is in complete control of the slaves. In Acts, God is honoured as the creator and sustainer. He is in complete control. Second, in the domain of 'possess, transfer, exchange', subdomain of 'have, possess, property, owner', both κύριος (57.12; Lk. 19.33; Jn 13.16) and δεσπότης (57.13; 2 Tim. 2.21) are owners of slaves. Louw and Nida emphasize 'high status and respect' for κύριος and 'absolute, and in some instances, arbitrary jurisdiction' for δεσπότης. This difference seems minimal and difficult to sustain on the examples cited alone. However, as we further consider these terms, a difference may become more pronounced.

whether or not it was a common form of address' ('Ἐπιστάτης', p. 623). There seems to be enough evidence to suggest that the word was known and used.

Even in the vocative, there seems to be a difference in the terms. As we have seen, κύριε could be used for friends and equals throughout the Roman period. However, δέσποτα is used almost always for superiors.[100]

Δεσπότης is not common in the New Testament. It occurs only ten times and in the Pauline corpus only in the Pastorals. Luke uses it twice to refer to God the Father (Lk. 2.29; Acts 4.24). It refers to God in Rev. 6.10 and probably in 2 Pet. 2.1 (or possibly Jesus). In Jude 4 it occurs with κύριος for Jesus. 1 Peter 2.18 refers to slave owners. In the Pastorals it is used three times for slave owners (1 Tim. 6.1, 2; Tit. 2.9) and once for God (2 Tim. 2.21). Thus, in New Testament usage when humans are referents, δεσπότης refers only to slave owners.

The slave owner nuance for δεσπότης can be seen also in Cassius Dio's record of the rejection of the title by Tiberius (57.8.1-2; this passage will be discussed further below). If Tiberius spoke these words, he likely did so in Latin. Thus, this passage is difficult to use for first-century evidence. However, in this context, Cassius Dio's use of the title demonstrates further evidence for the nuance of slave ownership (albeit in the third century).

When the two terms are considered together, many similarities are evident. However, there may be emphasized nuances that are stronger in one term than in the other. It seems that the *ownership* nuance may be more prominent with δεσπότης[101] and the *legal* nuance may be stronger with κύριος. This would explain the lack of evidence for the *authority over wife and daughter* nuance. It is here that the insights of Smith cited above are helpful. His examination of κύριος leads him to see the relationship between κύριος and a subordinate in a more legal sense.[102]

There may be many reasons why the New Testament authors chose κύριος instead of δεσπότης as a major title for Christ. Three may be suggested. First, with κύριος, the meaning of ownership is less prominent and it provides for inclusion of other types of relationships. However, it must be noted that there is much overlap in the two terms. Second, it may be a conscious effort to use emperor terminology that was familiar to the target readers. This may or may not be polemical. Although these two reasons may be involved, the most likely reason is the predominant use of κύριος in the Greek Old Testament. The influence of this source cannot be overestimated.

---

100. Dickey, 'Κύριε, Δέσποτα, *Domine*', p. 9.

101. See the prominence of this usage in BDAG.

102. Smith, 'Meaning', p. 157. However, as noted above, Smith takes his observations too far, minimizing other important evidence. For more detailed information on δεσπότης, see Karl Heinrich Rengstorf, 'Δεσπότης', (and cognates), in *TDNT*, II, pp. 44-49.

Additionally, passages such as Phil. 2.11 (see Chapter 5), explicitly suggest that the common Greek Old Testament title for God is now given to Jesus.[103]

c. *Greek and Latin*

In the previous section, κύριος was compared with ἐπιστάτης and, more importantly, δεσπότης. In this section the comparison will be with the Latin *dominus*. Some discussion of the vocative of this form occurred above; here the title will be discussed in more detail.

When discussing imperial cults, I described a common (although somewhat limiting) three-way geographical distinction. However, for lordship terminology there may be a more important distinction, namely linguistic. Although there was certainly much bilingualism, the western part of the empire (including Italy) primarily used Latin, and the eastern part primarily used Greek.

Thus, in Greek, *lord* terminology is expressed by either κύριος or δεσπότης. In Latin, *lord* terminology is primarily expressed by *dominus*, which may be used for both of the Greek terms. Although this may seem to be a simple matter of translation, the events surrounding the emergence of the imperial period under Augustus will result in different (or additional) pragmatic effects with the Latin as opposed to the Greek.

There are examples of both Augustus and Tiberius rejecting the title *lord*. However, since most business in Rome was conducted in Latin, the original events most likely took place in Latin, not Greek. Concerning Augustus, Suetonius says,

> He always shrank from the title Lord [domini] as reproachful and insulting. When the words O just and gracious Lord! [O dominum aequum bonum!] were uttered in a farce at which he was a spectator and all the people sprang to their feet and applauded as if they were said of him, he at once checked their unseemly flattery by look and gesture, and on the following day sharply reproved them in an edict. After that he would not suffer himself to be called Sire [dominumque] even by his own children or his grandchildren either in jest or earnest, and he forbade them to use such flattering terms among themselves (*Augustus* 53.1; trans. Rolfe, LCL).[104]

Although this event occurred in Latin, an abbreviated translated account in Greek occurs in Cassius Dio (55.12.2-3), which uses δεσπότης where

---

103. For later development of the relationship between these two terms, see D. Hagedorn and K.A. Worp, 'Von κύριος zu δεσπότης: Eine Bemerkung zur Kaisertitulatur im 3./4. Jhdt', *ZPE* 39 (1980), pp. 165-77. Further discussion will occur in the next section with a different focus.

104. See also Cassius Dio 55.12.2-3. For Tiberius, see Tacitus, *Annals* 2.87; Suetonius, *Tiberius* 27; Cassius Dio, 57.8.1-4.

the original conversation had *dominus*. This linguistic issue is worth further discussion. A number of factors may have contributed to Cassius Dio's choice of δεσπότης rather than κύριος. First, the passage about Tiberius may shed some light on the reason: 'he would not allow himself to be called master [δεσπότην] by the freemen, nor *imperator* except by the soldiers; the title of Father of His Country he rejected absolutely; . . . I am master [δεσπότης] of the slaves, *imperator* of the soldiers, and chief of the rest' (Cassius Dio, 57.8.1-2; trans. Cary, LCL). Cassius Dio seems to have interpreted Tiberius to be rejecting the title because it implied that he was the master of slaves (thus lowering the status of the people of Rome). This does not seem to be what the Latin passages are communicating. The Suetonius passage about Augustus is similar to the Latin passages about Tiberius. For example, Tacitus states: 'Yet he would not on that score accept the title "Father of his Country", . . . and he administered a severe reprimand to those who had termed his occupation "divine" and himself "Lord [dominum]"' (*Annals* 2.87; trans. Jackson, LCL; see also Suetonius, *Tiberius*, 27). As discussed above, although there is significant overlap between the words, κύριος seems to emphasize one who has power to dispose another where δεσπότης emphasizes ownership.[105] The passages about Tiberius in Tacitus and Cassius Dio seem quite different. Initially, they appear to be describing the same event because the title 'Father of his country' occurs in both. The Suetonius passage (*Tiberius*, 27) seems quite different as well (one difference is that it does not include the title 'Father of his Country'). It is difficult to see it as parallel with Cassius Dio; however, it seems parallel with Tacitus (despite the lack of the title 'Father of his country'). It may be a coincidence (or error) that, although recording the same event, the title occurs in the Cassius Dio passage. In any case, the passage as it reads in Cassius Dio demands δεσπότης. The same cannot be said of the other passages if translated directly into Greek. Although unlikely, it is also possible that the Tiberius quotation influenced the Augustus saying owing to similarities in content.

Second, although unlikely based on what was just stated about the differences of the terms, the two words may have been interchangeable in this context and Cassius Dio merely made a choice. Third, it is possible that the uses of δεσπότης in Cassius Dio are reflecting Cassius Dio's time and not necessarily what would have occurred in the first century. The title δεσπότης became more common as an imperial title and increasingly replaced κύριος in the late third century.[106] However, Cassius Dio's history

---

105. Foerster, 'Κύριος', p. 1045.

106. Dickey, 'Κύριε, Δέσποτα, *Domine*', pp. 4-5. Although this article primarily discusses the vocative, this section refers to the word more generally. See also, Foerster, 'Κύριος', p. 1046.

was completed in the early decades of the third century. It is possible that he is reflecting this shift early. Finally, if the usage shift has not taken place, it is also possible that Cassius Dio used δεσπότης because κύριος was commonly used for the emperors both in his time and in his Greek sources. The context of Cassius Dio presents this action by Augustus and Tiberius as positive. He does not wish to present the early emperors as rejecting a title now common for his contemporaries.

Certainty on this issue is impossible. What is important is that the original rejections of the title took place in Latin. There is little evidence of an emperor being called *dominus* before Domitian (e.g. Martial, *Epigram* 5.8.1; 8.2.6). However, κύριος appears for all the emperors in the Julio-Claudian and Flavian dynasties. This can be best explained by a specific resistance to or even abhorrence of the title *dominus* in Roman tradition. As we have seen and will revisit, Augustus promoted himself as a first citizen, *princeps*, of the principate. This may be seen as a contrast to a *dominus*. Rome had been a republic for centuries. It was first and foremost opposed to a ruling king (*rex*). Even Julius Caesar seemed to avoid this title. The eastern empire did not share this tradition or a negative view of kingship; it had been ruled by various kings and lords for centuries.

It seems likely that the aversion of the Romans to the title *dominus* could be avoided with the Greek title. The negative pragmatic effects associated with the Latin do not have a counterpart in Greek. These negative effects are actually not part of the semantic makeup of any term for *lord*. Rather, they are from Roman tradition. Once this tradition fades, the Latin term can be used for leaders. However, in the first century, these effects were firmly entrenched in the cognitive environment of Latin speakers in the empire. Use of the Greek terms for *lord* may be acceptable for an emperor if they avoid the negative association with the Latin. In the East this would be much more likely than in the West. Additionally, given the prominence of Greek everywhere, it is likely that the Greek term could be used even in the West without the offensive nuance that the Latin would evoke.

4. *Relational Nature of Κύριος*

Κύριος has been examined in detail with reference to its meaning and possible referents. This has led to the conclusion that the term essentially means 'one in [recognized] authority over another', or with inanimate objects, 'one who [legally] owns something'. This is helpful but fails to provide us with the most important insights concerning the term for our purposes. Implied in the meaning of the term is a *relational* nuance. Concerning deities, this observation in not missed by Bietenhard, 'Where *kyrios* was used of a god, the servant . . . who thus used it stood in a personal relationship of responsibility towards the god, who on his part exercised personal authority.'[107] However, this should not be limited to deity. Our examples above all suggest an implied relational nuance. The one called κύριος had a specific relationship with those who addressed him as such. Society placed expectations on both parties, and each had responsibilities towards the other. These responsibilities were somewhat defined by the specific roles of the κύριος and his subordinates. The slave owner and father had different responsibilities toward their subordinates, but the basic framework was the same. The κύριος was superior and had the authority to control the subordinate. However, in addition to this, the κύριος was responsible for caring for the subordinate while this relationship was intact. Even slave owners were expected to treat their slaves in a positive manner, as laws indicate. Of course, abuses occurred, and the law was not always followed or enforced. Slaves could be beaten or even killed. Nevertheless, in principle the relationship depended on defined responsibilities of both parties. In the eyes of society, beatings were discipline, which was viewed as benefiting both parties. Even if extreme abuse was carried out, namely killing the slave, some ancient societies would see this as the right of the κύριος. The action would end the relationship, which would not benefit either party.

The issues discussed in this section are related to those raised in *Semantics 2* above (pp. 175-82). It continues our analysis of κύριος from an external perspective. However, the importance of the relational aspect of the term makes it preferable to discuss related issues separately.

a. *Κύριος: Social and Relational Roles*

One of the problems with attempting to determine whether an anti-imperial polemic exists in Paul's use of κύριος is the multitude of potential referents possible. As demonstrated above, the word was used of various types of people who had authority over others such as masters of households, owners of slaves, civil leaders (e.g. Agrippa II), and although it was not very common, even gods could be so labelled (e.g. Zeus, Sarapis). All of these applications seem to have been used without offence to Caesar. How can this be? If offence can be given, what distinguishes such usages from these?

In order to answer these questions, we must look beyond the term itself. The first step is to develop the relational implications of the term. The second will be to go beyond the simple term itself, which will be done below. Here the relational aspect of the term will be explored. Particular societies include complex webs of social roles and functions that define relationships. Some relationships are clearly defined and others more ambiguous. The role(s) one plays in society will determine what type of κύριος one is. These roles are essentially relational. At least four status and relationship

---

107. Bietenhard, 'Κύριος', p. 511.

options can be discussed between κύριος and subordinates: (1) the relation-ship of the referent to the individual using the label; (2) the social status of the referent with respect to the individual using the label; (3) the social status and relationship of the referent to the local community to which the individual using the label belongs; and (4) the social status and relationship of the referent to the wider cultural context (e.g. the [known] world or the total sphere of influence).

When one is addressed with the title κύριος, these factors are important. For example, when a father with little means or influence is addressed by his son as κύριος, he is *lord* of his family. He is not *lord* of anything else. When the son uses this title, nothing more than this is implied. If Agrippa II is addressed as κύριος by the same boy, a broader type of lordship is implied. These roles are understood.

The relational aspect of the term κύριος takes on additional importance in the Roman empire when one considers the web of relationships held together by its patronage system. Benefactors in theory took care of others and in return received support from those who benefited from the patron (see *The Emperor in the Roman World,* p. 138 above). Although specific relationships may differ, in this system a benefactor may also be a κύριος. This would not necessarily be the case with a benefactor who gives a monu-ment to a city. However, for an individual who has a mutual relationship with others who are dependent on him at some level, he would function as a κύριος. Thus, the relational nature of κύριος makes the referent a patron to those who address him with this title. There is a mutual relationship between the two parties where both share some responsibility.

b. *Absolute and Modified Forms*

There appears to be difference between κύριος in its absolute form (with or without the article) and its occurrence with a genitive modifier. In other words, ὁ κύριος ('the lord') may have a more universal authority than ὁ κύριος μου ('my lord'), which has a genitive restricting the sphere of lordship. This may be demonstrated through usage, especially in places like the Greek Old Testament, where God is often 'the Lord', the unchal-lenged power of all (Gen. 18.13). When subordinate *lords* are mentioned, a modified usage (often a pronoun) is common (Gen. 18.12; 24.12; 4 Kgdms [Hebrew: 2 Kgs] 2.5). The New Testament also has such constructions. For example, Paul often uses κύριος ἡμῶν for Jesus (1 Cor. 1.2; Gal. 6.18). This convention may be a way of explicitly limiting the referent's lordship sphere (i.e. what the κύριος is lord over), which may have the result of not causing offence to readers who might dispute this. However, it seems that to some extent all uses of the title have an implied modifier, even if this may be a universal sphere. Thus, when God is called *the Lord* in the Greek Old Testament, the implied sphere of lordship may be *of all*.

Therefore, although there may be a difference between absolute and modified forms, it is unwise to make too significant an issue of this. As we will develop below, there are other, more important factors that will contribute to different spheres of lordship. Essentially, whether explicitly modified or not, a relationship is implied.

c. Κύριος as a Religious Term?

One striking observation of the usage of κύριος (and other terms for *lord*) that has arisen from this study is its general absence from religious contexts. As we have seen in this chapter, with the exception of the Greek Old Testament, the New Testament, literature strongly influenced by these and some second-century dining invitations, the term is not very common for divine beings, does not necessarily include a nuance of divinity, and is rarely found in contexts where some type of specific religious activity is taking place. It is not entirely absent from such contexts (e.g. SIG³ 814, 30-31, 55; POxy 1143.4; see Chapter 5); however, this is not common and the emperors in these passages are not the object of worship in a cultic setting.

As we have seen, the title is applied to gods. However, given other referents and usages, this application is minimal. It is not found in contexts of emperor worship. Even in the extant inscriptions for the provincial cult of the Flavians in Ephesus completed by Domitian, the title is not used. There appears to be no extant evidence of imperial priests in the first century being called, ἱερεὺς τοῦ κυρίου.[108]

A striking example of the title's absence is the inscriptions of the Arval brothers in Rome.[109] This college of twelve priests functioned during the republic[110] and probably revived under Augustus, who probably joined in 29 BCE.[111] They were responsible primarily for rituals dedicated to Dea Dia. However, their complex included other religious buildings, such as a shrine for emperor worship. They even appeared to have been involved in imperial sacrifices during the Julio-Claudian dynasty.[112] This group recorded its activities on its walls, and extant are inscriptions ranging from 21 BCE to the

---

108. "Foerster, 'Κύριος', p. 1056. Foerster notes one inscription from 263 CE.

109. The most comprehensive discussion of this group is John Scheid, *Romulus et ses frères.*

110. Archaology has revealed that they were in existence in the third century BCE (Beard, North and Price, *Religions of Rome. I. A History*, p. 194). This group apparently traced its root to Romulus (Turcan, *Gods of Ancient Rome*, p. 57). This appears to be the belief of Turcan but evidence supports only a republican origin.

111. Beard, North and Price, *Religions of Rome*, I, p. 194.

112. Beard, North and Price, *Religions of Rome*, I, p. 195. Liebeschuetz suggests that during the empire rites to Dea Dia were eclipsed by petition and thanks for the emperor (*Continuity*, p. 63).

mid-third century (although there is a fragment as late as 304 CE).[113] These *Acta* provide us with a wealth of information about the cult's activities. It is striking that, despite the use of κύριος for emperors elsewhere, no emperor is given the title "lord" (*dominus*) until the reign of Caracalla in 213 CE![114] Moreover, after this, it is not common.[115]

Although some of the reluctance to use *lord* terminology may be due to the Roman location of the cult or the negative connotations of *dominus* in Latin as described above, the Arval brothers may provide an insight into the nature of *lord* terminology. For the Romans, lordship was not primarily a religious concept. As already acknowledged, there is no strict distinction between religion and politics. Nevertheless, in the realm of those activities often associated with devotion to deity, the title is not common for gods or men. Rather, κύριος is a title usually used in spheres of relationships in the more general activities of life.

5. *Κύριος at the Conceptual Level*

A principal problem with attempting to determine whether κύριος in Paul may be polemical is the extensive number of potential referents. As noted in Chapter 1, to conclude that a polemic does or does not exist based on occurrences of the term may reveal more about one's presuppositions concerning Graeco-Roman influences than about the evidence. The way to get beyond this is to focus not on the term itself but to explore the conceptual level behind the term.

a. *Language in Layers: Concepts and Expressions*
Linguists have long recognized that utterances and texts are not language itself but expressions of language. What one actually sees or hears is the product of language. Some scholars, for example, Noam Chomsky, have postulated a deep and surface structure.[116] The communicator has a thought in mind (deep structure) and then expresses it with an appropriate utterance or text (surface structure). Other scholars, however, such as Sydney Lamb, have postulated a *concept* in the mind of an individual that then goes

---

113. Most recently collected in Scheid, *Commentarii Fratrum Arvalium qui supersunt* [abbreviated CFA].

114. 'CFA 99a.20 (213 CE); 99b.13 (214 CE). Although completely missing due to the fragmentary nature of the inscription, it is possible that 99b.6 (213 CE) has the title.

115. Scheid's edition of the extant inscriptions reveals only six more occurrences after this: three for Severus Alexander (CFA 105b.13, 24 [224 CE]; 107.2.9 [237 CE—date uncertain—it is after Severus Alexander's reign]) and three for Gordian III (CFA 113.1.5 [239 CE]; 114.1.20, 2.38 [240 CE]).

116. See, e.g., Noam Chomsky, *Aspects of the Theory of Syntax* (Cambridge, MA: MIT Press, 1965), pp. 16-18.

through a linguistic system (language elements such as syntax, morphology, and phonology) resulting in the written or spoken expression.[117] Although there are similarities between these approaches, the latter will be adopted here because it most explicitly makes a distinction between the concept and the expression (surface structure).

Sydney Lamb views language as a system of relationships. A thought or concept in the mind of a communicator must be brought through various related levels of language before an appropriate expression is produced. The further from the expression, the more abstract the language component. Thus, the phonology is relatively concrete because this system produced the final expression. The morphology behind the phonology is more abstract. The concept level is most abstract of all.

The importance of this approach for our discussion is twofold. First, it makes a distinction between a concept and specific expression. Second, and related, a concept may be expressed (realized[118]) differently depending on contextual features. In other words, a concept may be realized by more than one expression and a specific expression may realize more than one concept in different contexts.

There can be different levels of complexity between a concept and its expression. Some can be very simple. For example, the concept *tool with long straight "teeth" to organize hair* is simply expressed by the word 'comb'. Other situations can be much more complex. This is especially true for relational concepts. For example, in a business, the concept *head boss* may be expressed by a number of seemingly synonymous labels such as 'Chief Executive Officer', 'Company head' and so on. But the concept could also be expressed by more simple generic terms such as 'boss', 'leader' and the like. These terms can be seen as reflecting the concept because of the status of the individual within the societal context who fills the referent roles. Often the superlative nuance is simply implied. It is of course possible that these labels can be applied to a *head boss* without a superlative

117. Sydney M. Lamb, *Outline of Stratificational Grammar* (Washington, DC: Georgetown University Press, 1966); Lamb, *Pathways of the Brain: The Neurocognitive Basis of Language* (CILT, 170; Amsterdam: John Benjamins, 1999). See also David G. Lockwood, *Introduction to Stratificational Linguistics* (New York: Harcourt Brace Jovanovich, 1972). For an introduction to this approach, see Pamela Cope, *Introductory Grammar: A Stratificational Approach* (n.p.: SIL, 1994).

118. The term 'realize' refers to the expression of linguistic elements between layers of language—that is, how a linguistic element on a higher level is expressed at the next lower level. I am using it here synonymously with 'expression' to avoid confusion between expression as a way of communicating and expression as a specific surface structure. However, for consistency elsewhere in this work, I will use the more common (albeit more general) term 'express' with this more specific meaning of 'realize'. For an explanation of terminology, see Lockwood, *Introduction*, p. 27.

nuance intended. However, it may be difficult to determine this unless the context is clear.

For κύριος, this permits us to look at its usage in a more complex manner. We can focus on what specific concept may be offensive to the emperor and how such a concept would be expressed in the text.

b. *Concept: Supreme Lord*

Every κύριος is lord over something. A father is κύριος over his household. He is lord over a specific albeit minimal 'sphere'. A ruler such as Agrippa II may be a father and thus lord of his household. However, he is also lord of a larger 'sphere' that may include many households. When a father is addressed by his children as κύριος in Agrippa's presence, there is no offence to the local leader. The reason for this is that there is an *understood hierarchy* between the father and the local leader. Offence will be given only if a challenge is perceived. Above, four status and relationship options were introduced. The fourth is important for the present discussion, namely the social status and relationship of the referent to the wider cultural context (e.g. the [known] world or the total sphere of influence). If our notions of 'spheres of lordship' and 'hierarchy of lordship' are taken to their logical conclusion, we would arrive at an individual (or group) whose social status and relationship are at the top of the entire cultural context. This party is *supreme lord*. In other words, this individual is the top *lord*, the *lord of all other lords*. This would be one whose 'sphere' of lordship covers all other 'spheres' of lordship. Thus, this individual would be the supreme lord. This position would be held by a person who has authority over all possible 'spheres' in society. The usage of the term in this case would be a *superlative* usage.

Whether someone like this exists in any given society is debatable. One may argue that modern democracies do not include such an individual. *Balance of power* is an important concept in modern constitutions and is intended to avoid any one individual or group assuming the function of *supreme lord*. Nevertheless, given some flexibility, this concept did seem to function in many ancient societies.

The concept of *supreme lord*, like concepts in general described above, does not necessarily have any specific surface structure in a specific language. It seems that, when an individual has such a position, a term such as 'lord' is sufficient to communicate this. We have already accounted for this in two ways. First, it is possible that the address of such a person as *lord* includes an ellipsis and has an implied modifier such as 'of all'. Second, an implied social hierarchy may be present providing the understood *supreme* nuance from a social perspective. In any case, the concept is implied. When some party has the highest position in society, that individual or group when addressed as 'lord' is *supreme lord*. His subordinates may also be *lords* but only within the accepted hierarchy. They are not supreme *lord* despite the same term being used for both.

The four observations made above also highlight that different types of lordship exist side by side. One may have family lordship, civil lordship and so on. An individual may have more than one type of lordship. In all cases, these lordships are *relational*. Additionally, some lower-level lordships may maintain some of their authority even within larger spheres of lordship. For example, in most cases, a father will maintain his role within his household despite higher-level civic lords. Agrippa II, despite being lord of his kingdom, does not interfere with individual household activities. An exception to this may be if a perceived lack of loyalty to the king exists within the household, Agrippa II may intervene. However, usually the father would be held responsible for any problems within his sphere of lordship. As long as the household itself is loyal to the higher-ranking lord, harmony is maintained in the larger sphere of societal lordship.

c. *Supreme Lord as an Exclusive Concept*

The title κύριος was relatively common and had a wide distribution in ancient Rome. Its usage was as common as the number of 'spheres of lordship' in society. As long as the lordship of these 'spheres' was not contested, societal harmony was maintained. In a household, the father was *lord*. The mother may also function as *lord* for many, but the implied hierarchy maintained the structure. The mother may be *lord* over the slave, but the father was *lord* both of the slave and of the mother. If, however, the mother, a slave or a stranger entered the home and claimed to be *lord* of the household, either the father would need to submit and give up his lordship over the home or meet the challenge. More is taking place here than merely a challenge against the father. The societal hierarchy is being challenged. The father has society and the law on his side when he responds to the threat to his leadership.

Thus, the concept of *supreme lord* is an exclusive concept. Only one party may hold this position in a given sphere. Challenges to this position will be met. Three results are possible. First, the challenge may be stopped and things will remain as they are. Second, the challenge may be successful with the result that a new party will fill the role of *supreme lord*. Or it is possible that neither party will have the strength to overtake the other and some type of compromise will result. Either one party will be willing to submit to the other and possibly share a portion of the lordship, or the sphere of lordship will be divided. The result of either of these options will be a weakening of lordship, either through weakening the amount of power the top lord has or through dividing the original sphere into smaller sections.

The nature of the world is such that it is always difficult to speak in absolute terms about governments. Any society has a complex structure of power. However, some cultures have more defined supreme lordship than others. The British monarchy has progressed from near absolute power centuries ago to a more figurehead role. This occurred gradually. As monarchs needed funds and men for wars and other problems facing Britain, it yielded power to nobles. Thus, there are four tasks before us. First, we must determine whether first-century Rome had a *supreme lord,* and, if so, who filed this role. Next, we must determine under what circumstances the society saw a challenge to this position. Then, we must determine whether Paul's use of the term κύριος presented such a challenge. Finally, if it did present a challenge, under what circumstances did it do so.

Chapter 5

KYRIOS CHRISTOS AND KYRIOS KAISAR:
CHRIST'S CHALLENGE TO THE LIVING CAESAR

In Chapter 3 it was argued that the emperor's presence was pervasive throughout the Roman empire. It was even suggested that Rome was actively creating a cognitive environment in which they sought to control both context and people. In part, the goal has been to re-create this cognitive environment. This task is continuing in the present chapter. In Chapter 4, the meaning, usage and potential referents of the term κύριος were analysed, and the meaning of *lordship* was discussed in depth. Most importantly, it was concluded that κύριος was *relational*. Finally, the notion of a concept was developed that I labelled *supreme lord*. This concept represents the ultimate and highest *lord* in a specific cognitive environment. There may be many lords in a community, but there can generally be only one *supreme lord*. In this chapter I will examine the title used for the emperors and identify the default *supreme lord* for the general cognitive environment of the Roman empire. I will then explore under what circumstances one might present a challenge to this position and determine whether Paul presents Jesus as a challenge to Caesar for the position of *supreme lord*.

1. *Κύριος Caesar*

The first step in attempting to determine whether Paul may have intended a polemic against Caesar in his use of the title κύριος for Jesus must be to evaluate whether the title was used with any frequency for the living emperor at the time Paul's letters were written. This cannot prove a polemic. Nevertheless, only in this way is it possible to consider whether Paul's words could be perceived as a challenge.

With the possible exception of Nero, the extant evidence for κύριος as a title for the Julio-Claudian Caesars is not extensive. Nevertheless, the title was used for all of these emperors. Additionally, the emperors often functioned as κύριος whether or not the title was used. Much of the discussion in Chapter 3 is assumed here. In that chapter a general picture of the role of the emperor in society was presented. Here the focus will be much more specific. The living emperor as *lord* will be examined. I will proceed in two ways. First, extant evidence of the title for each of the Julio-Claudian emperors will be presented. The most important sources are non-literary materials such as papyri and ostraca.[1] Most of this evidence is from Egypt, produced during the reign of the emperor. Second, I will briefly discuss the role of the emperor generally and determine whether he could be considered a *lord* with or without titles. The purpose of this section is to determine whether the use of κύριος for the living emperor was within the cognitive environment of the readers. Whether or not he would fill the role of *supreme lord* will follow.

a. *Augustus (31 BCE–14 CE)*
There are at least three papyri from Egypt in which Augustus is given the title κύριος. In all cases, they also include the title θεός. POxy 1143.4 (1 CE) mentions sacrifices and libations, . . .

> . . . ὑπὲρ τοῦ θεοῦ καὶ κυρίου Αὐτοκράτορος

> . . . for the god and lord emperor[2]

This passage is of interest because of its cultic context. We have seen in Chapter 4 that the term κύριος is not very common in such contexts.

Although I argued previously that κύριος does not essentially attribute divinity to the referent, it nevertheless is a high honour and can be used of divine beings. I noted also that Augustus may have had an actual formulated response to requests wishing to grant him divine honours.[3] This response may have been followed by Tiberius and Claudius.[4] It was applicable only to formal requests and not to more informal situations. It was not applicable to documents such as papyri and ostraca circulating among Romans that were never intended for the emperor's eyes. Nevertheless, this attitude may have had some impact on the private use of the title. The rarity of the title for Augustus is further complicated by his apparent rejection of the title *dominus* (Suetonius, *Augustus* 53.1; see also Cassius Dio 55.12.2-3, which has δεσπότης).[5]

---

1. Among the sources cited in this chapter, Arch. f. Pap., PHeid, PLond, PMert, PMich, POslo, PStras, OBerl, OBrux, OStras, and OTheb were accessed through the PHI CD ROM #7. Dates were taken from Paul Bureth, *Les titulatures impériales dans les papyrus, les ostraca et les inscriptions d'Egypte (30 a.C.–284 p.C.)* (Brussels: Fondation égyptologique reine Elisabeth, 1964), pp. 21-45.

2. See also BGU 1197.15 (5–4 BCE); 1200.11 (2/1 BCE).

3. M.P. Charlesworth, 'The Refusal of Divine Honours: An Augustan Formula', *PBSR* 15 (NS 2) (1939), pp. 1-10.

4. Charlesworth, 'Refusal', pp. 2-6.

5. This incident will be discussed below.

b. *Tiberius (14–37 CE)*

There is less evidence of the title for Tiberius than for Augustus. Like Augustus, Tiberius is also recorded by later historians as having rejected *dominus*.[6] However, the one passage located is important because it was not found in Egypt (IGRR 3.1086.1 = OGIS 606.1; 29 CE):

τῶν κυρίων Σε[βαστῶν]

of the lords Sebastoi.

This passage describes both Tiberius and his mother Livia as *lords*. Additionally, it labels the god Kronos as *lord* (Κρόνῳ κυρίῳ) as well (line 10). This example is rare because it was found in Syria. It is the only extant example of a living emperor before Nero being called κύριος in a source written outside of Egypt.

c. *Gaius Caligula (37–41 CE)*

Presently there does not seem to be any extant contemporary source (inscriptions, papyri, or ostraca) officially labelling Caligula lord. However, there is evidence to suggest that he not only was called by this title but also desired it.

First, literary evidence suggests that the title was applied to Caligula. The Alexandrian Jew Philo had personal contact with the emperor and records a letter written by Agrippa I to Caligula. In this letter Caligula is addressed as δεσπότην . . . καὶ κύριον *(On the Embassy to Gaius* 286).[7] Also, in the beginning of their defence, the Jewish group addressed Caligula with the vocative, κύριε Γάιε *(Embassy* 356). Philo wrote shortly after the events and thus likely reflects accurate usage. Even if these words do not reflect the actual events, his use of the title for Caligula is earlier than the Pauline texts that will be considered below. Further, it is unlikely that the use of κύριος here reflects the superlative concept. As discussed in Chapter 4, the vocative usage may be slightly weaker than other usages. What is important is that this is an example of the application of the title to Caligula. This is further evidence of the title for a living emperor in the cognitive environment during Paul's time. There is one further point of importance. If Philo's words are accurate, although he was from Egypt, it is an example of the title's use in Rome itself. There is no indication that this was unnatural in this context.

---

6. Tacitus, *Annals* 2.87; Suetonius, *Tiberius* 27; see also Cassius Dio 57.8.1-4 (δεσπότης). This will be discussed below. Additionally, as noted above concerning Augustus, Tiberius may have followed the first emperor in his response to divine honours.

7. He is also addressed with the vocative δέσποτα (e.g. *Embassy* 276, 290; nominative: 271). Others in this book also addressed Caligula this way (e.g. 355; the accusative: 247).

Suetonius (*Caligula* 22) records Caligula applying a passage from the *Iliad* to himself: Εἶς κοίρανος ἔστω εἶς βασιλεύς ('let there be one lord, one king'; 2.204-205). The word is not κύριος; however, it is a term used in poetry for ruler or lord (LSJ). Suetonius's record of the quotation of the *Iliad* is in a context about Caligula's role as supreme leader. Suetonius notes that a number of surnames are given to Caligula. Then the emperor overhears a group of visiting kings discussing their own nobility and in reply Caligula quotes Homer. Suetonius continues by accusing Caligula of changing the appearance of the principate (*speciemque principatus*) into an outright monarchy. Significantly, κύριος does not occur in Homer. Thus, it is possible that this is the closest Homeric word to κύριος that is available. Finally, Aurelius Victor (mid to late fourth century) states that Caligula attempted to get others to call him *dominus* (*On the Caesars* 3).

Second, Caligula's character and actions would make such a title natural. We have already noted the passages from Philo and Suetonius about titles. In the latter, Suetonius notes that he was above all princes and kings and that he was claiming a divine type of monarchy. Other actions of his that would make the use of κύριος for him natural include associating himself with demigods, then later with the main deities, placing his image in places of worship and the like. Caligula abused power in countless ways.[8] The use of a title such as κύριος would be a minor incident in his reign. It was used for Augustus and Tiberius, so this practice was likely to have continued.

The lack of inscriptions and other contemporary examples of the use of *lord* for Caligula may be due to the brevity of his rule and the destruction of his memory (i.e. statues, images; see Cassius Dio 59.30).

d. *Claudius (41–54 CE)*

Claudius returned to the modesty of Augustus's and Tiberius's rule. Nevertheless, there are at least three extant Egyptian documents calling Claudius κύριος.[9] The first is from a lawsuit in which the title is used in the dating of the document (49 CE):

ζ (ἔτους) | Τιβερίου Κλαυδίου Καίσαρος τοῦ κυρίου (POxy 37.5-6)

in the seventh year of the lord Tiberius Claudius.

Dating is the primary use of the emperor's name and titles in this type of source. A longer example is extant from the end of Claudius's reign (54 CE):

ιδ Τιβερίου Κλαυδίου Καισαρος Σεβαστοῦ Αὐτογράτορος [*sic*] τοῦ κυρίου (OWilck 1038.4-6)

---

8. See the accounts in Suetonius, *Caligula*; Cassius Dio 59; and Philo, *On the Embassy to Gaius*.

9. A fourth is questionable: SB 4331.3.

in the fourteenth year of the lord Tiberius Claudius Caesar Augustus Emperor.

Finally, from the end of the Claudius's reign there is an ostracon in which Claudius is simply called

ιγ τοῦ κυρίου

in the thirteenth year of the lord (OPetr 209.3; 53 CE).[10]

There is little remaining of the source (three lines) to know whether the inclusion of only the title was merely a space-saving device or whether the referent was so common that it could stand alone. Fortunately, there is enough of the source extant to confirm that there was no more of the name and title than τοῦ κυρίου. Given the use of emperors' names and titles for dating these types of documents, the emperor would be the natural referent. Thus, what is gleaned from this evidence must be carefully extracted. This title for the emperor was apparently familiar enough in this context for the parties involved to use only the title. With the exception of the actual name of the emperor (e.g. Καῖσαρ for Augustus [the name he inherited from Julius Caesar]; Τιβέριος, Γαῖος,[11] Κλαύδιος,[12] Νέρων etc.), it is rare to have a one-label identification of an emperor. In Paul Bureth's comprehensive list of titles for emperors in non-literary sources in Egypt, only ὁ κύριος appears alone as a title for emperors from Augustus through Domitian.[13] A search through some common epigraphical sources suggests that this observation reflects the inscriptional data as well.[14] Thus, this ostracon is important. Among the rare uses of κύριος for the pre-Nero emperors, one example is the title κύριος alone. The use of an individual name only for an emperor is natural because a name is easily associated with the specific emperor. This is not the case with the title κύριος. This title can have multiple referents and thus has the potential to be ambiguous. In addition, research reveals no other title occurring alone in this context. There are a few examples of

10. For a justification of this identification, see the comments on this ostracon by editors of the Flinders Petrie ostraca collection (OPetr).

11. 'Gaius' is the name by which Caligula is usually identified in the sources. However, because this is a common name, I have primarily used 'Caligula' in this work.

12. Claudius is occasionally called only by his praenomen Τιβέριος (see PLond 1171; PMich 228, 340; however, in all cases, a fuller title also occurs in the document, making Claudius the obvious referent).

13. Bureth, *Les titulatures impériales*, pp. 21-45. This is true also for the immediately subsequent emperors. Additionally, this appears to be accurate for titles in the native Egyptian languages as well (Jean-Claude Grenier, *Les titulatures des empereurs romains dans les documents en langue égyptienne* [Papyrologica bruxellensia, 22; Brussels: Fondation égyptologique reine Élisabeth, 1989], pp. 9-45).

14. IGRR, OGIS, and SIG³.

titles such as θεὸς Καῖσαρ (e.g. Nero: POxy 1021.3) or θεὸς Σεβαστος (Augustus: BGU 1210; Claudius: PMich 244.15). However, the referents of these examples are much more restricted than the single κύριος. Given our limited sources, it is difficult to maintain that there were/are not other single-title examples; nevertheless, we must conclude that it is rare based on the evidence for emperors in the consulted sources, which, although limited, are fairly good. One might expect a title such as Αὐτοκράτωρ to occur alone because it is easily associated with the emperor. This does not appear to be the case. Since the reason for mentioning the emperor was to date documents, accurate identification would be important. These observations suggest that, despite the expectation of an emperor in this context, a certain association of the title with the emperor must have existed. This example is late in Claudius's reign—it is possible that people were familiar enough with his leadership at this point to refer to him with only the title. Or it is possible that the position of the emperor was what was familiar to the creators of this ostracon. In either case, the lack of a more personal identification suggests that the association of κύριος with the living emperor was strong.

Given our sources, we must conclude that the association of the title with the emperor reached a higher level of development with Claudius. As we will see, the use of the title continued to gain popularity. If development did occur under Claudius, it must be considered important because Claudius himself did not appear to encourage this. It is possible that Caligula made the use of such titles more common. Thus, Claudius simply inherited the situation. Yet it seems unlikely that Caligula was the most important factor. After Caligula was assassinated, Claudius probably would distance himself from the excesses of his nephew. This probably accounts for Claudius's return to the approach of Augustus and Tiberius concerning honours. It may be that this title was not necessarily an excess (especially in the East).

e. *Nero (54–68 CE)*

With Nero the evidence for the title increases dramatically. Contemporary inscriptions, papyri and ostraca all attest to Nero being called κύριος. The most common is simply:

Νέρωνος τοῦ κυρίου[15]

Nero the lord

---

15. In order to group sources by title, from this point on the letter representing the date will not be included in the examples. Additionally, in some cases, letters may be missing due to damage. This will not be individually noted. The examples below clearly reflect the wording they are supporting. The title will be written as it appears, but to avoid an awkward translation, it will be translated as if it were in the nominative case.

Spanning almost the entire reign of Nero, there are at least 109 papyri and ostraca with his name and this title.[16] These are often documents produced for business transactions. For example, POxy 246 (66 CE) is a certification of cattle registration. The reference to Nero as κύριος is in a second hand, probably that of an official.[17] Multiple hands are not uncommon, but since the emperor's name is usually being used for dating, the date of the κύριος occurrence is easily identified. Interestingly, Z.M. Packman observes that from the time of Nero, regnal formulas (essentially the name and titles of the emperor) were used for dating events within a document. These are considered secondary dating formulas in contrast to formulas that date the document itself. These secondary dating formulas use κύριος when abbreviated. In other words, instead of a long regnal formula, some titles are left out and κύριος is used.[18] Packman's observation about κύριος in shortened formulas seems correct. This example is very brief, but even in dating formulas below, titles are shorter than full regnal formulas. However, his suggestion that these are only in secondary dating formulas for this period is unsustainable. Returning to POxy 246, where three occurrences of

---

16. The date here reflects when κύριος was written (even if by a later hand [see below in the text]). PPrinc 152.1.3 (55–56 CE); OBerl 25.6-7; OStras 265.5 (56 CE); PPrinc 152.2.4 (56–57 CE); OBodl 663.2; OPetr 287.5-6; (57 CE); OStras 266.4; OWilck 1040.5; 1041.4 (58 CE); PHeid 257.4; PMert 12.27 SEG 8.500 (= SB 7813); OWilck 410.5 (59 CE); OBodl 664.4; OStras 84.2-3; OWilck 16.4 (60 CE); OPetr 289.4 (60–61 CE); OBodl 670.3-4; POslo 48.17 (61 CE); OBodl 1053.4-5; OCamb 30.3; ODeiss 22.2-3; 23.3-4; 36a.3; OPetr 290.6; 290.10; SB 9545.2.4; 9572.10; OStras 182.3-4; 241.4; OTheb 116.5 (62 CE); Arch f. Pap 5.p170.1.4; ODeiss 24.2-3; PHeid 258.4; OPetr 83.3; SB 3562.3; OStras 85.3; 267.3-4; PStras 290.4; OWilck 413.6; 414.7-8; 1623.3 (63 CE); OBerl 27.4-5; OBodl 424.3; 1054.6-7; OPetr 182.5; SB 1929.3; 6837.a.8; 9545.3.3; 9545.21.5; OStras 85.3; 267.3; OWilck 415.5 (64 CE); OWilck 1394.6 (64–65 CE); OBodl 1055.5; 1082.2-3; PLond 1215.7 [Bureth: 1215.4]; OPetr 84.3; 210.4; SB 9545.4.4; 9545.30.5; 9604.14.4; OTheb 41.3; OWilck 416.4 (65 CE); OWilck 17.4 (Bureth questions this one [*Les titulatures impériales*, p. 34]; I suspect that this is due to a missing word before Νέρωνος in line 3, which Wilcken supplies as Κλαυδίου); 771.3-4 (65–66 CE); Arch f. Pap 5.p172.8.2; 5.p172.8.6; OBodl 1174.5; POxy 246.30; OPetr 85.2; SB 6837.b.6; 9545.5.3; OStras 269.4 (66 CE); OWilck 18.4-5; 419.3-4; 1395.4; 1397.4; 1400.3-4; 1559.2 (66–67 CE); OBodl 488.3-4; 603.4-5; 961.2; 1056.4-5 (Nero's name is missing due to damage; this probably is why Bureth questions this example [*Les titulatures impériales*, p. 34]); OBrux 2.6 [Bureth: 2.5]; ODeiss 37.3-4; SB 9545.6.4; OStras 295.1-2; OTheb 71.3; OWilck 417.3-4; 418.4; 1325.4;1396.3-4; 1398.4 (67 CE); OWilck 420.7;1399.5 (67–68 CE); OBodl 489.3; 589.3-4; 604.4-5; ODeiss 25.2-3; 76.4-5; OPetr 86.4; OStras 88.3; OTheb 32.2; OWilck 19.4-5; 422.4-5 (68 CE). There are also three examples of this title that cannot be dated more specifically within Nero's reign: SB 6838.8; OStras 492.3; 499.2.

17. Deissmann, *Light from the Ancient East*, p. 173.

18. Z.M. Packman, 'Regnal Formulas in Document Date and in the Imperial Oath', *ZPE* 91 (1992), pp. 62-63.

shortened dating formulas probably occur (one is discussed above and the other two will be mentioned below), a full regnal formula for dating occurs within the document itself, Νέρωνο[ς] Κλαυδίου Καίσαρος Σεβαστοῦ Γερμανικοῦ Αὐτοκράτορος (Nero Claudius Caesar Augustus Germanicus Imperator; lines 11-14). This is used to date the actual registration. The briefer formulas with κύριος occur at the end by additional hands to date the signature and thus the document (all the same date).

A slightly longer form of identification also appears in our sources. The earliest is from 59 CE (OWilck 15.5-6):

Νέρωνος Καίσαρος τοῦ κυρίου

Nero Caesar the lord

There are at least six examples of this form.[19] The addition is probably insignificant and may be due to the personal style of the creator of the document.[20]

More significant are two ostraca from late in Nero's reign that have only the title κύριος to identify the emperor (OWilck 1560.2-3 [67 CE]; 667.3-4 [68 CE]). This is similar to OPetr 209 (53 CE) discussed above with Claudius. As with Claudius, these examples are from late in the emperor's reign and may indicate a solid association of the title with Nero. It is unlikely that the creators of the document would intentionally add anything ambiguous to a document. The title was used to date the transaction. It is more likely that the use of the title was developing in the cognitive environment of the first century.

For the first time an example occurs in which the title is anarthrous. In the fourth and bottom (remaining) line, ODeiss 39 (62 CE) simply has:

Νέρονος [*sic*] κυρίου

lord Nero

There are a number of reasons this example may exist. It is possible that the article was omitted in error. However, since this anarthrous wording is grammatically acceptable and the article is only one of three words in the most common form, error is unlikely. It is also possible that the ostracon was written by one unfamiliar with the normal pattern (for any number of reasons). This is impossible to know. Most likely, it is a stylistic varia-

---

19. In addition to the ostracon just cited, see OPetr 288.8 (61 CE); SB 9604.1.1 (63 CE); POxy 246.33-34; 246.36-37 (66 CE; these two examples, from the same cattle registration papyrus previous mentioned, are in a third and fourth hand [the final occurrence is marked as uncertain by the editors]); OPetr 293.6 (date missing).

20. That two of our six examples occur in a document (POxy 246) with the shorter version of the label in a different hand supports this observation.

tion demonstrating that the association of the living emperor was common enough to vary the usual formula in such documents.

There is at least one extant inscription that attributes to Nero the title κύριος. It does so in two places :

ὁ τοῦ παντὸς κόσμου κύριος Νέρων (SIG³ 814.30-31 [67 CE])

Nero, the lord of the entire world;

εἰς τὸν τοῦ κυρίου Σεβαστοῦ [Νέρωνος οἶκον] (SIG³ 814.55)

into the [house] of the lord Augustus [Nero].

This inscription was discovered in a small town called Acraephiae (modern Karditza) in Boeotia. It primarily records two related events. First, it records Nero's declaration made in Corinth on 28 November 67 CE granting the status of 'freedom' ('liberty') and tax relief for Greece (lines 1-26). Second, it includes a statement of gratitude by a priest of the Augusti for this action and a decree to consecrate an altar to Nero (who is called Zeus) (lines 27-58).[21] This inscription is important for at least seven reasons. First, simply, it is an inscription. This is rare (only one has been discussed thus far). Inscriptions had a more "official" character than papyri and ostraca. Second, and related, the title is not being used for dating. It is part of the content of the inscription. Third, it provides detail of what Nero is lord over: Nero is lord of the entire world. It is because of this that he is able to grant privileges to Greece. Fourth, the use of the title twice in the inscription seems to suggest that it was a common means of address. Fifth, unlike most other sources discussed, Nero is the subject of this inscription. It is about him. It records his words and actions. It also records the response of the people to him. Thus, it provides a glimpse into the explicit relationship between emperor and subjects. Sixth, this is the first extant example of an emperor being called κύριος in Greece. Seventh, because its subject matter took place in Corinth and was relevant for all Greece, it is likely that this inscription was set up throughout Greece (even in small towns like Acraephiae, where our example was found). Additionally, as important as Greece was in the empire, it is likely that this inscription was known beyond its borders. Thus, if the title was not well known, this inscription may have given it wider circulation; however, it is more likely that it reflected common usage in the empire and did not seem out of place to anyone.

The only literary example of the title κύριος being applied to Nero is that of Luke's record of Festus's words in the book of Acts:

---

21. For a discussion of this inscription, including a translation and notes, see Danker, *Benefactor,* pp. 281-86. For a discussion of this inscription including a comparison of Nero with Christianity, see Auffarth, 'Herrscherkult und Christuskult', pp. 294-300.

περὶ οὗ ἀσφαλές τι γράψαι τῷ κυρίῳ οὐκ ἔχω,

about whom I have nothing definite to write to my[22] lord (Acts 25.26a)

In Acts 25 and 26, Luke describes the apostle Paul's defence while a prisoner in Caesarea before the Roman governor (procurator) Porcius Festus and Herod Agrippa II (with his sister Berenice). Festus replaced Antonius Felix, who was recalled by Nero. Festus probably arrived in 59 CE.[23] One of the first things he did in his new position was go to Jerusalem, where Jewish leaders brought charges against Paul, who had been moved to a prison in Caesarea for his own safety during Felix's governorship (Acts 23.23-35). The leaders asked for the return of Paul to Jerusalem. The Jewish leaders' motives are described by Luke as deceptive. They planned to ambush and kill Paul on the trip from Caesarea. Festus refuses their suggestion but proposes that some of them accompany him back to Caesarea, where he will hear the case (Acts 25.1-5). During this hearing, according to Luke, Festus expresses a desire to do the Jews a favour and asks Paul if he is willing to return to Jerusalem and face charges there. Paul refuses and instead appeals to Caesar (25.6-12). Shortly thereafter, Agrippa II arrives, and Festus, seemingly confused about what to write about Paul, asks Agrippa to hear Paul and give his opinion (25.13-22). It is in this context that the statement is made.

Although this event can be dated to around 59–60 CE, its use for our analysis is questionable. First, there is no consensus on the date of Acts. Some would date it in the early sixties;[24] however, most maintain a later composition.[25] Second, we cannot know whether these words are exactly

22. For the article used as a possessive pronoun, see Wallace, *Greek Grammar beyond the Basics,* pp. 215-16.

23. The exact dates of Felix's recall and Festus's arrival in Caesarea and his governorship are disputed. For a discussion of the recall of Felix and the arrival of Festus, see Emil Schürer, *The History of the Jewish People in the Age of Jesus Christ (175 B.C.–A.D. 135)* (ed. Geza Vermes et al.; rev. ed.; 3 vols.; Edinburgh: T. & T. Clark, 1973–87), I, pp. 465-66 n. 42. It appears that Festus died approximately two years after he began his position (p. 468). Therefore, 59/60–62 seems a reasonable date for his governorship (see Loveday Alexander, "Chronology of Paul," pp. 116, 120; and Schürer *History of the Jewish People,* I, pp. 465-67).

24. Colin J. Hemer, *The Book of Acts in the Setting of Hellenistic History* (ed. Conrad Gempf; WUNT, 49; Tübingen: J.C.B. Mohr [Paul Siebeck], 1989), pp. 365-410 (argues for 62 CE).

25. See, e.g., Ben Witherington III, *The Acts of the Apostles: A Socio-Rhetorical Commentary* (Grand Rapids: Eerdmans, 1998), p. 62 (late seventies or early eighties CE); Hans Conzelmann, *Acts of the Apostles: A Commentary on the Acts of the Apostles* (ed. Eldon Jay Epp and Christopher Matthews; trans. James Limburg, A. Thomas Kraabel and Donald H. Juel; Hermeneia; Philadelphia: Fortress Press, 1987), p. xxxiii (80–100 CE). Some have proposed a second-century date for Acts. See, e.g., Richard Pervo, who

what Festus said. Even if we grant accuracy on the statement (*ipsissima vox*), whether he used simply τῷ κυρίῳ to refer to Nero is not possible to prove. Third, if Acts was completed long after the event, even with a contemporary source for this pericope, it is possible that the use of τῷ κυρίῳ for Nero betrays an anachronistic tendency by the author of Acts.[26] As we will see below, κύριος became very common under the Flavian dynasty and even the Latin *dominus* become a title for Domitian (81–96 CE). If this is the case, Luke, then writing at this time, may have placed a contemporary title for the emperor in the mouth of Festus in the late fifties or early sixties (who would not have used it in his day).[27]

This issue cannot be solved here. However, given the contemporary data of the title used for Nero and his predecessors, there is strong evidence suggesting that the statement could have been uttered by Festus. Nevertheless, owing to the uncertainty over this issue, it really can contribute little to our discussion.

Roman literature (non-New Testament) does not provide us with an example of Nero being called κύριος. This is to be expected, since after his overthrow and subsequent suicide little good is said of him. Most relevant sources were generally written after his rule (and much of it is in Latin). Nor is there evidence that Nero demanded the title. It is likely that later writers who might desire to paint a negative picture of Nero would have included such evidence if it was available.

Despite the lack of literary evidence outside of the book of Acts, it is clear that the title was used of Nero rather frequently. The evidence from Nero certainly supports a development of the use of the title for the living emperor that I suggested was occurring under Claudius. With Nero this development escalates significantly. First, it escalates in sheer quantity. One

argues for a date of 115 CE (or possibly 110–20) (*Dating Acts: Between the Evangelists and Apologists* [Santa Rosa, CA: Polebridge Press, 2006]; this is followed in his *Acts: A Commentary* [ed. Harold W. Attridge; Hermeneia; Philadelphia: Fortress Press, 2009], p. 5) and Joseph B. Tyson, *Marcion and Luke–Acts: A Defining Struggle* (Columbia: University of South Carolina Press, 2006). However, this seems unlikely (see Luke Timothy Johnson, *The Gospel of Luke* [SP 3; Collegeville, MN: Liturgical Press, 1991], p. 2 (arguing for both Luke and Acts).

26. See Conzelmann, *Acts*, p. 207, who may exhibit this view. Some commentators do not even mention the word as an issue (e.g. Johannes Munck, *The Acts of the Apostles: A New Translation with Introduction and Commentary* [AB 31; Garden City, NY: Doubleday, 1967], p. 238). Others are helpful: C.K. Barrett, *A Critical and Exegetical Commentary on the Acts of the Apostles* (ICC; 2 vols.; Edinburgh: T. & T. Clark, 1998), II, pp. 1147-48; Joseph A. Fitzmyer, *The Acts of the Apostles: A New Translation with Introduction and Commentary* (AB 31; New York: Doubleday, 1998), p. 752.

27. It could also be argued that if Acts was written as early as 62 CE, the title may be anachronistic, given the increase in extant examples beginning in the year 60 CE.

hundred and twenty-three references to Nero labelled κύριος were cited. Only eight could be cited for Augustus, Tiberius, and Claudius. One needs to rely on literature for examples of the title's use for Caligula. Additionally, development is supported by the increased use as Nero's reign progressed. Of those examples we can date, only fourteen can be dated to the early part of Nero's reign (54–59 CE). There are 105 that can be dated 60–68 CE. Second, the use of the title escalates in geographic distribution. Although only one source (two occurrences) was cited from outside Egypt, it was a significant source from Greece that likely had wide distribution. Third, it escalates in content. Again, although relying on only one source, Nero's lordship is defined as the lord of the entire world. Additionally, the anarthrous example provides a measure of diversity in use.

Adolf Deissmann suggests that the reason Nero is called κύριος is that he was proclaimed Ἀγαθὸς Δαίμων (*Agathos Daimon*, the god of the city of Alexandria)[28] in Egypt upon his ascension to the position of emperor.[29] This is supported by the vast amount of evidence for the title found in Egypt. Deissmann's thesis is possible; however, it seems preferable to view the increase as simply a development in the use of the title for the living emperor. Although I presented more evidence of the title for Nero's early reign (14) than for all previous emperors combined (8), one might expect a greater increase during the early reign if this proclamation was the impetus. Additionally, no example of the title can be produced from Nero's first year.

f. *The Flavian Dynasty (69–96 CE)*

It is likely that all three of the emperors who ruled briefly between Nero and Vespasian were called κύριος; however, it appears that there is evidence of the title only for Galba and Vitellius.[30] Lack of evidence for Otho is probably due to the paucity of extant primary sources for him. Given these emperors' short reigns and the constant warfare during this period, it is unlikely that any development in the use of the title occurred. Usage probably continued as it had during the later years of Nero.

In Chapter 3, it was observed that some development was necessary in the cults of the emperor under the Flavians. However, this was not extreme. The most significant period of development in emperor worship remained that of Augustus and Tiberius.

---

28. See POxy 1021.8-9 (54 CE); OGIS 666 (56 CE [date from Deissmann]). See the discussion in Deissmann, *Light from the Ancient East*, pp. 345n. 4, 353, 365 n. 2.

29. Deissmann, *Light from the Ancient East*, pp. 345 n.4, 353, 365 n.2.

30. Galba: SB 1930.4; CPJ 234.3-4; OWilck 21.4; 423.3-4 (68 CE); Vitellius: OPetr 294.6-7 (69 CE). Bureth cites OWilck 421.6 for Vitellius (*Les titulatures impériales*, p. 36); however, the published source for this ostracon indicates that line 6 is illegible. No title or name can be determined.

The use of κύριος continued to develop. The increase in usage that occurred under Nero continued at an even greater rate. In fact, the title in the papyri and ostraca became not only common but *normal*. In U. Wilcken's listing of ostraca, 44 of the 55 mentions of Vespasian include the title, three of five include the title for Titus, and an impressive 71 of 76 mentions of Domitian include κύριος (four of the five occurrences without the title mention Domitian only by his name). In Bureth's listing of titles from Egypt (which includes Wilcken's ostraca), the title's use is also impressive. If one omits the examples with just the emperor's name, ostraca and papyri with the title κύριος account for about half of the examples.[31]

In the literature, the early-second-century biographer Suetonius claims that Domitian *demanded* to be addressed as *Dominus et deus noster* ('our lord and [our] god'; *Domitian* 13.2). However, this may be an exaggeration or an attempt by Suetonius to please the reigning emperor Trajan by portraying Domitian poorly.[32] It would be in the interest of the reigning emperor to discredit the previous dynasty in order to emphasize the benefits of his own reign. The scepticism regarding Suetonius's record is supported by the fact that there is no other extant evidence of a *demand* by Domitian to be addressed in this manner. There are no extant official inscriptions or coins with this title. Additionally, despite the prevalence of the Greek title κύριος in the Egyptian ostraca and papyri, Bureth includes no example among his listing of Latin examples.[33] Nevertheless, Domitian was clearly called 'our lord god'. For example, Martial writes of the emperor *domini deique nostri* (*Epigram* 5.8.1; see also *Epigram* 8.2.6). The existence of the title applied to Domitian does not prove that Domitian *demanded* it. However, it also suggests that Domitian did not forbid it. This would be somewhat of a development because, although *dominus* was in some ways a Latin equivalent of κύριος, I argued in Chapter 4 that the Latin included certain negative pragmatic effects not present in the Greek.

The non-literary evidence makes it clear that the development of the use of the title κύριος for the living Roman emperors reached a level in which it was a *normal* means of referring to the ruler.

g. After the Flavian Dynasty
The significant increase in the use of the title κύριος for emperors began with Nero, and the title became common during the Flavian dynasty. This trend continued, and any brief view of indexes of inscriptions, papyri, and

---

31. Bureth, *Les titulatures impériales*, pp. 38-45.
32. See A.Y. Collins, *Crisis and Catharsis*, pp. 71-72; Friesen, *Imperial Cults*, pp. 147-48.
33. Bureth, *Les titulatures impériales*, pp. 44-45. The data for Latin are limited. There are nine different title forms and only a few examples of each.

ostraca confirms that the title was a normal part of the cognitive environment for emperors such as Trajan, Hadrian, and the others. One further important piece of evidence is worth noting in this development. In Arrian's published notes of Epictetus's teaching, Epictetus states,

ἀλλὰ τίς με δύναται ἀναγκάσαι, εἰ μὴ ὁ πάντων κύριος Καῖσαρ;
(*Discourses*, 4.1.12)

but who is able to constrain me, except the lord of all, Caesar?

This reference to Caesar is either to Trajan or Hadrian. Although much later than the Pauline texts, this passage helps to confirm that the title became as common a term for the emperor as any other.

h. *The Emperor Functioning as Lord*

In Chapter 3 (4. The Emperor in the Roman World, pp. 136-41), we considered the general role of the emperor in the Roman world. There I emphasized his pervasive presence in the lives of the people. Much of that discussion can be applied here. Essentially, the emperor, by virtue of his power and position, served as the *benefactor* of the people. By default, this was a lordship relationship between the emperor and *his* people. Many of the actions described there can be viewed as lord-like activities. These were proclaimed in inscriptions, on coins, and in literature. These will not be reviewed here. Despite the minimal use of the title, the emperor nevertheless functioned as lord.

As discussed previously, κύριος is a relational term. The κύριος has a certain relationship to those who call him by that title. Whether or not the term is used, where this relationship exists, the one exercising power is a functioning *lord*. After defeating Antony at Actium in 31 BCE, Octavian (later Augustus) stood as the only surviving leader without rival for supremacy in the Roman empire. His long reign (31 BCE–14 CE) as the supreme ruler of the Roman empire was outwardly the beginning of the principate. However, despite claims of giving up power and being granted a place in the Roman government as a result of a thankful people in 27 BCE (see Augustus's *Res Gestae*, especially section 34), he controlled the military and maintained absolute power. As long as this power was not challenged, it did not need to exert itself.

Subsequent emperors also held this position. Tiberius, although generally not liked by the senate, still wielded absolute power even when away for years from Rome at Capri. He was able to control events and even hold treason trials to quell any possible challenges (real or imagined) to his position. Caligula as well exerted the power of a *lord*. However, he failed to keep his part in the relationship and ultimately paid the price for this. Claudius returned to the example of Augustus and Tiberius and ruled fairly well.

Even Nero for much of his reign was tolerated as a *lord*. When the Julio-Claudian dynasty came to an end, the new Flavian dynasty continued this relationship. The very position these emperors held with the power at their disposal permitted them both to function as *lord* and to maintain that position.

A recently discussed inscription is worth revisiting here. In SIG³ 814, Nero grants Greece the status of 'freedom', which includes important tax benefits. In response to this act, a decree is issued in which Nero is mentioned as both Zeus and κύριος. It initially seems ironic that one granting freedom would be *lord* over those with the new status. However, this is the very nature of the lordship relationship. Although it is possible that some from outside a relationship with a people could grant this type of status (e.g. a god), it really is the function of a *lord* to grant and carry out. Nero is also addressed as deity in this inscription. This is important because it further reflects his status and power in relation to the people. However, it is the lordship relationship that is really necessary. Even gods could not necessarily make their will happen. Other gods and even men could disrupt their plans. However, a lord (whether human or divine) has the relationship with the people to accomplish things within his power. Nero was the Greek's κύριος. This relationship went two ways. The Greeks gave him loyalty and Nero was their benefactor. It is again interesting to note that the use of κύριος comes from below. It is not initiated by Nero. This is a response of the priest (representing the people) to Nero.

Given the actions of the emperor mentioned in Chapter 3 and the discussion here, it seems clear that the emperors functioned as κύριος.

i. *Caesar as Κύριος: Evaluation and Implications of the Explicit Title Evidence*

Although extant evidence of the title κύριος for the pre-Nero Julio-Claudian emperors is minimal, there is reason to conclude that it was part of the cognitive environment of the areas in which Paul carried out his correspondence. Although the bulk of the evidence comes from Egypt, this does not demand the conclusion that the title was localized. The nature of the sources and the accident of historical preservation have resulted in our extant primary sources.[34] I have noted that the more official material was rather restrained in its use of titles. One need only recall the very conservative use of titles in the Flavian provincial cult (Chapter 3). Despite the many references to these emperors as θεός and κύριος elsewhere, in their own provincial cult this language was not used. Thus, one would expect fewer inscriptional references than papyri and ostraca. This is indeed the case. The

---

34. The nature of the sources was discussed in Chapter 2.

presence of the title among more common sources is most important, for this material is closest to the original readers of Paul's letters.

Because of climate issues, the vast majority of papyri were found in Egypt. However, we cannot assume that all originated there. Egypt was an important centre in the Roman empire. Many people travelled through its great cities. Additionally, because it was an important centre, its influence would have been significant throughout the empire and especially in the Greek-speaking East. Although an argument from silence, the less-localized and more universal use of the title seems supported by Jean Claude Grenier's collection of imperial titles, which includes no example of a κύριος-equivalent applied to an emperor in the Egyptian language.[35] This evidence may suggest that the title was uncommon among locals; however, it is also possible that the title was usually associated with the Greek. We cannot be certain whether either of these options is correct, but one might expect the local population to use the title in its native tongue if it were specifically a local phenomenon.

Finally, the existence of even one inscription outside of Egypt applying this title to an emperor (IGRR 3.1086 = OGIS 606 [as cited above for Tiberius]) supports the notion that this is not exclusively an Egyptian phenomenon.

All that has been said above concerning the first four emperors can be applied to Nero. Here however the evidence is much stronger. More extant evidence of the title for Nero exists than for all of the previous emperors combined. Again, most examples are from less literary material and from Egypt, and most from the second half of Nero's reign.

Like those previously discussed, the sources are primarily papyri and ostraca from Egypt. The sheer volume of examples and the portability of these documents make it likely that some of these sources had their origin outside of Egypt. Further, I have noted the important inscription from Greece (SIG[3] 814), which likely was set up throughout Greece and may have been well known elsewhere. Thus, there is probably some geographic diversity.

The massive increase of sources in the second half of Nero's reign is difficult to explain. As demonstrated in Chapter 3, the common division between the good and poor halves of Nero's reign, if sustainable at all, is irrelevant for matters of Nero's character and for the use of titles by others for him. Additionally, it does not necessarily follow that the use of the title must be associated with "poor" government. In any case, with the exception of Nero's first year, there is fair representation of this title in his early reign. By comparison with Nero's later years, it is minimal, yet compared to the earlier emperors, it is relatively plentiful.

---

35. Grenier, *Les titulatures*.

The vast amount of evidence from Nero's later period could not have appeared instantly. Moreover, since the title is likely to have had some geographic diversity, its use may go back earlier than the bulk of primary sources suggests. Development must have taken place. It is thus likely that, given the title's use for previous emperors, it was also being used in a similar way in the early part of Nero's rule. It was also noted that the title during Nero's rule was used in regnal formulas. As noted above, when the title was used in a regnal formula for dating events in a document, it is a shortened form of a longer strings of titles.[36] Regarding these types of texts, Packman states, 'the title kyrios, in the overwhelming majority of occurrences, signals the omission of, or even in some sense replaces, elements eliminated from a fuller regnal formula recorded in the same text'.[37] Not all our sources with dating formulas have enough extant text to confirm the existence of longer formulas in the same text. Although certainty is impossible, it could be that the title κύριος was seen in part as a summary of the emperor's position, which is functionally one of relational lordship. For this reason, it could stand in place of a string of titles.

With the Flavian emperors there can be no doubt that κύριος was a common title. It is possible that the term has weakened from earlier periods. However, given our discussion in Chapter 4, this seems unlikely. A more likely explanation is that the relationship that was primarily implicit during earlier periods has now become more explicit. The fiction created by Augustus, in which the emperor appeared to be merely the *first citizen* of the republic, no longer needed to be sustained. The bloody civil war of 68–69 CE demonstrated at least two things. First, the Roman empire needed an emperor. The republic was now nothing more than a distant dream. In the absence of an emperor, some would risk everything for the position. Second, the emperor's position could be gained through strength. Military power had been important (e.g. Caligula was assassinated by his guards, and Claudius and Nero gave the military personnel incentives to remain loyal). Vespasian held power in 69 CE only after military victories. He was neither of the highest nobility nor did he have any connection to the imperial house. What he had was the loyalty of the strongest armies of the empire. This loyalty was a significant factor in his attaining the position of emperor and would also be the reason that his power would be sustained. After Domitian, the third and final Flavian emperor, was assassinated, no further Flavian could hold the position. The elderly Nerva received the office but in part because of his selection of Trajan as his adopted son and heir. Trajan was well liked by many, including the military.

---

36. Packman, "Regnal Formulas," p. 62.
37. Packman, "Regnal Formulas," p. 63.

The state of affairs really was unchanged. The reasons Augustus received and maintained power were the same as Vespasian. Most importantly, the emperor controlled the military. What was different was that the fiction Augustus had created was no longer necessary. In essence, Vespasian and Augustus had the same relationship with the state. Augustus however, at a vulnerable time for the imperial power, successfully created the illusion that he was not the *lord* of the empire. At least he was not given the outward trappings of lordship, which included titles. This was a major reason why he was able to keep those with republican sentiments and other possible supreme leaders from successfully either restoring the republic or taking his position. By the time of Vespasian, this fiction was no longer necessary. He still needed to maintain a modest outward appearance, but the position of emperor was secure. There would be an emperor; the question was simply, who would he be? Military power would be a very important factor in this equation.

Therefore, it was not a change in the meaning and usage of κύριος that accounts for the increased usage. Rather, the existing relationship between ruler and people was now becoming more explicit. This relationship was clear even under Augustus as the less literary and more unofficial evidence reveals. However, it was not part of the official ideological position of the early principate.

For the use of κύριος, Nero is a transitional figure. He is heir of a tradition in which the title was used sparingly. Lordship was a reality but was not 'official'. However, times had changed and the unofficial was now becoming more explicit. People began to state outwardly what everyone actually had known to be true for a while. It is important that this development need not have come from the emperor himself. Rather, as we have seen, both cities and individuals had reasons to attribute important titles to the emperors. For Nero, the external evidence is rather overwhelming. The many extant examples of the title and his own personality and character make it clear that it was appropriate to refer to him and to address him as κύριος.

That κύριος was a common title for the emperors is further supported by the nature of the sources. The vast majority of references to a living Caesar as κύριος are in non-literary documents, which have no chance of coming to the attention of the emperor. Numerous papyri and ostraca use the emperor as a means of dating the document. Many of these give the emperor the title κύριος. Dating is a common function and usually involves very familiar devices. Thus, it is unlikely that one would use a title that was not commonly associated with the emperor. Rather, one is likely to use wording that would be so common in such contexts as to not distract from the purpose of the document. These are not intended to honour the emperor; they are intended to keep daily life moving.

The existence of a few examples where only ὁ κύριος appears in dating formulas further suggests that the title was common for the living emperors. Usually late in the emperor's reign, such occurrences suggest that the title was common enough for people to omit other identifying names and titles. Apart from proper names, this appears to be the only identifier in our extant sources of this type for Augustus through Domitian.

If the title κύριος for the living emperor is a common dating device, it is probable that the title was familiar in the cognitive environment of Greek speakers in the empire. It seems justified to maintain that the living Caesar was κύριος in the cognitive environment of many in cities where Paul wrote to his communities. However, as we have seen, many potential referents could have this title. We need now to determine whether there is evidence that the living Caesar was the *supreme lord* of the Roman world.

Before continuing, one further point is worth mentioning. Given the development of the use of the title and the apparent lack of emperor-initiated use (with the possible exception of Domitian), it would be incorrect to see the use of the title κύριος as an abuse of power. Certainly, explicit demands of lordship over others (like monarchical actions) were discouraged. However, the evidence from the sources is generally produced from below, that is, from the people themselves. Thus, as demonstrated above, Caesar as κύριος in the cognitive environment of Romans would not necessarily have a negative connotation.

2. *Caesar as the Supreme Lord*

It can be said with some confidence that the emperor as κύριος was within the cognitive environment of the first-century Greek speakers. This is especially true beginning with Nero. However, does this evidence suggest that the living emperor was the referent of the concept developed in Chapter 4, the *supreme lord* for the sphere of the Roman empire (i.e. from the perspective of the subjects of the empire, *the world*)?

a. *The Existence of the Concept in First-Century Rome*
The existence of a *supreme lord* in one society does not demand that one exist in every society. Before determining whether Caesar filled this role, we must establish that it existed in the cognitive environment of Paul's world.

After the Romans revolted against their kings in the sixth century BCE, they established a republic. This form of government did not concentrate power in any one person for any length of time. With the exception of a temporary dictator for crises, the ancient Romans never had a *supreme ruler*. Even in such cases, the dictator was subject to the Roman constitution and would have to yield his power at the appropriate time. Thus, by definition, the role of *supreme lord* was not present during the republic. However, near its close, the existence and interests of strong men began to prepare Rome for the position. Men such as Pompey and Caesar fought to gain sole control of the empire. Once Caesar was victorious, he began to establish himself as sole ruler, even accepting the title 'dictator for life'.

Julius Caesar was the first to fill the role of *supreme lord*. This position can be determined only from his function and relationship to the people. Titles and honours were many but did not include *lord*. However, in him were concentrated all the powers, rights, and responsibilities of the relational concept. The Roman state was too large for the republic form of government to handle and needed a *supreme lord* to manage its affairs. The position was now established.

b. *The Role of the Emperor: Supreme Lord*

Given that many could be addressed as κύριος in the first century, is it possible to conclude that the living emperor fills the role as *supreme lord*? Let us return to the business analogy introduced in Chapter 4 to illustrate the existence of the concept. Although there were many who could be addressed as 'boss', only one could be the Chief Executive Officer and be addressed as 'boss' by all employees. What is it that permits this identification? To answer this, the term 'boss', the concept *supreme boss* (Chief Executive Officer), and the individual him or herself must be considered. 'Boss' is a relational word that makes explicit the relationship between the superior and worker. The concept *supreme boss* is an exclusive concept that can be filled by only one party. The referent either through ownership or by appointment holds a unique position that gives him or her (or them) both the rights and the responsibilities to act on behalf of the entire organization. This is most closely seen when the referent is an owner. The very nature of the referent himself or herself makes the use of the term 'boss' demand that the concept of *supreme boss* be assumed.

Although not a perfect analogy, this situation is similar to that of the living emperor. The same three areas must be considered: the term κύριος, the concept *supreme lord*, and the individual himself or herself. First, the *relational nature* of the term as previously developed is essential to this identification. The term κύριος is used primarily by one who is inferior in social class or rank to address his or her superior. This relationship of subordination could be rather formal (patronage and benefaction). Those participating in this relationship have different rights and responsibilities towards one another. In the case of the Roman emperor, he is responsible to protect his subjects and provide the means for them to carry on their lives. As the description of imperial propaganda suggested, the imperial role went beyond simple sustaining measures. The imperial regime presented itself as providing meaning for the subjects of the empire. In addition to supplying low-cost food and entertainment for many, participation in the Roman empire was promoted as being part of something great. The subjects, for their part, were obligated to participate in the empire and to submit themselves to the imperial regime and, specifically, to the ruling emperor. In addition to obedience to laws and participation in military campaigns as necessary, this would include for most the participation in imperial religious activities. The subjects must do what the *lord* requires of them.

Despite attempts by Augustus to claim that he had restored the republic, his position was actually *supreme ruler*. This is made clear by his own administration of certain provinces such as Egypt and his control over the military, and it is ultimately revealed in his action of providing a successor to himself. His role as *supreme lord* is confirmed also by the title granted him, *father of my country* (Augustus, *Res Gestae* 35; Suetonius, *Augustus* 58.1). In many ways the relational role of κύριος is present in the father–family relationship. The main difference is that the κύριος relationship is broader in scope.

Second, the *exclusive nature* of the concept of *supreme lord* leaves room for only one referent. In the Roman empire, the emperor was over all major areas of Roman life. This position is confirmed through recognition by the senate and, most importantly, by the military. Thus, not only could the emperor claim this role, but he functioned as supreme lord with or without official recognition. Additionally, he had the ability to sustain his position. Once the position of emperor was established, it was filled by only one. In rare instances, another would claim the position, but such circumstance could not last and could result in civil war (e.g. in 68–69 CE, when no fewer than five men [not all simultaneously] made claims to the role).

Unlike the linguistic and conceptual reasons above, the third area of consideration is purely pragmatic. When the emperor, backed up in his position by official recognition and the military, is addressed with the relational term κύριος, the exclusive concept supreme lord is most likely to be evoked. Unless there is a reason (e.g. the position of a child in relation to his emperor father), anything less than the position of supreme lord would seem almost insulting in view of the qualities of the person addressed. Thus, simply put, when the emperor is called κύριος, this term expresses the concept of supreme lord because of who the emperor is.

When one considers these points with the emperor's position at the apex of the Roman world, socially, politically, and religiously,[38] from the Roman perspective he is the only individual who could fill the role of supreme lord in the Roman world. Further, it seems unlikely that any use of the title for the emperor would not reflect the concept. The emperor is supreme lord

---

38. A distinction between these spheres is artificial and anachronistic, but it is helpful here to make the complex and comprehensive role of the emperor clear.

in his context. Thus, when he is addressed by the title κύριος, he is being addressed as supreme lord. The title κύριος for this individual in this context (i.e. the emperor in the Roman world) is expressing the concept of supreme lord.

c. *Support from Early Rejection of the Title*

Before we can conclude that the living emperor was the supreme lord of the Roman empire, we must revisit a passage (with parallels) introduced in the previous chapter. It was demonstrated that, despite similarities of meaning and translation, the Latin term *dominus* and the Greek κύριος had different pragmatic effects in the first-century Roman context. For certain historical and cultural reasons, the Latin term carried with it negative implications that were not present in the Greek. This was demonstrated partially through passages in which Augustus and Tiberius rejected the title *dominus*. However, at this stage in our discussion, our focus is on the *concept* supreme lord and not on a specific term. It is likely that in certain contexts the Latin *dominus,* like κύριος, expressed the concept of supreme lord. It may be argued that the living emperor could not possibly fill this role because both Augustus and Tiberius rejected the concept in the title *dominus*. Of Augustus, the Suetonius passage introduced in the last chapter is worth citing again,

> He always shrank from the title Lord [domini] as reproachful and insulting. When the words O just and gracious Lord! [O dominum aequum bonum!] were uttered in a farce at which he was a spectator and all the people sprang to their feet and applauded as if they were said of him, he at once checked their unseemly flattery by look and gesture, and on the following day sharply reproved them in an edict. After that he would not suffer himself to be called Sire [dominumque] even by his own children or his grandchildren either in jest or earnest, and he forbade them to use such flattering terms among themselves (*Augustus* 53.1; trans. Rolfe, LCL).[39]

This passage may initially seem to be problematic for our position, which suggests that the emperor was the supreme lord of the Roman world. Further, it seems difficult to argue for a polemic if the emperor himself rejects the concept. How could a polemic exist using terminology the emperors themselves reject? However, when the events are analysed more closely in their historical context, the rejection is natural. It can even be argued that these passages actually support both the existence of the concept of supreme lord and our contention that Caesar fills that role in the Roman empire.

The main reasons for discussing this passage are to demonstrate further the existence of the superlative concept and to support our position that living Caesar was the referent. Its role in the discussion of a polemic is really

---

39. Suetonius, *Augustus* 53.1 (trans. Rolfe, LCL); see also Cassius Dio 55.12.2-3. For Tiberius, see Tacitus, *Annals* 2.87; Suetonius, *Tiberius* 27; Cassius Dio 57.8.1-4.

secondary. However, before discussing this passage (and parallels) for its main purpose, three points will be made to show that it does not rule out a polemical usage in Paul. These points will also serve as background information for the primary discussion. First, these passages record Augustus and Tiberius rejecting the term. There is no record of Nero rejecting the title. Both Augustus and Tiberius were much more astute politicians than Nero.

Second, both Suetonius and Tacitus (the latter only for Tiberius) record this event in Latin as it was most likely to have occurred. The Latin *dominus* is broad and can be used to translate κύριος (however, it is not restricted to this translation). Additionally, we have already examined *dominus* in light of the 'political' climate under which Augustus founded the principate. This was a fiction. Augustus claimed to be first citizen (*princeps*) but in reality ruled as a king. His approach worked. He successfully ruled for more than 40 years. One consequence of this approach was the deliberate avoidance of terminology that made explicit Augustus's role in society. The title *dominus* was thus not common for an emperor. The climate probably added certain pragmatic effects not associated with the Greek terms for *lord*. Therefore, it was unlikely that Augustus or Tiberius would outwardly claim the title *dominus*. It would upset the successful balance that Augustus had worked to achieve.

Third, Cassius Dio, recording this passage in Greek (and probably having access to the Latin of Tacitus and Suetonius), used not κύριος but δεσπότης. Since the event occurred in Latin, Cassius Dio needed to translate (or use a source that translated) the passage. Thus, one could argue that this passage is irrelevant for the usage of κύριος since this term is not even used in the Greek. However, as pointed out above (see pp. 180-82, *Greek and Latin*), it is possible that in the first century, this could have been κύριος.

Thus, the rejection of title *lord* by Augustus and Tiberius does not rule out the possibility of a polemic in Paul. They were lord with or without the title. However, there is much to be gleaned from this passage for the present goals of establishing the existence of the superlative concept and to argue for the living emperor to be the referent of the concept. We are concerned with the conceptual level, and it appears that, in addition to the implications carried with *dominus*, the concept supreme lord is what is being rejected here. Concerning Cassius Dio, whether or not *dominus* would have been best translated as κύριος or δεσπότης is not as important as the evidence it provides for the superlative concept.

Why did Augustus and Tiberius reject the title *dominus*? We have already answered this from a linguistic perspective. A number of other reasons are possible. They may have truly disliked the title. They may have been too humble to accept the title. They may have been indifferent or even liked it but felt that acceptance would jeopardize their position with the senate and the people. It is common to find both Augustus and Tiberius rejecting certain honours during their lifetime.[40] Thus, as already stated, the rejection of *dominus* was all part of being *princeps*.

For Augustus, as a masterful politician, rejection of honours was a part of his rise to power. With reference to divine honours, neither Augustus nor Tiberius was successful in opposing them. Even Tiberius, who may have objected more than other emperors, never placed an absolute prohibition on the practice.[41] In light of the history of these men's rise to power, it is unlikely that they rejected the title from any humble motivation. Thousands had to die for Octavian to be hailed as 'saviour'. Tiberius's rule did not come without its sacrificial victims (e.g. Agrippa Postumus and, later, Germanicus etc.). Although Tiberius's role in these deaths is open to debate, his treason trials clearly demonstrate how far he would go to maintain his position. With reference to the wider issues of worship and the bestowal of divine honours, although some honours were rejected, when one takes into account the words of these men and the events and inscriptions available, it is difficult to conclude that they absolutely were opposed to the role made explicit by *dominus*. However, the use of this Latin term was not worth the potential problems it might cause among the Romans, especially the nobility.

It seems likely that Augustus and Tiberius understood that the acceptance of the title would be significant. The title made explicit their *relationship* to the people, which they preferred not to be seen as desiring. Even the titles 'god' or 'son of god' did not carry the *relational* implications of the title 'lord'. The rejection of the title *dominus* by these emperors suggests a usage for this term that must have superlative (or at least very unique) attributes. This does not deny other uses of the term. If, however, it was simply a matter of using a common title that could not give offence, failure to accept it would make little sense. But Augustus and Tiberius did reject it. They understood that is was not a simple common usage of a title being offered to them. They knew that they were being addressed as supreme lord with this title. What, then, gives the usage a superlative pragmatic effect? I suggest that it is that due to the issue discussed in Chapter 4, namely the *relational* nature of the term. The force of this title is directly proportionate to the position the referent holds in the community. Augustus and Tiberius were *supreme lords* in their respective reigns. However, they preferred to func-

---

40. Suetonius, *Augustus* 52 (though there is a minor concession here); Tacitus *Annals* 2.50; 4:37-38 (for Tiberius's actions); 4.55-56 (Tiberius). See also Lily Ross Taylor, 'Tiberius' Refusal of Divine Honors', *TAPA* 60 (1929), pp. 87-101; Kenneth Scott, 'Tiberius' Refusal of the Title "Augustus"', pp. 43-50; Charlesworth, 'Refusal', pp. 1-10. These articles are helpful only for illustrating the rejection of divine honours. Their reasons need to be read in light of the development in the study of emperor worship begun by Price.

41. Taylor, 'Tiberius' Refusal', pp. 100-101.

tion as supreme lords and allow others to relate to them in this manner without explicit acknowledgment. When given the opportunity, they wanted to be seen as rejecting this role.

We have discussed how the Latin *dominus* carried with it specific objectionable pragmatic effects that would have been explicitly offensive to some Romans. This accounts for its rather rare usage for emperor. The Greek terms did not necessarily carry with them the same pragmatic effects. This may account for why κύριος was more common (although not very common) in the East. When these terms are used of the emperors, it is likely that the concept of supreme lord was present. Because of Augustus's and Tiberius's sensitivities to issues of appearance, they may have rejected the Greek terms in a Roman context. However, to Greek ears these would not have been as problematic. Both terms expressed the concept of supreme lord in this context. This was a reality that these emperors preferred to remain implicit.

If both Augustus and Tiberius rejected the explicit address of this concept and they were the highest ranking individuals in the Roman empire (each was the supreme lord!), it follows that no other person should be able to fill this role.

d. *Consequences of the Identification*

The supreme lord of the Roman world was the living emperor. This identification has certain consequences for the use of the term κύριος and the superlative concept. First, the use of the term for the emperor usually expresses the concept supreme lord. Second, the emperor was unique in his position as lord. He had no superior. In general, he did not address any other person with this title. It is even unlikely that he would have addressed gods with the title κύριος, because this term was not normally associated with deities in the Roman context. Nevertheless, most emperors acknowledged some measure of dependence on certain gods. Third, as already noted, because of the emperor's important role in society as supreme lord, it is likely that any use of *lord* titles applied to him carried with it the superlative concept. Thus, the emperor is the default supreme lord. In other words, in the cognitive environment of the first-century Roman empire, when the concept of supreme lord was evoked, it naturally referred to the emperor. As default supreme lord, this concept could be expressed simply with the title. Thus, when the emperor is addressed as *lord*, this title is intended to include the meaning of supreme lord; the title expresses the concept.

3. *The Need for a More Powerful Method*

Based primarily on lexical parallels, some scholars, most notably Deissmann, have concluded that a polemic must have existed in some Pauline passages. To cite his conclusion again,

> It is sufficient for our purpose to have realised the state of affairs in the time of Nero and St. Paul. And then we cannot escape the conjecture that the Christians of the East who heard St. Paul preach in the style of Phil. ii. 9, 11 and I Cor. viii. 5, 6 must have found in the solemn confession that Jesus is 'the Lord' a silent protest against other 'lords,' and against 'the lord,' as people were beginning to call the Roman Caesar. And St. Paul himself must have felt and intended this silent protest.[42]

In Chapter 1 I suggested that Deissmann's discussion was too brief to warrant this level of confidence. The conclusion has been strengthened in the present study in three ways. First, much more evidence has been provided for the use of the term for Nero, Second, in my recreation of the cognitive environment of the first century, it was determined that the emperor's presence penetrated all levels of Roman life. Third, in addition to the lexical parallels, it was demonstrated that the emperor functioned as a *lord* figure in the Roman empire.

The greater contextual support strengthens the polemical case. N.T. Wright's positive position on this issue, although lexical parallels are important, seems strongly based in this type of contextual support.[43] However, will the additional evidence provided here answer those who are sceptical of a polemic usage? Does it answer Dunn's objections? He states,

> In Hellenistic culture, different lordships could be acknowledged in different spheres without implying conflict of loyalties. The sharp antithesis between 'Caesar is Lord' and 'Christ is Lord' (*Kyrios Kaisar* and *Kyrios Christos*), indicated later in *Martyrdom of Polycarp* 8.2, is not yet in evidence in Paul's time.[44]

I do not think that Dunn's objections have been fully met.[45] Dunn's comment reveals two major obstacles that hinder acceptance of a polemical position for many. At this point I am *not* making a judgment as to whether the evidence presented previously should be sufficient to conclude the existence of a polemic. I am merely answering potential objections from those not thus far persuaded. First, Dunn's statement about different lordships existing without contradiction is acknowledged. We have seen that κύριος can be used with many referents. It was used of various types of people

---

42. Deissmann, *Light from the Ancient East*, p. 355.

43. Wright, *What Saint Paul Really Said.* p. 88.

44. Dunn, *Theology of Paul the Apostle,* p. 247.

45. Dunn does not seem to be aware of developments in the study of imperial cults that Simon Price has helped the scholarly community to understand (see Chapter 3). Concerning emperor cults, Dunn says, 'it fulfilled a primarily political rather than religious function' (*Theology of Paul the Apostle*, p. 247). However, this does not make his concerns any less valid.

who had authority over others, such as masters of households,[46] owners of slaves[47] and civil leaders;[48] and, although not very common, even other gods were so labelled.[49] These examples do not appear to be offensive to Caesar. Second, Dunn's comparison of Paul's time with that of the writing of the *Martyrdom of Polycarp* reveals a problem of chronology. The primary-source evidence cited above was not very extensive. It was minimal for Augustus through Claudius. It began to become prominent under Nero. This is important, because it is during Nero's reign that the passages we will consider were written. However, although many examples of Nero being called κύριος were produced above, most of these do not occur before 60 CE. This makes the presence of a polemic less certain for κύριος in 1 Corinthians and Romans than for other terms that share both an imperial and a Christian context. Nevertheless, the title was used of earlier emperors, and there is extensive extant evidence of its use for Nero in 60 CE and later. As argued above, what is revealed in the sources for 60 CE and later must go back at least a little while. The Pauline letters were not written that much earlier.

Thus, problems of the existence of a polemic include many different potential referents for the term and minimal occurrences of the term for the referent that I am attempting to determine is being challenged. However, we have already provided important arguments that minimize these objections. First, κύριος is a relational term, and its use indicates a specific relationship between those calling someone κύριος and the κύριος himself or herself. Second, we postulated the existence of a concept, *supreme lord*. This role is filled by an individual who by his or her role in society commands a position superior to everyone else in the particular sphere of existence. Ultimate loyalty is given to this person. Third, this position was filled by the living Roman emperor in Paul's day.

These points minimize Dunn's objections by demonstrating that what needs to be proven is that the role of supreme lord is being claimed by or for another. Multiple referents and minimal titles for the emperors are not insurmountable problems. There are clearly many people who are lords over something in the Roman empire. However, all of these lords must be subordinate to the supreme lord. Additionally, it is not merely the presence of the term κύριος that determines whether one is supreme lord. This is determined by other factors. As we described above, the emperor by nature of his position, power, propaganda, cults and so on was presented as the supreme lord of the empire.

46. Demosthenes, *Oration* 47.60.
47. Aristotle, *Politics* 1269b, 10. Also the plural examples in Eph. 6.5, 9; Col. 3.22; 4.1.
48. OGIS 423, 425, 426 (Agrippa II).
49. OGIS 606 (first century CE; Kronos); POxy 523 (second century CE; Sarapis).

The question is no longer: How can this common term be offensive for one referent and not for others? Rather, now the question is: Does Christ challenge Caesar as the sole referent of the concept supreme lord? And if so, how can this be determined? Usages of terms alone cannot answer this question. Rather, insight from the communication process must be utilized to go beyond the surface structure of the text and shed light on issues involving the larger context of the passage.

4. *The Nature of the Polemic*

This study has been refocused on a more relevant question; it is now appropriate to consider what is actually meant by *polemic*. In Chapter 1, 'polemic' was defined as *a communicative act that challenges and/or gives offence in the form of a challenge to another;* or, slightly more specifically, it was defined as *a challenge of one party to another through a claim to a role held by the other*. These are rather general definitions and accommodate *polemics* of various strengths and various levels of directness. In light of the discussion above, we can now more precisely describe 'polemic' in our context. Given the responsibilities of running the state, the huge bureaucracy needed to carry out policies, the large population of the empire and the irrelevant nature of Christianity (from the Roman empire's perspective), how can one suggest that a few obscure words from Paul written a great distance from the city of Rome should be considered a polemic? We must consider what is specifically involved in the polemic.

First, any literature that may express a polemic against the emperor does not necessarily have to challenge the emperor directly. We have constructed a cognitive environment in which the emperor is the conceptual supreme lord. There are many in this system who benefit from (or even merely accept) this position and do not wish it to be challenged. We have seen that most of the honours given to emperors were not initiated by them. Further, we have seen that cities competed for prestige through this system. Therefore, challenges to the emperor do not have to offend the emperor directly to be a polemic. In fact, it is highly unlikely that Nero would have read Paul's works or even have heard of Paul's teaching in any detail. Therefore, we need only to determine whether a polemic challenges the position of the emperor in the cognitive environment. To rephrase the question(s) again: Does an individual or group with the emperor as their supreme lord perceive a challenge for this position in the figure of Christ? What textual evidence exists for this challenge to be perceived?

Second, and related to the first, a polemic against the emperor may be perceived as a polemic against the entire system that the emperor represents. In this case, a challenge to the emperor could be more widely personal and offensive than we might at first suspect. It is within discourse about and against the emperor that a more subtle polemic against the system is presented, a system in which most in the Pauline cities would be participating. Thus, within favourable rhetoric for the emperor there may be local issues in which some might wish to associate the name of the emperor. Thus, the emperor's person is evoked for added persuasive power in support of their programmes. This does not necessarily minimize a polemic against the emperor; however, there may be other factors and polemical charges being made within the discussion.

Finally, given the context of the Pauline Epistles, the main object of the polemic is the readers of the letters.[50] Therefore, even if no outward resistance may be immediately evident, the polemic is essentially intended to instruct the reader and community and not necessarily to change society (although such a purpose may be intended in some cases). Nevertheless, consequences will likely involve conflict. This conflict, however, may not be immediately evident.

5. *The Polemic Revealed*

The living Caesar was the supreme lord of the Roman empire. To be specific, for the readers of most of Paul's letters, Nero was the supreme lord. His position is such that he would universally so be acknowledged. This leads to the question, If someone were to challenge Nero for this position, how would it be done? Or more accurately, if someone were to replace Nero in this role in the cognitive environment, how would this be communicated in a text? In other words, what indicates a challenge to Nero for the position of supreme lord in the minds and hearts of a person or group?[51]

Everything discussed in this work has provided background and methodology to answer this question. I have noted the importance of perception over notions of historical truth or accuracy. Types of sources have been considered for their value and appropriately weighted in the discussion. Despite the value of all sources, the nature of the subject demands an emphasis on non-literary and more common sources (which tend to be more explicit in their use of *honour* language). Paul's influences have been considered. I have reconstructed important relevant aspects of the first-century world,

---

50. For a discussion of 'polemic' primarily in the Pastorals, see Lloyd K. Pietersen, *The Polemic of the Pastorals: A Sociological Examination of the Development of Pauline Christianity* (JSNTSup, 264. London: T. & T. Clark, 2004), pp. 14-23. Pietersen's work considers 'polemic' at a larger level than this project.

51. The focus here is literary. Of course, one could raise an army and challenge the ruling power by force. However, this is neither likely nor demanded for a threat to be perceived. We are exploring in what ways a challenge can be made through the communication process.

including a general view of religion in the empire, a specific understanding of imperial cults and their development, imperial cults in the framework of Roman religious experience and the role of the emperor more broadly in the empire. The role of social life, including the patronage system and city rivalries, was considered. City-specific issues in certain Pauline cites were also observed. The meaning and relational nature of κύριος has been examined. It was demonstrated that, in the Roman world, the term was not usually associated with contexts that we today view as religious. Evidence of the emperors being called by this title has been presented, including strong evidence of the title being used for Nero. A concept *supreme lord* has been suggested and defended. It has been argued that the emperor would be the default referent for this concept in the cognitive environment of the people. Thus, when the concept is evoked in the mind, the emperor would be thought of without further defining or identifying him. Finally, I refocused the question of the polemic and defined 'polemic' more precisely.

We are now in a position to determine whether a challenge to the emperor as supreme lord is present in the Pauline texts. Again, the questions: Does an individual or group with the emperor as their supreme lord perceive a challenge to this position in the figure of Christ? Does Christ challenge Caesar as the sole referent of the concept supreme lord? And if so, how can this be determined? In order to pursue these questions, we must consider the communication event itself.

a. *Relevance Theory: Relevance and Efficiency*
In Chapter 1, I introduced two observations from the communication theory known as *relevance theory*. For this project, these observations take the form of principles and provide the theoretical framework for understanding both whether a polemic exists and how it can be determined. The principles of *relevance* and *efficiency* suggest that a communicator adds to a communication situation content that relevantly furthers the discourse. It ideally adds only what is necessary to communicate what it intends. Communication most effectively proceeds when a communicative offering adds maximum relevant content for the least amount of processing effort.[52]

In the general cognitive environment reconstructed in this work, the living emperor is the supreme lord. He is the default person that fills this role. This is important because it suggests that, when a word is used to communicate this concept, the natural referent is Caesar. Therefore, unless context demands otherwise (such as Caesar's immediate household), only the title needs to appear. When κύριος is used for this concept, it can appear alone or with the article in an absolute form. Again, owing to the relational nature

---

52. Sperber and Wilson, *Relevance: Communication and Cognition,* 2nd edn, pp. 46-50, 118-72 (and throughout).

of the term and the position of the emperor, this is really the only meaning it can have. It may be modified or may appear in contexts that make this superlative nuance explicit; however, this is not necessary for the concept to be expressed. Such modifiers and other linguistic devices may be used for their own pragmatic effects, such as emphasis or flattery. The majority of occurrences of the title for Caesar mentioned above did not appear with any type of superlative addition. The exception to this was the inscription from 67 CE: ὁ τοῦ παντὸς κόσμου κύριος Νέρων ('Nero, the lord of the entire world'; SIG³ 814.30-31). This inscription essentially is an exception that makes explicit what the others intended.

Thus, if the living emperor is the natural referent of a term for *lord* when the concept of supreme lord is intended, how would one indicate a referent for this role who is not the living emperor? Something must be added to the context with the title to make explicit that the concept of supreme lord is being applied to another referent. If the title alone appears for another referent, there seems to be nothing to suggest that it is the supreme sphere being intended by the title's use. Unless there is something in the context that indicates a shift away from the default or natural referent of the supreme concept, the usage of the title must suggest a lower-level sphere of lordship and is not related to the supreme concept at all.

To return to the business analogy a final time, the referent of the concept *ultimate boss* fills this role no matter how one is addressed. This person will usually be referred to simply as 'boss', and the role is implied by the person's position in the business. No further linguistic detail is necessary. When others are referred to as 'boss', there is no intention for the addressees to fill the role of ultimate boss. The addressee is the boss of the one using the title but not necessarily the ultimate boss. This boss is subordinate to the ultimate boss. In the normal development of daily discourse in the office, the principle of *efficiency* assures that the hierarchy of bosses is maintained without needing additional terms. However, if one wishes to elevate another individual to the role of ultimate boss, some sort of additional information must be provided to make this explicit. Without this additional information, there will not be a perceived attempt to have someone else fill the role of ultimate boss. The default ultimate boss will still be assumed to fill this position. Information intended to shift the referent can be linguistic or non-linguistic. Linguistic information may include modifiers such as 'top' or 'highest'. Non-linguistic information may include a picture of the individual sitting in the chair of the ultimate boss, describing the individual in a way reserved only for the top executive, or even parking in the parking spot reserved for the supreme boss.[53]

---

53. Such actions can be perceived as humour in some instances (e.g. sitting in a boss's chair pretending to be the boss). Although possible, this type of communication

Are there indicators of this type in the Pauline texts that there is a challenge to the default supreme lord? As we have seen, many can be called κύριος without posing a challenge to the emperor's position in the lives of the subjects of the empire. However, there are at least three types of contexts in which Paul uses κύριος that seem to evoke a challenge to the established hierarchy. These contexts present Christ as κύριος and challenge the emperor as the referent of the natural supreme lord either with direct linguistic content or with other contextual features usually reserved for deities and/or the emperor. These three contextual indicators go beyond a simple use of the title and provide clues suggesting the challenge: superlative or unique modifiers, supreme loyalty expressed in creed-like statements, and a poetic or hymnic genre used officially for emperors. In some passages more than one of these apply and in all cases there are other contextual aspects that also add to these features.

When the discussion focuses on the conceptual level, apparent discrepancies between Polycarp's refusal to call Caesar "lord" (*Martyrdom of Polycarp* 8–9) and Tertullian's statement that he is willing to call Caesar lord can be explained.[54] Tertullian states,

> I will frankly call the Emperor Lord [*dominum*], but only in an ordinary way. but only when force is not brought to bear on me to call him Lord [*dominum*] in the sense of God [*dei*]. But I am a free man as far as the emperor is concerned; for my Lord [*Dominus*] is One (*Apology* 34.1; trans. Glover, LCL).

There are two things that need to be mentioned about this passage. First, for Tertullian, the term *dominus* can be associated with deity. A major feature of his argument in this and the previous section is the denial of divinity to the emperor. However, as we saw in the previous chapter, with κύριος (although divine beings can be lords) divinity is not necessarily a part of the semantic makeup of the word κύριος in the New Testament. Second, the relational nature of *lord* is clear by Tertullian's statement that he is 'free' with reference to the emperor. He is free because the Lord to whom he is bound is God. Further, Tertullian's statement reflects an implied understanding of hierarchy as developed in this work. In the next clause, Tertullian states that God is the emperor's Lord.

Thus, Tertullian's use of 'lord' for the emperor does not express the concept supreme lord. In his cognitive environment, the supreme lord is Jesus. Polycarp, on the other hand, understands that the Roman official is asking him to acknowledge Caesar as the supreme lord expressed by κύριος.

---

results only from certain relationships or a lack of social consciousness. This is not in view here.

54. It is possible that these two authors hold different views on this subject.

Acknowledgment of the social context of the writings is crucial. Although Polycarp's story is written by Christians, the view of the Roman official was being expressed. Readers would realize this and focus their cognitive environment appropriately. Tertullian, on the other hand, was a Christian writing to other Christians whose cognitive environment would be the same as his. Additionally, Tertullian wrote some decades after the martyrdom event took place. Christianity was better rooted in society; however, time alone does not account for the shift. The context of the writings is more important. Tertullian is instructing believers for life as a Christian in the empire. The *Martyrdom* was likely written to encourage believers who may find themselves in situations similar to that of Polycarp. Tertullian's time was not without persecution; however, this was not the major focus of his work.

In Paul's case, he is writing new material to relatively new converts. People came to Christianity from various religious experiences. There was a limited Christian teaching available, and it is unlikely that anyone had been a Christian from a young age (similar to a Christian today being raised in a Christian home). He is providing foundational teaching for future generations. In his world, the default supreme lord was Caesar. Thus, it may be that his letters were among the first to attempt to challenge and replace the default supreme lord in the cognitive environment of any who would listen.

b. *Superlative and Monadic Modifiers*

One forceful way to challenge the status quo regarding the supreme lord of a cognitive environment is to use modifiers that makes this explicit. If the default referent is intended, there is no need to add any further descriptive words to the title; κύριος is all that is necessary. However, since this title can be used for many throughout society without offence, if Paul wishes to challenge the normal state of affairs, he must do more than simply use the title. Modifiers such as 'only' or 'best' can be used to shake the default referent from his place in the cognitive environment. For example, given the relational nature of lordship, the exclusive nature of the concept supreme lord and the principles of relevance and efficiency, making a claim that another is the 'one lord', is a challenge and thus polemical.

Jerome Neyrey, in an article focusing on doxologies in 1 Timothy, has argued that ancient authors such as Aristotle, Cicero and Quintilian described and used a rhetoric of *uniqueness* that elevated one god, person or thing above others[55]. For example, concerning the practice of the rhetorician, Aristotle states,

55. Jerome H. Neyrey, '"First", "Only", "One of a Few", and "No One Else": The Rhetoric of Uniqueness and the Doxologies in 1 Timothy', *Bib* 86 (2005), pp. 59-87 (59-68).

we must also employ many of the means of amplification; for instance, if a man has done anything alone [μόνος], or first [πρῶτος], or with a few [μετ' ὀλίγων], or has been chiefly responsible for it [μάλιστα]; all these things render an action noble (*Rhetoric* 1.9.38 [1368a]; trans. Freese, LCL).

The emperor Augustus used this principle when describing his role in providing lands for veterans from his own money, 'I was the first [πρῶτος] and only one [μόνος] to do this of all those who up to my time settled colonies of soldiers in Italy or in the provinces' (*Res Gestae* 16).[56] Augustus is setting himself apart from all others. He is establishing in the readers' cognitive environment that he is the one who is above all others in these actions. He is unique.

The Jews in their writings also used the principle of *uniqueness*.[57] For example, the Hebrew Bible uses expressions such as -כְּ אֵין ('there is none like') to describe God, kings and other men as unique:

כִּי־אֵין כַּיהוָה אֱלֹהֵינוּ (Exod. 8.6)[58]

for there is no one like Yahweh our God

אֵין־כָּמוֹךָ בָאֱלֹהִים אֲדֹנָי וְאֵין כְּמַעֲשֶׂיךָ: (Ps. 86.8)[59]

there is no one like you among the gods, O' Lord, and there are no works like yours

כִּי אֵין כָּמֹהוּ בְּכָל־הָעָם (1 Sam. 10.24)

for there is no one like him [Saul] among all the people

כִּי אֵין כָּמֹהוּ בָּאָרֶץ (Job 1.8)

for there is no one like him [Job] in the land.

Examples using other Hebrew expressions can be cited as well.[60]

---

56. Although written in Latin, an inscription with a Greek translation was found in the temple of Rome and Augustus in Ankara, Turkey.

57. Neyrey, 'Rhetoric of Uniqueness', pp. 68-71. With reference to Yahweh, this can be labelled 'incomparability'; see C.J. Labuschagne, *The Incomparability of Yahweh in the Old Testament* (Pretoria Oriental Series 5; Leiden: E.J. Brill, 1966). For similarities to the approach of this work, see pp. 8-30.

58. The English translation reference of this verse is Exod. 8.10.

59. For Yahweh, see also 2 Sam. 7.22; 1 Chron. 17.20.

60. Neyrey's examples (which are only in English) are not limited to this Hebrew phrase. For example, he includes לֹא־הָיָה מֶלֶךְ כָּמֹהוּ ('there is no king like

The Greek Bible also has various ways of expressing uniqueness. For example, it often uses μόνος: ὁ μόνος βασιλεὺς καὶ χρηστός, ὁ μόνος χορηγός, ὁ μόνος δίκαιος καὶ παντοκράτωρ καὶ αἰώνιος ('[you are] the only king and good one, [you are] the only righteous one and all-powerful one and eternal one'; 2 Macc. 1.24-25). Neyrey suggests that this is a Greek, not a Hebrew, means of praise.[61]

Before turning to 1 Timothy specifically, Neyrey mentions three words that can express *uniqueness* in the New Testament: μόνος, εἷς, and οὐδείς.[62] These three words share the nuance of uniqueness by distinguishing the modified referent from others in its class, which often is made explicit by other modifying words and phrases (e.g. the **only** boy *to eat a full can of beans*). Other words or expressions that function in this manner can also be seen to express uniqueness.

Although Neyrey is not suggesting a polemic in 1 Timothy, his observations support the communication principles that have been developed in this work. Language is being used to set one individual apart from all others. The focus is on praise. However, as we have seen, this does not have to be in a formal setting and can be applied to a wide range of referents. Neyrey's examples include this principle applied to gods, heroes, men and even actions.[63]

When one considers this practice in light of Roman religious experience, which in worship emphasized the *relative status* between the worshipped and worshipper or the honoured and those doing the honouring, the application becomes clear. The very act of setting someone apart as unique demands a *relational superiority* between that individual and those against whom that one is set apart. Neyrey does not address (and this is not his purpose) what would happen if describing a certain individual as unique results in another referent being displaced. For him and his examples, the main emphasis is on uniqueness. However, uniqueness describing a relational word such as κύριος with many potential referents may include further nuances. If another would have held a certain position in the cognitive environment of those creating or exposed to the communicative offering, the use of uniqueness would demand that a challenge be present. Relationship, relevance, efficiency and exclusivity would all suggest that this is intended.

(1) *1 Corinthians 8.5-6: εἷς κύριος Ἰησοῦς Χριστός.* The most obvious place to observe a polemic in the Pauline corpus may be 1 Cor. 8.5-6:

him [Solomon]'; Neh. 13.26). Isaiah also uses a slightly different means of showing uniqueness (e.g. 43.11; 44.6, 8; 45.6, 21; these lack the preposition ‏כ‎ after ‏אין‎).

61. Neyrey, "Rhetoric of Uniqueness," p. 70.
62. Neyrey, "Rhetoric of Uniqueness," pp. 71-73.
63. Neyrey, "Rhetoric of Uniqueness," pp. 61-68.

καὶ γὰρ εἴπερ εἰσὶν λεγόμενοι θεοὶ εἴτε ἐν οὐρανῷ εἴτε ἐπὶ γῆς,
ὥσπερ εἰσὶν θεοὶ πολλοὶ καὶ κύριοι πολλοί, ἀλλ᾽ ἡμῖν εἷς θεὸς ὁ
πατὴρ ἐξ οὗ τὰ πάντα καὶ ἡμεῖς εἰς αὐτόν, καὶ εἷς κύριος Ἰησοῦς
Χριστὸς δι᾽ οὗ τὰ πάντα καὶ ἡμεῖς δι᾽ αὐτοῦ.

for even if [it is true] there are those called gods whether in heaven or
on earth, just as there are many gods and many lords, but to us there is
one God, the Father, from whom all things are and we exist in him, and
there is one Lord, Jesus Christ, through whom all things are and we exist
through him.

This passage is part of a discussion concerning whether a Christian is
permitted to eat meat sacrificed to idols. N.T. Wright points out that this
passage addresses how a Christian is to live in the midst of a pagan environment.[64] The question of the eating of certain meats is the specific issue.
Given the prevalence of meat sacrificed to idols, what should a Christian
do? Wright suggests that Paul is drawing on Jewish tradition, specifically
monotheism.[65] The verse immediately preceding this passage makes this
clear: Περὶ τῆς βρώσεως οὖν τῶν εἰδωλοθύτων, οἴδαμεν ὅτι οὐδὲν
εἴδωλον ἐν κόσμῳ καὶ ὅτι οὐδεὶς θεὸς εἰ μὴ εἷς ('now concerning eating food offered to idols, we know that an idol is nothing in the world and
that there is no God except one'). The ending of this verse is referring back
to Deut. 6.4, the Shema (ἄκουε Ἰσραηλ κύριος ὁ θεὸς ἡμῶν κύριος εἷς
ἐστιν, 'Hear, O Israel, the Lord your God is one'; this may be reflected
also in 1 Cor. 8.6a). Although the structure is not identical, the saying was
important enough in Jewish life that the association is almost certain. Nevertheless, there is a significant difference in the content of 1 Corinthians 8
that does not immediately occur in the citation in v. 4. The Shema includes
κύριος with the referent, God. Κύριος is the word used here to represent
the name of God (יהוה). However, Paul does not initially mention κύριος;
rather, he uses θεός. The use of κύριος does not happen until vv. 5-6, where
Jesus is specifically identified as the referent. In Deuteronomy, θεός and
κύριος had the same referent and were in apposition. In 1 Corinthians, the
referents of θεός and κύριος are explicitly different. Yet this is probably the
most clear and forceful expression of Jewish monotheism in Jewish tradition. This is not a departure from monotheism; much of Paul's argument is
dependent on it. Wright suggests that this is a "redefinition" of the Shema.[66]

---

64. Wright, *Paul: In Fresh Perspective*, p. 93.
65. Wright, *Paul: In Fresh Perspective*, pp. 93-94.
66. Wright, *Paul: In Fresh Perspective*, p. 94. See also Wright, *What Saint Paul
Really Said*, pp. 65-67. For a discussion of whether Paul implies a polemic against the
God of the Old Testament, see below.

There are many important issues associated with this passage, and there is little agreement on many of the particulars. Resolution of these issues is not important for the argument here.[67]

Paul appears to be acknowledging the existence of various gods and lords[68] but reminds (or instructs) the Corinthians that for them there is only one God (εἷς θεὸς ὁ πατήρ) and one Lord (εἷς κύριος Ἰησοῦς Χριστός). There are many reasons why this can be viewed as a polemical statement against the living emperor.

As discussed in Chapter 3, the city of Corinth was a Roman city with important ties to the family of the Caesars. It was refounded by Julius Caesar, and the emperor's presence was pervasive throughout as a result of the city's ties to Rome and the presence of important imperial religious activities (there was a large imperial provincial temple in the city). In addition, the ruling emperor, Nero, was very fond of Greece. He was probably more popular in the East than in the West. Also, there was a prominent temple in the city devoted to the cult of the imperial family. Thus, the emperor would have had a strong presence in the cognitive environment of the people of the city. They had benefited greatly from the imperial presence.[69]

Observations from our communication theory suggest that the use of the modifier εἷς can be seen as making a claim over and against other potential lords. The introduction of this modifier should add *relevant* content to the discussion. This modifier intentionally limits the referent of κύριος. Although many may be called 'lord', there is *one lord over all*. This reflects the relational nature of the term. As we saw in Chapter 4, although some may see the potential of many referents as a problem for a polemical view, close attention to the context helps focus not only the referent of the term but the nature of the lordship relationship. Paul is calling Jesus the 'one Lord' who is over all others who may be so titled. In addition to *relevance*, *efficiency* suggests that Paul's use of the modifier εἷς should be purposeful. He is not simply using it without consideration of what it is bringing to the context and its implications for his message. The notions of *relevance* and *efficiency* together with the uniqueness quality of εἷς suggest that Paul is setting Jesus up as the one and only true Lord, or, in order to be sensitive to the range of potential referents for κύριος, Paul is setting Jesus up as

67. For a detailed discussion of various views of this passage, see Fotopoulos, *Food Offered to Idols in Roman Corinth*, pp. 1-48.

68. It is not necessary for our purpose to determine the complete range of referents to which these labels refer. See Thiselton, *First Epistle to the Corinthians*, p. 632. Nor is it our purpose to determine whether this refers only to the subjective reality of some in the community (see Fee, *First Epistle to the Corinthians*, pp. 374-76). Our concern has to do with whether or not the emperor is included.

69. See pp. 142-44 above (*Corinth*).

the *supreme lord*. The fact that Paul uses this modifier to make this claim suggests that Jesus is not necessarily considered to be filling this role in the cognitive environments of his readers specifically or of society in general. The modifier is necessary to challenge the default supreme lord in these cognitive environments. If, as we have suggested, the living emperor fills the role of default supreme lord, Paul is demanding a shift in relationships. As a result, the inclusion of the modifier in this context suggests that the statement is polemical.

It may be argued that this has limited application because the lordship of Jesus is restricted to Paul and his readers (ἡμῖν). However, this cannot be sustained. First, κύριος reveals relationship and position between lord and subject, a relationship claimed by Rome in which Rome itself is to be the head. Second, κύριος is not primarily a term used in contexts that we associate with religious activities. In the Corinthian's cognitive environment, the realm of lordship was much broader and encompassed the greater part of life. The same cannot be said of θεός. Although the Romans saw their emperor as θεός, they honoured many gods and made concessions at times to some communities, such as the Jews, which permitted them not to participate. The modifier is also used for θεός and thus can be seen as polemical.[70] However, here the polemic is much broader and is against the entire Roman religious system. Thus, there is polemic, but it is not directed specifically at the emperor.

Context also provides support for a polemic. The opening phrase of 1 Cor. 8.5 includes at least two relevant phrases. First, the label λεγόμενοι θεοὶ ('so-called gods') has a derogatory tone toward the pagan gods. Second, with regard to the phrase ἐν οὐρανῷ εἴτε ἐπὶ γῆς ('in heaven or on earth'), two observations are helpful. First, the sphere referred to is essentially *everywhere*. It is limitless.[71] Second, the prepositional phrase ἐν οὐρανῷ ('in heaven') probably includes not only beings like Jupiter and the other major and minor deities (including mystery religion deities[72]) but likely includes the deified emperors, especially Augustus. This is supported by the following prepositional phrase ἐπὶ γῆς ('on earth'), which probably refers to the living emperor.[73] Although *lords* are not introduced until after

70. See Conzelmann, *1 Corinthians*, pp. 142-43. He begins by noting an anti-pagan polemic in the statement (from the readers) but suggests that Paul's development makes the polemic 'more difficult'.

71. This may refer to gods both in the upper world and in the underworld, but this does not rule out other possibilities (see David E. Garland, *1 Corinthians* [BECNT; Grand Rapids: Baker Book House, 2003], p. 374).

72. Deities from mystery religions are included as being both gods and lords. However, Fee's contention that '*kyrios* . . . is the normal title for the deities of the mystery religions' is too strong (*First Epistle to the Corinthians*, p. 373).

73. Bruce W. Winter, 'Acts and Roman Religion: B. The Imperial Cult', in *The Book*

the prepositional phrases, their inclusion here is likely. The *gods* and *lords* of this passage are grouped in such a way that they must have a higher status than the readers. Other earthly lords may be considered (e.g. local officials) but certainly the *ultimate lord* of the empire must maintain a dominant place in the polemic; otherwise, it would be pointless. There is little use for Christ to be superior to a local official and not supreme in the empire in the role of *lord*. The relational and hierarchal relationship expressed by the term and the concept makes this likely. Finally, as already noted, this passage may be reflecting the Shema (Deut. 6.4).[74] The polemical nature of Deut. 6.4 further supports a polemical intention here.

Despite the more polemically explicit nature of this text, for some a polemic may be difficult to sustain in 1 Corinthians. First Corinthians was written in the mid-fifties CE. This is before the increase of sources using the title for Nero. Nevertheless, given the history of the term described above and the strong explicit nature of Paul's words, it seems probable that, in the midst of a challenge to the Roman religious practices, he specifically challenged the default supreme lord of the empire. This is further supported by the emphasis on imperial religion described above (see pp. 142-44 [*Corinth*]). Finally, on a more general note, it may be possible that other aspects of 1 Corinthians are intended to challenge imperial ideology. For example, from a social-scientific approach, Mark Finney argues that Paul's crucifixion language is an inversion of imperial ideology.[75]

It is interesting that Wright does not emphasize this passage in his discussions of Paul's challenges to Caesar. It is lacking in his discussion of 'Paul and Empire',[76] and, in a detailed discuss of 1 Cor. 8.5-6 Wright emphasizes the Jewish monotheistic elements of the passage.[77] When discussing Jesus as lord as a challenge to Caesar, Wright uses Philippians 2.[78] This is of

---

of Acts in its Graeco-Roman Setting (ed. David W.J. Gill and Conrad Gempf; The Book of Acts in its First Century Setting, 2; Grand Rapids: Eerdmans, 1994), pp. 132, 174 (with discussion on pp. 126-31). For an outright rejection of this view without any real discussion, see Héring, *First Epistle of Saint Paul to the Corinthians,* p. 69. Also against this view, see Conzelmann, *1 Corinthians*, p. 143 n. 35.

74. Larry W. Hurtado, *One God, One Lord: Early Christian Devotion and Ancient Jewish Monotheism* (Edinburgh: T. & T. Clark, 2nd edn, 1998), p. 97; Robert M. Grant, *Paul in the Roman World: The Conflict at Corinth* (Louisville, KY: Westminster/John Knox Press, 2001), p. 71; Thiselton, *First Epistle to the Corinthians*, p. 636.

75. Finney, 'Christ Crucified', pp. 20-33. The early date of 1 Corinthians is also a problem for Finney's argument. Nevertheless, if my suggestion is correct concerning κύριος, other challenges to the emperor seem likely. Nevertheless, the tracing of a wider anti-imperial polemic in 1 Corinthians is beyond the scope of this project.

76. Wright, *What Saint Paul Really Said*, p. 88.

77. Wright, *Paul: In Fresh Perspective*, pp. 93-94.

78. Wright, *What Saint Paul Really Said*, p. 88.

course an important passage for this point; however, 1 Cor. 8.5-6 can add support. Also, the Jewish teaching from 1 Corinthians 8 may be more of a focus than the anti-imperial polemic; however, again, the passage would support his emphasis elsewhere.

A further issue must be raised in this section. In Chapter 4 I noted dining invitations on papyri that included reference to the god Sarapis (and Isis) with the title κύριος. Other gods appear in invitations, but not usually with the title κύριος (e.g. POxy 1485 [Demeter]). There is evidence of the Sarapis cult in Corinth at the time of Paul's correspondence (see Chapter 3), and these papyri display similarities to Paul's discussion of idol meat in 1 Cor. 8.1–11.1 (esp. 8.10; 10.21, 27). Is it possible that the main polemic here in 1 Cor. 8.5-6 is against this god?

Given the broad scope of the polemic in 1 Cor. 8.5-6, certainly Sarapis is included. However, it is difficult to maintain that any polemic against this god would overshadow the emperor. Despite the existence of the Sarapis cult in Corinth at the time of Paul, there is no evidence of dining facilities (although more archaeological work still needs to be done), making the direct association with 1 Cor. 8.1–11.1 more dubious.[79] Additionally, the earliest extant papyri are dated to the second century. We have already conceded a measure of uncertainty in our work, because it really was not until after 60 CE that the use of the title for the emperor began to increase and be used in a significant manner. The Sarapis evidence is even later. Further, the nature of the Roman religious experience was not exclusive; thus, it is less likely that a threat would be perceived in this context. It is likely participants were also honouring the emperor in appropriate ways.

Finally, as is important for all of our passages in this chapter, the focus of the polemic is not on the negative but on the positive confession. Conzelmann notes, 'Faith consists not in the thesis that there are no gods, but in the confession of the true God—a confession whose result is not to deny the "so-called" gods, but to overthrow them.'[80] This point is best discussed here because 1 Cor. 8.5-6 is the only passage discussed in which the author makes a negative statement against other lords. First Corinthians 12.3 follows a statement against idols and the readers' previous religious life (12.2). However, this is a reflection of the past, not of a present situation. First Corinthians 8.5-6 specifically states that Jesus is Lord and others are not. Nevertheless, the focus is on the positive confession about God and Jesus. This is the climax and goal of this passage. It is not enough to be against something. This is significant because in the remaining passages, the negative polemic must be implied by the positive statement. The relational nature of

79. See the discussion in Fotopoulos, *Food Offered to Idols in Roman Corinth*, pp. 93-128.

80. Conzelmann, *1 Corinthians*, p. 142.

κύριος and the exclusive nature of the concept *supreme lord* demand that to accept and/or confess one as supreme lord denies any others that position. No one else can assume the position, and anyone in the position must be displaced.

Given that this may be the most likely place for an imperial polemic to be evident, commentaries do not usually go beyond an acknowledgment of a challenge to all lords and gods.[81] This includes Caesar but little emphasis is placed on him in the discussion. The general polemic is important; however, given the apparent lengths described above to which the author went (e.g. 'lord on the earth') in order to bring the emperor into focus and the prominence of the emperor in the cognitive environment, further discussion of the imperial challenge should result in a more well-rounded understanding of this passage.

(2) *Ephesians 4.5: εἷς κύριος.* The Ephesian letter was likely intended as a circular letter for churches throughout Asia Minor.[82] Emperor worship was a prominent aspect of life in this area, and imperial temples and altars were virtually everywhere.[83] Emperor worship was a reflection of one's social status, community life and even city rivalry and pride. Additionally, Ephesus was part of the Greek East, and the ruling emperor was favourable to this area. The province of Asia had a functioning provincial cult in Pergamum devoted to Augustus. At the same time as this temple was given to Pergamum, Augustus instructed that a temple be constructed for Julius Caesar (*divus Julius*). However, it does not appear that this temple enjoyed much popularity. Additionally, Smyrna was the seat of Tiberius's provincial cult. The existence and operation of Tiberius's cult during our period, despite the fact that the emperor was never officially deified, may suggest just how important imperial religious activity was to this area.

It is likely, then, that the emperor played an important role in the cognitive environment of the original readers of the letter. It was at the time of this composition (60-62 CE) that a significant increase in the use of the title κύριος begins for Nero. Therefore, it is probable that the default supreme lord in the general cognitive environment was Nero.

---

81. See, e.g., Fee, *First Epistle to the Corinthians*, pp. 373-76; Garland, *1 Corinthians*, pp. 375-76. Also, the discussion of any imperial challenge is noticeably omitted from Richard A. Horsely, *1 Corinthians* (ANTC; Nashville: Abingdon Press, 1998), pp. 116-20.

82. See Chapter 2 and especially the appendix for a defence of this position.

83. Simon Price's important monograph is devoted to this area (*Rituals and Power*). See especially Price's maps identifying extant evidence of imperial religion (pp. xxii-xxv).

Although the modifier εἷς does include an exclusive nuance, the context of this passage makes it difficult to determine whether a polemic would be intended and understood by the readers. This passage is a string of such modifiers. Unlike in the previous passage, the modifier does not emphasize the distinction in as decisive a manner. Although the εἷς does communicate uniqueness here, it also communicates similarity among other terms so modified. This passage (4.4-6) may be a creedal formula or hymn,[84] which could add further support to a polemical nuance (see below); however, the context itself has no other elements that can be taken as anti-imperial. Verse 6 notes that God is over all. This certainly suggests that God is above all. However, this language is similar to Jewish language about God that the Romans had tolerated to some degree.

There is no agreement on the origin of the passage, whether it was written by the author of Ephesians or existed as a pre-Ephesian composition.[85] For those who maintain the latter, there are differences concerning the origin of the parts.[86] For our purposes we need only recognize the possible creedal or hymnic structure. We must deal with the passage as it exists in the text. Despite what will be said below about the potential polemical nature of creedal formulas and hymns, there are a number of elements in this passage that weaken the potential of polemic. First, unlike in the creedal statements below, the 'one Lord' is only one of seven points of confession and/ or belief. The entire package is in view. There is no particular focus on this one phrase. Ephesians 4.4-6 is comprehensive in nature. It involves more than Christology. Second, unlike the hymnic material below, this passage is not focused on Christ alone. Its focus is much more general. Finally, it is difficult to determine with any certainty whether this passage is intended to be a creedal statement, a hymn, or another specific genre.

Although the phrase εἷς κύριος is specific in its reference and focus on Jesus, the passage itself is much broader in nature. The result is that a pointed challenge to Caesar seems less likely in this context. With the exception of 1 Cor. 8.5-6, this and the other passages discussed in this work lack any direct negative attack against anything. However, as I have noted elsewhere, in certain contexts, a positive statement, when exclusive, must rule out others who claim the same position. In the case of Eph. 4.4-6, the context is least conducive to highlighting any specific opponent. Therefore,

---

84. Hoehner, *Ephesians*, pp. 513-14; Andrew T. Lincoln, *Ephesians* (WBC, 42; Dallas: Word Books, 1990), p. 238.

85. Compare Hoehner (*Ephesians*, pp. 513-14) and Peter O'Brien (*The Letter to the Ephesians* [PNTC; Grand Rapids: Eerdmans, 1999], pp. 280-81) (by the author of Ephesians) with Best (*Ephesians*, pp. 357-59) (pre-Ephesian).

86. See the discussion by Best (*Ephesians*, pp. 357-59).

we must acknowledge that any anti-imperial polemical pragmatic effect in this passage is likely weak.

Nevertheless, a polemic may be present for a number of reasons. First, as we have seen, the term κύριος is not generally a cultic term, and the separation between religion and politics is an artificial distinction. Second, the relational nature of the title and exclusive nature of the concept demand that, although readers can have many gods, they can have only one supreme lord. Finally, the inclusion of the modifier does result in a challenge to the default supreme lord. Whether or not this was intentional, it is a likely result. Therefore, it is best to conclude that a polemic may be intended and/or that the readers may have understood it; however, it is not a significant part of the intention of the passage. It is a weak implication.[87] Indeed, most commentators do not even suggest it as a possibility.[88] Ernest Best is an exception. He states, 'The title may then have been the one Christians learnt to use in indicating their new allegiance; this would require some identification of their new Lord over against the many non-Christian lords.'[89] Best then points out that unlike in other passages (Rom. 10.9; 1 Cor. 8.6; 12.3; Phil. 2.11), the 'lord' here is not specifically identified.[90] Nevertheless, the referent is clear and the structure (including parallelism) demands the short statement. Best is perhaps giving the challenge an appropriate amount of space, given its secondary nature in the passage. Nevertheless, the specific imperial connection and further implications of the challenge may have been fruitful to providing a fuller picture of the meaning of the passage.

Because the authorship and date of Ephesians are questioned, it is helpful to examine the passage in light of a post-Pauline date. The later the date of this epistle, the stronger a case can be made for a polemic. As we have seen, the use of κύριος continued to increase under the Flavians to the point where it became 'common'. This would only reinforce the identification of the emperor as κύριος. Additionally, if the book can be dated in the eighties or later, the presence of a provincial cult for the ruling emperors (Flavians) would have been a significant event in the city and throughout the province. The temple was dedicated in 89–90 CE during the reign of Domitian.[91] How-

87. Best suggests that it is a polemic against other religions, which have many lords (*Ephesians*, p. 368). Although the entire passage can be seen this way, the minimal use of the title in religious activities suggests that this phrase may not be best described in this manner.

88. See, e.g., Hoehner, *Ephesians*, p. 516; O'Brien, *Letter to the Ephesians*, pp. 283-84 (early Pauline date); Lincoln, *Ephesians*, p. 239 (later post-Pauline date).

89. Best, *Ephesians*, p. 368. Best maintains post-Pauline authorship; however, this statement is applicable to the passage during both the early and late date settings.

90. Best, *Ephesians*, p. 368.

91. Friesen, *Imperial Cults*, p. 46. For an extensive discussion of this temple and its activities, see Friesen's *Twice Neokoros*.

ever, preparations would have been taking place for some time. Although provincial cults had restrained language toward the emperors, the impact that this temple would have had on the cognitive environment during that period would have been enormous. Therefore, the reasons mentioned above for arguing that the polemic would be a weak implication during the early sixties are relevant here as well. However, the implication of a polemic at this later time would be stronger.[92]

As this passage is considered in its context, it seems clear that the polemical meaning is minimal (especially for the earlier dating); nevertheless, the structural clues make is likely that a claim to the exclusivity of the Christ is present. Thus, by implication, there is a challenge to Caesar.

c. *Loyalty and Creed Statement*

Values of loyalty and allegiance were important to Romans and especially to the imperial regime. As described in Chapter 3, the Roman people were consistently exposed to information that reminded people of the great deeds of Rome and the benefits that those within its borders enjoyed. Within this context, the emperor himself was portrayed in various ways that communicated his role as the head of this great empire. Clifford Ando's work discussed in Chapter 3 revealed Rome's own cognitive environment construction, which set out to define the world and control the subjects of the empire.[93]

In this empire-wide patronage system, the living Caesar was the great benefactor. Thus, the response that the people were expected to give the

---

92. First Timothy 6.15, another disputed Pauline passage, has a different type of superlative modifier: ὁ βασιλεὺς τῶν βασιλευόντων καὶ κύριος τῶν κυριευόντων. However, in this passage, the referent of κύριος is God the Father, not Jesus. God is 'the king over those who rule as kings and the lord over those who rule as lords'. The participle defines the spheres of kingship and lordship. Although slightly different in structure, there is likely Greek Old Testament influence here (see the Greek Deut. 10.17; Dan. 4.37; Ps. 135.3 [MT 136.3]; see also Rev. 17.14; 19.16). There is general agreement that this passage includes an anti-imperial polemic. This agreement includes both those who maintain Pauline authorship (e.g. J.N.D. Kelly, *A Commentary on the Pastoral Epistles: I Timothy, II Timothy, Titus* [BNTC; London: A. & C. Black, 1963], p. 146; William D. Mounce, *Pastoral Epistles* [WBC, 46; Nashville: Thomas Nelson, 2000], p. 361; Luke Timothy Johnson, *The First and Second Letters to Timothy: A New Translation with Introduction and Commentary* [AB, 35A; New York: Doubleday, 2001], pp. 308-309) and those who do not (e.g. Martin Dibelius and Hans Conzelmann, *The Pastoral Epistles: A Commentary on the Pastoral Epistles* [ed. Helmut Koester; trans. Philip Buttolph and Adela Yarbro; Hermeneia; Philadelphia: Fortress Press, 1972], p. 90; A.T. Hanson, *The Pastoral Epistles* [NCBC; Grand Rapids: Eerdmans, 1982], p. 112). This conclusion is strengthened by the use of imperial terminology in the context (see Price, 'Gods and Emperors', pp. 87-88).

93. Ando, *Imperial Ideology.*

state and its leader was loyalty and allegiance. This was necessary for the continued benefit for all.

Since the emperor was the great benefactor, loyalty to the state was essentially loyalty to him. There are many ways in which allegiance can be expressed. Imperial cults provided the emperor with a means of being *present* throughout the empire. They also served as a means for the people to relate to their physically distant ruler. Participation certainly demonstrated loyalty. However, certain acts, whether or not directly associated with emperor worship, expressed loyalty and allegiance more forcefully.

One important means of expressing allegiance was the swearing of an oath. This was a verbal means of expressing loyalty. One party swore their allegiance to another. This act was binding on the oath takers. Fortunately, many oaths survive from various parts of the empire. This permits us to get a fairly good understanding of their content and function. They could be sworn to both men and gods.[94] Essentially, this was an act of allegiance, and the divine or human status was not an important factor. The oath taker was bound to fulfil the oath. Oaths were sworn during the republic. For example, when fighting Hannibal in Italy, non-Roman allies swore an oath to obey the Roman leaders (Livy 22.38). After his defeat of Pompey, when Caesar returned to Rome, the magistrates swore an oath not to oppose Caesar's laws (Appian, *Civil Wars* 2.106). Cassius Dio informs us that included in the honours given to Julius Caesar in 44 BCE was the swearing of oaths to his Fortune (τύχη; Cassius Dio 44.6).[95] By the time of the empire, the practice of swearing an oath to a ruler was common.[96]

As early as 30 BCE, at dinners people were instructed to pour out libations to Augustus's Genius (Cassius Dio 51.19.7; see also Horace, *Odes* 4.5.33-35). In 14–12 BCE, the worship of Augustus's Genius became an official part of the state cult.[97] The reason this did not happen earlier is probably

---

94. For an example of an oath to a god, see Diodorus 37.11.

95. On oaths and Julius Caesar, see Lily Ross Taylor, *Party Politics in the Age of Caesar* (Sather Classical Lectures, 22; Berkeley: University of California Press, 1949), pp. 47, 174-75.

96. See the discussion in B.F. Harris, 'Oaths of Allegiance to Caesar', *Prudentia* 14 (1982), pp. 109-22 (109-11). For a discussion of oaths primarily but not exclusively in the late republic and early imperial periods, see Peter Herrmann, *Der römische Kaisereid: Untersuchungen zu seiner Herkunft und Entwicklung* (Hypomnemata, 20; Göttingen: Vandenhoeck & Ruprecht, 1968). For many examples of later imperial oaths in the papyri from various periods, see Z.M. Packman, 'Notes on Papyrus Texts with the Roman Imperial Oath', *ZPE* 89 (1991), pp. 91-102; Packman, 'Epithets with the Title Despotes in Regnal Formulas in Document Dates and in the Imperial Oath', *ZPE* 90 (1992), pp. 251-57; Packman, 'Still Further Notes on Papyrus Documents with the Roman Imperial Oath', *ZPE* 100 (1994), pp. 207-10.

97. Ovid, *Fasti* 5.145; Suetonius, *Augustus* 60; date from: Cerfaux and Tondriau, *Le*

that Augustus wished to wait until he had acquired the office of *pontifex maximus*.[98] In addition to these honours, people swore oaths to Augustus's Genius (and Numen). Around the time of Augustus's election as *pontifex maximus* in 12 BCE, Horace writes of Augustus, 'Upon you, however, while still among us, we give you honours, set up altars to swear by your *numen*, and confess that none like you has arisen or will arise again.'[99] The purpose of these actions was complex. One important aspect must have been a commitment from those taking these oaths to their benefactor.

Before defeating Antony, Octavian had entered into an oath agreement with the armies of the West and North Africa. This was an oath of allegiance in which the people gave their loyalty to Octavian in order that he might lead them against Antony. Much later, Augustus describes this oath as being initiated by the people (*Res Gestae* 25). This oath was due to practical and immediate needs; however, it foreshadowed imperial oaths to come.[100]

Imperial oaths were a means for the people to express their loyalty to their leader and a means for the emperor to acquire commitments of support from the people. According to Ando,

> These oaths had developed in a series of experiments between the final years of Caesar and the early 20s B.C. In form and content they duplicated and came to replace the Republican prayers for the health of the state (*vota pro rei publicae salute*). As such they participated in a gradual transference of focus in both popular and religious acts, from concern for the commonwealth to concern for the individual in whose care the commonwealth now resided.[101]

Thus, the emphasis in these oaths is firmly on the living emperor.

An inscription from Paphlagonia dated in 3 BCE provides a good example of an imperial oath for examination,

> 'I swear by Jupiter, Earth, Sun, by all the gods and goddesses, and by Augustus himself, that I will be loyal to Caesar Augustus and to his children and descendants all my life in word, in deed, and in thought, regarding as friends whomever they so regard, and considering as enemies whomever they so adjudge; that in defense of their interests I will spare neither body, soul, life, nor children, but will in every way undergo every danger in defense of their interests; that whenever I perceive or hear any-

cult des souverains, p. 318; Duncan Fishwick, '*Genius* and *Numen*', *HTR* 62 (1969), pp. 356-67 (356). (This article is revised in *ICLW,* II.1, pp. 375-87).

　　98. Taylor, *Divinity,* pp. 191-92.

　　99. Horace, *Epistle* 2.1.15-18; translation adapted and modernized from Fairclough, LCL. Fishwick suggests that *numen* here should be seen as the Genius ('*Genius* and *Numen*', p. 357; *ICLW,* II.1, p. 377). Fairclough's translation has 'name' for '*numen*'. However, this seems to be unjustified. It is left untranslated here.

　　100. Harris, 'Oaths', p. 112.

　　101. Ando, *Imperial Ideology,* p. 360.

thing being said or planned or done against them I will lodge information about this and will be an enemy to whoever says or plans or does any such thing; and that whomever they adjudge to be enemies I will by land and sea, with weapons and sword, pursue and punish. But if I do anything contrary to this oath or not in conformity with what I swore, I myself call down upon myself, my body, my soul, my life, my children, and all my family and property, utter ruin and utter destruction unto all my issue and all my descendants, and may neither earth nor sea receive the bodies of my family or my descendants, or yield fruits to them.'

The same oath was sworn also by all the people in the land at the altars of Augustus in the temples of Augustus in the various districts. In this manner did the people of Phazimon, who inhabit the city now called Neapolis, all together swear the oath in the temple of Augustus at the altar of Augustus. (OGIS 532 = ILS 8781; trans. Lewis and Reinhold).[102]

This oath is representative of other imperial oaths[103] and reveals a number of characteristics that are seen in this type of document. Five will be noted here. First, it is sworn before the witness of important gods. Interestingly, the living Augustus is included among those to whom this is sworn. In later oaths, he is often included as well (see an example below). Second, the one swearing the oath binds himself to the emperor and will take any measure to assure the well-being of the emperor. Third, if the swearer fails to keep the oath, he and his family will suffer gravely. Fourth, the oath was intended for all, both Roman and non-Roman. Fifth, it was intended to be administered in the temple of Augustus in each town in the region. The mention of the Augustan temple may suggest that there was an important connection between imperial oaths and imperial cults.[104] However, this does not need to be the case. If possible, places of imperial worship would be the logical place to swear such an oath. This was not only because of the obvious imagery that would be present but also because such places may be rather new and well situated to handle this act. We know little of how this oath was administered to large groups of people. It may have been through representatives. Below we will see that this practice happened in the senate, which was a relatively small body. Or it could have been administered in theatres or other large buildings. Concerning the oath in Thessalonica, Peter Oakes makes the following observation:

---

102. Translation in Naphtali Lewis and Meyer Reinhold (eds.), *Roman Civilization: Select Readings*. I. *The Republic and the Augustan Age* (New York: Columbia University Press, 3rd edn, 1990), p. 589. The date of this inscription is from Harris, 'Oaths', p. 112. See also Edwin A. Judge, 'The Decrees of Caesar at Thessalonica', *RTR* 30 (1971), pp. 5-6 (Judge also dates this to 3 BCE).

103. Harris, 'Oaths', p. 112. Part of another oath to Augustus from Samos survives (5 BCE). Much of this oath is missing, but it is clear that the magistrates administered the oath (Judge, 'Decrees', p. 7).

104. Harris, 'Oaths', p. 112.

The logistics of individuals swearing would seem impractical. If 50,000 Thessalonians took a minute each, it would require 170 officials to sit 5 hours (rapidly going insane), not to mention the other people required for crowd control and checking registration (which would itself be unworkably complex if it attempted to be universal). Even if this was scaled down to heads of household, the complexity of the exercise would surely prevent any city from trying it twice.[105]

I do not believe that an empire such as Rome, which was suspicious of large gatherings and attempted to avoid chaos, would attempt such a large-scale administration of oaths (not to mention an annually repeated act).[106] Of course, particulars probably differed in various areas (this may include various degrees of connection to local imperial cults). What is important is not the actual taking of the oath but rather the presence of the oath in the cognitive environment. All citizens were bound to the emperor whether they physically took the oath or not. No one could act contrary to the acts of the oath and then claim that he was not bound because he did not actually swear the oath. Such individuals would be condemned by the oath already and be open to punishment. The oath could be used in special individual cases where loyalty may be questioned (see below), but in general, it was not necessary.

If our contention is correct that the oath need only be in the cognitive environment to be effective, we must note its existence after the time of Augustus. When Tiberius began his rule after the death of Augustus in 14 CE, a similar oath was given to the officials and people (Tacitus, *Annals* 1.7).[107] An example survives from Cyprus.[108] Here again the oath shows the people committing themselves to Tiberius, an important step in acknowledging the new ruler. However, at this time he did forbid swearing by his Fortune (τύχη; Cassius Dio 57.8.3). Nevertheless, annual oaths in the senate were administered. It appears that, as time went on, the oath was taken by only one as a representative of the group. However, after Sejanus's plot was discovered, the entire senate swore individually (Cassius Dio 58.17.2). Tiberius appears to have been inconsistent in his demand for oaths sworn to obey or carry out imperial acts. In one case, he is recorded as refusing to allow the oath to be sworn (Tacitus, *Annals* 1.72). In another case, he excludes one from the senate for refusing to take an oath to carry out the

---

105. Oakes, 'Re-Mapping the Universe', p. 313.

106. It is interesting that the logistics of large-scale oaths are not normally considered. See Ando, *Imperial Ideology*, pp. 359-61.

107. However, Tiberius forbade an oath to be taken promising to fulfil his acts (Tacitus, *Annals* 1.72).

108. First published with Greek text, plate and English translation by T.B. Mitford, 'A Cypriot Oath of Allegiance to Tiberius', *JRS* 50 (1960), pp. 75-79.

acts of Augustus (Tacitus, *Annals* 4.42). This difference may partially be explained by when these occurred (and/or the role of Augustus). The further into his reign, Tiberius became more suspicious of others.

The oath practice continued under Caligula (ILS 190 [37 CE; Aritensian (Spain) oath];[109] SIG³ 797 [37 CE];[110] Cassius Dio 59.3.4). He did not include Tiberius's acts with the acts of Augustus and his own (Cassius Dio 59.91-93). He apparently demanded that people swear to his Genius or be put to death (Suetonius, *Caligula* 27.3). Even Claudius, who was reluctant to accept divine honours, still was the object of oaths for the empire (Cassius Dio 60.25.1-2; although he did not demand each individual senator to do so). He did not require people to swear by his own acts, but he did swear to uphold Augustus's acts (Cassius Dio 60.10.1). Nero probably also used this practice to have the people express loyalty to him.[111] Given the actions of his predecessors and his own somewhat dubious position (Claudius had a natural heir), it certainly is probable. However, I was unable to locate a specific example of an oath. Nevertheless, loyalty is implied in the announcement of his ascension.[112]

The evidence of oath taking by all of the emperors, whether restrained or extravagant in honours, demonstrates that this was an important means of expressing loyalty and allegiance to the emperor. In general, the sources described above present oaths in a neutral or positive light. The negative statement about Caligula in Suetonius (*Caligula* 27.3) is in a context of abuses and harsh punishments. The oath serves an important function. It expresses the relationship between emperor and people in the form of a commitment. Such expression was necessary to maintain peace in the empire. This is confirmed by the use of the oath during the civil wars of 68–69 CE. The oath made soldiers commit to one ruler against another. This at times was a difficult situation.[113]

109. For an English translation see Naphtali Lewis and Meyer Reinhold (eds.), *Roman Civilization: Select Readings*. II. *The Empire* (New York: Columbia University Press, 3rd edn, 1990), p. 8. This oath was administered 52 days after Tiberius's death (Lewis and Reinhold, *Roman Civilization*, II, p. 8 n. 11).

110. The oath is from Assus (Asia) and was sworn to Δία Σωτῆρα καί θεὸν Καίσαρα Σεβαστὸν καὶ πάτριον αγνὴν Παρθένον ('God the Saviour and god Caesar Augustus and the ancestral chaste Maiden'). The inclusion of Augustus is natural, since he was an official state deity at the time. Above in the Paphlagonia oath he was included while alive. It is interesting that Caligula is not included at this point in the oath. For an English translation of the entire oath, see Lewis and Reinhold, *Roman Civilization*, II, pp. 8-9 (he associates Δία with Zeus).

111. Harris, 'Oaths', p. 116 (with no evidence).

112. See POxy 1021 (54 CE).

113. Harris, 'Oaths', pp. 116-17.

Loyalty oaths, then, were an expression of allegiance. This allegiance was not towards participation in imperial cults but to the emperor himself.[114] The multifaceted purposes of imperial cults included loyalty. Thus, it is better to view both imperial cults and oaths as means (albeit related to various degrees) of demonstrating loyalty.[115] The important point of this discussion is that it was the expectation in the cities in which the Pauline communities were situated that all were to be loyal to the living Caesar. This was the assumed state of affairs—to use terminology from our lordship discussion, this was the default position. In this way our discussion of oaths is applicable to other means of expressing loyalty. Oaths or other means of expressing loyalty did not need to take place for this to be the assumed situation. If opportunities to express loyalty appeared, they needed to be fulfilled. However, without such opportunities, the obligation of loyalty was assumed.

The passage from the *Martyrdom of Polycarp* cited above was one such occasion. Polycarp's loyalty was questioned, and he was offered an opportunity to show his loyalty through swearing an oath and sacrificing to Caesar. A similar situation is described in Pliny's correspondence with the emperor Trajan just prior to Polycarp's death. Uncertain what to do with those accused of being Christians, he gave them an opportunity to show their loyalty by invoking Roman gods, offering wine and incense to Trajan's statue and reviling the name of Christ (*Epistles* 10.96.5). These were things that Pliny believed that those who were in truth (i.e. truly) Christians (*qui sunt re vera Christiani*) would not do.

What is at stake here is essentially the question of where the Christian's allegiance lies. Their failure to prove their loyalty to Caesar made them vulnerable to attack. The 'good' Roman must punish them, because this is what Romans are sworn to do. The Roman official and Pliny were doing what the empire expected. It is possible that a Christian could continue worshipping Christ as long as he/she gave Caesar his proper place. This was acceptable to the Roman system but not to the Christians. It was because of this conviction that there was conflict.

As for the general population, it is impossible to know whether individuals took these oaths seriously. This probably varied. The actions of the

114. Oakes, 'Re-mapping the Universe', p. 312.
115. Hubert Cancik explores the relationship between oaths and Roman ruler worship in 'Der Kaiser-Eid: Zur Praxis der römischen Herrscherverehrung', in Cancik and Hitzl (eds.), *Praxis der Herrscherverehrung*, pp. 29-45. To the present study, the question of the relationship between oaths and emperor worship is really not essential. Oaths preceded imperial religious expression. Also, on the one hand, it has been acknowledged that there is no distinction between religious experience and politics. On the other hand, both oaths and imperial religious practices point to the emperor. The emperor as the focal point in the cognitive environment is what is important.

soldiers during the civil war in 68–69 CE, when explicit loyalties were very important, suggest that it was significant to them. Whether this was due to fear of punishment or sincere conviction is uncertain (probably a mixture of both). However, in the passage cited above about senators individually taking the oath to Tiberius after the discovery of Sejanus's plot, Cassius Dio tacks on a final revealing clause, ὥσπερ τι παρὰ τοῦτο μᾶλλον εὐορκήσοντες ('as if because of this [they would be] keeping their oath more'; 58.17.2). Clearly Cassius Dio does not believe that the senators were sincere in their commitment to Tiberius.

As with the formal swearing of the oath, whether the oaths revealed what was in the heart of the people is less important than the actions themselves. We have already demonstrated that the Roman religious experience was primarily activity based. The visible outward appearance was probably more important than inward conviction (as long as it remained hidden). This is probably true for oath taking as well. The act of swearing the oath was the desired important action. Or, if I am correct that consistent large-scale oath taking was unlikely, general adherence to the oath was expected, and the willingness to take the oath when demanded was what was important. It committed the oath takers to the leader. All were responsibly bound to the oath no matter what they did or truly believed. The presence of the oath in the cognitive environment also gave the state (and others) reason to punish those who refused to express their loyalty when the opportunity arose.

It is possible that imperial oaths caused problems for the early Christian community. J.R. Harrison, following Edwin A. Judge and Karl Paul Donfried has suggested that Jews in Thessalonica 'fulfilled the spirit of the loyalty oaths in searching for Paul and Silas at Jason's house (Acts 17.5), reporting the Thessalonian believers to the politarchs (Acts 17.6-9), and then pursuing Paul to Berea with the same intent (17.13)'.[116] This certainly is possible but is far from provable. If accurate, it further substantiates the prevalence of the 'oath' content in the cognitive environment. Harrison also suggests that the imperial oaths may be influencing Paul's language in Rom. 6.12-23.[117] Again, if this is the case, it further validates the role of the oath in the general cognitive environment of the period.

It seems likely that the general content of the oath was strongly present throughout the Roman empire. Everyone knew of it and knew to whom they were to be loyal. The default object of allegiance in the cognitive environment was Caesar. The allegiance of the people of the empire was assumed.

116. J.R. Harrison, 'Paul and the Imperial Gospel at Thessaloniki', *JSNT* 25 (2002), pp. 71-96 (80). See also, Judge, 'Decrees', pp. 1-7; Karl Paul Donfried, 'The Cults of Thessalonica and the Thessalonian Correspondence', *NTS* 31 (1985), pp. 336-56.

117. J.R. Harrison, *Paul's Language of Grace in its Graeco-Roman Context* (WUNT, 2.172; Tübingen: J.C.B. Mohr [Paul Siebeck], 2003), pp. 234-42.

Later Christians certainly came into conflict with this. Is it possible that the conflict existed in the New Testament as well? If so, the communication principles of *relevance* and *efficiency* suggest that something would need to be communicated that would pose a challenge to the assumed allegiance of the day.

Although not exclusive of the other factors I am suggesting that can be used explicitly to challenge the object of loyalty, it seems likely that creedal statements function within the means of expressing allegiance. The phrase that Polycarp was asked to swear was Κύριος Καῖσαρ. In one of the ostraca cited above, Nero is called Νέρονος [*sic*] κυρίου (ODeiss 39; 62 CE). However, despite similarities in form, the use of the title in the ostracon cannot be seen as communicating anything more than the many articular uses listed above. More importantly, the Polycarp example demonstrates that this form, when placed in a context where loyalty may be expressed, is a means of confessing one's allegiance. Without intending to imply all the nuances of later usages of the term, I suggest that this form functions as a type of *creed*.

Additionally, although the predicate is δεσπότης, Josephus provides important evidence for creedal-type statements being used as expressions of loyalty. In *Jewish War* 7.10.1 §§417-19, Josephus describes Jews who, under terrible torture and even death, refused to call Caesar lord (Καίσαρα δεσπότην). The resolve of the Jews was so strong that it appears to have impressed those witnessing the suffering (especially of the Jewish children). Thus, when one considers the Polycarp and Josephus incidents, it seems clear that creedal-type statements can be viewed as expressions of loyalty.

Although we do not possess an example of κύριος in an imperial oath during the Julio-Claudian dynasty, it is possible an example may have existed. Packman discusses a number of papyri with imperial oaths that include κύριος.[119] However, these are all much later (most in the third or fourth century, some in the mid-second). Additionally, there were times when both date and oath formulas were identical. Above we saw a number of date formulas with the title in them. This was beginning to become common during Nero's reign. Packman's initial example on this subject includes the use of the title for the joint emperors during the Tetrarchy (turn of the fourth century CE):

τῶν κυρίων ἡμῶν Διοκλητιανοῦ καὶ Μαξιμιανοῦ Σεβαστῶν καὶ Κωνσταντίου καὶ Μαξιμιανοῦ τῶν ἐπιφανεστάτων Καισάρων

118. Correct spelling: Νέρωνος.

119. Packman, 'Notes on Papyrus Texts', pp. 93-98; Packman, 'Epithets', p. 251. Packman also discusses a number of late texts with δεσπότης ('Notes on Papyrus Texts', p. 95-100; 'Epithets', p. 251-53).

our lords Diocletian and Maximian Augusti and Constantius and Maximian distinguished Caesars.[120]

It is admitted that, given the history of development of the title κύριος,
the possibility of the title being used in oath formulas in the Julio-Claudian
period is slim. However, two points can be made to support a connection
between the title and the oath formula. First, its use at all suggests that the
title and the concept postulated above expressed by the title were natural in
oath formulas. Κύριος is a relational term, and the oath expresses this relationship. The reluctance to use the title may have been due to the continued
attempt to maintain the fiction created by Augustus, which was intended
to keep this relationship implicit. Second, later this fiction was no longer
necessary and the relationship could be made explicit. This is true whether
the title is used or not. The content and act of taking this oath expressed the
lordship relationship. It was always there. It was simply made explicit later.

Considering the relational nature of κύριος, the profession of one as *lord*
in a creedal statement would suggest that a claim is being made for supreme
lord. Because the concept of supreme lord is exclusive, it would appear that
the proclamation of Christ in such a context would be a challenge to the
default referent. If the Romans took pains to extract these statements from
others, it follows that an expression of another as Lord would be viewed as
a challenge.

Before proceeding, one grammatical issue must be discussed. We have
thus far translated the Polycarp passage as a creedal-type statement: 'Caesar is Lord.' However, given the identical case and implied equative verb,
translations such as '[the] lord is Caesar' or simply 'lord Caesar' may be
suggested. Such statements appear to be synonymous; however, these do
not really express a creedal notion in the way the original translation does.
This may be partially due to the nature of language translation, where one
expression (here in Greek) includes various nuances that the target language
cannot adequately reproduce. Nevertheless, the alternate English translations do not maintain the strong creedal nuance of the original translation.
In addition to the Polycarp passage, the remaining passages (including Phil.
2.11, not immediately discussed) all have this form.[121] There are two reasons why the original creedal translation best reflects the Greek. First, in the
Polycarp passage and the Pauline texts below, the statement is introduced in
contexts demanding a confessional or creedal-type statement. Second, when
two nominatives occur in an equative clause, the known entity is the subject
(the nominative being identified by the other).[122] Thus, in cases where there

120. CPR VII, 14 (cited in Packman, 'Epithets', p. 251).
121. However, in Rom. 10.9, the relevant expression is in the accusative case. This
will briefly be discussed with that passage.
122. Lane C. McGaughy, *Toward a Descriptive Analysis of Εἶναι as a Linking Verb*

is both a proper name and an anarthrous common noun in the nominative case, the proper name is the subject.[123] Therefore, the translations 'Caesar is lord' and 'Jesus is lord' are preferred.

(1) *1 Corinthians 12.3:* Κύριος Ἰησοῦς. 1 Corinthians 12.3 is part of an introductory section (12.1-3) to Paul's discussion of the use of spiritual gifts in the Christian assembly (chs. 12–14). After noting the ignorance of their pre-Christian existence and revealing his desire for the readers to be knowledgeable about spiritual gifts, Paul states:

διὸ γνωρίζω ὑμῖν ὅτι οὐδεὶς ἐν πνεύματι θεοῦ λαλῶν λέγει· Ἀνάθεμα Ἰησοῦς, καὶ οὐδεὶς δύναται εἰπεῖν· Κύριος Ἰησοῦς, εἰ μὴ ἐν πνεύματι ἁγίῳ.

> Therefore, I make known to you that no one speaking by the Spirit of God says, 'Jesus is accursed'; and no one is able to say 'Jesus is Lord', except by the Holy Spirit.

Paul contrasts the cursing of Jesus with the acknowledgment of Jesus as Lord. In their previous religious experience they were drawn to and led astray by idols.[124] However, they must realize that those who are led by the Spirit of God will acknowledge Jesus as Lord. Only through the Spirit can true commitment to Jesus be expressed. As in 1 Cor. 8.5-6, there are negative statements made in this section. However, unlike the earlier passage, in which the contrast was with different lords, this passage contrasts different approaches to Jesus. One led by the Spirit cannot curse Jesus, but only through the Spirit can one call Jesus 'Lord'.

The singular focus on Jesus in this passage may suggest that it is unlikely that an anti-imperial polemic is intended. The pagan religions are dealt with in a past manner. This was the life they lived previously. However, given our historical and linguistic (pragmatic and conceptual) discussion above, there is support for an anti-imperial polemic here.

---

in New Testament Greek (SBLDS, 6; Missoula, MT: Society of Biblical Literature, 1972), pp. 68-72. Rules for distinguishing between a subject and predicate nominative were suggested by Eugene van Ness Goetchius, *The Language of the New Testament* (New York: Charles Scribner's Sons, 1965), pp. 45-46. However, McGaughy found these insufficient (*Descriptive Analysis*, pp. 29-33). See also the developments by Wallace, *Exegetical Syntax*, pp. 42-46.

123. Wallace, *Exegetical Syntax*, pp. 43-44.

124. There are a number of exegetical difficulties in this passage. One such problem relates to the cursing of Jesus. Is this hypothetical? Did it or is it happening? For our purpose this issue need not be resolved. For a list of twelve options with discussion, see Thiselton, *First Epistle to the Corinthians*, pp. 918-27.

In addition to the strong imperial presence and increasingly common use of κύριος for Nero,[125] there are other reasons that a polemic may be present in this passage. This passage shares some features with the Polycarp confession. In addition to a similar form, there is a clear connection between making a statement and showing loyalty. The introductory statement identifies the following clause as confessional: οὐδεὶς δύναται εἰπεῖν· . . . ('no one is able to say . . .'). Also, when a context of some form of allegiance in the midst of conflict is postulated, it makes best sense of the entire passage:

διὸ γνωρίζω ὑμῖν ὅτι οὐδεὶς ἐν πνεύματι θεοῦ λαλῶν λέγει· Ἀνάθεμα Ἰησοῦς, καὶ οὐδεὶς δύναται εἰπεῖν· Κύριος Ἰησοῦς, εἰ μὴ ἐν πνεύματι ἁγίῳ.

Therefore, I make known to you that no one speaking by the Spirit of God says, 'Jesus is accursed'; and no one is able to say 'Jesus is Lord', except by the Holy Spirit.

It is unlikely that persecution such as that experienced during Polycarp's time was occurring. However, there were probably real threats to relationships, lifestyle, and social status. Additionally, there was also the possibility of physical harm (as Acts suggests). There would be temptation for Christians to curse Jesus and to distance themselves from the young movement. The repeated prepositional phrase ἐν πνεύματι is most likely instrumental (means).[126] It is possible that the application of this verse was what Pliny observed in the aforementioned passage (*Epistles* 10.96.5), namely that some cursed (*male dicerent*) Christ but a genuine (in truth or true) Christian (*re vera Christiani*) would neither offer incense to the emperor nor revile Christ.[127] Additionally, the expression of Jesus as κύριος must be more than merely words. It reflected a commitment of loyalty.[128] In the face of resist-

---

125. A brief statement about the imperial presence in Corinth was mentioned above under the discussion of 1 Cor. 8.5-6. Further comment is not necessary here.

126. Thiselton, *First Epistle to the Corinthians*, p. 917. Thiselton suggests both instrument and agency as usages for the prepositional phrase. However, a strict grammatical classification of agency for ἐν is rare and thus is unlikely here. Wallace, *Exegetical Syntax*, pp. 373-74. The classification of instrument or means does not demand that the object of the preposition be impersonal (Wallace, *Exegetical Syntax*, p. 373).

127. On Pliny's persecution, see Marta Sordi, *The Christians and the Roman Empire* (trans. Annabel Bedini; London: Croom Helm, 1986), pp. 59-65; Fergus Millar, 'The Imperial Cult and the Persecutions', in Willem den Boer (ed.), *Le culte des souverains dans l'empire romain* (Geneva: Fondation Hardt, 1973), pp. 152-53; F. Gerald Downing, 'Pliny's Persecutions of Christians: Revelation and 1 Peter', *JSNT* 34 (1988), pp. 105-23.

128. Thiselton uses speech act theory to make essentially this same point (*First Epistle to the Corinthians*, pp. 925-26). See also Archibald Robertson and Alfred

ance, it took the power of the Holy Spirit to make this commitment. This passage makes sense only if this confession was 'radical' in its context.[129] The confession was a commitment to Jesus as supreme lord replacing the default referent of the concept. If this was not the case, there would be little resistance and little need for such language.[130] Thiselton suggests that the statement is a *speech act:* 'it is *a spoken act of personal devotion and commitment which is part and parcel of Christ-centered worship and lifestyle.*[131]

One point of interest here is that if the Christian's confession of Jesus as κύριος does indeed include a polemic against Caesar, there is no indication that the Christian is to curse Caesar. This suggests two things. First, the confession of Jesus as lord was sufficient. It reflected an exclusive relationship to the confessor. Nothing more is needed. Second, the lack of explicit negative statements about Caesar may suggest that there was a role for Caesar in God's plan. This is an important aspect of our argument throughout. Any polemic is really only against Caesar when he usurps the role intended for Christ.

We noted above in a footnote that there are a number of difficulties associated with this passage. One is worth visiting here. Fee notes that some are troubled by this passage because anyone can literally say 'Jesus is Lord.'[132] Fee continues by suggesting that the 'absolute allegiance' demanded by this confession would result in pitting Christians against all others.[133] Fee is on the right track; however, acknowledging more of a direct challenge to the emperor (not to the exclusion of others) would strengthen his point. It was Caesar whose demand for allegiance was most prominent at this time. It stands to reason that acknowledging Jesus as Lord would be more challenging to imperial ideology than most other options (note the direct contrast to the 'Caesar is Lord' confessions). Switching one's alliance from Caesar to Jesus would be rejecting the lord who was responsible for so much that the imperial propaganda claimed was good in the empire. This would certainly result in some level of conflict.

Plummer, *A Critical and Exegetical Commentary on the First Epistle of St Paul to the Corinthians* (ICC; Edinburgh: T. & T. Clark, 2nd edn, 1914), pp. 261-62.

129. Fee, *First Epistle to the Corinthians*, p. 581. See also Barrett, *Commentary on the First Epistle to the Corinthians,* 279-80.

130. For an extensive discussion of this passage, see Thiselton, *First Epistle to the Corinthians*, pp. 916-27.

131. Thiselton, *First Epistle to the Corinthians*, p. 926 (italics in the original)

132. Fee, *First Epistle to the Corinthians*, p. 581.

133. Fee, *First Epistle to the Corinthians*, pp. 581-82. Also, Garland acknowledges that this passage 'declares absolute allegiance to [Jesus] and accepts his absolute authority over every aspect of life' (*1 Corinthians*, p. 572). However, there is no consideration of any imperial challenges and the resulting consequences.

(2) *Romans 10.9: κύριον Ἰησοῦν.* Romans 10.9 is in the context of a discussion about righteousness (10.5-13). It is filled with quotations of and allusions to the Old Testament. Given the significant usage of κύριος for God in the Old Testament, one may question whether a polemic from outside this context could be intended. However, this fails to consider the broader Old Testament context. God (יהוה) was often viewed against all other gods and objects of worship (e.g. Exod. 20.2-5; Isa. 44.9-20) as well as against nations and earthly rulers (e.g. Psalm 2; Daniel 4). In Rom. 10.13, Paul applies an Old Testament passage about God to Jesus (LXX Joel 3.5 [= English 2.32]). Thus, a connection between Jesus and God (יהוה) is made explicit. The gods and rulers have changed, but the theme is consistent: Jesus is Lord, no one else!

Much of the discussion concerning 1 Cor. 12.3 is applicable here. However, there are some important differences. First, unlike 1 Cor. 12.3, this passage is in the accusative case. Because of the context, including the introductory verb ὁμολογέω, it is likely a double accusative object–complement construction.[134] Determining the direct object and complement is essentially the same as determining the subject and predicative nominative discussed above.[135] Jesus, as the proper name, is the object of the verb, and κύριον is the complement.[136] The creedal or confessional statement 'Jesus is Lord' is preferred. The creedal nature of this passage is confirmed by a change in the text. This change is most importantly reflected in the fourth-century uncial codex Vaticanus. This manuscript adds το ῥῆμα after ὁμολογήσῃς and puts the creedal formula in the nominative case. The result is 'that you may confess *the word* with your mouth, namely that Jesus is Lord'. It is likely that this change reflects the desire to make the creedal formula more explicit.[137]

Second, the recipients of this letter are in the capital of Rome itself. Although I noted that differences between emperor worship in Rome and elsewhere are often exaggerated, there are nevertheless important differences between the capital and the rest of the empire. Although divinized

---

134. Daniel B. Wallace, 'The Semantics and Exegetical Significance of the Object–Complement Construction in the New Testament', *Grace Theological Journal* 6 (1985), pp. 91-112 (p. 96 n. 23, p. 109).

135. For an in-depth discussion of this issue, see Wallace, 'Semantics and Exegetical Significance', pp. 101-104. See also Wallace's *Exegetical Syntax*, pp. 182-89.

136. Wallace, 'Semantics and Exegetical Significance', pp. 108-11. Wallace also notes significance in the word order, suggesting that κύριον is likely to have a more definite nuance pointing more toward identification than quality (Wallace, 'Semantics and Exegetical Significance', pp. 109-11).

137. C.E.B. Cranfield, *A Critical and Exegetical Commentary on the Epistle to the Romans* (ICC; 2 vols.; Edinburgh: T. & T. Clark, 6th rev. edn, 1975, 1979), II, p. 527 n. 5. Dunn states that it is a 'well established creedal formula' (*Romans 9–16*, p. 607).

emperors were official state gods, the divinity of the living emperor tended to be euphemistically expressed (e.g. the worship of his Genius). Rome was the capital, and, especially among the elite, the emperor's divine status was not emphasized. Further, there appears to be no extant evidence of the titles κύριος or *dominus* used of an emperor in Rome before Domitian. Thus, in some ways the most difficult part of demonstrating a polemic in Rom. 10.9 is to prove convincingly that terminology such as κύριος and *dominus* would be associated with Caesar and would express his role as the default supreme lord in the cognitive environment of the capital.

Despite the lack of the use of κύριος and *dominus* for Caesar in Rome, there are a number of reasons why these terms would express Caesar's supreme lordship in as likely a manner in Rome as elsewhere. In general, this is a summary of aspects of the previous two chapters. First, as we already noted, the role of first citizen that Augustus created was a fiction. It was created to appease the nobility. Paul's letters were not intended for a community of the elite. However, it is highly unlikely that the common people ever needed the Augustan fiction. In addition to decades of time between the establishment of the principate and the composition of the letter, Rome had experienced the outward monarchical rule of Caligula, which essentially revealed the explicit role of the emperor. Second, there is not necessarily a dependence on imperial cults for the lordship of Caesar to be expressed. We have proposed that, in addition to their religious function, imperial cults were a means of communicating Caesar's position. However, the nature of lordship is not necessarily an aspect of the imperial rituals. Third and related, there is no necessary correlation between κύριος and divinity. Although we have maintained that Caesar was a god in Rome and gods may be labelled κύριος, the title itself does not demand this. Fourth, the difference in language is important. Although cities like Corinth and especially Philippi would have had a strong Latin influence, Rome was a Latin city. Certainly Greek was common there (as evidenced, among other things, by Paul's letter to the Romans which was written in Greek), but Latin and its influence were significant. The use of κύριος may not have included the negative nuances of *dominus*. Fifth, the role of the emperor as benefactor would be very explicit in Rome. He provided much for the locals there. Sixth, although this letter was written during the so-called positive part of Nero's reign (the same could be said for the Corinthian passages), it has been demonstrated that the character of Nero was not drastically different at this time from what it was later. Also, there is not a direct correlation between administration of Nero's government and his position as lord. He was as much κύριος at the beginning of his reign as he was at the end. The lordship of the emperor was a relationship that could be used for good or bad. The role itself was not necessarily negative.

Contextually, the passage is a creedal formula and expresses loyalty. Dunn states, 'It would indicate a transfer of allegiance, a change of acknowledged ownership.'[138] Loyalty itself is not necessarily polemical. After acknowledging that allegiance is involved in the statement, Dunn dismisses a polemic against Caesar because he believes that different spheres of lordship are in view.[139] Joseph Fitzmyer suggests that the statement may be an imitation of Κύριος Καῖσαρ as expressed in the later *Martyrdom of Polycarp* (8.2).[140] However, he denies a possible polemic because Rom. 10.9 'lacks the public and polemical connotation of the [*Martyrdom* passage]'.[141] However, by describing the relational nature of κύριος and the exclusiveness of the concept and developing the cognitive environment of the first century, I have satisfied the objections of Dunn and Fitzmyer. Robert Jewett's statement on this verse reflects the conclusion here, 'To "confess Jesus as Lord" was . . . to reveal one's own identity and commitment.'[142] Just prior to this, Jewett compares this passage with Καῖσαρα δεσπότην in Josephus, *Jewish War* 7.10.1 §418 (see above), which he considers a 'loyalty oath'.[143] I acknowledge that loyalty alone is not grounds for polemic. However, here there is loyalty to a specific κύριος. The use of a creedal formula connotes more than a simple loyalty. Without any further qualification, such a formula for a κύριος would imply supreme lord. Paul is not simply telling his readers about lord Jesus. Rather, he is telling them to confess (ὁμολογήσῃς) outwardly (ἐν τῷ στόματι, 'with [your] mouth') that *Jesus is Lord*.

The challenge to Caesar is strengthened by at least two other contextual features. First, the confession of Jesus as Lord results in salvation (σωθήσῃ, 'you will be saved'). Salvation was the responsibility of Caesar. He was the σωτήρ ('saviour'), the one who brings σωτηρία ('salvation') to the Roman people. This is most vividly expressed in the calendar inscription (9 BCE) of the province of Asia in which the living Augustus was honoured for (among other reasons) as the saviour (σωτῆρα) of the empire. (IPriene 105.35 = OGIS 458.36[144]). We also find Augustus described as τὸν εὐεργέτ[ην] καὶ σωτῆρα τοῦ σύμπαντο[ς] κόσμου ('benefactor and saviour of the whole world'; IGRR, III, 719). In addition, Tiberius is described the same way (IGRR, III, 721). And Philo uses these titles for Caligula

138. Dunn, *Romans 9–16*, p. 608.
139. Dunn, *Romans 9–16*, p. 608.
140. Fitzmyer, *Romans*, p. 591.
141. Fitzmyer, *Romans*, p. 591.
142. Robert Jewett, assisted by Roy D. Kotansky, *Romans: A Commentary* (ed. Eldon Jay Epp; Hermeneia; Minneapolis: Fortress Press, 2007), p. 630.
143. Jewett, *Romans*, pp. 629-30.
144. The word σωτῆρα was added to a damaged portion of the inscription. However, the addition is likely. See Danker, *Benefactor*, p. 220. For a portion of Danker's translation of this inscription, see p. 137 above.

(*On the Embassy to Gaius* 22). Although others could be described as saviour during Roman history,[145] during the empire it was the emperor himself who had this role.[146] Additionally, the quotation from LXX Joel 3.5 in Rom. 10.13 provides a universal principle:

πᾶς γὰρ ὃς ἂν ἐπικαλέσηται τὸ ὄνομα κυρίου σωθήσεται (Rom. 10.13)

for everyone who may call on the name of the Lord, will be saved[147]

This appears to be an open invitation for anyone, even Caesar himself. This statement must be seen as a challenge to the propositions expressed in the inscriptions just cited. Not only is Jesus the Lord, but it is he, not Caesar, who will provide salvation.[148]

Second, God has raised Jesus from the dead (ὁ θεὸς αὐτὸν ἤγειρεν ἐκ νεκρῶν; Rom. 10.9). Although this would be more difficult for the original readers to connect with the emperor (and thus weaker evidence for the polemic), it is possible that this action could be read in light of the *apotheosis* of the dead (deified) emperor. The senate could vote to honour an emperor as a god (i.e. *divus*) and the emperor would be transported to the sphere of the gods. The result was that the dead emperor was essentially gone from explicit daily affairs. However, Jesus was brought back to life. As lordship tends to be the domain of a present benefactor, Jesus, although he died, came back to life. This is something that even the great Augustus did not do.

Thus, the structure and context add the pragmatic information that suggests a challenge to Caesar is likely here. Nothing less than a loyalty commitment to Jesus is intended. However, it can only be seen if one considers the implications of the relational nature of lordship, acknowledges the pres-

---

145. See, e.g., during the late republic: Pompey (SIG³ 749, 751, 755); Cornelius Lentulus (SIG³ 750); Julius Caesar (SIG³ 759).

146. For Vespasian, see Josephus, *Jewish War*, 3.9.8 §459. In some cases, a close associate may have this title. In IGRR, III, 719 quoted above, Marcus Agrippa is also called by these titles, τὸν εὐεργέτην καὶ σωτῆρα τοῦ ἔθνους ('benefactor and saviour of the people [nation]'). However, the context of this inscription makes it clear that Augustus is superior.

147. With the exception of the conjunction, this is an exact quotation of LXX Joel 3.5. The use of an Old Testament passage may raise questions about whether this might be perceived as relevant to the Roman context. Throughout this work, I am not arguing for an exclusive Roman polemic against all other purposes of the passage. There is no reason to think that readers would not see this (at least partially) in light of their Roman context. This issue is discussed below for Phil 2:11. What is argued there would have at least as much relevance here in the Roman capital.

148. On the use of σωτήρ for emperors and others, see Cuss, *Imperial Cult*, pp. 63-71.

ence of the concept *supreme lord*, and considers the consequences of confessing Jesus as Lord. The structure and context of this passage suggest that
Jesus is filling the relational role of supreme lord. Despite Jewett's strong
acknowledgment that the notion of loyalty is in this passage, he does not
question whether anyone is displaced as lord.[149] Failing to consider such an
implication may result in this aspect of Paul's message being lost. Cranfield,
however, does acknowledge that the readers would understand the formula
in light of a similar confession for Caesar.[150] Even so, he does not consider
the implications of this. Rather, he devotes his discussion to whether or not
the confession is derived from (or a response to) the Caesar confession,[151] a
position he correctly rejects.[152] In Wright's commentary on Romans, a discussion of the specific confession for Jesus and Caesar is missing; however,
he acknowledges the implications and states that the confession 'from early
on, lay at the heart of the confrontation between the kingdom theology of
the early church and the ideology of imperial Rome'.[153]

d. *Poetic or Hymnic Material*
It has been suggested that certain modifiers and a specific structure contributed important information to the cognitive environment of Paul's original
readers that resulted in the communication of a challenge against the *lord*
of the world. We will explore one further such communicative intrusion.

It is not uncommon to produce poetry or hymns that exalt an individual
or group for doing something extraordinary. The great Homeric epics are
poems about great heroes and gods. Virgil's *Aeneid* and the works of other
Augustan poets praised the emperor and his family in exalted poetic language. In a Roman triumph, it was common for the soldiers to sing of the
exploits of the leader. Included in the songs about Julius Caesar were strong
insults (Suetonius, *Julius* 49.4; 51). Humans in these types of songs are
honoured, but there are not necessarily any implications beyond praise for
an action well done.

Hymns to gods were also common. The importance of songs in Jewish
life and worship is most vividly seen in the canonical book of Psalms. Additionally, the apocryphal Psalm 151 and the Thanksgiving and other hymns
from the Dead Sea Scrolls further emphasize the importance of this genre
in the praise of God. Songs to gods were common also in Greek and Roman

---

149. See Jewett, *Romans*, pp. 629-30.
150. Cranfield, *Romans*, II, pp. 527-28.
151. Cranfield, *Romans*, II, p. 528.
152. Cranfield, *Romans*, II, p. 528.
153. N.T. Wright, 'The Letter to the Romans: Introduction, Commentary, and
Reflections', *NIB* (ed. Leander Keck *et al.*; Nashville: Abingdon Press, 2002), X, pp.
393-770 (664).

religious life (see, e.g., the Homeric hymns). These hymns often included an introduction focusing the hymn on the deity and then a description of the deity's great deeds.

In some contexts, the inclusion of a person in a song or hymn can carry divine connotations. Cassius Dio tells us that after a long-standing dispute with the Parthians was settled in 29 BCE, Augustus's name was included in hymns ἐξ ἴσου τοῖς θεοῖς ('equally with the gods'; Cassius Dio 51.20.1). Although describing praise songs in general, Quintilian suggests, 'Some again may be praised because they were born immortal, others because they won immortality by their valour, a theme which the piety of our sovereign has made the glory even of these present times' (*Institutio Oratoria* 3.7.9; trans. Butler, LCL). The footnote to Butler's translation suggests that the second half of this statement refers to Domitian's deification of Vespasian and Titus.

With imperial cults, the inclusion of rulers in song reached a new level. There were already officials responsible for creating songs for gods.[154] Now however, positions were created in order to honour the emperor in song. The position of hymnode, already used in cults for the traditional gods, became part of many imperial cults.[155] Among other roles, these hymnodes (males) were responsible for singing hymns to the emperor.[156] Although we do not know who specifically wrote the hymns to the emperor, the existence of this role suggests that there was a formal means of praising the emperor in song. Songs of praise in worship were generally directed towards gods. An emperor was also lord. When a lord is praised in a worship context, it would be natural for this to refer to the emperor. He was really the only lord worthy of such an honour in the Roman empire.

(1) *Philippians 2.11*: κύριος Ἰησοῦς Χριστός. Paul's use of κύριος for Jesus in Phil. 2.11 is confessional and/or creedal and could have been discussed above with loyalty statements. However, this passage provides an opportunity to consider a further contextual element that contributes to a potential polemic.

Philippians 2.11 concludes a unit of poetic material introduced in v. 5. Ralph Martin, following Ernst Lohmeyer, and others have argued that this passage should be classified as an early Christian hymn.[157] Fee disagrees

---

154. Friesen, *Imperial Cults*, p. 104.

155. Friesen, *Imperial Cults*, pp. 104-5.

156. For a discussion of hymnodes and their responsibilities, see Friesen, *Imperial Cults*, pp. 104-13.

157. Ernst Lohmeyer, *Kyrios Jesus: Eine Untersuchung zu Phil. 2, 5-11* (Heidelberg: C. Winter, 1928; repr., Darmstadt: Wissenschaftliche Buchgesellschaft, 1961); Ralph P. Martin, *Hymn to Christ*, pp. 1-41 (see also the literature cited there). Recently, G. Walter

and suggests that it is better classified as exalted prose.[158] Adela Yarbro Collins argues that this passage should be classified as a prose hymn or prose encomium.[159] It seems difficult to make such fine distinctions between poetry, hymns, and exalted prose. What is certain is that in form and in content this passage is set apart as a unit from the rest of the book. It is essentially illustrative material to encourage the readers to set apart their differences and work together as a unified body. Thus, it really can serve a number of functions, and there is no reason to dismiss the possible use as a hymn. Despite Fee's objections, this is nearly a universal opinion.[160] This consensus does not necessarily mean complete agreement. For example, Stephen E. Fowl classifies this and other passages as 'hymns' but departs from the specificity sometimes associated with the label. Rather, these are 'hymns' in the 'general sense of poetic accounts of the nature and/or activity of a divine figure'.[161] Robert H. Gundry builds on the work of others such as Martin and emphasizes a chiastic structure.[162] Other questions, including whether or not Paul wrote it himself or merely used the hymn, are important. However, for the purpose of this study, we need only to acknowledge that Paul used these words for his intended purpose in the letter. Whether he wrote them himself or used them, he had control over the content as he communicated it to the Philippian church. A brief discussion of these issues is included in the appendix.

The use of a hymn form in Philippians adds pragmatic information that is likely to have drawn the attention of the readers. In their experience, only gods and the emperor had praise songs sung of them in the context of worship. Philippians was a book intended for a Christian community. Whether

Hansen concurs with the assessment that 'hymn' is the major view on this passage (*The Letter to the Philippians* [PNTC; Grand Rapids: Eerdmans, 2009], p. 122).

158. Gordon D. Fee, 'Philippians 2:5-11: Hymn or Exalted Pauline Prose?' *BBR* 2 (1992), pp. 29-46.

159. Adela Yarbro Collins, 'Psalms, Philippians 2:6-11, and the Origins of Christology', *BibInt* 11 (2003), pp. 361-72. Also classifying this passage as a encomium, John Reumann, *Philippians: A New Translation with Introduction and Commentary* (AYB, 33B; New Haven: Yale University Press, 2008), pp. 361-62.

160. In addition to Martin's important monograph already mentioned, see his brief comment in his revision of Hawthorne's commentary on Philippians, which includes a brief discussion of Fee's argument (Ralph P. Martin and Gerald F. Hawthorne, *Philippians* [WBC, 43; Nashville: Thomas Nelson, rev. edn, 2004], pp. 99-100).

161. Stephen E. Fowl, *The Story of Christ in the Ethics of Paul: An Analysis of the Function of the Hymnic Material in the Pauline Corpus* (JSNTSup, 36. Sheffield: Sheffield Academic Press, 1990), p. 45. See also pp. 31-44; 50-101 on Fowls's defintion of a hymn and on Phil 2.6-11 specifically).

162. Robert H. Gundry, 'Style and Substance in Philippians 2:6-11', in *The Old Is Better: New Testament Essays in Support of Traditional Interpretations* (WUNT, 178; Tübingen: J.C.B. Mohr [Paul Siebeck], 2005), pp. 272-91.

The Lord of the Entire World

or not 2.6-11 is a pre-Pauline hymn, it could clearly be used by the community for their purpose. Although this passage may lack some formal features of hymns, such as an invocation or prayer, it is still likely to be seen as a hymn. Collins suggests that such features were omitted either because the passage was modified to fit the context of the book or was composed specifically for Philippians.[163] However, Gundry exploits the structure of this passage in a way that helps fit all the parts together in a more sophisticated manner. He develops a detailed chiastic structure that serves to highlight relationships between the parts of the hymn.[164] Gundry notes the contrast between κύριος and δοῦλος and 'anticipates the identification of Jesus Christ's name as κύριος'.[165] Although Gundry never suggests that an anti-imperial polemic is present, his work serves to highlight the use of κύριος in context. Whether precisely structured or more loosely put together, Jesus' placement in this type of context adds to the polemical dimension of the passage. Not only do the words challenge Caesar, but the form does also. Although gods can be sung about in this form, the content usually expresses their elevated status in relation to the singers. However, when the relational lordship terminology is employed, it expresses a relationship between the worshipper and lord. Caesar is the only lord who is usually sung about in this context. The suggestion that another is lord in a context reserved for lord Caesar is likely to have been a challenge to the usual referent.[166]

In addition to the formal attributes of the passage, there is evidence from the background of the hymn to support a polemical aspect in Paul's intention. First, broadly speaking, the background of this hymn may have in view imperial ideology and specifically the emperor as a contrast to Christ. In the two studies introduced in Chapter 1, Mikael Tellbe and Peter Oakes place the passage in its context and suggest that anti-imperial messages contribute to the overall argument of the book. Tellbe argues that both the titles κύριος and σωτήρ provide a challenge to the imperial ideology of the emperor of the day. Thus, Paul's Christology is a challenge to imperial ideology.[167] For Tellbe, Philippians is 'one of Paul's most political letters',[168] and 'the conflict at Philippi focused on certain tensions between Christian theology and

---

163. Collins, 'Psalms, Philippians 2:6-11', p. 370.

164. Gundry, 'Style and Substance', pp. 272-91.

165. Gundry, 'Style and Substance', p. 276.

166. For a discussion of this passage in light of Jewish monotheism, see Richard Bauckham, 'The Worship of Jesus in Philippians 2:9-11', in Ralph P. Martin and Brian J. Dodd (eds.), *Where Christology Began: Essays on Philippians 2* (Louisville, KY: Westminster/John Knox Press, 1998), pp. 128-39. Although there is clear Jewish influence most vividly illustrated by the use of Isa. 45.23 in this passage, this does not rule out Roman comparisons. See Oakes, *Philippians*, p. 172.

167. Tellbe, *Paul between Synagogue and State*, pp. 350-59.

168. Tellbe, *Paul between Synagogue and State*, p. 276.

imperial ideology and propaganda as promoted in Philippi'.[169] For Oakes, the Philippians were experiencing suffering. The letter was intended to promote unity in the midst of this suffering.[170] Christ's example of sacrifice and suffering in Phil. 2.6-11 is in contrast to the emperor's example; in fact, Christ is above the emperor.[171] Some have proposed that a specific emperor such as Caligula is in view.[172] Tellbe and Oakes reject the suggestion that a specific emperor is intended.[173] This interpretation is preferred. Emperors such as Caligula or Nero may seem to be the most offensive and easiest to contrast with Christ. However, as we saw in Chapter 3, the entire system with its imperial lord was offensive, and more innovation in emperor worship took place during the reigns of Augustus and Tiberius than during those of Caligula, Nero and Domitian. Further, if a specific emperor was in view, the hymn would lack its potency once that emperor was forgotten.

Second, regarding the social background, Joseph Hellerman has argued that this passage should be read in light of the Roman value and quest for honour in the process of the ascension to higher and higher public offices.[174] Extant evidence from Philippi suggests that everyone in the city, whether elite or non-elite, even slaves, were concerned with honour and esteem.[175] Based on his work on the social context, Hellerman's examination of 2.6-11 leads him to conclude that Christ goes against the accepted values and the means of gaining honour. Philippians 2.6-8 reverses the prevailing manner of the process by stating that Christ began as 'equal to God' but descended to the position of a slave and finally to a position in which he accepted the most dishonourable of deaths.[176] Christ's example would be shocking to Romans, Hellerman states. 'Such a utilization of power—indeed, a voluntary relinquishing of power and prestige—would have struck members of the Roman elite as abject folly.'[177] Nevertheless, Phil. 2.9-11 continues the

---

169. Tellbe, *Paul between Synagogue and State*, p. 277.

170. Oakes, *Philippians*, pp. 77-102.

171. Oakes, *Philippians*, pp. 188-210.

172. Karl Bornhäuser and David Seeley argue that Caligula was in view (Karl Bornhäuser, *Jesus imperator mundi [Phil. 3,17-21 und 2,5-12]* [Gütersloh: Bertelsmann, 1938]; and David Seeley 'The Background of the Philippians Hymn (2:6-11)', *Journal of Higher Criticism* 1 [1994], pp. 49-72). For Seeley however it may not be limited to Caligula (pp. 62-64) and the emperor is not the only background. He also sees Isaiah 45 and stories about suffering righteous people (including stories in 2 Maccabees and *4 Maccabees*).

173. Tellbe, *Paul between Synagogue and State*, pp. 255-56. Oakes, *Philippians*, p. 131 (they reject Caligula and do not suggest another emperor).

174. Hellerman, *Reconstructing Honor*.

175. Hellerman, *Reconstructing Honor*, pp. 88-109.

176. Hellerman, *Reconstructing Honor*, pp. 129-48.

177. Hellerman, *Reconstructing Honor*, p. 148.

story and reveals that Christ is exalted and attained the highest position of authority and honour.[178] Thus, the social background of this hymn is a critique of, or, more appropriately for our purposes, a polemic against, the Roman system of honour and its quest. This critique of the Roman system must go all the way to the top of the empire, to the one with the 'highest honour', the emperor himself. Indeed, when Hellerman discusses Phil. 2:11 and the title κύριος, the emperor comes to the forefront in the discussion.[179] The emperor's manner of exaltation was one of seizing power and using violence; Christ's was one of relinquishing position and self-sacrifice.[180]

Studies such as those by Tellbe, Oakes and Hellerman are important because they show that the entire passage (Phil. 2.6-11) can be seen as a challenge to the emperor. In general, Tellbe and Oakes, in addition to describing the background, place the passage in the context of the epistle and Hellerman places it in the context of its social environment. Since the passage is seen as a challenge to the emperor, it can be argued that the particulars are also so intended.

In addition to the form and observations about the social background of the passage in which this use of κύριος occurs, there are at least five other reasons this passage may be seen as polemical. First, what was discussed about creedal structure and uniqueness applies here. There are no modifiers present but the passage definitely sets Christ apart from all others. Second, in Chapter 3 I noted the strong Roman presence in Philippi. More than most Eastern colonies, Philippi would have had a very Roman flavour. Although not necessarily central, imperial worship was an important aspect of city life. The emperor was a very strong presence in the cognitive environment. Third, and related to what was observed about the background of the passage above, the text contains other elements that can be seen as challenging the emperor. Thus, the immediate context of Phil. 2.11 (i.e. 2.6-11) can be viewed as anti-imperial. Although a specific emperor may not be in view,[181] the hymn mirrors imperial aspirations.[182] The passage includes words and phrases that have parallels in imperial religion. Although not identical to ἴσα θεῷ in Phil. 2.6, the emperor's cult, according to Simon Price 'could be described as *isotheoi timai*'.[183] Price continues, 'An *isotheos* was one "equal

---

178. Hellerman, *Reconstructing Honor*, pp. 148-56.

179. Hellerman, *Reconstructing Honor*, pp. 151-53.

180. Hellerman, *Reconstructing Honor*, p. 153.

181. For example, as already mentioned, Bornhäuser argues that Caligula is in view (*Jesus imperator mundi*).

182. For an excellent discussion of the comparison of Christ with the emperors, see Oakes, *Philippians*, pp. 147-74.

183. Price, 'Gods and Emperors', p. 88. See also, Reumann, *Philippians*, pp. 344-45.

(*isos*) to the gods" and *isotheoi timai* can thus be paraphrased as "honours equivalent to those paid to the gods".[184] Further, Hellerman states,

> A variety of sources specifically associates the idea of equality with God with the position of a king or emperor, using language similar to Paul's. And given the centrality of the imperial cult in the social and religious life of the colony at Philippi, it is quite likely that Paul has emperor veneration directly in view in ἐῖναι ἴσα θεῷ in Phil 2:6.[185]

Fourth, Jesus was in the form of God (ἐν μορφῇ θεοῦ) and did not seek to exalt himself.[186] However, the emperors were men and were portrayed as divine. A portion of Oakes's conclusion about this passage's comparison of Christ and the emperor is relevant to this entire study,

> Whatever they would have made of the details of verses 9-11, the hearers are likely to have heard the Imperial shape of the events, i.e., at their most basic level: raised to power on account of deeds, universal submission, universal acclamation as Lord. This shape fits an Imperial figure much more closely than it does any other figure.[187]

Fifth, the exaltation of Jesus is comprehensive and complete. Everyone everywhere will acknowledge the lordship of Jesus.[188] The hymn has gone out of its way to emphasize that it is Jesus who fills the role of supreme lord. This must include anyone for whom this role is also claimed, including Caesar. Thus, the default supreme lord Caesar is being challenged by both words and form.

In light of the Old Testament Psalms and the word κύριος for Yahweh in the Greek Old Testament, is it possible that Paul also intended a polemic against Yahweh? Philippians makes use of Isa. 45.23, where Yahweh is the referent of the title. However, this is unlikely for at least three reasons. First, Paul's theology has consistently demonstrated a cooperation or unity between Yahweh and Christ. It is God (Yahweh) who exalts Jesus to his position as κύριος (Phil. 2.9). Second, the presentation of Christ here does not depart from Jewish monotheism. Concerning Phil. 2.9-11, Bauckham states,

---

184. Price, 'Gods and Emperors', p. 88.

185. Joseph H. Hellerman, 'ΜΟΡΦΗ ΘΕΟΥ as a Signifier of Social Status in Philippians 2:6', *JETS* 52 (2009), pp. 779-97 (788).

186. For a relevant discussion of this phrase, see Hellerman, 'ΜΟΡΦΗ ΘΕΟΥ', pp. 779-97

187. Oakes, *Philippians*, p. 174.

188. Verses 10-11: ἵνα ἐν τῷ ὀνόματι Ἰησοῦ πᾶν γόνυ κάμψῃ ἐπουρανίων καὶ ἐπιγείων καὶ καταχθονίων καὶ πᾶσα γλῶσσα ἐξομολογήσεται ὅτι κύριος Ἰησοῦς Χριστὸς εἰς δόξαν θεοῦ πατρός ('that at the name of Jesus, every knee might bow in heaven and on earth and under the earth and every tongue will confess that Jesus Christ is Lord').

> They [the early Christians] preserved Jewish monotheism by including
> Jesus in the unique identity of the one God as Jewish monotheism under-
> stood this. Participating in God's unique sovereignty over all things and
> bearing the unique divine name, the exalted Jesus belongs to the unique
> divine identity, which is precisely what monotheistic worship recognizes.[189]

Finally, the context itself makes clear that Jesus' reception of the title
κύριος glorifies God the Father (εἰς δόξαν θεοῦ πατρός; 2.11c).

This passage is not an intended polemic against either Jewish monotheism or against Yahweh. Rather, Paul's use of the Old Testament and the
title for Jesus is part of a development from within monotheism. Larry
Hurtado argues that early Christology comes from Jewish monotheism.
From this source it underwent a 'mutation' or 'innovation'.[190] However,
this mutation or innovation occurred among early Jewish Christians (thus
from within Jewish monotheism), not as the result of later pagan converts.[191] Wright sees early Christianity as 'redefining' Jewish monotheism.[192] Thus, Paul did not intend κύριος language to be a polemic against
Jewish monotheism.[193] However, whether some Jews perceived it as such
is another matter.

Given the lexical connections, structure and contextual information, an
anti-imperial polemic is highly likely in this passage (probably only slightly
less, if at all, than in 1 Cor. 8.5-6). Thus, it is not surprising that some
commentators see an anti-imperial connection here.[194] Marcus Bockmuehl
acknowledges the imperial challenge and makes a connection with later
martyrs,

> one who says 'Jesus Christ is *Lord*' cannot also agree that 'Caesar (or any
> other potentate) is Lord': a Christian is forbidden to render to other pow-
> ers, or to require from them, the allegiance that belongs to Christ alone.
> This conviction is unmistakable in the accounts of early Christian mar-
> tyrs.[195]

---

189. Bauckham, 'Worship', pp. 126-39.

190. Hurtado, *One God,* pp. 99-104. Hurtado has done much work in this area. See
also his *Lord Jesus Christ: Devotion to Jesus in Earliest Christianity* (Grand Rapids:
Eerdmans, 2003), pp. 27-78. On Jewish monotheism, see Hurtado, 'First-Century
Jewish Monotheism', *JSNT* 71 (1998), pp. 3-26.

191. Hurtado, *One God,* p. 100.

192. Wright, *Paul: In Fresh Perspective,* pp. 83-107.

193. On Phil. 2.9-11, see Hurtado, *One God,* p. 97.

194. See, e.g., Reumann, *Philippians,* p. 359; and Gordon D. Fee, *Paul's Letter to
the Philippians* (NICNT; Grand Rapids: Eerdmans, 1995), p. 222 (in the discussion of
2.9 [referencing 2.11]; the issue is lacking in the discussion of 2.11 [Fee, *Philippians,*
pp. 225-26]).

195. Marcus Bockmuehl, *The Epistle to the Philippians* (BNTC; London: A. & C.
Black, 4th edn, 1997), p. 147.

However, not all commentators mention an imperial challenge despite acknowledgment of the universal lordship involved.[196] Nevertheless, among commentators who see a polemic in this passage, it does not appear that they have incorporated implications of this insight into the message of the passage itself. There is little difference among the commentaries concerning the significance of the confession.

e. *A Subtle Polemic?*

When one contrasts the Pauline texts above with the dramatic Polycarp event, one must ask whether there is truly a challenge to Caesar in Paul and if so whether it is more subtle. If there was a challenge, why did it go unanswered? These questions are fair and need to be addressed. First, unlike the narrative of the *Martyrdom of Polycarp*, Paul's letters give no indication of how these texts may have been read and what response actually occurred. In other words, the narrative nature with its description of the event records an incident in which Polycarp explicitly understands the implications of the confession and refuses to proclaim Caesar as lord. This genre difference cannot be overstated. The *Martyrdom of Polycarp* is reporting events, telling a story; Paul is giving instruction. There is no record of how the recipients of Paul understood and responded to his teaching. I believe I have demonstrated that in the cognitive environment, a challenge would have been perceived. What happened after this is lost to history. Nevertheless, the Polycarp incident suggests that there was a rejection of this confession for Caesar by at least some Christians. This could be rooted in the New Testament. It is the only extant evidence available.

Second, we do not know whether those outside the church read Paul's letters and, if so, how they would have understood Paul's message. These letters were not intended for those outside the churches, and since they were written to a relatively insignificant group, it is unlikely that they would have come to the attention of many. Based on our reconstruction of the cognitive environment, it is likely that, if the letters were read by outsiders, they would have perceived a challenge and may have viewed it as offensive. However, it is more likely that any contact with Paul's teaching would have been through the lives of the readers. In light of the relationship between Paul and his recipients as seen in the letters, it seems likely that the readers would have followed his instruction (especially in Philippians). It is also possible that an initial polemic may have been felt only by the original readers. Consequences and resistance could follow, but they may or may not have been immediate.

---

196. See, e.g., Martin and Hawthorne, *Philippians*, pp. 125-26 (on v. 9), 128-31.

Third, if Harrison is correct about imperial oaths and the Thessalonian church, it is possible that Luke is recording a conflict that may have involved some sort of positive confession of loyalty to Christ and a negative assertion against Caesar. The creedal-type statements discussed here could have been a part of this. However, for some reason Luke does not record the specifics. If any portion of Luke's purpose included an attempt to show Christianity in a positive light before the Romans, such details would be counterproductive.

Fourth, when the creedal statements were written by Paul, the church was insignificant in the eyes of Rome. Gallio wonders why Paul is brought before him. To him this was a Jewish matter (Acts 18.12-17). Even Felix, Festus, Agrippa II and Berenice appear to see Paul as no significant threat (Acts 24.10–26.32). Paul's defence before them gives Luke a chance to present Paul's message to his readers; however, there is no reason to view this event as fabricated. It would be a natural thing for Paul to present his views before those who could sit in judgment against him. The overall impression is that the officials knew little of Paul and the Christian movement. It was new and not much of a threat.

Fifth, there were probably various levels of local persecution but no empire-wide threat against the movement. Nero's persecution in Rome (64 CE) probably increased the Christians' visibility. Although there were problems for Christians under Domitian, as noted in Chapter 3, charges of a large-scale persecution at that time are probably exaggerated.[197] In the second century, the church's influence was spreading. Pliny sees Christians as a threat. However, the way in which he describes them to Trajan is as one who is just now beginning to learn about the movement (*Epistles* 10.96). Trajan's response suggests that they are little more than a nuisance (*Epistles* 10.97). Nevertheless, they are on the Roman radar. There is a gradual increase in visibility of the church. The conflicts with Rome are due not to a new message but rather to the growing perception that Christians may be a threat.

Sixth, concerning the response to Paul's teaching, it seems unwise to assume that the challenge was not answered by the Romans because we lack explicit evidence of such a response. It is likely that at least some would have followed Paul's teaching. The book of Revelation makes it clear that there was serious conflict between the church and the authorities. Thus, the initial response of Rome may be lost. But, given the cognitive environment reconstructed here and the observations just made, it is not unlikely that there was a response from Rome when necessary.

---

197. This does not minimize the strong language in the book of Revelation. However, this book was written from a perspective of Christians and much more than harsh physical abuse can be viewed as persecution.

Thus, the question of whether the Pauline polemic is a more subtle form than what is seen in Polycarp's *Martyrdom* needs to be answered in two ways. First, the polemic was as strong in Paul as it was later. We do not know what happened to the churches after they received this teaching. In fact, we cannot even be certain how the recipients would have responded. Second, as visibility of the church increased, so did the potential for conflict. The polemic is unchanged; the more noticeable presence could have resulted in more potential for conflict. Also, as time progressed, a consistent lifestyle of Christians may have become more and more suspicious. What once was overlooked now was attracting attention. Further, it seems possible that the initial polemic aimed at the original readers began to be practised more and more. The Polycarp incident is a logical consequence of the earlier teaching. As the church put Paul's words into practice, and as it grew and became more influential, increased resistance in a cognitive environment with Caesar as the supreme lord was natural. Regarding the second question, why the challenge went unanswered, the same observations apply. We do not know what happened in the communities where Paul wrote, and thus it is wrong to suggest that the challenge went unanswered. In fact, it is likely that it did, and the Polycarp incident is later evidence of an earlier conflict.

The task here was to attempt to determine whether a challenge to Caesar was an aspect of the Pauline message in certain passages where Jesus is called κύριος. By reconstructing relevant aspects of the first-century world based on extant evidence, I have been able to argue that a challenge was likely part of the original intended message. It was explicit and not subtle. What is uncertain is how this message was received and practised.

f. Addendum: Romans 13 Revisited
In Chapter 1, Rom. 13.1-7 was introduced. It was acknowledged that it presents a positive view of government. However, this positive view has been the source of abuse for centuries by brutal regimes that have argued, based on this passage, that people must submit to their authority. The results can be disastrous. Some approaches to this problem were introduced in Chapter 1. However, now that our study of κύριος is coming to an end, we can ask, Does our study shed any light on this passage's use today?[198]

I believe it does. As mentioned in Chapter 1, a major problem with this passage has been its application by authorities to demand obedience from their subjects or to legitimize their rule. This is an incorrect application

---

198. This discussion is intentionally brief and does not attempt to further reconstruct the relevant cognitive environment for this passage specifically. For a detailed discussion and attempt to understand this passage in its imperial context, see Harrison, *Paul and the Imperial Authorities,* pp. 271-323. Even if Harrison's conclusions are not accepted, his discussion of the context is illuminating.

of the passage. Traditionally, it has been read as requiring Christians to (unquestionably?) follow authorities (this is different from giving authorities the right to demand obedience or to legitimize their position; see below). This is a possible reading. However, I believe that this study provides some evidence to help one understand this passage in context. Before directly discussing the contribution of this study, five brief observations are necessary to consider when approaching this passage. These are not interpretative keys in themselves. Rather, they are observations that should be considered before interpreting and applying this difficult passage. An approach that desires to apply Rom. 13.1-7 directly to government today must at least consider these observations. Following these, the results of this study will be incorporated into an understanding of this passage.

First, the passage was written to a community without power providing instruction on how to live in peace with the ruling power. The powerless nature of the early church is often lost on modern readers. Few of us have experienced this in any meaningful manner. Living in a society in which one has little or no power demands that one (or a group) negotiate one's place in a very careful manner.

Second, can it be assumed that the governmental authorities mentioned in Rom. 13.1-7 can be representative of all governments at any time? The Roman government had a specific role in the functioning of the empire. In many ways this was much more limited than governments today. Although the Roman empire demanded allegiance of its subjects and settled a large range of matters for its people, it was not involved in many of the activities of many present governments (e.g. health care, copyright laws, etc.). I am not suggesting that the roles of modern governments are wrong or that we should adopt a Roman-style government. I am merely pointing out that the role of the government of Rome was different in some ways from the roles of governments today. Can we assume that the more expansive role for government today could be assumed under the commands in passages like Romans 13?

Third, the reason for the instruction must be considered. In this passage and other passages in the New Testament that seem to instruct obedience to government, the focus is not obedience for its own sake but obedience as a means of minimizing conflict in order for Christians to focus on Christ. Thus, the primary concern is not good citizenship but Christian peace and survival. This does not remove the aspect of obedience but puts it in perspective. As introduced in the discussion of Romans 13 in Chapter 1, Stanley Porter suggests that this passage instructs obedience to just authorities but permits disobedience to unjust authorities. This maintains the biblical directive and provides Christians with the ability to respond to unjust rule.[199]

---

199. Porter, 'Romans 13:1-7 as Pauline Political Rhetoric', pp. 115-39.

Fourth, rulers are not the addressees of this passage, and it is unlikely that it was ever intended for use *by* authority. If the paradigm in other Pauline literature can serve as an example, the author's method is to address parties concerning their own responsibilities. Husbands are told to love their wives and wives are told to respect their husbands; children are told to obey their parents and parents are told to avoid provoking their children; and slaves are told to obey their masters and masters are told to treat their slaves well (Eph. 5.22–6.9; Col. 3.18–4.1). The author does not instruct husbands that they should be respected, wives that they should be loved, slaves that they should be treated well and so on. It seems that if Romans followed this pattern, authorities would be instructed to be just, avoid abuse and the like. This is the Old Testament and Apocrypha example (Dan. 4.24-37; Wis. 6.1-11). However, authorities are not addressed explicitly because they were not among the addressees.

Fifth, as discussed in Chapter 3, it is generally believed that Nero's reign before approximately 60 CE was rather fair. Thus, it can be argued that this moderate rule should be supported by the readers. Failure to pay taxes or other disruptive acts could only harm the Christian community. After the decline in Nero's reign and his persecution of Christians, would Paul have written this? We cannot know. Also, it is not possible to know if Paul would have modified his teaching if he wrote later. We cannot know how 'good' this period actually was for Christians. Nor can we assume that Paul was not thinking universally (some emperors will be good, others bad—all should be obeyed in the same way). Nevertheless, in light of Paul's belief in an imminent Christ event (e.g. 1 Thess. 4.16–5.4), the local nature of much of his writing and the lack of such teaching in the context of known persecution, we cannot assume that this teaching would be applied in other circumstances.

The study here suggests that Paul challenges the living emperor for the role of supreme lord of all, including the Roman empire. Christ, not Caesar, is supreme lord. Passages such as Phil. 2.9-11 suggest that this is more than the personal lord of an individual Christian. It is universal lordship.[200] If I am correct to see a polemic in Rom. 10.9, it is likely the reader is urged already to view the living emperor as a subordinate lord to Christ, the supreme lord. This seems reinforced by Rom. 13.1b-c, 4. The emperor's (and the government's) role is to accomplish God's will on earth. What is to be done if God's power is usurped? To a powerless community like the one to which Paul wrote, little can be done. We simply do not know if this instruction would have been different if the recipients could have responded in a different manner or were under different cir-

---

200. Ephesians also vividly describes the universal reign of God.

cumstances (i.e. active persecution). What we do know is that Paul saw a role for government. This is supported by the observation made above in the discussion of 1 Cor. 12.3. The polemic is stated only in the positive: Jesus is Lord. There is no instruction to curse Caesar. For Paul, Caesar and government play a role in Christ's administration of his lordship—even though the government to which he was subject could be unpredictable and cruel. It appears that at the time Paul wrote Romans, things were fairly good. However, this could change rapidly, as it did a few years later when Nero blamed Christians for the fire in Rome. Nevertheless, the Roman authorities were established by God (Rom. 13.1c).

The word κύριος is not used in Rom. 13.1-7. Nevertheless, the relational elements we have described earlier are in place. The people are subordinate to government, and the government and the people are subordinate to God. Romans 13 was not intended to be used by governments to justify the abuse of their subjects. Any such (ab)use should be resisted by those who submit to Paul's supreme lord.

What, then, does Paul say to rulers and governments? It has already been noted that the addressees of Romans 13 do not include the government as an institution or rulers. It is instruction to the governed. Again, what does Paul say to rulers and governments? When one surveys his writings, one finds very little that could be used as specific instruction to governing authorities. This is generally the case in much of the New Testament. Matthew 25.31-46 presents a story in which nations will be judged based on their treatment of others. Nations in this story are judged based on their active kindness and mercy. Even the clearly anti-imperial Apocalypse emphasizes judgment based on how nations treat people, especially the people of God. There is a theme of judgment against idolatry, but this too seems to be somewhat related to how people are treated. The nation that forces people into idolatry is harming the people. This is not to minimize the anti-idolatry theme, but it seems there is an interrelationship between treatment of people and idolatry.

As noted above, the recipients of Paul's letters were generally not in a position of power.[201] Thus, the need did not arise for instruction. However, it is possible that Paul, as a Jewish teacher (and other New Testament writers), assumed Old Testament principles directed to the nations. The nations were judged in light of how they treated others. This often meant the Jews (e.g. Jeremiah 46–51; Ezekiel 25–32; Amos 1). However, both the nations and Jewish states were judged on their treatment of others (e.g. Amos 1–2). There is judgment for unfaithfulness to Yahweh, but this

---

201. For a postcolonial treatment of how Romans 13 fits within Paul's wider anti-imperial message, see John W. Marshall, 'Hybridity and Rereading Romans 13', *JSNT* 31 (2008), pp. 157-78.

is primarily (although not exclusively) a judgment against the Jewish states (e.g. Hosea). The notion in Romans 13 of government being raised up and used for God's will is throughout Old Testament teaching (e.g. 2 Chron. 36.22-23; Isa. 45.1; Jer. 25.9).

If one wishes to ask what Paul would say to the rulers and governments, it does not seem a stretch to suggest that he would instruct rulers and governments to rule with justice, kindness and mercy. They must take care of their own people, especially those without means, and be kind to outsiders. One might even add that they should not hinder believers in their worship of God nor demand loyalty reserved for God. In all types of modern forms of government, it seems easy to overlook the voiceless in one's own society and to ignore any negative consequences of policies on those outside of one's own state. Christ is κύριος, and God has established governments to exercise authority on earth. They rule at his pleasure. This is what rulers should be thinking about. They should not be using passages like Romans 13 to force people to submit to them.[202]

6. Conclusion

Given the above discussion, we must now ask whether objections such as those raised by Dunn have been answered. Central to his objection was the existence of different lordships without apparent conflicting loyalties. Thus, he concluded that there was no polemical usage in Paul's time. This seems essentially based on the potential for many referents for κύριος. In other words, because the term was used for many, it must be assumed that different loyalties existed side by side. The *Martyrdom of Polycarp*, a clear example of the polemic, is cited to show that later a conflict clearly took place. What has changed? Was κύριος no longer used with many potential referents? My discussion of imperial cults has demonstrated that the most important developments occurred in the earliest period. The role of the emperor was essentially the same. He was still first citizen in name but lord in practice. Even if one sees a rather subdued outward and explicit emphasis on the lordship role of the emperor under Augustus and Tiberius, the fact of the matter is that this was more imperial propaganda than reality. Also, it is not correct to associate loyalty only with the use of the term κύριος. Loyalty involves much more than the explicit use of one term.

By recreating a portion of the cognitive environment, I have attempted to determine the place of the emperor in the first-century world. His presence was prevalent. Cults, art, literature, coins and so on made him and his

---

202. For a detailed discussion and attempt to understand this passage in its imperial context, see Harrison, *Paul and the Imperial Authorities,* pp. 271-323.

family an important part of the daily life of many. Additionally, I defined what is actually involved in a polemic. Although possible, a polemic against the emperor does not necessarily challenge the emperor directly in Rome but rather may be perceived as such a challenge by the local power structures. Initially, this polemic may be seen only by the original readers of the letters of Paul with possible consequences to follow. Observations from *relevance theory* highlighted features of the Pauline texts that would be perceived as contributing a nuance of challenge to the emperor and his system. Given the relational nature of κύριος and the exclusive nature of supreme lord, using the title for Christ with explicit features such as unique modifiers, creedal formulas, and praise hymns would be viewed by the original readers as challenging the default supreme lord.

Chapter 6

Conclusion and Perspective

After a reconstruction of a portion of the first-century cognitive environment, it was determined that the living emperor was an important part of the world of Paul's readers. The title κύριος was examined and its relational nature was highlighted. I also postulated and defended the existence of a superlative concept, *supreme lord*, that could be expressed by κύριος and other means. Finally, it was determined that the living Caesar would have been the default referent of this concept in the cognitive environment of the target readers of Paul's letters in the first century.

Using communication principles from *relevance theory*, I demonstrated that an author could include certain contextual clues that would suggest a challenge to the default referent by another. Certain modifiers and structures in the Pauline text led to the conclusion that in some cases Paul intended a polemic against the living emperor.

As this study concludes, it is important to step back again and focus on the larger picture. This study has been narrowly focused. It was a tree in the midst of the forest. I concluded that a polemic does exist in Paul's letters. However, I do not claim that this is the only or even the primary intention of Paul in these texts. The influence of the Greek Bible was very strong, and implications from this source were only remotely considered. Nevertheless, these discoveries are important and add a further dimension to the rich fabric of the message of the New Testament.

Epilogue

. . . The words of the letter, ἀλλ᾽ ἡμῖν . . . εἷς κύριος Ἰησοῦς Χριστός ('but for us, there is one Lord, Jesus Christ'; 1 Cor. 8.6), catch Demetrios somewhat by surprise. So much so that he momentarily loses track of the argument about eating idol meat, a subject of interest to him because he has always enjoyed the food and discussion around the table, a table often supplied with food that was dedicated to local deities. This passage troubles Demetrios, could his newfound faith demand that he make a choice between it and his loyalty to the Roman state, including his family's patron, Nero? This question is entertained for a only few moments. It seems clear, the apostle says that for us there can be only *one Lord*—what else could it mean? How would this work out in practice?

Demetrios sat quietly through the remainder of the reading. It was interesting, especially the discussion of resurrection. However, his mind returned over and over again to the earlier words: 'for us there is one Lord'. Although he did not like it, the meaning seemed clear. He had always been subject to lords in one way or another. However, this was different. Caesar was the lord over all lords. Demetrios had a lot to think about. He made his way back home quietly and spent much of the week considering the implications of these words.

Demetrios did not return to the group for a few weeks. However, he was welcomed back eagerly when he finally returned. Demetrios was glad to see his friends again and enjoyed his participation in the meeting. At the end of the meeting, the host announced a collection for a group in a similar gathering in another city. This group had suffered socially for their belief in Jesus, and many in their number had lost their employment. One man was actually put in prison temporarily. Gatherings from all over the province were taking up a collection to help. Demetrios was sad because he did not have any spare money.

People lingered for a little while, and then Demetrios thanked his host and began to leave. However, something stopped him. He saw the collection basket near the door with a modest amount of change in it. He stood still staring at it. Fortunately he was alone. If someone had been looking at him, they might have thought he was considering stealing some of the money. Demetrios opened up his money bag and took out the only coin in there. The picture of Augustus was still distinct. He looked up, dropped the coin in the basket and left.

Appendix

Further Discussion on the Provenance and Date of Philippians and the Authorship and Date of Ephesians

In Chapter 2 it was suggested that Philippians was written during Paul's Roman imprisonment usually dated 60–62 CE. Additionally, although controversial, it was argued that Ephesians was written by Paul and dated 60–62 CE as well. This appendix will further defend the positions taken in Chapter 2.

1. Philippians: Provenance, Date, Unity, and the Form of 2.6-11

Paul wrote Philippians. This identification is rarely challenged. However, the letter's date and place of composition are less certain. These are linked. When the provenance is determined, the date can generally be concluded. It was clearly written from prison (1.7, 13, 14, 17); however, the identification of this prison has been disputed. The traditional view has claimed Rome as the place of origin of this epistle.[1] However, the view has been questioned primarily because the number and distance of journeys recorded in the letter are difficult to place within the time frame available (see 2.19-30; 4.18). Therefore, Ephesus[2] and, to a lesser extent, Caesarea[3] have been

---

1. See, e.g., McDonald and Porter, *Early Christianity,* pp. 373-74, 470; Guthrie, *New Testament Introduction,* pp. 545-55; Bockmuehl, *Epistle to the Philippians,* pp. 25-32; Fee, *Paul's Letter to the Philippians,* pp. 34-37; O'Brien, *Epistle to the Philippians,* pp. 19-26; Moisés Silva, *Philippians* (BECNT; Grand Rapids: Baker Book House, 2nd edn, 2005), pp. 5-7 (reluctantly). See also the classic description by J.B. Lightfoot, who assumes Rome as the place of composition (*St Paul's Epistle to the Philippians: A Revised Text with Introduction, Notes and Dissertations* [London: Macmillan, 1913; repr., Grand Rapids: Zondervan, 1953], pp. 1-29).

2. For a detailed defence of an Ephesian provenance for all of the prison epistles, see Duncan, *St Paul's Ephesian Ministry.* More recently, see Brown, *Introduction to the New Testament,* p. 496 (reluctantly); Carolyn Osiek, *Philippians, Philemon* (ANTC; Nashville: Abingdon Press, 2000), pp. 27-31. Kümmel sees both Ephesus and Caesarea as possibilities (*Introduction to the New Testament,* pp. 324-32).

3. See, e.g., Ernst Lohmeyer, *Der Brief an die Philipper* (KEK; Göttingen:

suggested as alternatives.[4] I will not rehash this debate in significant detail. The representative sources for each position cited above argue their cases well. However, it is worth defending the position taken in the text in more detail than was presented there. I maintain that Rome is the least problematic option of the three for the following six reasons. First, although not exclusive to a Roman context, references to πραιτωρίῳ ('Praetorium'; 1.13) and Καίσαρος οἰκίας ('Caesar's household'; 4.22) are best understood in a Roman context. Second, the rather optimistic view of prison presented in the epistle reflects the situation recorded by Luke in Acts 28.14-31. Third, although Paul spent much time in Ephesus (1 Cor. 15.32; 16.8; Acts 18.19-21; 19.1-41; 20.17-38), there is no evidence he was ever imprisoned there. It is possible that such an imprisonment occurred (possibly referred to in 1 Cor. 15.32?) but there is no explicit early record of such a captivity and therefore this option suffers a serious drawback. Fourth, although Paul was clearly a prisoner in Caesarea (Acts 23.23–26.32), the problem of the distance and journeys is not resolved. Caesarea is as far from Philippi as Rome. Therefore, since this option is unable to solve the principal problem of the traditional position and, given point 1 above,[5] namely that πραι–τωρίῳ (1.13) and Καίσαρος οἰκίας (4.22) are best explained in a Roman context, the Caesarean option seems least likely. Fifth, the letter's optimism concerning release is best understood in Rome, where through due process

Vandenhoeck & Ruprecht, 1929), pp. 3-4; John A.T. Robinson, *Redating the New Testament*, pp. 57-61; and especially Hawthorne, *Philippians*, pp. xxxvi-xliv. Hawthorne's original commentary (cited here) maintained Caesarea as the provenance; however, the revised edition by Martin, which maintains much of what Hawthorne had done, backs off from this conclusion and supports an Ephesian origin, although suggesting that the reader decide (Martin and Hawthorne, *Philippians*, pp. xxxix-l, esp. p. 1). In his own earlier commentary on the letter, Martin described in detail all three positions and concluded that either Rome or Ephesus is possible (*The Epistle of Paul to the Philippians: An Introduction and Commentary* [TNTC; Leicester: InterVarsity Press, rev. edn, 1987], pp. 20-37). Also, as noted above, Kümmel considers both Ephesus and Caesarea to be possibilities (*Introduction*, p. 332).

4. S. Dockx has suggested a Corinthian provenance ('Lieu et date de l'épître aux Philippiens', *RB* 80 [1973], pp. 230-46). This has persuaded few and has numerous problems not least of which is that there is no evidence of a Corinthian imprisonment for Paul. See Ralph P. Martin, *Philippians* (NCBC; London: Marshall, Morgan & Scott, 1976; repr., Grand Rapids: Eerdmans, 1985), pp. 44-45; and McDonald and Porter, *Early Christianity*, p. 376.

5. Though point 2 (compatibility of Philippians with Acts 28.14-31) is suggested here in favour of Rome, it may also be said that the imprisonment of Paul in Caesarea as recorded in Acts 23.23–26.32 is also compatible with the conditions presented in Philippians. Therefore, although point 2 is used here in support of Rome, it is really not an argument against another position. The same could be said of Caesarea.

Paul is appealing to the highest authority; no further appeals are possible.[6] Six, until recently the general history of interpretation has almost exclusively considered Rome to be the city of origin. This reason on its own is not strong enough to be persuasive; nevertheless, it cannot be ignored without good cause.

The strongest argument in favour of the Ephesian option is the lengthy distance between Rome and Philippi. The journeys mentioned in the letter are difficult to fit into the time frame usually reconstructed for the writing. However, the problem is not insurmountable for the Roman position. The travel was possible within the time frame given.[7] Recently, Frank Thielman has argued for an Ephesian provenance based on internal evidence. Among other points, he notes that an earlier Ephesian context for the letter better explains the two different types of opposition represented in Phil. 3.2 and 3.18-19, respectively. The former appears to be an attack against nomism, and the latter an attack on antinomianism.[8] The earlier date provides a closer link to Galatians and 1 Corinthians (the latter was written from Ephesus; 1 Cor. 16.8). Thielman's approach is attractive. However, it cannot overcome the strong evidence for Rome and the difficulty of establishing an Ephesian imprisonment in the earliest records. All things considered, Rome seems the strongest of the three positions. Therefore, it is likely that Philippians should be dated during Paul's Roman imprisonment, for which Acts 28 is the only source.[9] This is usually dated between 60 and 62 CE (or 61–63). A date in the later stage of this period is possible (62 CE), given Paul's optimistic words in 1.21-26, which seem to suggest an imminent resolution of his predicament. However, since we know little of Paul's imprisonment and Paul's attitude throughout (he may always have felt that release was imminent), it is best to avoid dating the letter more specifically than 60–62 CE.[10]

There are two further introductory matters that may affect dating that demand brief attention. First, the unity of the epistle has been questioned. It is claimed that our present epistle contains as many as three separate let-

---

6. McDonald and Porter, *Early Christianity*, p. 470.

7. Bockmuehl, *Epistle to the Philippians*, pp. 31-32; Fee, *Paul's Letter to the Philippians*, pp. 36-37, 277-78.

8. Frank S. Thielman, 'Ephesus and the Literary Setting of Philippians', in Amy M. Donaldson and Timothy B. Sailors (eds.), *New Testament Greek and Exegesis: Essays in Honor of Gerald F. Hawthorne* (Grand Rapids: Eerdmans, 2003), pp. 215-23.

9. This position still maintains significant support. In addition to the works mentioned above, see the recent commentaries by Fee, *Paul's Letter to the Philippians*, pp. 34-37; Bockmuehl, *Epistle to the Philippians*, pp. 25-32.

10. If Ephesians is the place of origin, the date would probably be 54–56 CE; if Caesarea, 58–60 CE.

ters (A: 4.1-10; B: 3.1b-to somewhere later such as 3.19;[11] 4.1[12]; 4.3[13]; C: 1.1–3:1a and possibly part of the later portion of ch. 4).[14] These theories have arisen to account for the content of the epistle, which at times seems random. Also, Τὸ λοιπόν ('finally'; 3.1a) seems to indicate that the letter is coming to an end; however, this phrase occurs about halfway through the work.

Despite an apparent reference in Polycarp's *Epistle to the Philippians* (3.2)[15] to ἐπιστολάς (plural 'letters') written by Paul to the Philippians, there is little if any support for such reconstructions. First, there is no textual support to favour any position other than that the letter is a unity. One may postulate many reasons why the letter seems disjointed. For example, Paul's own passion/emotion over the issues could account for changes in content. Also, the apparent delay in ending after 3.1a may be due to its closing being postponed for some reason (interruption, further thoughts Paul wished to add, etc.). When looking at other ancient letters (even 1 Thess. 4.1), we find that this phrase does not demand an immediate ending.[16] Second, when the letter is considered among other ancient (Hellenistic) letters[17] or subjected to modern discourse analysis, its unity seems defensible (even likely). For example, Jeffrey T. Reed's discourse analysis considers the structure (including the literary genre and epistolary form) and texture (including the microstructure of the book such as grammatical and semantic meaning) of Philippians and concludes that it is a cohesive letter that does not need multi-letter theories to explain its contents.[18] Thus, form and content favour

11. J. Hugh Michael, *The Epistle of Paul to the Philippians* (MNTC; London: Hodder & Stoughton, 1928), pp. xi-xii.

12. F.W. Beare, *A Commentary on the Epistle to the Philippians* (HNTC; Peabody, MA: Hendrickson, 1959), p. 5 (actually Beare sees the fragment beginning at 3.2).

13. Kirsopp Lake, 'The Critical Problems of the Epistle to the Philippians', *Exp* Eighth Series 7 (1914), pp. 481-93 (486-87). Lake is less precise on the beginning of the interpolation; he suggests 3.1 or 3.2.

14. For general arguments, see the works cited in the previous three notes.

15. See also 11.3 (*epistulae*; there is no extant Greek for this passage). However, Michael Holmes emends the clause in which this word occurs with Greek, and this emendation has the singular (Holmes [ed. and trans.], *Apostolic Fathers*). Holmes is not specifically interested in this word but is concerned with the entire clause. He believes his emendation is probably original. He thinks a change may have occurred early in the transmission of the Greek or in the translation process into Latin (Michael W. Holmes, 'A Note on the Text of Polycarp *Philippians* 11.3', *VC* 51 [1997], pp. 207-10 [208]). Additionally, the meaning of this verse is less certain than 3.2.

16. Alexander, 'Hellenistic Letter-Forms', pp. 96-97 (see also the literature cited there).

17. Alexander, 'Hellenistic Letter-Forms', pp. 87-101.

18. Reed, *Discourse Analysis of Philippians*.

its unity.[19] Third, the disagreement among scholars over the different letters (especially letter B) raises questions concerning the entire enterprise of
attempting to find individual letters within the letter.[20] Fourth, it is difficult
to explain the motivation for bringing these letters together.[21] Finally, Polycarp's reference is uncertain. Even if Polycarp has more than one letter in
mind, given the unified manuscript evidence on this matter, it is more likely
that an additional (lost) letter(s) accounts for the plural than that the present
letter is an amalgamation of a number of letters. Further, Polycarp could be
referring to other known letters of Paul that had circulated to Philippi before
he wrote his letter. The fact that letters circulated may suggest that they
were considered to be written to a wider audience than Paul first intended
(Col. 4.16 may suggest that this was his intention in at least some cases).[22]

In addition to the unity of the epistle, because my analysis will include
Phil. 2.11, for dating reasons, I must also briefly consider the proposal that
2.5-11 is a pre-Pauline hymn/poem.[23] If this is the case, one may question
whether an argument suggesting that κύριος is a Pauline polemic against
Caesar is sustainable in this passage. If this passage has an earlier pre-
Pauline (or pre-Philippian) history, the consideration of a polemic can proceed for at least two reasons. First, whatever the history of the passage, one
cannot limit Paul's use only to that for which it was originally intended.
Paul used this passage to illustrate Christ's great humility as an argument
for unity in the Philippian church. If this was an early (isolated) hymn or
poem, it is unlikely that it was composed for any other reason than praise
of Jesus.[24] Additionally, assuming that the original work was a hymn or
poem of praise to Jesus, it may originally have included an implied polemic

19. Note however the concerns of Bockmuehl over these types of approaches
(*Epistle to the Philippians*, pp. 23-24).

20. Fee, *Paul's Letter to the Philippians*, p. 21.

21. McDonald and Porter, *Early Christianity*, pp. 466-67.

22. Lightfoot argues that the plural may be used for the singular to stress the
importance of the letter (*St Paul's Epistle to the Philippians*, pp. 140-41). However, this
seems unlikely. All eight of the plural occurrences in the New Testament refer to more
than one letter (Acts 9.2; 22.5; 1 Cor. 16.3; 2 Cor. 3.1; 10.9, 10, 11; 2 Pet. 3.16). See also
the discussion in BDAG.

23. See, e.g., Martin, *Hymn to Christ,* pp. 42-62; O'Brien, *Epistle to the Philippians*,
pp. 186-202. Since my concern is primarily one of word usage and reference, with one
exception (see below), I do not need to enter the debate on the classification of this
passage (i.e. whether it is a formal poem, formal hymn, poetic language, or prose). This
was briefly discussed in Chapter 5. See the previously mentioned works in support of a
hymn form. For a challenge to this view see Fee, 'Philippians 2:5-11', pp. 29-46 (also
Fee, *Paul's Letter to the Philippians*, pp. 40-43). See also the approach of A. Y. Collins,
'Psalms, Philippians 2:6-11', pp. 361-72.

24. I will not discuss in any detail the meaning of the passage here. This is developed
in Chapter 5.

against Caesar. Thus, the entire passage (not only our term) may be polemi-cal.[25] As I have said previously, I am not suggesting the polemic is the only (or indeed the main) factor in Paul's use of κύριος. This principle applies also to the entire passage. Second, in light of the development of the emper-or's role in the empire and imperial cults in the first century, and especially the use of κύριος as a title for him, it is more difficult to prove my case in earlier periods. However, the polemic may still be involved, given the right contextual clues. In addition to these two points, I must acknowledge that, if this passage was an earlier work used by Paul, he certainly could have modified it for his purpose. Even if there was no intentional polemic in the original, Paul, being aware of the political climate, may have known the implications and intended a polemic in his use of the poem/hymn. Without an extant example of the original or a copy closer to the source, we have no way of knowing if or how it may have been modified. Therefore, even if this passage did originate earlier than the letter, it still may prove to be an excellent example of an anti-imperial polemic.

Having argued that this passage may include an anti-imperial polemic as used in Philippians even if it predates the letter, I now suggest that it may not be necessary to view this passage as pre-Pauline at all. First, if this passage is an early hymn or poem, there are no parallels in Greek lit-erature.[26] Moreover, it does not exhibit the characteristics of the Psalms or other New Testament hymns (e.g. Luke 1.46-55, 68-79; 1 Tim. 3.16b).[27] Without a formal parallel, one wonders whether it is justifiable to suggest an existence outside the letter. Second, given the importance of the unity issue in Paul's mind, the passage could have been composed (as a hymn, poem, poetry, or prose) for the intended readers. After an extensive study of this passage, Peter Oakes states, 'There are very few scholarly options that my study on 2.6-11 has absolutely excluded. It has, however, led me to think that the most likely view about the nature of the passage is that it was composed especially for the people of Philippi and, more specifically, for the letter written to their church.'[28] My discussion here has described only one contextual feature (unity) in order to demonstrate the likelihood of

---

25. K. Bornhäuser maintains that this passage was a polemic against the emperor Gaius Caligula, who ruled Rome shortly after Jesus death (37–41 CE) (*Jesus imperator mundi*).

26. Fee, 'Philippians 2:5-11', p. 31.

27. Fee, 'Philippians 2:5-11', p. 31.

28. Oakes, *Philippians: From People to Letter,* p. 210. See also Stephen E. Fowl's discussion concerning the difficulty of determining whether a passage includes quotations and/or is a reconstructed hymn of some sort (*Story of Christ,* pp. 37-44).

simultaneous composition. Oakes has an extended discussion of the nature of the passage in its Philippian context.[29]

The poetic nature of this passage is no reason to conclude that it is pre-Pauline. Additionally, it is interesting that many scholars tend to see highly developed Christology as a sign of later development within the early Christian community. In this case, some wish to suggest that one of the most lofty christological passages in the New Testament is very early. This of course is not an argument for Pauline authorship of this passage, nor is it an argument against the existence of an early high Christology. It merely reveals the irony of the pre-Pauline position. Finally, if we grant that this is a relatively impressive passage demonstrating much consideration on the part of the author, Paul (with a lot of time on his hands [as a prisoner] and a deep concern for the unity of a community) would be an excellent candidate to write such a poem/hymn. Therefore, given his position and the absolute lack of any evidence of the passage outside Philippians, it seems prudent to maintain that it was written by Paul as part of his letter to the church at Philippi.

Whether, as maintained here, the passage was written by Paul for the Philippians or it was written earlier and used by him, the important issue is that it was included in the letter as it was sent to the church at Philippi. Paul composed it or used it for his own purposes. Essentially, it can be said that he made it his own. The position here is that the letter was completed, sent, and read within the period of 60–62 CE.

2. *The Authenticity of Ephesians*

The authorship and dating of Ephesians pose more difficulty than the three other letters from which passages in this study are drawn. Many scholars view this letter as post-Pauline.[30] If Ephesians was not written by Paul, it would be considered an example of ancient pseudepigrapha. The nature of this literature with special reference to letters will be discussed. Finally, I will conclude by suggesting the probable date for this epistle.[31] Despite my conclusions, I will acknowledge the post-Pauline position and discuss the implications for the polemic of a later date.

---

29. Oakes, *Philippians: From People to Letter*, pp. 207-10.

30. The seven undisputed Pauline letters are Romans, 1 Corinthians, 2 Corinthians, Galatians, Philippians, 1 Thessalonians, and Philemon.

31. As stated above, this issue is very complex and I cannot do justice to all of the arguments here. I will be selective, highlighting arguments I deem most important. For an excellent discussion of this issue and the history of interpretation, see Best, *Ephesians*, pp. 6-36.

a. *Authorship of Ephesians*

First, there are differences in vocabulary and style between Ephesians and the undisputed Pauline letters. There are a number of words unique to this letter in the Pauline corpus (and the New Testament as a whole). Additionally, there are some common Pauline words that do not occur.[32]

Second, theological emphases differ. Most prominently, Ephesians emphasizes the church in contrast to the more soteriological (and other) focuses in the undisputed letters. It also has been argued that in Ephesians the discussion of Christ differs, emphasizing the resurrection and exaltation (e.g. Eph. 2.20-23) in contrast to the emphasis on Christ's death in the undisputed letters (e.g. Rom. 3.23; 2 Cor. 5.14-16; Gal. 2.20).[33]

Third, Ephesians is often compared to Colossians (another disputed letter) because of its apparent similarities and differences.[34] The similarities are striking. In addition to the overall content and structure, see especially the relational instruction (Eph. 5.22–6.9; Col. 3.18–4.1). Also, there seem to be significant differences within similar discussions. Among the differences, Ephesians seems more dependent on the Old Testament than Colossians. In Colossians, the 'mystery' is Christ in the believer (1.27) but in Ephesians it is the uniting of Jew and Gentile (3.3-6). In Ephesians, the author exhorts his readers 'to be filled with the Spirit' (5.18), but Colossians instructs the reader 'to let the word of Christ dwell within them' (3.16). Some find it difficult to accept that one man would have written two works that are so similar yet so different, and they suggest that this demonstrates the existence of a Pauline school.[35]

Fourth, for a church in which Paul spent much time (Ephesus), there is minimal personal detail included in the letter. There is little information on Paul's life. Nor does the letter include a final greeting such as concludes some other letters (e.g. Rom. 16.1-16).

Many other arguments could be mentioned; however, these seem to be the most important ones. Those who conclude that Ephesians is not authentic do not do so based on one argument. It is the cumulative effect of many arguments.[36] However, these arguments are not as strong as they appear.

---

32. Best, *Ephesians*, pp. 27-32; Lincoln, *Ephesians,* pp. lxv-lxvi.

33. For a detailed discussion of these differences, especially christological and soteriological, see Lincoln, *Ephesians*, pp. lxiii-lxv. Lincoln discusses a wide variety of differences (many more than are mentioned here).

34. Lincoln, *Ephesians*, pp. lxvi-lxviii.

35. Best, *Ephesians*, pp. 32-40.

36. Best, *Ephesians*, p. 36. Although Lincoln does not use the term 'cumulative', his experience is instructive. In 1975 he completed his PhD dissertation at the University of Cambridge. In the revision published in 1981 (on which these comments are based), he noted the problem of authorship but nevertheless stated his position in favour of Pauline authorship (*Paradise Now and Not Yet: Studies in the Role of the Heavenly Dimension*

Each may be answered, and when problems with pseudepigraphy are considered, the cumulative argument seems to favour authenticity.

First, arguments based on vocabulary and style prove nothing more than that the vocabulary and style differ. They say little about authorship. There are many factors that need to be considered before accepting this argument. First, it is clear that Paul used secretaries in his letter-writing process (e.g. Rom. 16.22). This was a common practice in Paul's day. Recent research suggests that letter writers used secretaries in different ways and gave them varying degrees of control over the final product.[37] What impact does this have when comparing a personally written letter with one written with a secretary? I acknowledge that function words (e.g. conjunctions, prepositions, etc.) could be used to reveal similarities and differences in style, which may lead to decisions on authorship. Function words are used rather uniformly by a single author.[38] However, again, this may reveal only different secretaries. Second, in general, context dictates the choice of non-function word vocabulary. The emphases of the undisputed Paulines are quite different

in Paul's Thought with Special Reference to his Eschatology [SNTSMS, 43; Cambridge: Cambridge University Press, 1981], p. 8). He developed a possible setting of Ephesians as a Pauline letter (pp. 135-39). However, already by the time of publication in 1981 (or the writing of the preface in 1978), Lincoln had changed his mind and could no longer support Pauline authorship. This is indicated in an endnote to the very statement cited above in which Lincoln favours Pauline authorship (p. 197 n. 29; this refers to Lincoln's statement on p. 8). As already noted, in his commentary (*Ephesians* [1990]), Lincoln gives a lengthy defence of his post-Pauline position. Lincoln's experience is illuminating in the sense that it is an example of a scholar attempting to come to terms with a difficult issue and only changing his mind after careful consideration of many issues related to the problem.

37. See Markus Barth, *Ephesians: Introduction, Translation and Commentary on Chapters 1–3* (AB, 34; Garden City, NY: Doubleday, 1974), p. 40. On secretaries, see E. Randolph Richards, *The Secretary in the Letters in Paul* (WUNT 2 42. Tübingen: Mohr Siebeck, 1991). See also his more recent but less technical volume, *Paul and First-Century Letter Writing: Secretaries, Composition, and Collection* (Downers Grove, IL: InterVarsity Press, 2004). In addition to secretaries, Richards's discussion of the letter-writing process reveals other factors such as editing, input from others and so on that could impact the final form of the letter (see, e.g., his discussion of the physical place of composition, pp. 36-46).

38. Although without interest in determining authorship, Stephen Levinsohn's approach to discourse analysis could be used to help determine whether two works are written by the same author (*Discourse Features of New Testament Greek*). His approach focuses on the use and distribution of function words in specific letters, for example, his discussion of τότε in the Gospels and Acts (pp. 94-98). This approach may not be conclusive in itself; however, it can be one piece of evidence toward solving the problem. Additionally, there may be similarities in a writer's uses of a specific function word. The more specific examples of different function words being used similarly or differently will make one's position stronger.

from those of Ephesians. Therefore, differences in vocabulary would be expected. Third, there is a gap in time between the writing of Ephesians and most of the undisputed Paulines. This should result in some difference in vocabulary and style. Fourth, even granting that these factors can contribute to a decision about authorship, there is no remotely objective means of establishing how much difference in vocabulary and style would be needed to demonstrate different writers. To my knowledge no major study has been undertaken to provide criteria for this type of claim. Such a study would need to begin by choosing undisputed works by (preferably ancient) authors writing within a single field but concerning different subjects over a period of time. Each author's work would need to be subjected to vocabulary and style comparisons similar to those that the disputed Pauline epistles have undergone. Only after many such authors are studied would one have any kind of external criteria for determining whether a document is not authentic.[39] Of course, there are still questions of secretaries and other unique elements in Paul's works not factored into the proposed study. Nevertheless, it is a start to be able to use this criterion of vocabulary and style as a determining factor in this debate.

Second, the argument based on differing theological emphases must demonstrate that the differences are not due to the purpose(s) of the letters and/or to theological development. Those using theological emphases to disprove Pauline authorship must demonstrate a contradiction. If, as I will propose (see below), Ephesians was a circular letter, an emphasis on the universal church is to be expected. Additionally, as Paul's ministry proceeded, he may have felt a need to be more explicit about the teaching of the universal church. Also, concerning Ephesians and the undisputed Paulines, the christological emphases mentioned above are just that, *emphases*. In Ephesians, the death of Christ is evident (e.g. 1.7) and in the undisputed Paulines, the resurrection and exaltation are not lacking (e.g. Rom. 4.25; and esp. Phil. 2.6-11). These complementary themes occur throughout Paul's works.

Third, the relationship between Ephesians and Colossians is complex. However, there is nothing contradictory in the examples suggested. A single author may have wished to say things somewhat differently to two separate audiences, being aware of their unique situation. Is the Colossian call to 'allow the word of Christ to dwell within the reader' (3.16a) really much different from the Ephesian exhortation 'to be filled with the Spirit' (5.18)? Both phrases are somewhat difficult to understand on their own. The participles explaining similar results or (less likely) causes (Col. 3.16b and

---

39. It would be interesting for any writer to place his or her own work under the same scrutiny. In any case, it may be an opportunity to distance oneself from that embarrassing paper, thesis, or book written years ago.

Eph. 5.19-21) suggest that these passages may be two ways of saying the same or similar things. Can the mystery as defined in Colossians as 'Christ in you' (1.27) be the individual emphasis (or the emphasis important to the Gentile perspective) of the same phenomenon mentioned in Eph. 3.3-6? In the latter, the author is concerned with unity and has just completed a discussion of a remarkable new situation, namely, that the Gentiles and Jews are now one in Christ. For the Colossian church, the Jewish emphasis may not be as necessary, and the author chose to mention a certain aspect of the event, namely the more personal and directed part of this teaching, which has made the more racially unifying teaching in Ephesians possible. Also, it is possible that despite similar contexts, the statements are in fact different.[40]

Additionally, it seems problematic to postulate the existence of a Pauline school to account for both the similarities and differences. Initially, this hypothesis seems attractive because it proposes a number of potential contributors to writings that share certain beliefs but may express them differently. Also, real differences may be accounted for because members may knowingly or unknowingly have differences that are expressed in their works.[41] However, there are at least three problems with this proposal First, there is no evidence that such a school existed. To suggest that it did because of letters such as Ephesians and Colossians, which do not identify the creators as such, is rather circular reasoning. Second, development of doctrine in the later first-century church was minimal. The tendency was to look back at what had already been given, not to develop it further (see, e.g., 1 John). Third, a Pauline school does not alleviate the problems we will discuss below concerning pseudonymity.

Fourth, the accusation that Ephesians is not personal and therefore not Pauline can be answered in a number of ways. First, Paul's letters exhibit a varying level of personal content, and some do not include specific greetings in the conclusion. For example, although in Galatians Paul discusses himself, he does not make any personal comments to anyone specifically. Second, if Ephesians was not written by Paul, one might wish to include such greetings to make it look more like an authentic letter.[42] Third, the reason that Paul did not include much personal data about himself may be explained in the letter. Near the end of the letter the author mentions that he is sending Tychicus in order to inform the readers of his circumstances (Eph. 6.21-22). There is no need (and/or other reasons) to duplicate this information in the letter. Finally, the most persuasive argument may be that

40. No attempt will be made here to determine whether or not Eph. 5.18-21 and Col. 3.16 are discussing the same or different phenomena using similar but different language.

41. See the case presented by Best (*Ephesians*, pp. 36-40).

42. This comment previews further discussion below on the nature of pseudonymity.

the letter was intended to be circular.[43] The phrase ἐν ᾿Εφέσῳ is most likely a later addition to the text. It is lacking in the oldest and most important manuscripts of this passage (e.g. p[46] [c. 200 CE], the original hands of ℵ and B [fourth century] and the later [tenth century] but important minuscule 1739). However, the phrase was added by the seventh-century corrector of ℵ and the sixth/seventh century corrector of B. The earliest extant Greek manuscript with the phrase is A (fifth century), and it has the support of the Western (D, F, G) and Byzantine traditions (included within gothic M). The former has a tendency to include additions, and the latter has a tendency to harmonize. Also, the omission is favoured because it is the shorter and possibly more difficult reading. Finally, it is difficult to explain why it would have been deleted if original. Therefore, given both internal and extant external evidence, the original text of Ephesians does not identify a destination.

This in itself does not demand that we consider it a circular letter. In fact, the sending of Tychicus, as noted above (Eph. 6.21-22), seems to imply an intended audience. Also, one must explain how the location phrase became inserted into the text. When one considers all the factors, the following reconstruction seems to account for the details. The letter was intended as a circular letter for the churches throughout Asia Minor. There are a number of reasons why Ephesus would be an ideal initial destination for the letter. First, Ephesus was probably the most important city in the province. Second, it had a port and thus was an ideal first stop on a trip to Asia Minor. Third, the church there was probably one of the more established Pauline churches. Finally, the church was very close personally to Paul. For these reasons Ephesus probably had the resources and could be trusted to circulate a letter containing important teaching that Paul desired all to know. Tychicus thus brought the letter there and explained Paul's desire and instruction. Additionally, it may even be speculated that Tychicus, after stopping in Ephesus, took the letter with him to Laodicea and then went on to Colossae. Tychicus's instructions about relating Paul's circumstances are repeated in Col. 4.7, which supports the notion that the letters were simultaneously dispatched. Thus, the letter coming from Laodicea mentioned in Col. 4.16 was in fact our circular letter. If this is the letter Marcion called the letter to the Laodiceans, this can explain Marcion's title (certainly based partially on Col. 4.16), although he was incorrect if he assumed that the Laodiceans were the primary recipients. Since Colossians was specifically addressed to the church at Colossae, it was to be read there first. Paul then instructs the church to have the letter (Colossians) read in Laodicea. The role of the Ephesian church in this process resulted in its name being attached to the letter.

43. Best, *Ephesians*, pp. 1-2, 98-101; O'Brien, *Letter to the Ephesians,* pp. 48, 85-87.

This reconstruction is highly speculative, and I acknowledge that it also raises a number of problems. It is also impossible to prove (or disprove). Additionally, our attempt to trace Tychicus's travel route is even more tenuous and is not necessary for our more general reconstruction to be accurate. Nevertheless, this suggestion (with or without the Colossian connection) is plausible and does provide explanations for some of the problems raised by those who cannot justify Pauline authorship. The circular nature of the letter may also explain some of the differences with the letter to the Colossians, which was primarily directed to a specific church.

Thus, it is reasonable to maintain Pauline authorship for Ephesians.[44] In fact, even in present New Testament scholarship there are strong voices for authenticity. Although the major commentaries by Best in the International Critical Commentary series and Lincoln in the Word Biblical Commentary series favour pseudonymity,[45] two other recent commentaries, those by O'Brien and Hoehner, defend Pauline authorship.[46] Additionally, Hoehner has compiled a list of commentaries and other important works from ancient to modern times with their position on Pauline authorship noted. There has been division over this issue for some time. Nevertheless, even in modern times, although one position may be slightly favoured over the other from decade to decade, there is consistently around a fifty-fifty split over this issue.[47]

b. *Ancient Pseudonymity*

If Paul did not write Ephesians, it must be assumed that it is an example of ancient pseudepigraphy because it claims to have been written by Paul. This type of writing usually uses the name of a prestigious person as the author. Two different views of pseudonymity in the ancient world exist. Some maintain that it is a deliberate attempt to pass a work off as another's, usually to communicate their message under the authority of the falsely named author. In other words, it is intentionally deceptive.[48] Others suggest that it was a genre understood in the ancient world and that readers would

---

44. For an example of a similar approach, see McDonald and Porter, who acknowledge difficulties but conclude that authenticity is reasonable (*Early Christianity*, pp. 465-67).

45. Best, *Ephesians*; Lincoln, *Ephesians*.

46. O'Brien, *Letter to the Ephesians*; Hoehner, *Ephesians*. Also, see the significant work by Markus Barth in the Anchor Bible series, though it is older (*Ephesians 1–3*).

47. Hoehner, *Ephesians*, pp. 9-20.

48. Eduard Verhoef, 'Pseudepigraphy and Canon', *BibNotiz* 106 (2001), pp. 90-98.

not have objected to its practice.[49] Briefly, I will discuss pseudonymity and its implications.[50]

First, pseudonymity was common in the ancient world. It was not unusual for someone to use the name of a well-known person as a literary device to present a message. In Jewish literature, there were many apocalyptic works that claimed an ancient biblical character as the mediator of the vision (e.g. *1 Enoch, Apocalypse of Abraham,* etc.). We also find the same type of literature among Christians (e.g. *Apocalypse of Peter, Apocalypse of Paul*). In addition, there are a number of Gospels that use this form (e.g. *Gospel of Thomas, Gospel of Peter,* etc.). However, pseudonymity in letters appears to be rare. There are three possible Jewish examples (none is accepted as canonical by the Jews), namely the *Letter of Jeremy,* the *Letter of Baruch,* and the *Letter of Aristeas.* None of these can be viewed as an actual letter. Setting aside the possibility of pseudepigraphic letters in the New Testament itself,[51] examples of early Christian epistolary works are rare. The few possible examples include *3 Corinthians* (in the *Acts of Paul*) and the *Letter to the Laodiceans.* It is not difficult to understand why epistolary literature would be uncommon. The letter often has a different function from a Gospel or an apocalypse. An actual letter is usually directed to a specific group or individual, and the author's role is often an important part of the acceptance of the message by these groups. One can understand why one would like to use pseudonymity; however, those doing so would not necessarily want their work to be considered (or exposed) as such.

The influential work of David Meade on the subject has attempted to demonstrate that pseudonymity was an accepted practice in the first century and thus any New Testament examples would have been understood in this context. No deceit is intended.[52] In some ways this conclusion has provided New Testament scholars with a third and attractive option in a debate that previously demanded a decision for authenticity or forgery. However, this work has not convinced everyone that pseudonymity was a harmless and

---

49. David G. Meade, *Pseudonymity and Canon: An Investigation into the Relationship of Authorship and Authority in Jewish and Earliest Christian Tradition* (WUNT, 39; Tübingen: J.C.B. Mohr [Paul Siebeck], 1986).

50. In addition to commentaries and other sources cited below on this issue, see Guthrie, *New Testament Introduction,* pp. 1011-28; and D.A. Carson and Douglas J. Moo, *An Introduction to the New Testament* (Grand Rapids: Zondervan, 2nd edn, 2005), pp. 337-53. Pseudepigraphy and the canon cannot be discussed in any detail here. The purpose of this section is to determine the date of Ephesians. For a sober approach to pseudepigraphy and canon, see McDonald and Porter, *Early Christianity,* pp. 640-41.

51. This is a methodological decision because every New Testament book labelled pseudonymous is disputed, and I maintain that, to make a case against New Testament books, one should use certain external examples as a first priority.

52. Meade, *Pseudonymity.*

accepted practice during New Testament times.[53] This will be discussed further below.

The only discussion of pseudonymity from early church sources is negative. First, 2 Thessalonians markedly rejects pseudonymity (2.2) and, to back up this rejection, Paul explicitly mentions that he is writing the greeting in his own hand (3.17). It may be argued that these are the types of comments one might include if one was attempting to forge a letter. There is merit in this claim, but such an argument is problematic. A lack of personal information has contributed to the rejection of Ephesians as authentic. In 2 Thessalonians, 1 Timothy, 2 Peter and elsewhere, such details have been used to argue against authenticity. Interestingly, Abraham Malherbe has recently published a major commentary supporting Pauline authorship for 2 Thessalonians.[54] It is worth asking in what way other than as expressed by 2 Thess. 2.2 one might warn about a forged letter. Also, even if this letter was an example of pseudonymity, these passages favour a view that the practice was not acceptable at the time of writing this letter.

Second, the Muratorian canon (late second century) mentions forged letters as unacceptable in the canon. It states, 'There is current also (an epistle) to the Laodiceans, another to the Alexandrians, forged in Paul's name for the sect of Marcion, and several others, which cannot be received in the catholic Church; for it will not do to mix gall with honey' (lines 63-66; trans. W. Schneemelcher and R. Wilson[55]).

Third, Eusebius described an event in which Serapion of Antioch (late second century) discovered the use of the *Gospel of Peter* in Cilicia. Serapion wrote to them, 'We receive both Peter and the other apostles as Christ, but the writings which falsely bear their names we reject, as men of experience, knowing that such were not handed down to us' (*Church History* 6.12.2-3; trans. Oulton, LCL).

Finally, Tertullian mentions one who produced the *Acts of Paul (and Thecla)*. This work includes stories about Paul and a letter called *3 Corinthians.* However, Paul is not the source of this information. Even though Tertullian concedes that the writer produced the work from a love for Paul, the man was still removed from office (*On Baptism* 17).

---

53. See, e.g., Verhoef, 'Pseudepigraphy', pp. 90-98.

54. Abraham J. Malherbe, *The Letters to the Thessalonians: A New Translation with Introduction and Commentary* (AB, 32B; New York: Doubleday, 2000), pp. 349-74.

55. This translation was originally in German by Wilhelm Schneemelcher and was then translated and checked against the original by R. McL. Wilson. (Wilhelm Schneemelcher [ed.], *New Testament Apocrypha*. I. *Gospels and Related Writings* [English translation edited by R. McL. Wilson]; Cambridge: James Clarke, rev. edn, 1991), p. 36.

Admittedly, all but 2 Thessalonians are at least one hundred years later than our period of interest. However, a drastic shift in the attitude toward pseudonymity must be explained if one attempts to maintain that it was an acceptable practice in the first century. Meade suggests that, as the Jewish influence faded and especially as the debate over doctrine became important, the church's attitude toward this practice changed.[56] However, as attractive as this is, Meade offers no tangible support for this construct. Indeed, his view has recently been seriously challenged. Pseudonymity could be intentionally deceptive in the first century, and the earliest church did reject the practice.[57] Therefore, the situation of the first century was not drastically different from that in the second.

All that can be proven is that pseudonymity was rejected during New Testament times. We cannot prove that there is no example of pseudonymity in the New Testament. However, there are grounds for arguing that if pseudepigraphy existed, it was intentionally deceptive. Therefore, Meade's third option mentioned above has been effectively removed, and we have returned to an either/or situation.

I would suggest that the burden of proof rests with those who reject authenticity for three reasons. First, the early church was not an uninterested party in these matters. It is possible that they were fooled into accepting a forgery, but this would not necessarily have been easy. Second, although I support the recent emphasis not to limit the study of early Christianity to the New Testament, in the mind of the early church there does seem to be something special about the books that ultimately became the New Testament. The early circulation of Pauline letters (Col. 4.16), the tremendous number of quotations and allusions in the earliest post-New Testament writings and the relatively early canonical lists (which cannot be attributed only to a reaction against heretics) suggest that the early community placed a high value on certain books. Thus, it would be somewhat remarkable for a forgery to be counted among them. Even if it has occurred, one wonders if so many (six Pauline letters alone) could have crept in unnoticed.

Third, the well-noted differences between Ephesians and other letters of Paul would seem to make it a likely candidate for rejection. It seems that it would need better than average support to make it into the canon.

Therefore, it is not unreasonable to maintain that Ephesians is an authentic letter of Paul. I have treated it as such in this work. However, I have

---

56. Meade, *Pseudonymity*, p. 206.

57. Terry L. Wilder, *Pseudonymity, the New Testament, and Deception: An Inquiry into Intention and Reception* (Lanham, MD: University Press of America, 2004). See also Jeremy Duff, *A Reconsideration of Pseudepigraphy in Early Christianity* (DPhil thesis, Oxford University, 1998).

accommodated the view that it was written later by acknowledging implications of the late date (see below for further development of this point).

c. *Date of Writing*

Having presented a case for Pauline authorship for Ephesians, I reiterate the date of the letters. Ephesians was written from prison (3.1; 6.20). As the discussion about Philippians revealed, there are three general suggestions for the origin of the prison epistles. Unlike with Philippians, we do not have the contextual clues to link the letter to a specific location. However, the emphasis on the universal church and the realized eschatology seem to favour a date later than Romans and Galatians. Indeed, I suggest that there is a development and a shift in emphasis in Paul's writing to partially explain the differences between Ephesians and the undisputed Pauline letters. Although one cannot be certain, the Roman imprisonment also seems the likely setting for this letter (60–62 CE), and, as with Philippians, there is no compelling evidence to demand that we narrow this period. Therefore, I will suggest 60–62 CE as the time of composition.

3. *Conclusion*

My conclusions concerning Philippians and Ephesians can be summarized as follows:

Letter	Date	Addressees
Philippians	60–62 CE	church at Philippi
Ephesians	60–62 CE	churches in Asia Minor

However, as discussed in Chapter 2 concerning Ephesians, owing to the large number of modern scholars who reject Pauline authorship, the argument of this study is considered *both* with the Pauline date as argued here and with a later post-Pauline date. Those who do not maintain Pauline authorship for Ephesians date it anywhere from 60 to 100 CE,[58] although it seems that the later part of this period is generally preferred. Thus, in addition to the date proposed above, the argument of this work is considered from the perspective of a late-first-century date for Ephesians. In addition, in this case, the addressees are broadened from the traditional designation (Ephesus [or Asia Minor]) to include much of the entire church (although probably mainly in the East).

---

58. Best, *Ephesians*, p. 45 (80-90 CE); however, if Paul was the author, Best suggests that a date in the early 60s from Rome would be most probable.

BIBLIOGRAPHY

Abaecherli, Aline L., "The Institution of the Imperial Cult in the Western Provinces of the Roman Empire", *Studi e materiali di storia delle religioni* 11 (1935), pp. 153-86.

Achtemeier, Paul J., *Romans* (Interpretation: A Bible Commentary for Teaching and Preaching; Atlanta: John Knox Press, 1985).

Akmajian, Adrian, Richard Demers and Robert M. Harnish, *Linguistics: An Introduction to Language and Communication* (Cambridge, MA: MIT Press, 2nd edn, 1984).

Aland, Barbara, Kurt Aland, Johannes Karavidopoulos, Carlo M. Martini and Bruce M. Metzger (eds.), *The Greek New Testament* (Stuttgart: Deutsche Bibelgesellschaft, 4th rev. edn, 1993).

—*Novum Testamentum graece* (Stuttgart: Deutsche Bibelgesellschaft, 27th rev. edn, 1993).

Aland, Kurt (ed.), *Synopsis of the Four Gospels: Completely Revised on the Basis of the Greek Text of the Nestle–Aland 26th Edition and Greek New Testament 3rd Edition: The Text Is the Second Edition of Revised Standard Version* (New York: United Bible Societies, 1982).

Aland, Kurt, and Barbara Aland, *The Text of the New Testament: An Introduction to the Critical Editions and to the Theory and Practice of Modern Textual Criticism* (trans. Erroll F. Rhodes; Grand Rapids: Eerdmans, 2nd edn, 1989).

Alexander, Loveday, "Chronology of Paul", in Hawthorne *et al.* (eds.), *Dictionary of Paul and his Letters,* pp. 115-23.

—'Hellenistic Letter-Forms and the Structure of Philippians', *Journal for the Study of the New Testament* 37 (1989), pp. 87-101.

—'Paul and the Hellenistic Schools: The Evidence of Galen', in Engberg-Pedersen (ed.), *Paul in his Hellenistic Context,* pp. 60-82.

Alexander, Philip S., 'Hellenism and Hellenization as Problematic Historiographical Categories', in Engberg-Pedersen (ed.), *Paul beyond the Judaism/Hellenism Divide,* pp. 63-80.

Alföldy, Géza, *The Social History of Rome* (trans. David Braund and Frank Pollock; Totowa, NJ: Barnes & Noble, 1985).

Altman, Marion, 'Ruler Cult in Seneca', *Classical Philology* 33 (1938), pp. 198-204.

Anderson, J.G.C., 'Trajan on the Quinquennium Neronis', *Journal of Roman Studies* 1 (1911), pp. 173-78.

Ando, Clifford, *Imperial Ideology and Provincial Loyalty in the Roman Empire* (Classics and Contemporary Thought, 6; Berkeley: University of California Press, 2000).

Antonaccio, Carla M., *An Archaeology of Ancestors: Tomb Cult and Hero Cult in Early Greece* (Lanham, MD: Rowman & Littlefield, 1995).

—'Contesting the Past: Hero Cult, Tomb Cult, and Epic in Early Greece', *American Journal of Archaeology* 98 (1994), pp. 389-410.

Auffarth, Christoph, 'Herrscherkult und Christuskult', in Cancik and Hitzl (eds.), *Praxis der Herrscherverehrung*, pp. 283-317.

Aune, David E., 'Human Nature and Ethics in Hellenistic Philosophical Traditions and Paul: Some Issues and Problems', in Engberg-Pedersen (ed.), *Paul in his Hellenistic Context*, pp. 291-312.

Badian, E., 'Alexander the Great between Two Thrones and Heaven: Variations on an Old Theme', in Small (ed.), *Subject and Ruler*, pp. 11-26.

Bagnall, Roger S., *Reading Papyri, Writing Ancient History* (Approaching the Ancient World; London: Routledge, 1995).

Balsdon, J.P.V.D., 'The "Divinity" of Alexander', *Historia* 1 (1950), pp. 363-88.

Barceló, Pedro. 'Beobachtungen zur Verehrung des christlichen Kaisers in der Spätantike', in Cancik and Hitzl (eds.), *Praxis der Herrscherverehrung*, pp. 319-39.

Barr, James, *The Semantics of Biblical Language* (Oxford: Oxford University Press, 1961; repr., London: Xpress Reprints [SCM Press], 1996).

Barrett, Anthony A. *Caligula: The Corruption of Power* (New Haven: Yale University Press, 1989).

Barrett, C.K., *A Commentary on the Epistle to the Romans* (Harper's New Testament Commentaries; Peabody, MA: Hendrickson, 1957).

—*A Commentary on the First Epistle to the Corinthians* (Harper's New Testament Commentaries; Peabody, MA: Hendrickson, 1968).

—*A Critical and Exegetical Commentary on the Acts of the Apostles* (International Critical Commentary; 2 vols.; Edinburgh: T. & T. Clark, 1998).

Barth, Markus, *Ephesians: Introduction, Translation and Commentary on Chapters 1–3* (Anchor Bible, 34; Garden City, NY: Doubleday, 1974).

Bauckham, Richard, 'The Worship of Jesus in Philippians 2:9-11', in Ralph P. Martin and Brian J. Dodd (eds.), *Where Christology Began: Essays on Philippians 2* (Louisville, KY: Westminster/John Knox Press, 1998), pp. 128-39.

Baudissin, Wolf W.G., *Kyrios als Gottesname im Judentum und seine Stelle in der Religionsgeschichte* (ed. Otto Eissfeldt; 4 vols.; Giessen: Alfred Töpelmann, 1929).

Bauer, Walter, *A Greek–English Lexicon of the New Testament and Other Early Christian Literature* (rev. and ed. Frederick W. Danker; Chicago: University of Chicago Press, 3rd edn, 2000).

Beard, Mary, 'Priesthood in the Roman Republic', in Beard and North (eds.), *Pagan Priests*, pp. 17-48.

Beard, Mary, and John A. North (eds.), *Pagan Priests: Religion and Power in the Ancient World* (London: Duckworth, 1990).

Beard, Mary, John A. North and Simon R.F. Price, *Religions of Rome*. I. *A History*. II. *A Sourcebook* (Cambridge: Cambridge University Press, 1998).

Beare, F.W., *A Commentary on the Epistle to the Philippians* (Harper's New Testament Commentaries; Peabody, MA: Hendrickson, 1959).

Beile, Rüdiger, *Zwischenruf aus Patmos: Eine neue Gesamteinschätzung der Apokalypse des Johannes von Ephesus* (Göttingen: V&R unipress, 2005).

Béranger, Jean, *Recherches sur l'aspect idéologique du principat* (Schweizerische Beiträge zur Altertumswissenschaft, 6; Basel: Reinhardt, 1953).

Bernett, Monika, *Der Kaiserkult in Judäa unter den Herodiern und Römern* (Wissenschaftliche Untersuchungen zum Neuen Testament, 203; Tübingen: Mohr Siebeck, 2007).

Best, Ernest, *A Critical and Exegetical Commentary on Ephesians* (International Critical Commentary; Edinburgh: T. & T. Clark, 1998).

Beurlier, E., *Le culte impérial: son histoire et son organisation depuis Auguste jusqu'à Justinien* (Paris: Ernest Thorin, 1891).

Bevan, Edwyn Robert, 'The Deification of Kings in the Greek Cities', *English Historical Review* 16 (1901), pp. 625-39.

Bickerman, Elias, 'Consecratio', in den Boer (ed.), *Le culte des souverains dans l'empire romain*, pp. 1-37.

Bietenhard, H., 'Κύριος', in Colin Brown (ed.), *The New International Dictionary of New Testament Theology* (4 vols.; Grand Rapids: Zondervan, 1975–85), II, pp. 510-20.

Black, David Alan, Katherine Barnwell and Stephen H. Levinsohn (eds.), *Linguistics and New Testament Interpretation: Essays on Discourse Analysis* (Nashville: Broadman, 1992).

Black, Matthew, *Romans* (New Century Bible; Grand Rapids: Eerdmans, 2nd edn, 1989).

Blackburn, Simon, *The Oxford Dictionary of Philosophy* (Oxford: Oxford University Press, 1994).

Blakemore, Diane, *Relevance and Linguistic Meaning: The Semantics and Pragmatics of Discourse Markers* (Cambridge Studies in Linguistics, 99; Cambridge: Cambridge University Press, 2002).

—*Semantic Constraints on Relevance* (Oxford: Basil Blackwell, 1987).

—*Understanding Utterances* (Oxford: Basil Blackwell, 1992).

Bock, Darrell L., 'New Testament Word Analysis', in McKnight (ed.), *Introducing New Testament Interpretation*, pp. 97-113.

Bockmuehl, Marcus, *The Epistle to the Philippians* (Black's New Testament Commentaries; London: A. & C. Black, 4th edn, 1997).

Boer, Willem den (ed.), *Le culte des souverains dans l'empire romain* (Geneva: Fondation Hardt, 1973).

Bookidis, Nancy, 'Religion in Corinth: 146 B.C.E. to 100 C.E.', in Schowalter and Friesen (eds.), *Urban Religion in Roman Corinth*, pp. 141-64.

Bormann, Lukas, *Philippi: Stadt und Christengemeinde zur Zeit des Paulus* (Supplements to *Novum Testamentum*, 78; Leiden: E.J. Brill, 1995).

Bornhäuser, Karl, *Jesus imperator mundi (Phil. 3,17-21 und 2,5-12)* (Gütersloh: Bertelsmann, 1938).

Botha, Jan, *Subject to Whose Authority? Multiple Readings of Romans 13* (Emory Studies in Early Christianity, 4; Atlanta: Scholars Press, 1994).

Botha, P.J.J., 'Assessing Representations of the Imperial Cult in New Testament Studies', *Verbum et ecclesia* 25 (2004), pp. 14-45.

Bousset, Wilhelm, *Kyrios Christos* (trans. John E. Steely; Nashville: Abingdon Press, 5th edn, 1970).

Bowersock, G.W., *Augustus and the Greek World* (Oxford: Clarendon Press, 1965).

—'Divine Might: Review of Price, *Rituals and Power* and Lambert, *Beloved and God'*, *New Republic* (11 February 1985), pp. 35-38.

Boyarin, Daniel, *Dying for God: Martyrdom and the Making of Christianity and Judaism* (Figurae: Reading Medieval Culture; Stanford, CA: Stanford University Press, 1999).

Braund, David, 'Function and Dysfunction: Personal Patronage in Roman Imperialism', in Wallace-Hadrill (ed.), *Patronage in Ancient Society*, pp. 137-52.

Bréhier, Louis, and Pierre Batiffol, *Les survivances du culte impérial romain: A propos des rites shintoïstes* (Paris: Auguste Picard, 1920).

Brent, Allen, *The Imperial Cult and the Development of Church Order: Concepts and Images of Authority in Paganism and Early Christianity before the Age of Cyprian* (Supplements to *Vigiliae christianae,* 45; Leiden: E.J. Brill, 1999).

Brown, Raymond E., *Introduction to the New Testament* (New York: Doubleday, 1996).

Bruce, F.F., *Romans* (Tyndale New Testament Commentaries; Leicester: InterVarsity Press, 2nd edn, 1985).

Bultmann, Rudolf, *Theology of the New Testament* (trans. Kendrick Grobel; 2 vols.; New York: Charles Scribner's Sons, 1951).

Bureth, Paul, *Les titulatures impériales dans les papyrus, les ostraca et les inscriptions d'Egypte (30 a.C.–284 p.C.)* (Brussels: Fondation Egyptologique Reine Elisa-beth, 1964).

Burk, Denny, 'Is Paul's Gospel Counterimperial? Evaluating the Prospects of the "Fresh Perspective" for Evangelical Theology', *Journal of the Evangelical Theological Society* 51 (2008), pp. 309-37.

Burkert, Walter, *Ancient Mystery Cults* (Cambridge, MA: Harvard University Press, 1987).

Burns, Lanier, *Aspects of Babylonian Theocracy as Background for the Biblical Polemic* (ThD diss., Dallas Theological Seminary, 1979).

Burrell, Barbara, *Neokoroi: Greek Cities and Roman Emperors* (Cincinnati Classical Studies, NS 9; Leiden: E.J. Brill, 2004).

—*Neokoroi: Greek Cities of the Roman East* (PhD diss., Harvard University, 1980).

Byrne, Brendan, *Romans* (Sacra pagina, 6; Collegeville, MN: Liturgical Press, 1996).

Cadbury, Henry J., 'The Titles of Jesus in Acts', in F.J. Foakes Jackson and Kirsopp Lake (eds.), *The Beginnings of Christianity. Part 1: The Acts of the Apostles,* V (London: Macmillan, 1933), pp. 354-75.

Cancik, Hubert, 'Der Kaiser-Eid: Zur Praxis der römischen Herrscherverehrung', in Cancik and Hitzl (eds.), *Praxis der Herrscherverehrung,* pp. 29-45.

Cancik, Hubert, and Konrad Hitzl (eds.), *Die Praxis der Herrscherverehrung in Rom und seinen Provinzen* (Tübingen: Mohr Siebeck, 2003).

Cannadine, David, 'Introduction: Divine Rites of Kings', in David Cannadine and Simon R.F. Price (eds.), *Rituals of Royalty: Power and Ceremonial in Traditional Societies* (Cambridge: Cambridge University Press, 1987), pp. 1-19.

Carr, E.H., *What Is History? The George Macaulay Trevelyan Lectures Delivered in the University of Cambridge, January–March 1961* (London: Penguin Books, 2nd edn, 1987).

Carson, D.A., *Exegetical Fallacies* (Grand Rapids: Baker Book House, 2nd edn, 1996).

Carson, D.A., and Douglas J. Moo, *An Introduction to the New Testament* (Grand Rapids: Zondervan, 2nd edn, 2005).

Carson, D.A., Douglas J. Moo and Leon Morris, *An Introduction to the New Testament* (Grand Rapids: Zondervan, 1992).

Carson, D.A., Peter T. O'Brien and Mark A. Seifrid (eds.), *Justification and Variegated Nomism* (2 vols.; Tübingen: Mohr Siebeck, 2001, 2004).

Carston, Robyn, and Seiji Uchida (eds.), *Relevance Theory: Applications and Impli-cations* (Pragmatics & Beyond, New Series, 37; Amsterdam: John Benjamins, 1997).

Carter, Warren, 'Contested Claims: Roman Imperial Theology and Matthew's Gospel', *Biblical Theology Bulletin* 29 (1999), pp. 56-67.

—*Matthew and Empire: Initial Explorations* (Harrisburg, PA: Trinity Press International, 2001).

—*Matthew and the Margins: A Sociopolitical and Religious Reading* (Maryknoll, NY: Orbis Books, 2000).

—Review of *Christ and Caesar: The Gospel and the Roman Empire in the Writings of Paul and Luke* (Grand Rapids: Eerdmans, 2008), by Seyoon Kim, *Review of Biblical Literature* (2009) [http://www.bookreviews.org].

—'Toward an Imperial-Critical Reading of Matthew's Gospel', in *Society of Biblical Literature 1998 Seminar Papers* 37 (Atlanta: Scholars Press, 1998), I, pp. 296-324.

Cassidy, Richard J., *Christians and Roman Rule in the New Testament: New Perspectives* (Companions to the New Testament; New York: Crossroad, 2001).

Casson, L., *Everyday Life in Ancient Rome* (Baltimore: Johns Hopkins University Press, rev. and exp. edn, 1998).

Cerfaux, L., and J. Tondriau, *Le cult des souverains dans la civilization gréco-romaine* (Bibliothèque de théologie, série III, 5; Paris: Desclée, 1957).

Champlin, Edward, *Nero* (Cambridge, MA: Harvard University Press, 2003).

Charlesworth, M.P., 'The Refusal of Divine Honours: An Augustan Formula', *Papers of the British School at Rome* 15 (NS 2) (1939), pp. 1-10.

—'Some Observations of Ruler-Cult, Especially in Rome', *Harvard Theological Review* 28 (1935), pp. 5-44.

Chomsky, Noam, *Aspects of the Theory of Syntax* (Cambridge, MA: MIT Press, 1965).

Cineira, David Alvarez, *Die Religionspolitik des Kaisers Claudius und die paulinische Mission* (Herders Biblische Studien, 19; Leiden, Brill, 1999).

Clark, Gillian, 'Let Every Soul Be Subject: The Fathers and the Empire', in Loveday Alexander (ed.), *Images of Empire* (JSOTSup, 122; Sheffield: JSOT Press, 1991), pp. 251-75.

Clauss, Manfred, '*Deus praesens:* Der römischer Kaiser als Gott', *Klio* 78 (1996), pp. 400-433.

—*Kaiser und Gott: Herrscherkult im römischen Reich* (1999; repr., Munich: K.G. Saur, 2001).

—*The Roman Cult of Mithras: The God and his Mysteries* (trans. Richard Gordon; New York: Routledge, 2000).

Clay, Diskin, *Archilochos Heros: The Cult of Poets in the Greek Polis* (Hellenic Studies, 6; Cambridge, MA: Harvard University Press, 2004).

Coldstream, J.N., 'Hero-Cults in the Age of Homer', *Journal of Hellenic Studies* 96 (1976), pp. 8-17.

Cole, Spencer, , 'Elite Scepticism in the *Apocolocyntosis*: Further Qualifications', in K. Volk and G.D. Williams (eds.), *Seeing Seneca Whole: Perspectives on Philosophy, Poetry and Politics* (Leiden: Brill, 2006), pp. 175-82.

Collart, Paul, *Philippes, ville de Macédoine: depuis ses origines jusqu'à la fin de l'époque romaine* (Travaux et mémoires, 5; 2 vols.; Paris: Ecole française d'Athènes, 1937).

Collins, Adela Yarbro, *Crisis and Catharsis: The Power of the Apocalypse* (Philadelphia: Westminster Press, 1984).

—'Psalms, Philippians 2:6-11, and the Origins of Christology', *Biblical Interpretation* 11 (2003), pp. 361-72.

—'The Worship of Jesus and the Imperial Cult', in Carey C. Newman, James R. Davila and Gladys S. Lewis (eds.), *The Jewish Roots of Monotheism: Papers from the St*

Andrews Conference of the Historical Origins of the Worship of Jesus (*Journal for the Study of Judaism* Supplement, 63; Leiden: E.J. Brill, 1999), pp. 234-57.

Collins, John J., 'Judaism as *Praeparatio Evangelica* in the Work of Martin Hengel', *Religious Studies Review* 15 (1989), pp. 226-28.

Conzelmann, Hans,. *1 Corinthians: A Commentary on the First Epistle to the Corinthians* (ed. George W. MacRae; trans. James W. Leitch; Hermeneia; Philadelphia: Fortress Press, 1975).

—*Acts of the Apostles: A Commentary on the Acts of the Apostles* (ed. Eldon Jay Epp and Christopher Matthews; trans. James Limburg, A. Thomas Kraabel and Donald H. Juel; Hermeneia; Philadelphia: Fortress Press, 1987).

Cook, John G., *The Structure and Persuasive Power of Mark: A Linguistic Approach* (Semeia Studies; Atlanta: Scholars Press, 1995).

Cope, Pamela, *Introductory Grammar: A Stratificational Approach* (n.p.: SIL, 1994).

Cranfield, C.E.B., *A Critical and Exegetical Commentary on the Epistle to the Romans* (International Critical Commentary; 2 vols.; Edinburgh: T. & T. Clark, 1975, 1979).

Crawford, Michael, 'Numismatics', in Crawford (ed.), *Sources for Ancient History*, pp. 185-233.

Crawford, Michael (ed.), *Sources for Ancient History: Studies in the Use of Historical Evidence* (Cambridge: Cambridge University Press, 1983).

Crossan, John Dominic, 'Roman Imperial Theology', in Richard A. Horsley (ed.), *In the Shadow of Empire: Reclaiming the Bible as a History of Faithful Resistance* (Louisville, KY: Westminster/John Knox Press, 2008), pp. 59-73.

Currie, Bruno, *Pindar and the Cult of Heroes* (Oxford Classical Monographs; Oxford: Oxford University Press, 2005).

Cuss, Dominique, *Imperial Cult and Honorary Terms in the New Testament* (Fribourg, Switzerland: University Press, 1974).

Danker, Frederick W., *Benefactor: Epigraphic Study of a Graeco-Roman and New Testament Semantic Field* (St Louis: Clayton, 1982).

Danove, Paul L., *Linguistics and Exegesis in the Gospel of Mark: Applications of a Case Frame Analysis and Lexicon* (*Journal for the Study of the New Testament:* Supplement Series, 218; Studies in New Testament Greek, 10; London: T. & T. Clark, 2001).

Davies, Jason P., *Rome's Religious History: Livy, Tacitus and Ammianus on their Gods* (Cambridge: Cambridge University Press, 2004).

Davies, Penelope J.E., *Death and the Emperor: Roman Imperial Funerary Monuments from Augustus to Marcus Aurelius* (Cambridge: Cambridge University Press, 2000; repr., Austin: University of Texas Press, 2004).

Davies, W.D., *Paul and Rabbinic Judaism: Some Rabbinic Elements in Pauline Theology* (Philadelphia: Fortress Press, 4th edn, 1980).

Deissmann, Adolf, *Light from the Ancient East: The New Testament Illustrated by Recently Discovered Texts of the Graeco-Roman World* (trans. Lionel R. Strachan; New York: George H. Doran, 1927; repr., Peabody, MA: Hendrickson, 1995).

DeMaris, Richard, 'Cults and the Imperial Cult in Early Roman Corinth: Literary versus Material Record', in Labahn and Zangenberg (eds.), *Zwischen den Reichen*, pp. 73-91.

DeWitt, Norman Wentworth, *St Paul and Epicurus* (Minneapolis: University of Minnesota Press, 1954).

Dibelius, Martin, and Hans Conzelmann, *The Pastoral Epistles: A Commentary on the Pastoral Epistles* (ed. Helmut Koester; trans. Philip Buttolph and Adela Yarbro; Hermeneia; Philadelphia: Fortress Press, 1972).

Dickey, Eleanor, 'Κύριε, Δεσπότα, *Domine*: Greek Politeness in the Roman Empire', *Journal of Hellenic Studies* 121 (2001), pp. 1-11.

Dobbins, John, 'The Imperial Cult Building in the Forum at Pompeii', in Small (ed.), *Subject and Ruler,* pp. 99-114.

Dockx, S., 'Lieu et date de l'épître aux Philippiens', *Revue biblique* 80 (1973), pp. 230-46.

Dodd, C.H., *The Epistle of Paul to the Romans* (London: Hodder & Stoughton, 1932; repr., London: Collins, 1959).

Donfried, Karl Paul, 'The Cults of Thessalonica and the Thessalonian Correspondence', *New Testament Studies* (1985), pp. 336-56.

Downing, F. Gerald, 'A bas les aristos: The Relevance of Higher Literature for the Understanding of the Earliest Christian Writing', *Novum Testamentum* 30 (1988), pp. 212-30.

—'Pliny's Persecutions of Christians: Revelation and 1 Peter', *Journal for the Study of the New Testament* 34 (1988), pp. 105-23.

Duff, Jeremy, *A Reconsideration of Pseudepigraphy in Early Christianity* (DPhil thesis, Oxford University, 1998).

Duncan, George S., *St Paul's Ephesian Ministry: A Reconstruction with Special Reference to the Ephesian Origin of the Imprisonment Epistles* (London: Hodder & Stoughton, 1929).

Dundas, Gregory S., 'Augustus and the Kingship of Egypt', *Historia* 51 (2002), pp. 433-48.

—*Pharaoh, Basileus and Imperator: The Roman Imperial Cult in Egypt* (PhD diss., University of California, Los Angeles, 1994).

Dunn, James D.G., 'ΚΥΡΙΟΣ in Acts', in *The Christ and the Spirit: Collected Essays of James D.G. Dunn*. I. *Christology* (Grand Rapids: Eerdmans, 1998), pp. 241-53. Reprinted from Christof Landmesser, Hans-Joachim Eckstein and Hermann Lichtenberger (eds.), *Christus als die Mitte der Schrift: Studien zur Hermeneutik des Evangeliums* (Beihefte zur *Zeitschrift für die neutestamentliche Wissenschaft und die Kunde der älteren Kirche,* 86; Berlin: W. de Gruyter, 1997).

—*Romans*. I. *Romans 1–8*. II. *Romans 9–16* (Word Biblical Commentary, 38a, 38b; 2 vols.; Dallas: Word Books, 1988).

—*The Theology of Paul the Apostle* (Grand Rapids: Eerdmans, 1998).

Ebner, Martin, and Elisabeth Esch-Wermling (eds.), *Kaiserkult, Wirtschaft und Spectacula: Zum politischen und gesellschaftlichen Umfeld der Offenbarung* (Novum Testamentum et orbis antiquus/Studien zur Umwelt des Neuen Testaments, 72; Göttingen: Vandenhoeck & Ruprecht, 2011).

Edwards, Douglas R., *Religion and Power: Pagans, Jews, and Christians in the Greek East* (Oxford: Oxford University Press, 1996).

Egger, Wilhelm, *How to Read the New Testament: An Introduction to Linguistic and Historical-Critical Methodology* (ed. Hendrikus Boers; trans. Peter Heinegg; Peabody, MA: Hendrickson, 1996).

Ehrenberg, Victor, 'Caesar's Final Aims', in Victor Ehrenberg, *Man, State and Deity: Essays in Ancient History* (London: Methuen, 1974), pp. 127-42.

Elliott, Neil, *Liberating Paul: The Justice of God and the Politics of the Apostle* (Bible and Liberation; Sheffield: Sheffield Academic Press, 1995).

Elton, G.R., *The Practice of History* (Glasgow: Fontana, 1984).

Engberg-Pedersen, Troels, 'Introduction: Paul beyond the Judaism/Hellenism Divide', in Engberg-Pedersen (ed.), *Paul beyond the Judaism/Hellenism Divide,* pp. 1-16.

—*Paul and the Stoics* (Louisville, KY: Westminster/John Knox Press, 2000).

—'Stoicism in Philippians', in Engberg-Pedersen (ed.), *Paul in his Hellenistic Context,* pp. 256-90.

Engberg-Pedersen, Troels (ed.), *Paul beyond the Judaism/Hellenism Divide* (Louisville, KY: Westminster/John Knox Press, 2001).

—(ed.), *Paul in his Hellenistic Context* (Minneapolis: Fortress Press, 1995).

Engels, Donald, *Roman Corinth: An Alternate Model for the Classical City* (Chicago: University of Chicago Press, 1990).

Epp, Eldon Jay, 'The Significance of the Papyri for Determining the Nature of the New Testament Text in the Second Century: A Dynamic View of Textual Transmission', in Eldon Jay Epp and Gordon D. Fee (eds.), *Studies in the Theory and Method of New Testament Textual Criticism* (Grand Rapids: Eerdmans, 1993), pp. 274-97.

Esler, Philip F., 'Paul and Stoicism: Romans 12 as a Test Case', *New Testament Studies* 50 (2004), pp. 106-24.

Etienne, Robert, *Le culte impérial dans la péninsule ibérique d'Auguste à Dioclétien* (Bibliothèque des écoles françaises d'Athènes et de Rome, 191; Paris: E. de Boccard, 1958).

Evans, Craig A., *Ancient Texts for New Testament Studies: A Guide to the Background Literature* (Peabody, MA: Hendrickson, 2005).

—*Noncanonical Writings and New Testament Interpretation* (Peabody, MA: Hendrickson, 1992).

Falk, Julia S., 'Semantics', in Virginia P. Clark, Paul A. Escholz and Alfred F. Rosa (eds.), *Language: Introductory Readings* (New York: St Martins Press, 1981), pp. 319-417.

Fantin, Joseph D., 'Background Studies: Grounding the Text in Reality', in Darrell L. Bock and Buist M. Fanning (eds.), *Interpreting the New Testament Text: Introduction to the Art and Science of Exegesis* (Wheaton, IL: Crossway, 2006), pp. 167-96.

—*The Greek Imperative Mood in the New Testament: A Cognitive and Communicative Approach* (Studies in Biblical Greek, 12; New York: Peter Lang, 2010).

—Review of *Christ and Caesar: The Gospel and the Roman Empire in the Writings of Paul and Luke* (Grand Rapids: Eerdmans, 2008), by Seyoon Kim, *Bryn Mawr Classical Review* (2009) [http://bmcr.brynmawr.edu].

—Review of 'The Imperial Cult in the Pauline Cities of Asia Minor and Greece', *Catholic Biblical Quarterly* 72 (2010), pp. 314-31, by Colin Miller, *Bibliotheca Sacra* 168 (2011), pp. 98-99.

Farnell, Lewis Richard, *Greek Hero Cults and Ideas of Immortality* (Gifford Lectures 1920; Oxford: Clarendon Press, 1921; repr., Chicago: Ares, 1995).

Faust, Eberhard,. *Pax Christi et pax Caesaris: Religionsgeschichtliche, traditionsgeschichtliche und sozialgeschichtliche Studien zum Epheserbrief* (Novum Testamentum et orbis antiquus, 23; Göttingen: Vandenhoeck & Ruprecht, 1993).

Fee, Gordon D., *The First Epistle to the Corinthians* (New International Commentary on the New Testament; Grand Rapids: Eerdmans, 1987).

—*Paul's Letter to the Philippians* (New International Commentary on the New Testament; Grand Rapids: Eerdmans, 1995).

—'Philippians 2:5-11: Hymn or Exalted Pauline Prose?' *Bulletin for Biblical Research* 2 (1992), pp. 29-46.

Ferguson, Everett, *Backgrounds of Early Christianity* (Grand Rapids: Eerdmans, 3rd edn, 2003).

Filson, Floyd V., *The New Testament against its Environment: The Gospel of Christ the Risen Lord* (Studies in Biblical Theology, 3; Chicago: Henry Regnery, 1950).

Finney, Mark T., 'Christ Crucified and the Inversion of Roman Imperial Ideology in 1 Corinthians', *Biblical Theology Bulletin* 35 (Summer 2005), pp. 20-33.

Fishwick, Duncan, 'The Development of Provincial Ruler Worship in the Western Roman Empire', in H. Temporini and W. Haase (eds.), *Aufstieg und Niedergang der römischen Welt: Geschichte und Kultur Roms im Spiegel der neueren Forschung*, II.16.2 (Berlin: W. de Gruyter, 1979), pp. 1201-53.

—'*Genius* and *Numen*', *Harvard Theological Review* 62 (1969), pp. 356-67.

—'The Imperial Cult in Roman Britain', *Phoenix* 15 (1961), pp. 159-73.

—'The Imperial Cult in Roman Britain (Cont.)', *Phoenix* 15 (1961), pp. 213-29.

—*The Imperial Cult in the Latin West: Studies in the Ruler Cult of the Western Provinces of the Roman Empire* (3 vols. [vols. 1-2: Etudes preliminaires aux religions orientales dans l'empire romain; vol. 3: Religions in the Graeco-Roman World]; Leiden: E.J. Brill, 1987-2005).

—'Studies in Roman Imperial History' (Unpublished work, 1977).

—'The Temple of Divus Claudius at Camulodunum', *Britannia* 26 (1995), pp. 11-27.

Fitzmyer, Joseph A., *The Acts of the Apostles: A New Translation with Introduction and Commentary* (Anchor Bible, 31; New York: Doubleday, 1998).

—*Romans: A New Translation with Introduction and Commentary* (Anchor Bible, 33; New York: Doubleday, 1993).

Foerster, Werner, and Georg Fohrer, 'Σῴζω' [and Cognates], in Kittel and Friedrich (eds.), *Theological Dictionary of the New Testament*, VII, pp. 965-1024.

Foerster, Werner, Georg Fohrer and Gottfried Quell, 'Κύριος' [and Cognates], in Kittel and Friedrich (eds.), *Theological Dictionary of the New Testament*, III, pp. 1039-98.

Fotopoulos, John, *Food Offered to Idols in Roman Corinth: A Social-Rhetorical Reconsideration of 1 Corinthians 8:1–11:1* (Wissenschaftliche Untersuchungen zum Neuen Testament, 2.151; Tübingen: Mohr Siebeck, 2003).

Fowl, Stephen E., *The Story of Christ in the Ethics of Paul: An Analysis of the Function of the Hymnic Material in the Pauline Corpus* (*Journal for the Study of the New Testament:* Supplement Series, 36; Sheffield: Sheffield Academic Press, 1990).

Fredricksmeyer, E., 'Three Notes on Alexander's Deification', *American Journal of Ancient History* 4 (1979), pp. 1-9.

Frenschkowski, Marco, 'Kyrios in Context: Q 6:46, the Emperor as "Lord", and the Political Implications of Christology in Q', in Labahn and Zangenberg (eds.), *Zwischen den Reichen*, pp. 95-118.

Friesen, Steven J., *Imperial Cults and the Apocalypse of John: Reading Revelation in the Ruins* (Oxford: Oxford University Press, 2001).

—'Satan's Throne, Imperial Cults and the Social Settings of Revelation', *Journal for the Study of the New Testament* 27 (2005), pp. 351-73.

—*Twice Neokoros: Ephesus, Asia, and the Cult of the Flavian Imperial Family* (Religions in the Graeco-Roman World, 116; Leiden: E.J. Brill, 1993).

Furlong, Anne, *Relevance Theory and Literary Interpretation* (PhD thesis, University College London, 1995).

Gabba, Emilio, 'Literature', in Crawford (ed.), *Sources for Ancient History,* pp. 1-79.

Galinsky, Karl, *Augustan Culture: An Interpretive Introduction* (Princeton, NJ: Princeton University Press, 1996).

Garland, David E., *1 Corinthians* (Baker Exegetical Commentary on the New Testament; Grand Rapids: Baker Book House, 2003).

Garlington, Donald B., 'The New Perspective on Paul: An Appraisal Two Decades Later', *Criswell Theological Review* ns 2 (2005), pp. 17-38.

Garnsey, Peter, and Richard P. Saller, *The Roman Empire: Economy, Society and Culture* (Berkeley: University of California Press, 1987).

Garnsey, Peter, and Greg Woolf, 'Patronage of the Rural Poor in the Roman World', in Wallace-Hadrill (ed.), *Patronage in Ancient Society,* pp. 153-70.

Garriguet Mata, José A., *El culto imperial en la Córdoba romana: una aproximación arqueológica* (Córdoba: Diputación de Córdoba, 2002).

Gasque, W. Ward, 'Tarsus', in David Noel Freedman (ed.), *The Anchor Bible Dictionary* (6 vols.; New York: Doubleday, 1992), VI, pp. 333-34.

Georgi, Dieter, *Theocracy in Paul's Praxis and Theology* (trans. David E. Green; Minneapolis: Fortress Press, 1991).

—''Who Is the True Prophet?' in Horsley (ed.), *Paul and Empire,* pp. 36-46.

Gerdmar, Anders, *Rethinking the Judaism–Hellenism Dichotomy: A Historiographical Case Study of Second Peter and Jude* (Coniectanea biblica: New Testament Series, 36; Stockholm: Almqvist & Wiksell International, 2001).

Gesche, Helga, *Caesar* (Erträge der Forschung, 51; Darmstadt: Wissenschaftliche Buchgesellschaft, 1976).

—*Die Vergottung Caesars* (Frankfurter althistorische Studien, 1; Kallmünz/Opf.: Michael Lassleben, 1968).

Goetchius, Eugene van Ness, *The Language of the New Testament* (New York: Charles Scribner's Sons, 1965).

Gordon, Richard, 'From Republic to Principate: Priesthood, Religion and Ideology', in Beard and North (eds.), *Pagan Priests,* pp. 177-98.

—'The Veil of Power: Emperors, Sacrificers and Benefactors', in Beard and North (eds.), *Pagan Priests,* pp. 199-231.

Gradel, Ittai, *Emperor Worship and Roman Religion* (Oxford Classical Monographs; Oxford: Oxford University Press, 2002).

Gradl, Hans-Georg, 'Kaisertum und Kaiserkult: Ein Verleich zwischen Philos *Legatio ad Gaium* und der *Offenbarung des Johannes*', *New Testament Studies* 56 (2010), pp. 116-38.

GRAMCORD Greek New Testament for Windows 2.4cx with Database 5.3 (Battle Ground, WA: Gramcord Institute, 1999).

Grant, Michael, *The Jews in the Roman World* (London: Weidenfeld & Nicolson, 1973; repr., London: Phoenix Press, 1999).

—*Roman History from Coins: Some Uses of the Imperial Coinage to the Historian* (Cambridge: Cambridge University Press, 1958).

Grant, Robert M., *Paul in the Roman World: The Conflict at Corinth* (Louisville, KY: Westminster/John Knox Press, 2001).

Green, Steven J., 'Undeifying Tiberius: A Reconsideration of Seneca, *Apocolocyntosis* 1.2', *Classical Quarterly* 60 (2010), pp. 274-76.

Grenier, Jean Claude, *Les titulatures des empereurs romains dans les documents en langue égyptienne* (Papyrologica bruxellensia, 22; Brussels: Fondation Egyptologique Reine Elisabeth, 1989).

Grether, Gertrude, 'Livia and the Roman Imperial Cult', *American Journal of Philology* 67 (1946), pp. 222-52.

Grice, H. Paul, 'Further Notes on Logic and Conversation', in P. Cole (ed.), *Syntax and Semantics. IX. Pragmatics* (New York: Academic Press, 1978), pp. 113-27.

—'Logic and Conversation', in P. Cole and J. Morgan (eds.), *Syntax and Semantics. III. Speech Acts* (New York: Academic Press, 1975), pp. 41-58.

—'Meaning', *Philosophical Review* 66 (1957), pp. 377-88.

—*Studies in the Way of Words* (Cambridge, MA: Harvard University Press, 1989).

Griffin, Miriam T., *Nero: The End of a Dynasty* (New Haven: Yale University Press, 1984).

—'Urbs Roma, Plebs and Princeps', in Loveday Alexander (ed.), *Images of Empire* (*Journal for the Study of the Old Testament:* Supplement Series, 122; Sheffield: JSOT Press, 1991), pp. 19-46.

Gundry, Robert H., 'Style and Substance in Philippians 2:6-11', in Robert H. Gundry, *The Old Is Better: New Testament Essays in Support of Traditional Interpretations* (Wissenschaftliche Untersuchungen zum Neuen Testament, 178; Tübingen: Mohr Siebeck, 2005), pp. 272-91.

Guthrie, Donald, *New Testament Introduction* (Downers Grove, IL: InterVarsity Press, 4th edn, 1990).

Gutt, Ernst-August, *Relevance Theory: A Guide to Successful Communication in Translation* (Dallas: Summer Institute of Linguistics; New York: United Bible Societies, 1992).

—*Translation and Relevance: Cognition and Context* (Manchester: St Jerome, 2nd edn, 2000).

—'Unravelling Meaning: An Introduction to Relevance Theory', *Notes on Translation* 112 (1986), pp. 10-20.

Habicht, Christian, 'Die augusteische Zeit und das erste Jahrhundert nach Christi Geburt', in den Boer (ed.), *Le culte des souverains dans l'empire romain*, pp. 39-99.

—*Gottmenschentum und griechische Städte* (Zetemata, 14; Munich: Beck, 2nd edn, 1970).

Hack, Roy Kenneth, 'Homer and the Cult of Heroes', *Transactions and Proceedings of the American Philological Association* 60 (1929), pp. 57-74.

Hagedorn, D., and K.A. Worp, 'Von Κύριος zu Δεσπότης: Eine Bemerkung zur Kaisertitulatur im 3./4. Jhdt.', *Zeitschrift für Papyrologie und Epigraphik* 39 (1980), pp. 165-77.

Hagner, Donald A., 'The New Testament, History, and the Historical-Critical Method', in Black, David Alan, and David S. Dockery (eds.), *New Testament Criticism and Interpretation* (Grand Rapids: Zondervan, 1991), pp. 73-96.

Hahn, Ulrike, *Die Frauen römischen und ihre Ehrungen im griechischen Osten anhand epigraphischer und numismatischer Zeugnisse von Livia bis Sabina* (Saarbrücker Studien zur Archäologie und alten Geschichte, 8; Saarwellingen, Germany: Saarländische Druckerei und Verlag, 1994).

Hanhart, Robert, 'Introduction: Problems in the History of the LXX Text from its Beginnings to Origen', in Martin Hengel, *The Septuagint as Christian Scripture: Its Prehistory and the Problem of its Canon* (Edinburgh: T. & T. Clark, 2002), pp. 1-17.

Hänlein-Schäfer, Heidi, *VENERATIO AUGUSTI: Eine Studie zu den Tempeln des ersten römischen Kaisers* (Archaeologica, 39; Rome: Giorgio Bretschneider, 1985).

Hannestad, Niels, *Roman Art and Imperial Policy* (trans. P. J. Crabb; Jutland Archaeological Society Publications, 19; Højbjerg, Denmark: Jutland Archaeological
Press, 1986).

Hansen, G. Walter, *The Letter to the Philippians* (Pillar New Testament Commentary;
Grand Rapids: Eerdmans, 2009).

Hanson, A.T., *The Pastoral Epistles* (New Century Bible; Grand Rapids: Eerdmans,
1982).

Hardin, Justin K., *Galatians and the Imperial Cult: A Critical Analysis of the First-
Century Social Context of Paul's Letter* (Wissenschaftliche Untersuchungen zum
Neuen Testament, 2.237; Tübingen: Mohr Siebeck, 2008).

Harland, Philip A., *Associations, Synagogues, and Congregations: Claiming a Place in
Ancient Mediterranean Society* (Minneapolis: Fortress Press, 2003).

—'Honouring the Emperor or Assailing the Beast: Participation in Civic Life among
Associations (Jewish, Christian and Other) in Asia Minor and the Apocalypse of
John', *Journal for the Study of the New Testament* 77 (2000), pp. 99-121.

—'Honours and Worship: Emperors, Imperial Cults and Associations at Ephesus (First
to Third Centuries C.E.)', *Studies in Religion/Sciences religieuses* 25 (1996),
pp. 319-34.

—'Imperial Cults within Local Cultural Life: Associations in Roman Asia', *Ancient History Bulletin* 17 (2003), pp. 85-107.

Harris, B.F., 'Oaths of Allegiance to Caesar', *Prudentia* 14 (1982), pp. 109-22.

Harrison, James R., *Paul and the Imperial Authorities at Thessalonica and Rome: A
Study in the Conflict of Ideology* (Wissenschaftliche Untersuchungen zum Neuen
Testament, 273; Tübingen: Mohr Siebeck, 2011).

—'Paul and the Imperial Gospel at Thessaloniki', *Journal for the Study of the New Testament* 25 (2002), pp. 71-96.

—*Paul's Language of Grace in its Graeco-Roman Context* (Wissenschaftliche Untersuchungen zum Neuen Testament, 2.172; Tübingen: J.C.B. Mohr [Paul Siebeck],
2003).

Hasel, Gerhard, *New Testament Theology: Basic Issues in the Current Debate* (Grand
Rapids: Eerdmans, 1978).

Hatch, Edwin, and Henry A. Redpath, *A Concordance to the Septuagint and Other Greek
Versions of the Old Testament (Including the Apocrypha)* (3 vols. in 2; Oxford:
Clarendon, 1897–1906; repr., Grand Rapids: Baker Book House, 1983).

Haverfield, F., 'Note on the Above by Prof. F. Haverfield', *Journal of Roman Studies* 1
(1911), pp. 178-79.

Hawthorne, Gerald F., *Philippians* (Word Biblical Commentary, 43; Waco, TX: Word
Books, 1983).

Hawthorne, Gerald F., Ralph P. Martin and D.G. Reid (eds.), *Dictionary of Paul and his
Letters* (Downers Grove, IL:; InterVarsity Press, 1993).

Hazzard, R., 'Did Ptolemy I Get his Surname from the Rhodians in 304 B.C.?', *Zeitschrift
für Papyrologie und Epigraphik* 93 (1992), pp. 52-56.

Hellerman, Joseph H., 'ΜΟΡΦΗ ΘΕΟΥ as a Signifier of Social Status in Philippians
2:6', *Journal of the Evangelical Theological Society* 52 (2009), pp. 779-97.

—*Reconstructing Honor in Roman Philippi: Carmen Christi as Cursus Pudorum* (Society for New Testament Studies Monograph Series, 132; Cambridge: Cambridge
University Press, 2005).

Hemer, Colin J., *The Book of Acts in the Setting of Hellenistic History* (ed. Conrad Gempf; Wissenschaftliche Untersuchungen zum Neuen Testament, 49; Tübingen: J.C.B. Mohr [Paul Siebeck], 1989).

Hengel, Martin, *Crucifixion in the Ancient World and the Folly of the Message of the Cross* (trans. John Bowden; Philadelphia: Fortress Press, 1977).

—*Judaism and Hellenism: Studies in their Encounter in Palestine during the Early Hellenistic Period* (trans. John Bowden; London: SCM Press, 1974; repr., London: Xpress Reprints [SCM Press], 1996).

—*The Septuagint as Christian Scripture: Its Prehistory and the Problem of its Canon* (trans. Mark E. Biddle; Old Testament Studies; Edinburgh: T. & T. Clark, 2002).

Hengel, Martin, in collaboration with Roland Deines, *The Pre-Christian Paul* (trans. J. Bowden; London: SCM Press, 1991).

Héring, Jean, *The First Epistle of Saint Paul to the Corinthians* (trans. A.W. Heathcote and P.J. Allcock; London: Epworth, 1962).

Herrmann, Peter, *Der römische Kaisereid: Untersuchungen zu seiner Herkunft und Entwicklung* (Hypomnemata, 20; Göttingen: Vandenhoeck & Ruprecht, 1968).

Hock, R.F., 'Paul and Greco-Roman Education', in Sampley (ed.), *Paul in the Greco-Roman World*, pp. 198-227.

Hoehner, Harold W., *Ephesians: An Exegetical Commentary* (Grand Rapids: Baker Book House, 2002).

Holmes, Michael W., 'New Testament Textual Criticism', in McKnight (ed.), *Introducing New Testament Interpretation*, pp. 53-74.

—'A Note on the Text of Polycarp *Philippians* 11.3', *Vigiliae christianae* 51 (1997), pp. 207-10.

Holmes, Michael W. (ed. and trans.), *The Apostolic Fathers: Greek Texts and English Translation* (3rd edn,. after the earlier work of J.B. Lightfoot and J.R. Harmer; Grand Rapids: Baker Book House, 2007).

Hornblower, Simon, and Antony J.S. Spawforth (eds.), *The Oxford Classical Dictionary* (Oxford: Oxford University Press, 3rd edn, 1996).

Horrell, David G., 'Introduction', *Journal for the Study of the New Testament* 27 (2005), pp. 251-55.

Horrocks, Geoffrey C., *Greek: A History of the Language and its Speakers* (Longman Linguistic Library; London: Longman, 1997).

Horsley, Richard A., *1 Corinthians* (Abingdon New Testament Commentaries; Nashville: Abingdon Press, 1998).

—'General Introduction', in Horsley (ed.), *Paul and Empire*, pp. 1-8.

Horsley, Richard A. (ed.), *Paul and Empire: Religion and Power in Roman Imperial Society* (Harrisburg, PA: Trinity Press International, 1997).

—*Paul and Politics: Ekklesia, Israel, Imperium, Interpretation. Essays in Honor of Krister Stendahl* (Harrisburg, PA: Trinity Press International, 2000).

—*Paul and the Roman Imperial Order* (Harrisburg, PA: Trinity Press International, 2004).

Horsley, Richard A., and Neil Asher Silberman, *The Message and the Kingdom: How Jesus and Paul Ignited a Revolution and Transformed the Ancient World* (New York: Grosset/Putnam, 1997; repr., Minneapolis: Fortress Press, 2002).

Howgego, Christopher, *Ancient History from Coins* (Approaching the Ancient World; London: Routledge, 1995).

Hurtado, Larry W., 'First-Century Jewish Monotheism', *Journal for the Study of the New Testament* 71 (1998), pp. 3-26.

—*Lord Jesus Christ: Devotion to Jesus in Earliest Christianity* (Grand Rapids: Eerdmans, 2003).

—'New Testament Christology: A Critique of Bousset's Influence', *Theological Studies* 40 (1979), pp. 306-17.

—*One God, One Lord: Early Christian Devotion and Ancient Jewish Monotheism* (Edinburgh: T. & T. Clark, 2nd edn, 1998).

Huzar, Eleanor G., 'Emperor Worship in Julio-Claudian Egypt', in H. Temporini and W. Haase (eds.), *Aufstieg und Niedergang der römischen Welt: Geschichte und Kultur Roms im Spiegel der neueren Forschung*, II.18.5 (Berlin: W. de Gruyter, 1995), pp. 3092-3143.

Ifantidou, Elly, *Evidentials and Relevance* (Pragmatics & Beyond NS, 86; Amsterdam: John Benjamins, 2001).

Jellicoe, Sydney, *The Septuagint and Modern Study* (Oxford: Clarendon Press, 1968).

Jewell, E.J., and F. Abate (eds.), *The New Oxford American Dictionary* (Oxford: Oxford University Press, 2nd edn, 2005).

Jewett, Robert, *Dating Paul's Life* (London: SCM Press, 1979).

Jewett, Robert, assisted by Roy D. Kotansky, *Romans: A Commentary* (ed. Eldon Jay Epp; Hermeneia; Minneapolis: Fortress Press, 2007).

Jobes, Karen H., and Moisés Silva, *Invitation to the Septuagint* (Grand Rapids: Baker, 2000).

Johansson, Daniel, '*Kyrios* in the Gospel of Mark', *Journal for the Study of the New Testament* 33 (2010), pp. 101-24.

Johnson, Carl Garth, '*OGIS* 98 and the Divination of the Ptolemies', *Historia* 51 (2002), pp. 112-16.

Johnson, Luke Timothy, *The First and Second Letters to Timothy: A New Translation with Introduction and Commentary* (Anchor Bible, 35A; New York: Doubleday, 2001).

—*The Gospel of Luke* (Sacra pagina, 3; Collegeville, MN: Liturgical Press, 1991).

Johnson, Terry, and Christopher Dandeker, 'Patronage: Relation and System', in Wallace-Hadrill (ed.), *Patronage in Ancient Society*, pp. 219-41.

Jones, A.H.M., *Augustus* (ed. M.I. Finley; Ancient Culture and Society; London: Chatto & Windus, 1970).

Jones, Christopher P., *New Heroes in Antiquity: From Achilles to Antinoos* (Revealing Antiquity; Cambridge, MA: Harvard University Press, 2010).

Jones, Donald L. 'Christianity and the Roman Imperial Cult', in H. Temporini and W. Haase (eds.), *Aufstieg und Niedergang der römischen Welt: Geschichte und Kultur Roms im Spiegel der neueren Forschung*, II.23.2 (Berlin: W. de Gruyter, 1980), pp. 1023-54.

—'The Title *Kyrios* in Luke–Acts', in *Society of Biblical Literature 1974 Seminar Papers* 2 (ed. George W. MacRae; Cambridge, MA: Scholars Press, 1974), pp. 85-101.

Judge, Edwin A., 'The Decrees of Caesar at Thessalonica', *Reformed Theological Review* 30 (1971), pp. 1-7.

Kahle, Paul Eric, *The Cairo Geniza* (Oxford: Basil Blackwell, 2nd edn, 1959).

Kallas, James, 'Romans xiii. 1-7: An Interpolation', *New Testament Studies* 11 (1964–65), pp. 365-74.

Kantiréa, Maria, *Les dieux et les dieux augustes: le culte impérial en Grèce sous les Julio-claudiens et les Flaviens: études épigraphiques et archéologiques* (Meletemata, 50; Athens: Centre de recherches de l'antique grecque et romaine, 2007).

Keil, Josef, 'Die erste Kaiserneokorie von Ephesos', *Numismatische Zeitschrift* NF 12 (1919), pp. 115-20.

Keller, Marie Noël, *Choosing What Is Best: Paul, Roman Society and Philippians* (ThD diss., Lutheran School of Theology at Chicago, 1995).

Kelly, J.N.D., *A Commentary on the Pastoral Epistles: I Timothy, II Timothy, Titus* (Harper's New Testament Commentaries; Peabody, MA: Hendrickson, 1963).

Kennedy, H.A.A., 'Apostolic Preaching and Emperor Worship', *The Expositor* 7 (April 1909), pp. 289-307.

Kezbere, Ilze, *Umstrittener Monotheismus: Wahre und falsche Apotheose im lukanischen Doppelwerk* (Novum Testamentum et orbis antiquus/Studien zur Umwelt des Neuen Testaments, 60; Göttingen: Vandenhoeck & Ruprecht, 2007).

Kim, S., *Christ and Caesar: The Gospel and the Roman Empire in the Writings of Paul and Luke* (Grand Rapids: Eerdmans, 2008).

Kittel, Gerhard, and Gerhard Friedrich (eds.), *Theological Dictionary of the New Testament* (trans. Geoffrey W. Bromiley; 10 vols.; Grand Rapids: Eerdmans, 1964–76).

Klauck, Hans-Josef, *The Religious Context of Early Christianity: A Guide to Graeco-Roman Religions* (trans. Brian McNeil; Studies of the New Testament and its World; Edinburgh: T. & T. Clark, 2000).

Knox, John, *Chapters in the Life of Paul* (New York: Abingdon–Cokesbury Press, 1950).

Köberlein, Ernst, *Caligula und die ägyptischen Kulte* (Beiträge zur klassischen Philologie, 3; Meisenheim am Glan: Anton Hain, 1962).

Koukouli-Chrysantaki, Chaido, 'Colonia Iulia Augusta Philippensis', in Charalambos Bakirtzis and Helmut Koester (eds.), *Philippi at the Time of Paul and after his Death* (Harrisburg, PA: Trinity Press International, 1998), pp. 5-35.

Kraybill, J. Nelson, *Apocalypse and Allegiance: Worship, Politics, and Devotion in the Book of Revelation* (Grand Rapids: Brazos, 2010).

—*Imperial Cult and Commerce in John's Apocalypse* (*Journal for the Study of the New Testament:* Supplement Series, 132; Sheffield: Sheffield Academic Press, 1996).

Kreitzer, Larry J., *Striking New Images: Roman Imperial Coinage and the New Testament World* (*Journal for the Study of the New Testament:* Supplement Series, 134; Sheffield: Sheffield Academic Press, 1996).

Krentz, Edgar, *The Historical-Critical Method* (Philadelphia: Fortress Press, 1975).

Kümmel, Werner Georg, *Introduction to the New Testament* (trans. Howard Clark Kee; Nashville: Abingdon Press, rev. edn, 1975).

Kwong, Ivan Shing Chung, *The Word Order of the Gospel of Luke: Its Foregrounded Messages* (Library of New Testament Studies, 298; Studies in New Testament Greek, 12; London: T. & T. Clark, 2005).

Labahn, Michael, and Jürgen Zangenberg (eds.), *Zwischen den Reichen: Neues Testament und römische Herrschaft. Vorträge auf der ersten Konferenz der European Association for Biblical Studies* (Texte und Arbeiten zum neutestamentlichen Zeitalter, 36; Tübingen: Francke, 2002).

Labuschagne, C.J., *The Incomparability of Yahweh in the Old Testament* (Pretoria Oriental Series, 5; Leiden: E.J. Brill, 1966).

Lacey, D.R. de, '"One Lord" in Pauline Christology', in Harold H. Rowdon (ed.), *Christ the Lord: Studies in Christology Presented to Donald Guthrie* (Downers Grove, IL: InterVarsity Press, 1982), pp. 191-203.

Lake, Kirsopp, 'The Critical Problems of the Epistle to the Philippians', *The Expositor,* Eighth Series 7 (1914), pp. 481-93.

Lamb, Sydney M., *Outline of Stratificational Grammar* (Washington, DC: Georgetown University Press, 1966).

—*Pathways of the Brain: The Neurocognitive Basis of Language* (Current Issues in Linguistic Theory, 170; Amsterdam: John Benjamins, 1999).

Lambert, Royston, *Beloved and God: The Story of Hadrian and Antinous* (Secaucus, NJ: Meadowland, 1984).

Lanci, John R., 'The Stones Don't Speak and the Texts Tell Lies: Sacred Sex at Corinth', in Schowalter and Friesen (eds.), *Urban Religion in Roman Corinth*, pp. 205-20.

Larson, Jennifer, *Greek Heroine Cults* (Madison: University of Wisconsin Press, 1995).

Leech, Geoffrey N., *Principles of Pragmatics* (London: Longman, 1983).

Levinsohn, Stephen H., *Discourse Features of New Testament Greek: A Coursebook on the Information Structure of New Testament Greek* (Dallas: Summer Institute of Linguistics, 2nd edn, 2000).

Levinson, Stephen C., *Pragmatics* (Cambridge Textbooks in Linguistics; Cambridge: Cambridge University Press, 1983).

—Review of *Relevance: Communication and Cognition* (Oxford: Basil Blackwell, 1986), by Dan Sperber and Dierdre Wilson, *Journal of Linguistics* 25 (1989), pp. 455-72.

Lewis, Naphtali, and Meyer Reinhold (eds.), *Roman Civilization: Select Readings*. I. *The Republic and the Augustan Age*. II. *The Empire* (New York: Columbia University Press, 3rd edn, 1990).

Liddell, Henry George, and Robert Scott, *A Greek–English Lexicon* (rev. and augmented by Henry Stuart Jones and Roderick McKenzie, with a revised supplement, 1996, ed. R.G.W. Glare and A.A. Thompson; Oxford: Clarendon Press, 9th edn, 1940).

Liebeschuetz, J.H.W.G., *Continuity and Change in Roman Religion* (Oxford: Clarendon Press, 1979).

Liertz, Uta-Maria, *Kult und Kaiser: Studien zu Kaiserkult und Kaiserverehrung in den germanischen Provinzen und in Gallia Belgica zur römischen Kaiserzeit* (Acta Instituti Romani Finlandiae, 20; Rome: Institutum Romanum Finlandiae, 1998).

Lightfoot, J.B., *St Paul's Epistle to the Philippians: A Revised Text with Introduction, Notes and Dissertations* (London: Macmillan, 1913; repr., Grand Rapids: Zondervan, 1953).

Lincoln, Andrew T., *Ephesians* (Word Biblical Commentary, 42; Dallas: Word Books, 1990).

—*Paradise Now and Not Yet: Studies in the Role of the Heavenly Dimension in Paul's Thought with Special Reference to his Eschatology* (Society for New Testament Studies Monograph Series, 43; Cambridge: Cambridge University Press, 1981).

Lockwood, David G., *Introduction to Stratificational Linguistics* (New York: Harcourt Brace Jovanovich, 1972).

Lohmeyer, Ernst, *Der Brief an die Philipper* (Kritisch-exegetischer Kommentar über das Neue Testament; Göttingen: Vandenhoeck & Ruprecht, 1929).

—*Christkult und Kaiserkult* (Tübingen: J.C.B. Mohr [Paul Siebeck], 1919).

—*Kyrios Jesus: Eine Untersuchung zu Phil. 2, 5-11* (Heidelberg: C. Winter, 1928; repr., Darmstadt: Wissenschaftliche Buchgesellschaft, 1961).

Louw, Johannes P., *Semantics of New Testament Greek* (Semeia Studies; Atlanta: Scholars Press, 1982).

Louw, Johannes P., and Eugene A. Nida (eds.), *Greek–English Lexicon of the New Testament Based on Semantic Domains* (New York: United Bible Societies, 1988).

Lozano, Fernando, 'The Creation of Imperial Gods: Not Only Imposition versus Sponta-
    neity', in P. Iossif (ed.), *Royal Cult and Emperor Worship* (Athens, forthcoming).
—'*Divi Augusti* and *Theoi Sebastoi*: Roman Initiatives and Greek Answers', *Classical
    Quarterly* 57 (2007), pp. 139-52
—*La religión del poder: el culto imperial en Atenas en época de Augusto y los empera-
    dores Julio-Claudios* (British Archaeological Reports, International Series, 1087;
    Oxford: John and Erica Hedges, 2002).
—'*Thea Livia* in Athens: Redating *IG* II² 3242', *Zeitschrift für Papyrologie und Epi-
    graphik* 148 (2004), pp. 177-80.
Luedemann, Gerd, *Paul, Apostle to the Gentiles: Studies in Chronology* (trans. F. Stanley
    Jones; Philadelphia: Fortress Press, 1984).
Lyons, John, *Introduction to Theoretical Linguistics* (London: Cambridge University
    Press, 1968).
—*Language and Linguistics* (London: Cambridge University Press, 1981).
—*Linguistic Semantics: An Introduction* (Cambridge: Cambridge University Press,
    1995).
—*Semantics* (2 vols.; Cambridge: Cambridge University Press, 1977).
MacKenzie, Ian, *Paradigms of Reading: Relevance Theory and Deconstruction* (Bas-
    ingstoke, UK: Palgrave Macmillan, 2002).
Maier, Harry O., 'A Sly Civility: Colossians and Empire', *Journal for the Study of the
    New Testament* 27 (2005), pp. 323-49.
Malherbe, Abraham J., 'Determinism and Free Will in Paul: The Argument of 1 Cor-
    inthians 8 and 9', in Engberg-Pedersen (ed.), *Paul in his Hellenistic Context*,
    pp. 231-55.
—*The Letters to the Thessalonians: A New Translation with Introduction and Commen-
    tary* (Anchor Bible, 32B; New York: Doubleday, 2000).
Malina, Bruce J., *The New Testament World: Insights from Cultural Anthropology* (Lou-
    isville, KY: Westminster/John Knox Press, 3rd rev. and exp. edn, 2001).
Malitz, Jürgen, *Nero* (trans. Allison Brown; Malden, MA: Blackwell, 2005).
Marshall, John W., 'Hybridity and Rereading Romans 13', *Journal for the Study of the
    New Testament* 31 (2008), pp. 157-78.
Martin, Alain-Georges, 'La traduction de κύριος en syriaque', *Filología neotestamen-
    taria* 12 (1999), pp. 25-54.
Martin, Dale B., 'Paul and the Judaism/Hellenism Dichotomy: Toward a Social History
    of the Question', in Engberg-Pedersen (ed.), *Paul beyond the Judaism/Hellenism
    Divide,* pp. 29-61.
Martin, Ralph P., *The Epistle of Paul to the Philippians: An Introduction and Commen-
    tary* (Tyndale New Testament Commentaries; Leicester: InterVarsity Press, rev.
    edn, 1987).
—*Hymn to Christ: Philippians 2:5-11 in Recent Interpretation and in the Setting of
    Early Christian Worship* (Cambridge: Cambridge University Press, 1967; repr.,
    Downers Grove, IL: InterVarsity Press, 1997).
—*Philippians* (New Century Bible Commentary; London: Marshall, Morgan & Scott,
    1976; repr., Grand Rapids: Eerdmans, 1985).
Martin, Ralph P., and Gerald F. Hawthorne, *Philippians* (Word Biblical Commentary,
    43; Nashville: Thomas Nelson, 2004).
Martin, Ronald, *Tacitus* (London: Batsford, 1981).
Martin-Asensio, Gustavo, *Transivity-Based Foregrounding in the Acts of the Apostles:
    A Functional-Grammatical Approach to the Lukan Perspective* (*Journal for the*

Study of the New Testament: Supplement Series, 202; Studies in New Testament Greek, 8; Sheffield: Sheffield Academic Press, 2000).

Marwick, Arthur, *The New Nature of History: Knowledge, Evidence, Language* (Chicago: Lyceum, 2001).

Mateos Cruz, Pedro (ed.), *El 'Foro Provincial' de Augusta Emerita: un conjunto monumental de culto imperial* (Anejos de Archivo Español de Arqueología, 142; Madrid: Instituto de Arqueología de Mérida, 2006).

McDonald, Lee Martin, and Stanley E. Porter (eds.), *Early Christianity and its Sacred Literature* (Peabody, MA: Hendrickson, 2000).

McGaughy, Lane C., *Toward a Descriptive Analysis of Εἶναι as a Linking Verb in New Testament Greek* (Society of Biblical Literature Dissertation Series, 6; Missoula, MT: Society of Biblical Literature, 1972).

McKnight, Scot (ed.), *Introducing New Testament Interpretation* (Grand Rapids: Baker Book House, 1989).

McLaren, James S. 'The Jews and the Imperial Cult: From Augustus to Domitian', *Journal for the Study of the New Testament* 27 (2005), pp. 257-78.

Meade, David G., *Pseudonymity and Canon: An Investigation into the Relationship of Authorship and Authority in Jewish and Earliest Christian Tradition* (Wissenschaftliche Untersuchungen zum Neuen Testament, 39; Tübingen: J.C.B. Mohr [Paul Siebeck], 1986).

Meeks, Wayne A., 'Judaism, Hellenism, and the Birth of Christianity', in Engberg-Pedersen (ed.), *Paul beyond the Judaism/Hellenism Divide,* pp. 17-27.

Mellor, Ronald, ΘΕΑ ΡΩΜΗ: *The Worship of the Goddess Roma in the Greek World* (Hypomnemata, 42; Göttingen: Vandenhoeck & Ruprecht, 1975).

Metzger, Bruce M., and Bart D. Ehrman, *The Text of the New Testament: Its Transmission, Corruption, and Restoration* (Oxford: Oxford University Press, 4th edn, 2005).

Mey, Jacob L., *Pragmatics: An Introduction* (Oxford: Basil Blackwell, 1993).

Michael, J. Hugh, *The Epistle of Paul to the Philippians* (Moffatt New Testament Commentary; London: Hodder & Stoughton, 1928).

Michel, Otto, *Der Brief and die Römer* (Kritisch-exegetischer Kommentar über das Neue Testament; Göttingen: Vandenhoeck & Ruprecht, 5th edn, 1978).

Millar, Fergus, *The Emperor in the Roman World (31 BC–AD 337)* (London: Duckworth, 1977).

—'Epigraphy', in Crawford (ed.), *Sources for Ancient History,* pp. 80-136.

—'The Imperial Cult and the Persecutions', in den Boer (ed.), *Le culte des souverains dans l'empire romain,* pp. 143-75.

—*A Study of Cassius Dio* (Oxford: Oxford University Press, 1964).

Miller, Colin, 'The Imperial Cult in the Pauline Cities of Asia Minor and Greece', *Catholic Biblical Quarterly* 72 (2010), pp. 314-31.

Mirón Pérez, María Dolores, *Mujeres, religión y poder: el culto imperial en el occidente mediterráneo* (Granada: University of Granada, 1996).

Mitford, T.B., 'A Cypriot Oath of Allegiance to Tiberius', *Journal of Roman Studies* 50 (1960), pp. 75-79.

Momigliano, Arnaldo, 'Roman Religion: The Imperial Period', in Arnaldo Momigliano, *On Pagans, Jews, and Christians* (Middletown, CT: Wesleyan University Press, 1987), pp. 178-201. Reprinted from *The Encyclopedia of Religion* (ed. Mircea Eliade; New York: Macmillan, 1986).

Moo, Douglas J., *The Epistle to the Romans* (New International Commentary on the New Testament; Grand Rapids: Eerdmans, 1996).

Moore, Hamilton, and Philip McCormick, 'Domitian (Part i)', *Irish Biblical Studies* 25 (2003), pp. 74-101.

—'Domitian (Part ii)', *Irish Biblical Studies* 25 (2003), pp. 121-45.

Morris, Leon, *The Epistle to the Romans* (Pillar New Testament Commentary; Grand Rapids: Eerdmans, 1988).

Morrison, Clinton D., *The Powers That Be* (Studies in Biblical Theology, 29; London: SCM Press, 1960).

Moulton, James Hope, and George Milligan, *The Vocabulary of the Greek Testament: Illustrated From the Papyri and Other Non-Literary Sources* (London: Hodder & Stoughton, 1930; repr., Grand Rapids: Eerdmans, 1985).

Mounce, William D., *Pastoral Epistles* (Word Biblical Commentary, 46; Nashville: Thomas Nelson, 2000).

Müller, Mogens, *The First Bible of the Church: A Plea for the Septuagint* (*Journal for the Study of the Old Testament:* Supplement Series, 206; Sheffield: Sheffield Academic Press, 1996).

Munck, Johannes, *The Acts of the Apostles: A New Translation with Introduction and Commentary* (Anchor Bible, 31; Garden City, NY: Doubleday, 1967).

Munro, Winsome, 'Romans 13:1-7: Apartheid's Last Biblical Refuge', *Biblical Theology Bulletin* 20 (1990), pp. 161-68.

Murphy-O'Connor, Jerome, *St Paul's Corinth: Texts and Archeology* (Good New Studies, 6; Wilmington, DE: Michael Glazier, 1983).

—*St Paul's Corinth: Texts and Archeology* (Collegeville, MN: Liturgical Press, 3rd rev. and exp. edn, 2002).

Musurillo, Herbert (ed.), *Acts of the Christian Martyrs: Introduction, Texts and Translations* (Oxford Early Christian Texts; Oxford: Oxford University Press, 1972).

Myers, Ched, *Binding the Strong Man: A Political Reading of Mark's Story of Jesus* (Maryknoll, NY: Orbis Books, 1988).

Nanos, Mark D., *The Mystery of Romans: The Jewish Context of Paul's Letter* (Minneapolis: Fortress Press, 1996).

Naylor, Michael, 'The Roman Imperial Cult and Revelation', *Currents in Biblical Research* 8 (2010), 207-39.

Neill, Stephen, and N.T. Wright, *The Interpretation of the New Testament 1961–1986* (Oxford: Oxford University Press, new edn, 1988).

Neyrey, Jerome H., '"First", "Only", "One of a Few", and "No One Else": The Rhetoric of Uniqueness and the Doxologies in 1 Timothy', *Biblica* 86 (2005), pp. 59-87.

Nock, Arthur Darby, 'Notes on Ruler-Cult, I–IV', *Journal of Hellenic Studies* 48 (1928), pp. 21-43.

—'Religious Developments from the Close of the Republic to the Death of Nero', in S.A. Cook, F.E. Adcock and M.P. Charlesworth (eds.), *The Augustan Empire: 44 B.C.–A.D. 70* (Cambridge Ancient History, 10; Cambridge: Cambridge University Press, 1934).

Nogales Basarrate, Trinidad, and Julián González (eds.), *'Culto imperial: política y poder'. Actas del congreso international* (Hispania Antigua, Serie Arqueológica, 1; Rome: L'Erma di Bretschneider, 2007).

Noguera Celdrán, Jośe Miguel (ed.), *Foro Hispaniae: paisaje urbano, arquitectura, programas decorativos y culto imperial en los foros de las ciudades hispanorrama-*

nas (Monografías del Museo Arqueológico de Murcia, 3; Murcia, Spain: Museo Arqueológico de Murcia, 2009).

Nygren, Anders, *Commentary on Romans* (Philadelphia: Fortress Press, 1949).

Oakes, Peter, 'Christian Attitudes to Rome at the Time of Paul's Letter', *Review and Expositor* 100 (2003), pp. 103-11.

—*Philippians: From People to Letter* (Society for New Testament Studies Monograph Series, 110; Cambridge: Cambridge University Press, 2001).

—'Re-Mapping the Universe: Paul and the Emperor in 1 Thessalonians and Philippians', *Journal for the Study of the New Testament* 27 (2005), pp. 301-22.

Oakes, Peter (ed.), *Rome in the Bible and the Early Church* (Carlisle: Paternoster Press, 2002).

Oates, John F., *et al.*, 'Checklist of Editions of Greek, Latin, Demotic and Coptic Papyri, Ostraca and Tablets', Web edition: http://scriptorium.lib.duke.edu/papyrus/texts/clist.html (updated 11 September 2008).

O'Brien, Peter T., *The Epistle to the Philippians: A Commentary on the Greek Text* (New International Greek Testament Commentary; Grand Rapids: Eerdmans, 1991).

—*The Letter to the Ephesians* (Pillar New Testament Commentary; Grand Rapids: Eerdmans, 1999).

O'Donnell, Matthew Brook, *Corpus Linguistics and the Greek of the New Testament* (New Testament Monographs, 6; Sheffield: Sheffield Phoenix Press, 2005).

Oepke, Albrecht, 'Ἐπιστάτης', in Kittel and Friedrich (eds.), *Theological Dictionary of the New Testament,* II, pp. 622-23.

Ogden, C.K., and I.A. Richards, *The Meaning of Meaning: A Study of the Influence of Language upon Thought and of the Science of Symbolism* (New York: Harcourt, Brace & World, 8th edn, n.d.).

Ogilvie, R.M., *The Romans and their Gods* (London: Chatto & Windus, 1969; repr., London: Pimlico, n.d.).

Oliver, James H., 'The Divi of the Hadrianic Period', *Harvard Theological Review* 42 (1949), pp. 35-40.

Olsen, Mari Broman, *A Semantic and Pragmatic Model of Lexical and Grammatical Aspect* (Outstanding Dissertations in Linguistics; New York: Garland, 1997).

Osborne, Grant R., *The Hermeneutical Spiral: A Comprehensive Introduction to Biblical Interpretation* (Downers Grove, IL: InterVarsity Press, rev. and exp. edn, 2006).

Osiek, C., *Philippians, Philemon* (Abingdon New Testament Commentaries; Nashville: Abingdon Press, 2000).

Oster, Richard, 'Christianity and Emperor Veneration in Ephesus: Iconography of a Conflict', *Restoration Quarterly* 25 (1982), pp. 143-49.

The Oxford English Dictionary (ed. J.A. Simpson, and E.S.C. Weiner; 20 vols.; Oxford: Clarendon Press, 2nd edn, 1989).

Packman, Z.M., 'Epithets with the Title Despotes in Regnal Formulas in Document Dates and in the Imperial Oath', *Zeitschrift für Papyrologie und Epigraphik* 90 (1992), pp. 251-57.

—'Notes on Papyrus Texts with the Roman Imperial Oath', *Zeitschrift für Papyrologie und Epigraphik* 89 (1991), pp. 91-102.

—'Regnal Formulas in Document Date and in the Imperial Oath', *Zeitschrift für Papyrologie und Epigraphik* 91 (1992), pp. 61-76.

—'Still Further Notes on Papyrus Documents with the Roman Imperial Oath', *Zeitschrift für Papyrologie und Epigraphik* 100 (1994), pp. 207-10.

Pattemore, Stephen,*The People of God in the Apocalypse: A Relevance-Theoretic Study* (PhD thesis, University of Otago, 2000).

—*The People of God in the Apocalypse: Discourse, Structure, and Exegesis* (Society for New Testament Studies Monograph Series, 128; Cambridge: Cambridge University Press, 2004).

Peppel, Matthias, 'Gott oder Mensch? Kaiserverehrung und Herrschaftskontrolle', in Cancik and Hitzl (eds.), *Praxis der Herrscherverehrung*, pp. 69-95.

Pervo, Richard I., *Acts: A Commentary* (ed. Harold W. Attridge; Hermeneia; Philadelphia: Fortress Press, 2009).

—*Dating Acts: Between the Evangelists and Apologists* (Santa Rosa, CA: Polebridge Press, 2006).

Pfeiffer, Stefan, *Der römische Kaiser und das Land am Nil: Kaiserverehrung und Kaiserkult in Alexandria and Ägypten von Augustus bis Caracalla (30 v. Chr.–217 n. Chr.)* (Historia – Einzelschrift, 212; Stuttgart: Franz Steiner, 2010).

PHI Greek Documentary Texts [CD ROM #7. Software database] (Los Altos, CA: Packard Humanities Institute, 1991–96).

Pietersen, Lloyd K., *The Polemic of the Pastorals: A Sociological Examination of the Development of Pauline Christianity* (*Journal for the Study of the New Testament:* Supplement Series, 264; London: T. & T. Clark, 2004).

Pilhofer, Peter, *Philippi. II. Katalog der Inschriften von Philippi* (Wissenschaftliche Untersuchungen zum Neuen Testament, 119; Tübingen: Mohr Siebeck, 1st edn, 2000; 2nd edn, 2009).

Pippidi, D.M., *Recherches sur le culte impériale* (Institut roumain d'études latines collection scientifique; Paris: Les Belles Lettres, 1939).

Pleket, H.W., 'An Aspect of the Emperor Cult: Imperial Mysteries', *Harvard Theological Review* 58 (1965), pp. 331-47.

Porter, Stanley E., *Idioms of the Greek New Testament* (Biblical Languages: Greek, 2; Sheffield: JSOT Press, 2nd edn, 1994).

—'Romans 13:1-7 as Pauline Political Rhetoric', *Filología neotestamentaria* 3 (1990), pp. 115-39.

—*Verbal Aspect in the Greek of the New Testament with Reference to Tense and Mood* (Studies in Biblical Greek, 1; New York: Peter Lang, 2nd edn, 1993).

Porter, Stanley E., and Andrew W. Pitts, 'New Testament Greek Language and Linguistics in Recent Research', *Currents in Biblical Research* 6 (2008), pp. 214-55.

Porter, Stanley E., and D.A. Carson (eds.), *Biblical Greek Language and Linguistics: Open Questions in Current Research* (*Journal for the Study of the New Testament:* Supplement Series, 80; Sheffield: JSOT Press, 1993).

—*Discourse Analysis and Other Topics in Biblical Greek* (*Journal for the Study of the New Testament:* Supplement Series, 113; Sheffield: Sheffield Academic Press, 1995).

Porter, Stanley E., and Jeffrey T. Reed (eds.), *Discourse Analysis and the New Testament: Approaches and Results* (*Journal for the Study of the New Testament:* Supplement Series, 170; Studies in New Testament Greek, 4. Sheffield: Sheffield Academic Press, 1999).

Price, Simon R.F., 'Between Man and God: Sacrifice in the Roman Imperial Cult', *Journal of Roman Studies* 70 (1980), pp. 28-43.

—'From Noble Funerals to Divine Cult: The Consecration on Roman Emperors', in David Cannadine and Simon R.F. Price (eds.), *Rituals of Royalty: Power and*

Ceremonial in Traditional Societies (Cambridge: Cambridge University Press, 1987), pp. 56-105.

—'Gods and Emperors: The Greek Language of the Roman Imperial Cult', *Journal of Hellenic Studies* 104 (1984), pp. 79-95.

—'Religious Pluralism in the Roman World: Pagans, Jews, and Christians' (Unpublished paper delivered at the Annual Meeting of the Society of Biblical Literature, Nashville, Tennessee, 2000).

—'Response', in Horsley (ed.), *Paul and the Roman Imperial Order*, pp. 175-83.

—'Rituals and Power', in Horsley (ed.), *Paul and Empire*, pp. 47-71.

—*Rituals and Power: The Roman Imperial Cult in Asia Minor* (Cambridge: Cambridge University Press, 1984).

Radford, Andrew, *Transformational Syntax* (Cambridge Textbooks in Linguistics; Cambridge: Cambridge University Press, 1981).

Ramage, Edwin S., 'Augustus' Treatment of Julius Caesar', *Historia* 34 (1985), pp. 223-45.

Ratté, Christopher, Thomas N. Howe and Clive Foss, 'An Early Imperial Pseudodipteral Temple at Sardis', *American Journal of Archaeology* 90 (1986), pp. 45-68.

Reed, Jeffrey T., *A Discourse Analysis of Philippians: Method and Rhetoric in the Debate over Literary Integrity* (*Journal for the Study of the New Testament:* Supplement Series, 136; Sheffield: Sheffield Academic Press, 1997).

Reid, Sara Karz, *The Small Temple: A Roman Imperial Cult Building in Petra, Jordan* (Gorgias Dissertations, 20; Near Eastern Studies, 7; Piscataway, NJ: Gorgias Press, 2005).

Rengstorf, Karl Heinrich, 'Δεσπότης' [and Cognates], in Kittel and Friedrich (eds.), *Theological Dictionary of the New Testament*, II, pp. 44-49.

Reumann, John, *Philippians: A New Translation with Introduction and Commentary* (Anchor Yale Bible; New Haven: Yale University Press, 2008).

Richards, E. Randolph, *Paul and First-Century Letter Writing: Secretaries, Composition, and Collection* (Downers Grove, IL: InterVarsity Press, 2004).

—*The Secretary in the Letters in Paul* (Wissenschaftliche Untersuchungen zum Neuen Testament, 2.42; Tübingen: Mohr Siebeck, 1991).

Richey, L.B., *Roman Imperial Ideology and the Gospel of John* (Catholic Biblical Quarterly Monograph Series, 43; Washington, DC: Catholic Biblical Association of America, 2007).

Rives, James B., 'Graeco-Roman Religion in the Roman Empire: Old Assumptions and New Approaches', *Currents in Biblical Research* 8 (2010), pp. 240-99.

Robert, Louis, 'Le culte de Caligula à Milet et la province d'Asie', *Hellenica* 7 (1949), pp. 206-38.

Roberts, C.H., *Two Biblical Papyri in the John Rylands Library Manchester* (Manchester: Manchester University Press, 1936).

Roberts, Lawrence D., 'Relevance as an Explanation of Communication', *Linguistics and Philosophy* 14 (1991), pp. 453-72.

Robertson, Archibald, and Alfred Plummer, *A Critical and Exegetical Commentary on the First Epistle of St Paul to the Corinthians* (International Critical Commentary; Edinburgh: T. & T. Clark, 2nd edn, 1914).

Robinson, Henry S., *Corinth: A Brief History of the City and a Guide to the Excavations* (Athens: American School of Classical Studies, 1964).

Robinson, John A. T., *Redating the New Testament* (Philadelphia: Westminster Press, 1976).

Rock, Ian E., *The Implications of Roman Imperial Ideology for an Exegesis of Paul's Letter to the Romans: An Ideological Literary Analysis of Exordium, Romans 1:1-17* (PhD thesis, University of Wales, 2007).

Rogers, Guy, *The Sacred Identity of Ephesos: Foundation Myths of a Roman City* (London: Routledge, 1991).

Rose, H.J., *The Gods and Heroes of the Greeks: An Introduction to Greek Mythology* (New York: World Publishing, 1958).

Rouchota, Villy, and Andreas H. Jucker (eds.), *Current Issues in Relevance Theory* (Pragmatics & Beyond NS, 58; Amsterdam: John Benjamins, 1998).

Rowe, C. Kavin, *Early Narrative Christology: The Lord in the Gospel of Luke* (Beihefte zur Zeitschrift für die neutestamentliche Wissenschaft, 139; Berlin: W. de Gruyter, 2006).

—'Luke–Acts and the Imperial Cult: A Way through the Conundrum?' *Journal for the Study of the New Testament* 27 (2005), pp. 279-300.

Rubin, Benjamin B., *(Re)presenting Empire: The Roman Imperial Cult in Asia Minor, 31 BC–AD 68* (PhD diss, University of Michigan, 2008).

Said, Edward W., *Culture and Imperialism* (New York: Vintage Books, 1993).

Sampley, J.P. (ed.), *Paul in the Greco-Roman World: A Handbook* (Harrisburg, PA: Trinity Press International, 2003).

Sanders, E.P., *Paul and Palestinian Judaism* (Minneapolis: Fortress Press, 1977).

—*Paul, the Law, and the Jewish People* (Minneapolis: Fortress Press, 1983).

Sanders, G.D.R., 'Urban Corinth: An Introduction', in Schowalter and Friesen (eds.), *Urban Religion in Roman Corinth*, pp. 11-24.

Sandmel, Samuel, 'Parallelomania', *Journal of Biblical Literature* 81 (1962), pp. 1-13.

Sandys, John Edwin, *Latin Epigraphy: An Introduction to the Study of Latin Inscriptions* (London: Cambridge University Press, 1927; repr., Chicago: Ares, n.d.).

Saunders, Ross, 'Paul and the Imperial Cult', in Stanley E. Porter (ed.), *Paul and his Opponents* (Pauline Studies, 2; Leiden: E.J. Brill, 2005), pp. 227-37.

Sauter, Franz, *Der römische Kaiserkult bei Martial und Statius* (Tübinger Beiträge zur Altertumswissenschaft, 21; Stuttgart: W. Kohlhammer, 1934).

Scheid, John, *Commentarii Fratrum Arvalium qui supersunt: Les copies épigraphiques des protocoles annuels de la Confrérie Arvale (21 AV.–31 AP. J.-C.)* (Roma Antica, 4; Rome: Ecole Française de Rome, Soprintendenza Archeologica di Roma, 1998).

—*An Introduction to Roman Religion* (trans. Janet Lloyd; Edinburgh: Edinburgh University Press, 2003).

—*Romulus et ses frères: le collège des Frères Arvales, modèle du culte public dans la Rome des empereurs* (Bibliothèque des écoles françaises d'Athènes et de Rome, 265; Rome: Ecole Française de Rome, 1990).

Scherrer, Peter, 'The City of Ephesos from the Roman Period to Late Antiquity', in Helmut Koester (ed.), *Ephesos: Metropolis of Asia. An Interdisciplinary Approach to its Archaeology, Religion, and Culture* (Harvard Theological Studies, 41; Valley Forge, PA: Trinity Press International, 1995), pp. 1-25.

Schneemelcher, Wilhelm (ed.), *New Testament Apocrypha. I. Gospels and Related Writings* (English translation edited by R. McL. Wilson; Cambridge: James Clarke, rev. edn, 1991).

Schowalter, Daniel N., *The Emperor and the Gods: Images from the Time of Trajan* (ed. Margaret R. Miles and Bernadette J. Brooten; Harvard Dissertations in Religion, 28; Minneapolis: Fortress Press, 1993).

Schowalter, Daniel N., and Steven J. Friesen (eds.), *Urban Religion in Roman Corinth: Interdisciplinary Approaches* (Harvard Theological Studies, 53; Cambridge, MA: Harvard University Press, 2005).

Schürer, Emil, *The History of the Jewish People in the Age of Jesus Christ (175 B.C.–A.D. 135)* (rev. and ed. Geza Vermes, Fergus Millar, Matthew Black, Martin Goodman, and Pamela Vermes; 3 vols.; Edinburgh: T. & T. Clark, rev. edn, 1973–87).

Schwartz, Seth, *Were the Jews a Mediterranean Society? Reciprocity and Solidarity in Ancient Judaism* (Princeton, NJ: Princeton University Press, 2010).

Schweitzer, Albert, *The Mysticism of Paul the Apostle* (trans. William Montgomery; London: A. & C. Black, 2nd edn, 1953).

Scott, James C., *Domination and the Arts of Resistance: Hidden Transcripts* (New Haven: Yale University Press, 1990).

Scott, Kenneth, *The Imperial Cult under the Flavians* (Ancient Religion and Mythology; Stuttgart: W. Kohlhammer, 1936; repr., New York: Arno Press, 1975).

—'Tiberius' Refusal of the Title "Augustus"', *Classical Philology* 27 (1932), pp. 43-50.

Seeley, David, 'The Background of the Philippians Hymn (2:6-11)', *Journal of Higher Criticism* 1 (1994), pp. 49-72.

Segal, Alan F., *Paul the Convert: The Apostolate and Apostasy of Saul the Pharisee* (New Haven: Yale University Press, 1990).

Séve, M., and P. Weber, 'Un monument honorifique au forum de Philippes', *Bulletin de correspondance hellénique* 112 (1988), pp. 467-79.

Sherk, Robert K. (ed. and trans.), *The Roman Empire: Augustus to Hadrian* (Translated Documents of Greece and Rome, 6; Cambridge: Cambridge University Press, 1988).

Silva, Moisés, *Biblical Words and their Meanings* (Grand Rapids: Zondervan, 1983).

—'Old Testament in Paul', in Hawthorne *et al.* (eds.), *Dictionary of Paul and his Letters*, pp. 630-42.

—*Philippians* (Baker Exegetical Commentary on the New Testament; Grand Rapids: Baker Book House, 2nd edn, 2005).

Simpson, C.J., 'Caligula's Cult: Immolation, Immortality Intent', in Small (ed.), *Subject and Ruler*, pp. 63-71.

—'The Cult of Emperor Gaius', *Latomus* 40 (1981), pp. 489-511.

Small, Alistair (ed.), *Subject and Ruler: The Cult of the Ruling Power in Classical Antiquity. Papers Presented at a Conference Held in the University of Alberta on April 13-15, 1994, to Celebrate the 65th Anniversary of Duncan Fishwick* (Ann Arbor: Journal of Roman Archaeology, 1996).

Smallwood, E. Mary, *The Jews under Roman Rule from Pompey to Diocletian: A Study in Political Relations* (Studies in Judaism in Late Antiquity, 20; Leiden: E.J. Brill, 2nd edn, 1981).

Smith, J.A., 'The Meaning of Κύριος', *Journal of Theological Studies* 31 (1929–30), pp. 155-60.

Smith, Jay E., 'The New Perspective on Paul: A Select and Annotated Bibliography', *Criswell Theological Review*, NS 2 (2005), pp. 91-111.

Smith, Kevin Gary, *Bible Translation and Relevance Theory: The Translation of Titus* (DLitt diss., University of Stellenbosch, 2000).

Snodgrass, Anthony, 'Archaeology', in Crawford (ed.), *Sources for Ancient History*, pp. 137-84.

Sordi, Marta, *The Christians and the Roman Empire* (trans. Annabel Bedini; London: Croom Helm, 1986).

Spawforth, Antony J.S., 'The Achaean Federal Cult Part I: Pseudo-Julian, Letters 198', *Tyndale Bulletin* 46 (1995), pp. 151-68.

—'Corinth, Argos and the Imperial Cult: Pseudo-Julian, *Letters* 198', *Hesperia* 63 (1994), pp. 211-32.

Sperber, Dan, and Deirdre Wilson, 'Mutual Knowledge and Relevance in Theories of Comprehension', in N.V. Smith (ed.), *Mutual Knowledge* (London: Academic Press, 1982), pp. 61-85.

—*Relevance: Communication and Cognition* (Oxford: Basil Blackwell, 1986; 2nd edn, 1995).

Stendahl, Krister, 'The Apostle Paul and the Introspective Conscience of the West', in Krister Stendahl, *Paul among Jews and Gentiles and Other Essays* (Philadelphia: Fortress Press, 1976), pp. 78-96. Reprinted from *Harvard Theological Review* 56 (1963), pp. 199-215.

Stepper, Ruth, 'Der Kaiser als Priester: Schwerpunkte und Reichweite seines oberpontifikalen Handelns', in Cancik and Hitzl (eds.), *Praxis der Herrscherverehrung*, pp. 157-87.

Stirewalt, M. Luther, Jr, *Paul, the Letter Writer* (Grand Rapids: Eerdmans, 2002).

Stowers, Stanley K., 'Does Pauline Christianity Resemble a Hellenistic Philosophy?', in Engberg-Pedersen (ed.), *Paul beyond the Judaism/Hellenism Divide*, pp. 81-102.

—*A Rereading of Romans: Justice, Jews, and Gentiles* (New Haven: Yale University Press, 1994).

Strong, Eugenia Sellers, 'Lecture I: Divus Augustus: The Influence of the Imperial Apotheosis on Antique Design', in Eugenia Sellers Strong, *Apotheosis and After Life: Three Lectures on Certain Phases of Art and Religion in the Roman Empire* (Freeport, NY: Books for Libraries Press, 1969), pp. 30-111.

Stuhlmacher, Peter, *Paul's Letter to the Romans* (trans. Scott J. Hafemann; Edinburgh: T. & T. Clark, 1994).

Süss, Jürgen, 'Kaiserkult und Urbanistik: Kultbezirke für römische Kaiser in kleinasiatischen Städten', in Cancik and Hitzl (eds.), *Praxis der Herrscherverehrung*, pp. 249-81.

Sweet, Louis Matthews, *Roman Emperor Worship* (Boston: Richard G. Badger, 1919).

Syme, Ronald, *Tacitus* (2 vols.; Oxford: Oxford University Press, 1958).

Taeger, Fritz, *Charisma: Studien zur Geschichte des antiken Herrscherkultes*, II (Stuttgart: W. Kohlhammer, 1960).

Tarn, W.W., 'The Hellenistic Ruler Cult and the Daemon', *Journal of Hellenic Studies* 48 (1928), pp. 206-19.

Taylor, Joan E., 'Pontius Pilate and the Imperial Cult in Roman Judaea', *New Testament Studies* 52 (2006), pp. 555-82.

Taylor, Lily Ross, 'Artemis of Ephesus', in F.J. Foakes Jackson and Kirsopp Lake (eds.), *The Beginnings of Christianity*. Part I. *The Acts of the Apostles*, V (London: Macmillan, 1933), pp. 251-56.

—*The Divinity of the Roman Emperor* (ed. Joseph William Hewitt; American Philological Association Monograph Series, 1; Middletown, CT: American Philological Association, 1931; repr., New York: Arno Press, 1975).

—*Party Politics in the Age of Caesar* (Berkeley: University of California Press, 1949).

—'The Proskynesis and the Hellenistic Ruler Cult', *Journal of Hellenic Studies* 47 (1927), pp. 53-62.

—'Tiberius' Refusal of Divine Honors', *Transactions and Proceedings of the American Philological Association* 60 (1929), pp. 87-101.

—'The Worship of Augustus in Italy during his Lifetime', *Transactions and Proceedings of the American Philological Association* 51 (1920), pp. 116-33.

Tellbe, Mikael, *Paul between Synagogue and State: Christians, Jews, and Civic Authorities in 1 Thessalonians, Romans, and Philippians* (Coniectanea biblica: New Testament Series, 34; Stockholm: Almqvist & Wiksell International, 2001).

Terry, Ralph Bruce, *A Discourse Analysis of First Corinthians* (Dallas: Summer Institute of Linguistics, 1995).

Thesaurus lingua graecae [CD ROM E. Software database] (Los Altos, CA: Packard Humanities Institute, 1999).

Thielman, Frank S., 'Ephesus and the Literary Setting of Philippians', in Amy M. Donaldson and Timothy B. Sailors (eds.), *New Testament Greek and Exegesis: Essays in Honor of Gerald F. Hawthorne* (Grand Rapids: Eerdmans, 2003), pp. 205-23.

Thiselton, Anthony C., *The First Epistle to the Corinthians: A Commentary on the Greek Text* (New International Greek Testament Commentary; Grand Rapids: Eerdmans, 2000).

Thompson, Leonard L., *The Book of Revelation: Apocalypse and Empire* (New York: Oxford University Press, 1990).

Tilborg, Sjef van, *Reading John in Ephesus* (Supplements to *Novum Testamentum,* 83; Leiden: E.J. Brill, 1996).

Trebilco, Paul, *The Early Christians in Ephesus from Paul to Ignatius* (Wissenschaftliche Untersuchungen zum Neuen Testament, 166; Tübingen: Mohr Siebeck, 2004).

Tripolitis, Antonia, *Religions of the Hellenistic-Roman Age* (Grand Rapids: Eerdmans, 2002).

Troeltsch, Ernst, 'Historical and Dogmatic Method in Theology', in Ephraim Fischoff and Walter Bense (eds.), *Religion in History* (Minneapolis: Fortress Press, 1991), pp. 11-32).

Tsalampouni, Ekaterini [Τσαλαμπουνη, Αικατερινη], *Η Μακεδονια στην Εποχη της Καινης Διαθηκης* [Macedonia during the Period of the New Testament] (Βιβ–λικη Βιβλιοθηκη, 23; Thessaloniki: Pournaras Press, 2002).

Turcan, Robert, *The Gods of Ancient Rome: Religion in Everyday Life from Archaic to Imperial Times* (trans. Antonia Nevill; Edinburgh: University of Edinburgh Press, 2000).

Turner, E.G., *Greek Papyri: An Introduction* (Oxford: Oxford University Press, 2nd edn, 1980).

Tyson, Joseph B., *Marcion and Luke–Acts: A Defining Struggle* (Columbia: University of South Carolina Press, 2006).

Uchida, Seiji, 'Text and Relevance', in Carston and Uchida (eds.), *Relevance Theory,* pp. 161-78.

Verhoef, Eduard, 'Pseudepigraphy and Canon', *Biblische Notizen* 106 (2001), pp. 90-98.

Villard, U. Monneret de, 'The Temple of the Imperial Cult at Luxor', *Archaeologia* 95 (1953), pp. 85-105.

Waddell, W.G., 'The Tetragrammaton in the LXX', *Journal of Theological Studies* 45 (1944), pp. 158-61.

Wallace, Daniel B., *Greek Grammar beyond the Basics: An Exegetical Syntax of the New Testament* (Grand Rapids: Zondervan, 1996).

—'The Semantics and Exegetical Significance of the Object–Complement Construction in the New Testament', *Grace Theological Journal* 6 (1985), pp. 91-112.

Wallace-Hadrill, Andrew (ed.), *Patronage in Ancient Society* (London: Routledge, 1989).

—'Patronage in Roman Society: From Republic to Empire', in Wallace Hadrill (ed.), *Patronage in Ancient Society*, pp. 63-87.

Walton, Steve, 'The State They Were in: Luke's View of the Roman Empire', in Oakes (ed.), *Rome in the Bible and the Early Church*, pp. 1-41.

Weinstock, Stefan, *Divus Julius* (Oxford: Clarendon Press, 1971).

Wendland, Ernst R., 'On the Relevance of "Relevance Theory" for Bible Translation', *The Bible Translator* 47 (1996), pp. 126-37.

Westfall, Cynthia Long, *A Discourse Analysis of the Letter to the Hebrews: The Relationship between Form and Meaning* (Library of New Testament Studies, 297; London: T. & T. Clark, 2005).

White, John L., *The Apostle of God: Paul and the Promise of Abraham* (Peabody, MA: Hendrickson, 1999).

White, Peter, 'Julius Caesar in Augustan Rome', *Phoenix* 42 (1988), pp. 334-56.

Wilder, Terry L., *Pseudonymity, the New Testament, and Deception: An Inquiry into Intention and Reception* (Lanham, MD: University Press of America, 2004).

Williams, Charles K., II, 'A Re-Evaluation of Temple E and the West End of the Forum of Corinth', in Susan Walker and Averil Cameron (eds.), *The Greek Renaissance in the Roman Empire: Papers from the Tenth British Museum Classical Colloquium* (London: University of London Institute for Classical Studies, 1989), pp. 156-62.

Wilson, Deirdre, and Dan Sperber, 'On Grice's Theory of Conversation', in Paul Werth (ed.), *Conversation and Discourse: Structure and Interpretation* (London: Croom Helm, 1981), pp. 155-78.

—'An Outline of Relevance Theory', *Notes on Linguistics* 39 (1987), pp. 5-24.

—'Remarques sur l'interprétation des énoncés selon Paul Grice', *Communications* 30 (1979), pp. 80-94.

Winedt, Marlon Domingo, *A Relevance-Theoretic Approach to Translation and Discourse Markers: With Special Reference to the Greek Text of the Gospel of Luke* (PhD diss., Free University Amsterdam, 1999).

Winter, Bruce W., 'The Achaean Federal Imperial Cult II: The Corinthian Church', *Tyndale Bulletin* 46 (1995), pp. 169-78.

—'Acts and Roman Religion: B. The Imperial Cult', in David W.J. Gill and Conrad Gempf (eds.), *The Book of Acts in its Graeco-Roman Setting* (Book of Acts in its First Century Setting, 2; Grand Rapids: Eerdmans, 1994), pp. 93-103.

—*After Paul Left Corinth: The Influence of Secular Ethics and Social Change* (Grand Rapids: Eerdmans, 2001).

—'The Imperial Cult and the Early Christians in Roman Galatia (Acts XIII 13-50 and Galatians VI 11-18)', in Thomas Drew-Bear, Mehmet Taşlialan and Christine M. Thomas (eds.), *Actes du Ier congres international sur Antioche de Pisidie* (Lyon: Université Lumière-Lyon 2, 2002), pp. 67-75.

—'Roman Law and Society in Romans 12-15', in Oakes (ed.), *Rome in the Bible and the Early Church*, pp. 67-102.

Wiseman, James, 'Corinth and Rome I: 228 B.C.–A.D. 267', in H. Temporini and W. Haase (eds.), *Aufstieg und Niedergang der römischen Welt: Geschichte und Kultur Roms im Spiegel der neueren Forschung*, II.7.1 (Berlin: W. de Gruyter, 1979). pp. 438-548.

Witherington, Ben, III, *The Acts of the Apostles: A Socio-Rhetorical Commentary* (Grand Rapids: Eerdmans, 1998).

Witulski, Thomas, *Kaiserkult in Kleinasien: Die Entwicklung der kultisch-religiösen Kaiserverehrung in der römischen Provinz Asia von Augustus bis Antoninus Pius* (Novum Testamentum et orbis antiquus/Studien zur Umwelt des Neuen Testaments, 63; Göttingen: Vandenhoeck & Ruprecht, 2007).

Woolf, Greg, 'Divinity and Power in Ancient Rome', in Nicole Brisch (ed.), *Religion and Power: Divine Kingship in the Ancient World and Beyond* (Oriental Institute Seminars, 4; Chicago: University of Chicago Press, 2008), pp. 243-59.

Wright, N.T., 'The Letter to the Romans: Introduction, Commentary, and Reflections', in Leander Keck *et al.* (eds.), *The New Interpreter's Bible* (Nashville: Abingdon Press, 2002), X, pp. 393-770.

—*Paul: In Fresh Perspective* (Minneapolis: Fortress Press, 2005).

—*What Saint Paul Really Said: Was Paul of Tarsus the Real Founder of Christianity?* (Grand Rapids: Eerdmans, 1997).

Würthwein, Ernst, *The Text of the Old Testament: An Introduction to the Biblica Hebraica* (trans. Erroll F. Rhodes; Grand Rapids: Eerdmans, 2nd edn, 1995).

Yegül, Fikret Kutlu, 'A Study in Architectural Iconography: *Kaiseraal* and the Imperial Cult', *Art Bulletin* 64 (1982), pp. 7-31.

Zanker, Paul, *The Power of Images in the Age of Augustus* (trans. Alan Shapiro; Ann Arbor: University of Michigan Press, 1988).

Zeller, Dieter, 'New Testament Christology in its Hellenistic Reception', *New Testament Studies* 46 (2001), pp. 312-33.

Zerwick, Maximilian, *Biblical Greek Illustrated by Examples* (trans. Joseph Smith; Scripta Pontificii Instituti Biblici, 114; Rome: Pontificio Istituto Biblico, 1963).

Zimmermann, Christiane, *Die Namen des Vaters: Studien zu ausgewählten neutestamentlichen Gottesbezeichnungen vor ihrem frühjüdischen und paganen Sprachhorizont* (Ancient Judaism and Early Christianity, 69; Leiden: E.J. Brill, 2007).

INDEXES

INDEX OF REFERENCES

Index of Modern Authors